Salvation through Temptation

THE CATHOLIC UNIVERSITY OF AMERICA PRESS
Washington, D.C.

Salvation through Temptation

MAXIMUS THE CONFESSOR AND THOMAS AQUINAS
ON CHRIST'S VICTORY OVER THE DEVIL

Benjamin E. Heidgerken   Foreword by Paul M. Blowers

Copyright © 2021
The Catholic University of America Press
All rights reserved

Image on title page: *Temptation of Christ* by Surikov Vasily. Used with permission of Alamy.

Cataloging-in-Publication data available from the Library of Congress
ISBN 978-0-8132-3412-0 (cloth)

FOR CHRISTINE AND THE BOYS
Isaac, Eli, and Jacob

AND IN MEMORY OF PATRICK HERMAN LEE
Pte San Wasté

CONTENTS

Foreword by Paul M. Blowers   ix

Acknowledgments   xiii

List of Abbreviations   xv

INTRODUCTION   1

Modern Studies of Both Maximus and Thomas   3
Christ's Demonic Temptation in Modern Studies of Maximus   6
Christ's Demonic Temptation in Modern Studies of Thomas   13

1 SOURCES FOR MAXIMUS'S PRESENTATION
   OF CHRIST'S TEMPTATION   21

Maximus's Anthropological Sources   21
Maximus's Christological Sources   41

2 MAXIMUS'S ANTHROPOLOGY OF TEMPTATION   48

Adam's Created State and Fall   50
Human Nature and Demonic Temptation after the Fall   57
Providence and Affectivity in an Eschatological Perspective   90

3 MAXIMUS'S VIEW OF CHRIST'S TEMPTATION   98

Christ's Humanity, Human Fallenness, and the Devil   99
The Perfections of Christ's Humanity and His Temptation   106
Salvation through Temptation: Christ's Victory over the Devil   120

4 SOURCES FOR THOMAS'S PRESENTATION OF CHRIST'S TEMPTATION   132

John of Damascus as the Historical Link between Maximus and Thomas   133
Western Patristic Thought on Christ's Temptation by the Devil   148
High Medieval Sources on Christ's Temptation by the Devil   162

5 THOMAS'S ANTHROPOLOGY OF TEMPTATION   179

The Created and Fallen States   180
Fleshly and Internal Demonic Temptation   199
Demonic Temptation, Virtue, and Providence   231

6 THOMAS'S VIEW OF CHRIST'S TEMPTATION   243

Christological Synecdoche in Thomas's Soteriology of Temptation   244
Christ's Perfections and Voluntary Defects   254
Christ's Temptation and the Three Medieval Temptations   267

CONCLUSION: CHRIST IN CHRISTIAN TRADITIONS OF TEMPTATION   284

Bibliography   295

Index   313

FOREWORD

Paul M. Blowers

Benjamin Heidgerken's comparative study of Maximus the Confessor and Thomas Aquinas on Christ's temptation and subjection to passions comes at an auspicious time. Not only is there broad and increased interest in overcoming centuries-old mutual suspicion and alienation between the great systems of constructive theology East and West, but given the continuous retrieval of Aquinas in Western Christian thought and the reiterations of "Neo-Thomism" that have powerfully registered themselves in Catholic theology in our own time, there has also been an ever more sustained concern to bring Maximus into conversation with contemporary theology—perhaps most notably in the prolific work of the late Hans Urs von Balthasar. Heidgerken furthermore capitalizes on some of the groundbreaking work of scholars like Antoine Lévy in comparing and contrasting the theological projects of Aquinas and Maximus, who has been rivaled only by John of Damascus as the virtual "Thomas Aquinas of the East." There is always room for caution here given the obvious differences in how Thomas and Maximus respectively approach and "write" theology. Thomas has bequeathed a *Summa* of extraordinary proportions and scope, whereas Maximus wrote in much briefer, densely packed scholia and *sententiae*. In addition, as Lars Thunberg and others have shown, some of the pioneering scholarship comparing the two thinkers was that of Roman Catholic Thomists who tended to force Maximus's thought into Thomistic categories of nature and grace without nuancing the real differences, which are substantial.

That said, there is just too much to be gained from disciplined comparison of these two prolific and influential Christian thinkers. Heidgerken plumbs an exceedingly interesting sub-theme in the Christology of the two theologians: the nature and emotional anatomy of Jesus's temptation, a point on which the deified humanity of Christ and his identification with fallen humanity crucially intersect. Indeed, the issue takes us into the substructure of Christ's composite hypostasis and the important question of Christ's appropriation of human passibility but not peccability. Heidgerken has good reasons for exploring the peculiar significance of Christ's temptation by the Devil in Maximus and Thomas, for such temptation, not restricted solely to the episode recounted in the desert story in the Synoptic Gospels (Mt 4:1–11 et par.), thoroughly dramatizes the depth of Christ's kenotic condescension, as the writer of Hebrews already observed in the apostolic age (Heb 4:15). Both Maximus and Thomas clearly recognized the extraordinary claim that the Savior was "in every respect tempted as we are, yet without sin," as well as the need to expound the subtleties of that claim. A peculiar kind of salvific vulnerability was operative in Christ in his openness to demonic assault, and Heidgerken shows us how both Maximus and Thomas patiently and carefully sought to tease out its broader implications. The issues here were not merely technical matters of Christology and anthropology; they extended to the lived life of the faithful, the Christian's experience of engagement with the powers and principalities, the dark forces of evil that sought to obfuscate a believer's moral vision, and capacities of choice and action. Both Maximus and Thomas, after all, were monastic theologians, and they built upon the foundation of longstanding traditions of Eastern and Western monastic wisdom concerning spiritual warfare and conquest, in which the dynamics of demonic infestation in the moral psychology and wellbeing of the soul had become a veritable science.

Though the actual historical lines of literary or intellectual connection between Maximus, in the Byzantine East in the seventh century, and Thomas, in thirteenth-century Europe, are quite limited, Heidgerken investigates the mediating role of John Damascene and seeks exhaustively to identify whatever links are available. Meanwhile, the comparison of the two writers on the temptation of Christ is still worthy in its own right, as both Maximus and Thomas were deeply invested in demonstrating how Christ entered the fray of human existence to stabilize the soul from within, to restore its moral and affective faculties, and to extend to all believers a gracious empowerment to countermand the assaults of the Evil One. Heidgerken brings to light here the important insights and nuances of both theologians, including the internal and external dimensions of Christ's definitive engagement with the Devil and its full salvific effects, and helpfully concludes his study by reflecting on the continuing significance of Christ's temptation and "passibility" for the life and worship of the Church. Heidgerken's work will hopefully inspire further such comparative explorations of Maximus and Thomas. Much work on this topic has yet to be done.

ACKNOWLEDGMENTS

I first thank those who contributed most directly to this work. Matthew Levering read and reread drafts of this project throughout its early stages, offering substantial improvements in my chapters on Thomas Aquinas. Paul Blowers helped significantly with my chapters on Maximus the Confessor. The anonymous readers from CUA Press gave feedback that greatly strengthened the final version.

At the outset of this project, Fred Jenkins and Fr. Silviu Bunta offered help with Latin and Greek, respectively, and Charlotte Kingston helped corroborate some of my work on Gregory the Great. More recently, members of the Minnesota Association of Patristic Scholars graciously read and provided feedback on chapters 2 and 3.

Along the way, I owe debts to professors, committee members, and friends. At St. Olaf, Charles Wilson, Elizabeth Galbraith, and Gregory Walter were early theological inspirations. At Princeton Seminary, George Hunsinger and Bruce McCormack helped shape my perception of the anthropological and Christological matters explored at the theological crux of this book. At the University of Dayton, Brad Kallenberg, William Portier, and Sandra Yocum were later guiding lights. Gloria Dodd and Dennis Doyle were helpful and supportive committee members; Fr. Francois Rossier, who has since passed away, also served on my committee with joy and enthusiasm. Joshua Brown, Jason Heron, Elizabeth Huddleston, Alan Mostrom, Robert Parks, Julia Parks, and Katherine Schmidt continue to be friends on the academic journey.

Institutionally, the resources of Roesch Library and the Marian Library at the University of Dayton, Ireland Library at St. Paul Seminary, and Rolvaag Library at St. Olaf College contributed to my research. St. Olaf College has supported travel to conferences that allowed me to present research connected with this book. My students at the University of Dayton, St. Olaf College, and the St. Paul Seminary have all endured my questioning and prodding on any number of issues related to this project; their engagement and consideration have inspired me to continue my research and writing. The editorial team at CUAP, especially John Martino, has also provided invaluable assistance as the project drew to a close.

More foundationally, my family has held me up throughout this process. In their own ways, my parents have supported and, from time to time, encouraged my academic trajectory. My three young sons are all very alive (keeping me coming back to the pot for more coffee) and completely fulfilling (quenching much deeper thirsts). Finally, my wife, Christine, has constantly demonstrated, as Maximus and Thomas exhort, the virtues of patience, fortitude, and temperance as setbacks, obstacles, and joys mingle. Her work outside the home has provided stability for our family, and her love has kept me (to mix some metaphors) both grounded and buoyed.

Late in publication, a dear childhood friend, Patrick Herman Lee, Pte San Wasté (the Good Grey Buffalo), passed away. This work is dedicated to his memory. May Our Lady, the White Buffalo Calf Woman, lead him down the end of the Good Red Road to the Great Spirit, Wakan Tanka.

The remaining errors in the work are my own. For the unrecalled and forgotten debts that helped bring it to fruition: *ab occultis meis munda me.*

ABBREVIATIONS

AL	Maximus the Confessor, *The Ascetic Life*
Amb. Io.	Maximus the Confessor, *Ambigua to John*
Amb. Thom.	Maximus the Confessor, *Ambigua to Thomas*
CCSG	Corpus Christianorum, Series Graeca
CCSL	Corpus Christianorum, Series Latina
CL	Maximus the Confessor, *Centuries on Love*
CT	Maximus the Confessor, *Centuries on Theology*
DFO	John of Damascus, *De Fide Orthodoxa*
PG	Migne, Patrologia Graeca
PL	Migne, Patrologia Latina
QD	Maximus the Confessor, *Questions and Doubts*
QT	Maximus the Confessor, *Questions from Thalassios*
Sent. Comm.	Thomas Aquinas, *Commentary on the Sentences*
ST	Thomas Aquinas, *Summa Theologica*
TPO	Maximus the Confessor, *Theological and Polemical Opuscula*

Salvation through Temptation

INTRODUCTION

In light of the biblical claim that Christ was "tempted like us in every way, yet without sin" (Heb 4:15), Christ's emotionality and temptation are a recurring locus for both popular and academic study of Christian theology, practice, devotion, and contemplation. As an aid to Christian reflection on this topic, contemporary theological exploration of Christ's temptation strives to elaborate an appropriate understanding of temptation and sin as they relate to Christ and his followers. Theologians across ecclesial commitments have presented Christ's temptation as soteriologically significant—yet in ways that are often mutually irreconcilable.[1] Indeed, such a basic question as *who* or *what* tempted Jesus remains a matter of dispute. Karl Barth and Helmut Thielicke, for instance, appear to identify the source of Christ's temptation as his very humanity; Joseph Ratzinger states that Jesus wrestles with his mission; and Kallistos Ware identifies the devil as the source of the temptation.

1. Robert W. Jenson, "Evil as Person," in *Lutheran Theological Seminary Bulletin* 69, no. 1 (1989): 33–40; Benedict XVI, *Jesus of Nazareth: From the Baptism in the Jordan to the Transfiguration* (New York: Doubleday, 2007), 26–28; Karl Barth, *Church Dogmatics* I.2, trans. G. T. Thomson and Harold Knight (Peabody, Mass.: Hendrickson Publishers, 2010), 158; Helmut Thielicke, *Between God and Satan*, trans. C. C. Barber (Grand Rapids, Mich.: William. B. Eerdmans Publishing Company, 1960), especially 18; Kallistos Ware, "The Imitation of Christ according to Saint Maximus the Confessor," in *A Saint for East and West: Maximus the Confessor's Contribution to Eastern and Western Christian Theology*, ed. Daniel Haynes, 73–74 (Eugene, Ore.: Cascade Books, 2019). See also John E. McKinley, *Tempted for Us: Theological Models and the Practical Relevance of Christ's Impeccability and Temptation* (Colorado Springs, Colo.: Paternoster, 2009) and Gerald Vann and P. K. Meagher, *The Temptations of Christ* (New York: Sheed and Ward, 1957), especially 7–43.

The central significance of modern theological investigation of Christ's emotionality and temptation derives from questions pertaining to key soteriological convictions: How can Christ be both sinless and tempted? How is Christ fully human, sharing in a fully human emotionality? How does Christ's emotional life express solidarity with the fallen condition of humanity? How is Christ's emotional life to be imitated as the perfect example of human existence? How does Christ govern his passions in a universally praiseworthy manner? The life of the Christian believer, shaped as an *imitatio Christi*, is closely bound to a proper understanding of Christ's perfectly praiseworthy emotionality, yet such an understanding proves difficult to articulate within the concrete minutiae of the human experience of the affective life.

The current study expands theological insight into human emotionality and the exemplary emotionality of Christ by attending to the way in which two figures of the Christian theological tradition—St. Maximus the Confessor and St. Thomas Aquinas—approach these problems concerning Christ's temptation. Each of these thinkers provides sustained attention to human passibility (the human susceptibility to a wide range of positive and negative affective experiences) and to the appropriate relationship of that passibility to Christ's own human experience. While recent studies of Maximus and Thomas have devoted sustained attention to Christ's emotional life and to his relationship with fallen human passibility, the specific contention of this study is that a correct understanding of Maximus's and Thomas's views of Christ's saving emotionality cannot be complete without considering the figure that both Maximus and Thomas recognize as the quintessential Tempter of the human race: Satan.

Perhaps due to modern reticence regarding discussion of the demonic, modern studies have tended to downplay or ignore the standing that Maximus and Thomas grant the devil in human temptation. Yet Maximus and Thomas provide detailed analysis of the devil's role in the temptation of Christ and other human beings. This analysis is intimately bound to the questions of human passibility that are at stake in other recent studies of their thought. Although consideration of demonic temptation may seem to be an esoteric journey into the far reaches of ancient and medieval cosmology, Maximus and Thomas's reflection on Christ's confrontation with the devil cuts to the heart of Christian claims about the salvific life and death of Jesus Christ. My hope, then, is that a historical and theological approach to Christ's temptation by the devil can enrich the modern conversation and offer a unique yet deeply traditional navigation of these ongoing Christological and anthropological challenges.

At the same time, in bringing Maximus and Thomas into conversation, certain theological developments in the description of the devil's temptation must be acknowledged. I argue that Maximus, along with early Greek monasticism as a whole, views temptation primarily from an externalized and demonological framework: the ascetic's emotional life is articulated as a battle against personified, malicious spirits. Thomas, on the other hand, is a well-developed example of a Latin tradition that frames fallen human temptation primarily as an internal or anthropological struggle against the "flesh," rooted in concupiscence, or the *fomes peccati*. In this framework, the devil's temptation is in some ways dependent on that logically prior corruption of human nature. I argue that this shift in anthropological framework between these two thinkers results in distinct articulations of human virtue and of the exemplarity of Christ's temptation for the Christian believer. Thus, investigation of these two figures can help us to understand more clearly the historical and theological development of Christian conceptions of the Fall, particularly insofar as Maximus and Thomas represent somewhat diverging Greek and Latin schools of thought on the subject.

At the outset, I make some note of recent academic literature, including studies that juxtapose Maximus and Thomas as theologians and recent work on Christ's passibility in each of the scholarly communities around Maximus and Thomas.

Modern Studies of Both Maximus and Thomas

The choice to juxtapose a seventh-century ascetic and a thirteenth-century university professor merits some comment. Historically, one must concede that Thomas Aquinas never substantively read the works of Maximus the Confessor. Only two citations in Thomas's corpus can be attributed to Maximus with certainty, and those come not directly from Maximus's works but from a popular florilegia. Other citations of his name (about a dozen in all) are references to the *Scholia* on Maximus's texts, the authorship of which has been significantly disputed since 1940.[2]

Nevertheless, scholars have uncovered important reasons to compare these two figures. In a broad sense, Marcus Plested, Christiaan Kappes, and Matthew Briel have investigated how both Eastern Orthodoxy and Catholicism have developed vibrant and interrelated scholastic traditions.[3] The work of these scholars points to a convergence and mutual recognition of Eastern and Western traditions that popular dichotomies of "Eastern mysticism versus Western scholasticism" do not allow. Plested and Briel, in particular, show that Aquinas is received in the Greek East in ways that undercut the presumption of a strong dichotomy on this front. Cumulatively, these scholars indicate that a sustained comparison of Maximus and Aquinas as systematic Christian thinkers has much to commend itself.

In a narrower sense, twentieth- and twenty-first-century French-language scholars already have undertaken comparative theological studies of Maximus and Thomas, most prominently R.-A. Gauthier, Antoine Lévy, and Jean-Miguel Garrigues. These thinkers alternately justify their subject matter historically and systematically. Gauthier, writing in the mid-twentieth century, provides the most important historical and systematic justification for the subject matter of the current study.[4] According to Gauthier, Thomas's account of the mor-

---

2. This comparative work is drawn from Antoine Lévy, *Le Créé et l'Incréé: Maxime le Confesseur et Thomas d'Aquin, aux Sources de la Querelle Palamienne* (Paris: Librairie Philosophique J. Vrin, 2006), 36–40. Since the authorship of the *Scholia* is disputed, I do not make reference to them in this work.

3. Marcus Plested, *Orthodox Readings of Aquinas* (Oxford: Oxford University Press, 2014); Christiaan Kappes, *The Immaculate Conception: Why Thomas Aquinas Denied, While John Duns Scotus, Gregory Palamas, and Mark Eugenicus Professed the Absolute Immaculate Existence of Mary* (New Bedford, Mass.: Academy of the Immaculate, 2014); and Matthew Briel, *A Greek Thomist: Providence in Gennadios Scholarios* (unpublished PhD diss., Fordham University, 2016).

4. R.-A. Gauthier, "Saint Maxime le Confesseur et la Psychologie de l'acte humain," in *Recherches de Théologie Ancienne et Médiévale* XXI (1954): 51–100.

al act is substantively a gloss on the moral psychology of Maximus. Gauthier argues that John of Damascus's role in the *De Fide Orthodoxa* is largely that of a compiler, depending almost entirely on Maximus for the substance of his moral psychology. In this way, Gauthier shows that Thomas's theological ethics is at least partially indebted to that of Maximus. However, it should be noted that Gauthier's analysis is sharply critical of certain psychological distinctions that he traces to Maximus, thereby attempting to drive a wedge between a proper reading of Maximus and modern Thomistic studies.

Whereas Gauthier is interested in critically tracing the historical roots of Thomas's moral psychology, more recent studies of Maximus and Thomas are motivated by ecumenical questions that aim to unite rather than divide the two figures. First, Jean-Miguel Garrigues's *Le Dessein Divin d'Adoption et le Christ Rédempteur* treats God's providential plan for the universe, particularly in light of human sin, the coming of Christ in response to that sin, and the means by which God restores a filial relationship with fallen human beings.[5] Garrigues's work does not historically or textually justify its comparison of Maximus and Thomas. Rather, he notes the systematic similarities between the two thinkers: both structure some of their major works around God's providential plan for the world.[6] While Garrigues's text is broadly Christological, his work remains much more cosmologically focused than the current study. I broach questions regarding God's providential permission of human temptation, but my concern in this regard is much narrower than that of Garrigues.

Second, Antoine Lévy's *Le Créé et l'Incréé: Maxime le Confesseur et Thomas d'Aquin, aux Sources de la Querelle Palamienne* rises out of a desire for rapprochement between Latin and Greek Christianity.[7] The ecumenical subject matter of Lévy's text does not necessitate historical justification, yet Lévy nevertheless provides the valuable textual analysis of Thomas's use of Maximus indicated at the outset of this

---

5. Jean-Miguel Garrigues, *Le Dessein Divin d'Adoption et le Christ Rédempteur* (Paris: Éditions du Cerf, 2011), 19–20.
6. Garrigues, *Le Dessein Divin*, 17.
7. Antoine Lévy, *Le Créé et l'Incréé*.

section. While this study shares Lévy's ecumenical concerns, the subject of his inquiry does not overlap substantially with mine. While the Palamite theory of uncreated energies concerns the economy of God's action in the world, the Christological and soteriological focus of the present work is wholly distinct from Lévy's subject matter.

Finally, on the basis of the convictions of Lévy's text, the recent English-language collection, *A Saint for East and West: Maximus the Confessor's Contribution to Eastern and Western Christian Theology*, offers a variety of scholars' attempts to consider Maximus's potential in helping arbitrate later ecumenical issues in metaphysics, ontology, and beyond.[8] While interest in Aquinas is not at the center of that volume, its ecumenical goal gives rise to many essays that fruitfully bring Aquinas into conversation with Maximus. Except for the essay by Kallistos Ware cited above, none of the essays discuss Christ's temptation at any length.

In light of these studies, this work investigates new territory in the comparative literature of Maximus and Thomas. Substantive consideration of Christ's emotional life has not been attempted in the comparative literature between Maximus and Thomas: heretofore, it has only taken place in the respective scholarly communities around Maximus and Thomas.

Christ's Demonic Temptation in Modern Studies of Maximus

Christ's struggle in the Garden of Gethsemane has been the crucial locus of modern analysis of the Maximus's Christological thought.[9] Many scholars have made an effort to analyze Maximus's interpretations of this passage in order to understand how Maximus upholds

---

8. Haynes, ed., *A Saint for East and West*. The volume places the Palamite controversy at the center of Maximus's ecumenical significance, and for that reason, Maximus's theory of the *logoi*—often juxtaposed with Aquinas's reflections on created and uncreated grace—is a recurring matter of discussion in the volume.

9. For a general treatment of the passions in Maximus's thought, see Paul M. Blowers, "The Dialectics and Therapeutics of Desire in Maximus the Confessor," in *Vigiliae Christianae* 65 (2011): 425–51.

Christ's full humanity while maintaining his perfect sinlessness. These scholars have described the problem as *anthropological* and *Christological*, requiring an understanding of fallen human beings in general and of Christ's unique relationship to that fallenness.

Yet some scholars express dissatisfaction with Maximus's final solution to the Christological component of this dilemma. Most importantly, Paul Blowers has repeatedly raised concern in the scholarly Maximian community regarding Maximus's denial of a *gnomic* will in Christ. Blowers asks: if Christ lacks precisely that concrete experience of will that other fallen human beings experience—that of a vacillating or deliberative will—then how can Christ redeem that experience?[10] Blowers's reading leans on Maximus's earlier works that ontologize the *gnomic* will of fallen human beings (as part of the human λόγος, our nature). In these works, a case can be made that Maximus sees the *gnomic* will as explaining the vacillation human beings experience with respect to the good. But when Maximus later revises this opinion and considers the *gnomic* will as a mode of willing that cannot be present in Christ, he appears to have created a disjunction between the fallen human experience of the affective life and Christ's affectivity. Blowers believes that this gap between Christ's experience and ours should lead scholars today to continue to investigate the nature of Maximus's resolution of this soteriological conundrum.

Other scholars indicate an inner tension in the way Maximus speaks of Christ's "natural" resistance to God's will in Gethsemane. Christ's fully elicited will is to do the will of the Father, yet these scholars acknowledge that this decision is made *eventually*, not absolutely immediately and spontaneously. Francois-Marie Léthel, for instance, says that Christ's acceptance indicates that he "no longer" rejects the cup.[11] Similarly, Demetrios Bathrellos says that Christ "eventually"

---

10. See, for example, Paul Blowers and Robert Louis Wilken, "Introduction," in *On the Cosmic Mystery of Jesus Christ* (Crestwood, N.Y.: St. Vladimir's Seminary Press, 2003), 37. More recently, see Paul M. Blowers, "Maximus the Confessor and John of Damascus on Gnomic Will (γνώμη) in Christ: Clarity and Ambiguity," *Union Seminary Quarterly Review* 63, no. 3–4 (2012): 44–50, and Paul M. Blowers, *Maximus the Confessor: Jesus Christ and the Transfiguration of the World* (Oxford: Oxford University Press, 2016), 156–65.

11. Francois-Marie Léthel, "La Prière de Jésus à Gethsémani," in *Maximos Confessor: Acts*

subjected his will to the Father's and "overcame" the instinctive desire to avoid death.[12] Pierre Piret also speaks of a preliminary rejection and a subsequent acceptance that completely destroys our egoistic fear of death, but he remains ambiguous as to whether the natural fear itself had to be *extinguished* in Christ's case, remaining content to affirm that Christ does not hesitate in performing God's will.[13] For the first two of these authors, there is a lack of clarity concerning what happened *before* that ultimate submission, and in Piret's case, it appears as if Christ's natural human fear (and related activation of the natural will) is something that has to be resisted as such. Yet Andrew Louth has reminded us that, for Maximus, human nature itself (and certainly the natural will) *cannot* resist God.[14] The idea that virtue is natural is at the heart of Maximus's theological vision of the human person. A natural resistance to God's will, then, would contradict the fundamental orientation of created nature toward its Creator and could ultimately

---

du Symposium sur Maximue le Confesseur Fribourg, 2–5 septembre 1980, ed. Felix Heinzer and Christoph Schönborn, 212 (Fribourg: Éditions Universitaires, 1982).

12. Demetrios Bathrellos, *The Byzantine Christ: Person, Nature, and Will in the Christology of St. Maximus the Confessor* (New York: Oxford University Press, 2004), 147. One might also note Guido Bausenhart in this list. He maintains the presence in Christ of an "instinctive drive for self-preservation" and an "already active natural, spontaneous, pre-reflective ... movement," neither of which immediately directs itself toward the highest goods of God's plan. See Guido Bausenhart, *"In allem uns gleich außer der Sünde" Studien zum Beitrag Maximos' des Bekenners zur altkirchlichen Christologie* (Mainz: Matthias-Grünewald-Verlag, 1992), 153–54.

13. Pierre Piret, *Christ et la Trinité selon Maxime le Confesseur* (Paris: Beauchesne, 2012), 280, 282, and 283. The following interpretations also fail to take seriously Maximus's explicit statements about the demonic component of Christ's human passibility. See Lévy, *Le Créé et l'Incréé*, 339; Adam G. Cooper, *The Body in St. Maximus the Confessor: Holy Flesh, Wholly Deified* (New York: Oxford University Press, 2005), 144, 160, and 225; Bathrellos, *The Byzantine Christ*, 147; throughout Marcel Doucet, "La Volonté Humaine du Christ, Spécialement en son Agonie. Maxime le Confesseur, Interprète de l'Écriture," *Science et Esprit* 37, no. 2 (1985): 123–59; and Christoph Schoenborn, "Plaisir et Douleur dans l'Analyse de S. Maxime, d'après les Quaestiones ad Thalassium," in *Maximus Confessor*, 278–79. Other examples point to a demonological resolution of this situation without articulating it fully. See John Meyendorff, "Free Will in Saint Maximus the Confessor," in *The Ecumenical World of Orthodox Civilization: Russia and Orthodoxy: Volume III*, ed. Andrew Blane, 75 (Paris: Mouton, 1974), and Claire-Agnes Zernheld, "Le Double Visage de la Passion: Malédiction due au Péché et/ou Dynamisme de la Vie," in *Philohistor: Miscellanea in Honorem Caroli Laga Septuagenarii*, ed. A. Schoors and P. Van Deun, 361–80 (Leuven: Uitgeverij Peeters, 1994). Finally, Blowers, *Maximus the Confessor*, 245–46, also reviews recent attempts to navigate the natural quality of Christ's resistance.

14. Andrew Louth, "Introduction," in *A Saint for East and West*, xxii–xxiv. This problem is also noted by Adam Cooper in that same work, 89–93. Cooper's resolution strives to uphold the unity of the *Logos* as both divine and human; still, more attention to the nature of Christ's demonstrated resistance is needed in response to Louth's observation.

call into question the orthodoxy of Maximus's dyothelite Christology. Surely Christ's human nature could not be a counterexample to this fundamental rule of creation? In the attempt to remove a Christological problem (Christ's resistance to God's will in Gethsemane), the secondary literature has only been able to substitute it with an equally unacceptable anthropological problem (human nature's natural resistance to God's will).

In response to these Christological difficulties and ambiguities, this work argues that a full articulation of Maximus's understanding of Gethsemane is not only anthropological and Christological but also *demonological*.[15] In various places, Maximus manifests a consistent demonological mode of reflection within his anthropological thought. This demonology is in continuity with that of Maximus's intellectual predecessors who were, in turn, concerned with clarifying and modifying the Stoic category of "what is up to us" (τὰ ἐφ' ἡμῖν) in light of Christian cosmology.[16] With the exception of Kallistos Ware's recent essay on the imitation of Christ,[17] this demonological framework is not adequately affirmed in the secondary literature. The mitigation of this strand of Maximus's thought goes back at least to Polycarp Sherwood, who follows a common Western distinction between internal and external forms of temptation. Sherwood argues that Maximus's

---

15. There is little modern discussion of Maximus's demonology. A brief treatment can be found in E. Mangenot, "Démon d'après les Pères," in *Dictionnaire de Théologie Catholique*, vol. 4 (Paris: Librairie LeTouzey et Ané, 1939), 377, but he receives no discussion in the otherwise wonderful presentation of monastic views of demonic temptation by Antoine and Claire Guillaumont, "Démon: Dans la Plus Ancienne Littérature Monastique," in *Dictionnaire de Spiritualité* (Paris: Beauchesne, 1957), 189–212.

16. Particularly important among recent studies concerning early Christian demonology are Jeffrey Burton Russell, *Satan: The Early Christian Tradition* (Ithica, N.Y.: Cornell University Press, 1981), especially 39–45 and 135–37; David Brakke, *Demons and the Making of the Monk: Spiritual Combat in Early Christianity* (Cambridge, Mass.: Harvard University Press, 2006), especially chapter 3; and Nienke Vos, "Demons Without and Within: the Representation of Demons, the Saint, and the Soul in Early Christian Lives, Letters and Sayings," in *Demons and the Devil in Ancient and Medieval Christianity*, ed. Nienke Vos and Willemien Otten, 3–36 (Boston: Brill, 2011). For the development of Jewish and Christian interest in Stoic conceptions of the passions, see Richard Sorabji, *Emotion and Peace of Mind: From Stoic Agitation to Christian Temptation* (Oxford: Oxford University Press, 2003), 343–418.

17. Kallistos Ware, "The Imitation of Christ," 73–74. Ware recognizes Maximus's demonological parallels between the general human experience of temptation and Christ's experience of it.

Christology conforms to this distinction, thereby implying that Maximus departed from his ascetic inheritance.[18] Accordingly, Sherwood states that while Maximus views demons as active internally within the affectivity of fallen human beings, Maximus's conception of Christ restricts the devil's activity to an external temptation.[19] In reality, Maximus's corpus simply does not support this distinction.[20]

More recent scholarship expands Sherwood's conclusions by downplaying Maximus's view of the devil's role in the anthropology of postlapsarian temptation. Ian A. McFarland and Jean-Claude Larchet, for example, favorably compare Maximus's anthropology to that of Augustine but in the process ignore the demonological aspects of the key proof-texts for this ecumenically oriented position.[21] Though Guido Bausenhart does not seek Western comparisons, his account of human sinfulness shares the anthropological focus of McFarland and Larchet.[22] Other scholars, such as Jean-Miguel Garrigues and Adam Cooper, discuss Maximus's view of self-love in relatively Western terms without attending to the demonological associations that

---

18. Polycarp Sherwood, OSB, "Introduction," in Maximus the Confessor, *The Ascetic Life, The Four Centuries on Charity*, trans. and annotated by Polycarp Sherwood (Westminster, Md.: Newman Press, 1955), 84–87.

19. Sherwood's supporting argument is that only *desert* monasticism is concerned so much with demons and that Maximus's career was too cosmopolitan to share this eremitic concern: "Maximus never even came to Egypt" (*The Ascetic Life*, 86). The incorrect assumption of this argument is that Maximus sees the demons' work as *exclusively* associated with the desert. Dayna S. Kalleres, "Demons and Divine Illumination: A Consideration of Eight Prayers by Gregory of Nazianzus," *Vigiliae Christianae* 61, no. 2 (2007): 157–88, shows that already by the fourth century, demons were by no means exclusively associated with the desert.

20. See my discussion of the *Ambigua to John* and *Questions from Thallasius* in chapters 2 and 3 (see pages X). Because of the way Maximus often tends to flow from anthropology to Christology while at the same time shifting from anthropology to demonology, it would be easier to get the (still incorrect) impression that Maximus associates demons with Christ's temptation *more* than with that of other human beings.

21. See Ian A. McFarland, "'Naturally and by Grace': Maximus the Confessor on the Operation of the Will," *Scottish Journal of Theology* 58 (4): 410–33 (2005), especially 412 and 416, where no reference is made to demonic powers. Jean-Claude Larchet, *Maxime le Confesseur Médiateur entre l'Orient et l'Occident* (Paris: Éditions du Cerf, 1998) is more reserved, though aims at the same comparison. See 121, where Larchet separates passibility from demonic temptation in order to compare Maximus's conception of the former with Augustine. While one must respect Larchet's ecumenical approach, the texts that he cites for the complete separability of these two realities do not bear the weight of his claim (see 88–89).

22. Bausenhart, *"In allem uns gleich außer der Sünde,"* 152–54. In his account, sinful human willing takes place through "disorientation" and "concupiscence" without reference to the demonic (153).

self-love has in Maximus's corpus.[23] And while still other scholars—including Demetrios Bathrellos, Lars Thunberg, and Jean Claude Larchet—acknowledge Maximus's affirmation of the devil's role in human temptation, these authors often fail to systematize this role.[24] A proper understanding of Maximus in relation to these authors is found in chapter 2, where I show the central and systematic importance of demonology in Maximus's view of fallen human temptation. For Maximus as well as for his ascetic forebears, demons constitute a decisive and distinctively Christian factor in establishing the boundaries of "what is up to us" (τὰ ἐφ' ἡμῖν), which in turn shapes their reflection on moral praise, responsibility, and virtue.

Putting aside the subsidiary anthropological question for the moment, however, this work attempts to resolve the Christological problems of the *gnomic* will and "natural" resistance to God's will through attention to Maximus's demonology in connection with his Christology and anthropology. Whereas Blowers is concerned that Christ's experience of will might not be identical to that of fallen human beings (in that Christ lacks a *gnomic* will), this study argues that the basic experiential categories of temptation (and thereby of will) as Maximus

---

23. See Jean-Miguel Garrigues, *Maxime le Confesseur: La Charité, Avenir Divin de l'Homme* (Paris: Ed. Beauchesne, 1976), 90, where no reference is made to Maximus's demonology in the analysis of self-love, yet Garrigues notes the importance of demons for that self-love on 109. See also Cooper, *The Body in St. Maximus the Confessor*, 208, 215, 244–46, and 208, where passing references to the devil (disposable in the course of Cooper's argument) can be found. In other places, Cooper wholly ignores the demonic aspect of possibility; see 222–23. See 148 and 159–60 for passages in which Maximus discusses demons, but Cooper's analysis does not. Cooper's "Freedom and Heteronomy" leans heavily on concepts of instinct and impulse to explain Christ's resistance but thereby avoids reference to Maximus's explicitly demonic approach to Christ's Gethsemane prayer.

24. Bathrellos, *The Byzantine Christ*, 159, downplays the devil's role in humanity's original temptation. See also Lars Thunberg, *Microcosm and Mediator: The Theological Anthropology of Maximus the Confessor* (Lund: Hakan Ohlssons Boktryckeri, 1965), 155, which emphasizes Adam's freedom to the detriment of the portrayal of the demonic associations of his temptation. In other places, Thunberg ignores the devil in his account of human fragility (227) and the Evagrian and Maximian association of demons with vice (248). Finally, Jean-Claude Larchet, *La Divinisation de l'Homme selon Saint Maxime le Confesseur* (Paris: Éditions du Cerf, 1996) at times demonstrates more interest in emphasizing human freedom than explaining Maximus's demonology, such as in his discussion of the demonic associations of possibility in Maximus's thought (197, 238, and 240–41). The concern for human responsibility in the face of demonic temptation precedes Maximus as well; see the discussion of earlier Christian views in David Bradshaw, *Aristotle East and West: Metaphysics and the Division of Christendom* (New York: Cambridge University Press, 2004), 123–24.

understood them should be framed less in terms of the *gnomic* will and more in terms of the oppression of angelic powers hostile to God through desire and aversion.[25] In my analysis, I follow Maximus's developed position that the *gnomic* will is strictly a *tropos* of human willing that merely *describes* the way human beings in fact activate their will (instead of explaining why they do so). Such a reading renders the exclusion of the *gnomic* will from Christ soteriologically tenable: if it is not properly constitutional, it is not necessarily a part of the *logos* of human nature that Christ must assume. Since modern scholarship is in agreement that Maximus ultimately denied a *gnomic* will in Christ, I have chosen to read Maximus generously on this point and seek an alternate solution to the experiential problem in Maximus's demonology. If one takes Maximus's demonology perfectly seriously, the fundamental temptations experienced by the monk are essentially identical with those experienced by Christ. The soteriological problems raised by Blowers are thereby reframed in a way that makes them more structurally soluble.

Whereas some scholars above noted that Christ "eventually" submits to God's will, I argue that Maximus, especially in his earlier nonpolemical writing, does not deflect that "eventually" onto human nature but rather onto the devil. Maximus does not say that the "Not my will" expressed in Gethsemane is merely a natural appetite. Rather, it is an appetite that is also a demonic temptation. Because of this additional component, the devil (and not human nature) is ultimately responsible for the emphatic resistance recounted in the Gospel accounts of Gethsemane. On the one hand, the "will" that is expressed is still in essential accord with nature; in this way, it is still a natural ap-

---

25. My assessment of this Christological solution to human fallenness is also expressed in Demetrios Bathrellos, "Passions, Ascesis, and the Virtues," in *The Oxford Handbook of Maximus the Confessor*, ed. Pauline Allen and Bronwen Neil, 287–305 (Oxford: Oxford University Press, 2015). Bathrellos notes clearly the demonological character of Maximus's *solution* to human passibility found in Christ's temptation (289–90), but his exposition of the *problem* of human passibility makes no reference whatsoever to demonic action in fallen humanity (287–88). In Bathrellos' exposition of Maximus, sin breaks human *passibility*, but Christ instead fixes humanity's relationship to *demons*: an odd incongruity between the Fall and Christ's saving action. I argue in chapters 2 and 3 that Maximus's view of the problem *and* the solution should be articulated in demonological categories.

petite and not at all blameworthy. But Maximus nevertheless affirms that the devil "lurks behind" these appetites so that they become an object of moral discernment. The reconciliation of this position with Maximus's dyothelite readings of Gethsemane will require some attention in the coming chapters. Even though Gethsemane appears only occasionally in my analysis, one component of my task is to render Maximus's demonology compatible with that later locus of Maximus's theological efforts.

Christ's Demonic Temptation in Modern Studies of Thomas

With respect to Thomistic studies, the modern conversation is somewhat different. The medieval tradition leading up to and including Thomas acknowledges that the devil can tempt in two ways: both from external suggestion and by internal means. Yet a difficulty for Thomas's interpreters arises from Thomas's direct consideration of Christ's temptation in *ST* III 41, where he does not explicitly address the internal means available to the devil. On the one hand, Thomas denies that Christ was tempted by the flesh: Christ possessed a perfection of grace that excludes the possibility of Christ's temptation by concupiscence, or the *fomes peccati*. On the other hand, Thomas affirms that Christ was tempted by the devil, since such temptation does not imply sinfulness. Thomas tersely affirms that "temptation which comes from an enemy can be without sin because it comes about by merely outward suggestion,"[26] without clarifying Christ's relationship to the devil's *interior* suggestion.

To explain Thomas's view on this matter, two basic positions have developed in the recent literature, each motivated by distinct modern theological concerns. The first position downplays the devil's role in temptation, both in general and in Christ's case. More specifically,

---

26. Thomas Aquinas, *Summa Theologica* III 41.1, reply 3 (hereafter, *ST*). See Thomas Aquinas, *Summa Theologiae: First Complete American Edition*, 3 vols., translated by Fathers of the English Dominican Province (Cincinnati, Ohio: Benzinger Brothers, 1947).

these authors deny or consider unimportant the idea that the devil can affect the human mind. Often, the reason for this dismissal is a worry that serious consideration of the devil's activity would lead to a diminished sense of personal responsibility for sin.[27] When Thomas's own theological underpinnings clash with the modern tendency toward demythologization, these authors tend to side with the latter as an apologetic to our times.

This first position can be seen in writings by Joseph Wawrykow and Nicholas Lombardo. Joseph Wawrykow's *Westminster Handbook to Thomas Aquinas* does not discuss internal demonic temptation and even denies its possibility in his purely anthropological consideration of temptation.[28] Wawrykow states: "No angel can work inwardly on a human; the inward moving of the person is reserved to God."[29] As will be clear in chapter 5, however, this assertion contradicts Thomas's explicit view of demonic temptation, at least in the postlapsarian condition. Admittedly, there is a restricted sense in which Wawrykow's statement would be true, but his denial is far too broad and is in need of substantial clarification and correction.[30] Wawrykow's consideration of Christ's temptation consequently does not address whether the devil tempted Christ internally.

Nicholas Lombardo's *The Logic of Desire: Aquinas on Emotion* also denies any significant place for a discussion of the devil's inter-

---

27. This position is explicit in the very brief treatment of the demonic in Rudi A. te Velde, "Evil, Sin, and Death: Thomas Aquinas on Original Sin," in *The Theology of Thomas Aquinas*, ed. Rik van Nieuwenhove and Joseph Wawrykow, 151–52 (Notre Dame, Ind.: University of Notre Dame Press, 2005). Velde downplays the demonic with an argument about the maintenance of human culpability. Perhaps in this same vein, Jean Porter, "Right Reason and the Love of God: The Parameters of Aquinas' Moral Theology" in *The Theology of Thomas Aquinas*, ed. Rik van Nieuwenhove and Joseph Wawrykow, 171–86 (Notre Dame, Ind.: University of Notre Dame Press, 2005) introduces the devil as an external agent of temptation but does not treat Satan's role in the moral life in the substantive discussion that follows.

28. Joseph Wawrykow, *Westminster Handbook to Thomas Aquinas* (Louisville, Ky.: Westminster John Knox Press, 2005). Throughout the text, Wawrykow allows the distinction between inner and outer temptation to correspond perfectly with that between the flesh and the devil. Yet this explanation ignores Aquinas's claims that the devil also employs internal bodily organs for the same purpose.

29. Wawrykow, *Westminster Handbook*, 38, 147.

30. If Wawrykow had restricted this statement to movement of the will and intellect (both of which are immaterial faculties and thus beyond the meddling of demonic powers), he would be correct.

nal temptation. As such, Lombardo's discussion of Christ's internal temptation by the devil is confined to a single brief footnote.[31] In the main text, Lombardo repeats Thomas's basic distinction: "the temptations that Christ experienced were always 'exterior'; Christ never experienced 'interior' temptation."[32] But Lombardo provides no substantial Christological discussion of the internal assault of the devil. As with Wawrykow's text, the root of this Christological omission is anthropological in nature given Lombardo's similarly brief treatment of the devil's internal temptation in his purely anthropological chapters. Unlike Wawrykow, Lombardo adequately acknowledges that the devil *can* tempt internally, yet he denies that this sort of internal temptation is anthropologically *significant*. Considering a subtreatise on Aquinas's demonology to be a significant digression from his central subject matter, Lombardo ignores the topic almost entirely:

> According to Aquinas, the devil can arouse desires and passions, but he does not have a monopoly on any particular passion or temptation.... Demonic temptation ... does not constitute its own category of subjective human experience. It can only exaggerate the preexisting inclinations of nature. Demons manipulate matter; they do not occupy a permanent niche in our psyche. In a sense, there is nothing mysterious about diabolic temptation in Aquinas's account: preternatural agents are involved, but they act through natural causes. Consequently, even when temptation involves more than natural causes, its demonic origin is largely irrelevant to practical questions about virtue and vice, because human nature operates according to its own principles even when demonic activity is involved.[33]

Important criticisms must be leveled against these assertions. First, Lombardo seems to commit something of a category error in describing angels as "preternatural agents" who act as "more than natural causes." In a Thomistic account, angels and demons are wholly *natural* agents; *only* God is properly a supernatural agent. His discussion of angels in *ST* I calls angelic natures higher than human nature, but not

---

31. Nicholas Lombardo, *The Logic of Desire: Aquinas on Emotion* (Washington, D.C.: The Catholic University of America Press, 2011), 211.
32. Lombardo, *The Logic of Desire*, 211.
33. Lombardo, *The Logic of Desire*, 123.

preternatural, beyond nature.[34] As such, demons are fully part of the broader "nature" within which human beings act (see Eph 6:12)—not superfluous ephemera that the Christian agent can safely ignore or treat as if they didn't exist.

Second, if demonic powers are a part of the natural Christian landscape, they are certainly relevant to discussion of virtue and vice—a point Lombardo denies. Even if they do not occupy a "permanent niche in our psyche," Thomas acknowledges that demons nevertheless bombard the fallen human being though imagination and desire. The latter of these temptations depend upon the *fomes peccati*, but, as I show in chapter 5, temptations that manipulate the imagination are formally distinct. In those cases, it is not possible to reduce such temptations to "the preexisting inclinations of nature" (as Lombardo suggests), since demons would be capable of impressing wholly new images or ideas that have no intrinsic relationship to the independent (affective?) inclinations of nature. No analogy, let alone identification, of this sort of demonic temptation with the human subject's own natural use of imagination would suffice to describe that subject's moral circumstances.

Third, perhaps the most significant piece of evidence against Lombardo's claim that demonic temptation is irrelevant to virtue and vice is found in Thomas's own organization of the *Summa Theologica*. There, Aquinas devotes significant and lengthy attention to the role of the devil as an internal tempter, and he does so *within the treatise on vice* in *ST* I-II. Thomas's placement of this discussion makes clear that the phenomena of demonic temptation require a *moral* response, grounded in his broader theory of virtue and vice. It is not, as Lombardo contends, "largely irrelevant to practical questions about virtue and vice." While Lombardo's dismissal of internal demonic temptation may have been necessary for the brevity and focus of his study, his reasons for that dismissal do not sufficiently bear the weight of his claims.

The second position in the recent literature acknowledges Thom-

---

34. *ST* I 112.1, obj. 4.

as's view of the devil's interior temptation in a truncated form. These authors note that the devil can affect the human imagination in Thomas's system, but they stop short of the more robust forms of interior demonic temptation that Thomas discusses. Here, the modern motivation is soteriological: they acknowledge Thomas's position precisely to the extent that it allows them to affirm Christ's solidarity with the fallen human condition. When Thomas's view departs from an affirmation of this solidarity (which at times it does), these authors fall silent.

This tendency is seen in the work of Paul Gondreau and Jean-Pierre Torrell. Among works in English, Paul Gondreau's *The Passions of Christ's Soul in the Theology of St. Thomas Aquinas* is unsurpassed in the length of discussion granted to the topic of Christ's temptation in general and of his temptation by the devil in particular. The chief benefit of Gondreau's treatment is that it attempts to create, in a Thomistic framework, as close a correspondence as possible between Christ's affectivity and that of his followers. Gondreau argues that Thomas assigns the devil the same sort of power over Christ's internal states as the devil has over other fallen human beings: "Aquinas recognizes that the manner by which Satan attacks the affective dimension of human life ... was certainly operative in his assault on Jesus."[35] As part of this affirmation, Gondreau clarifies what Thomas leaves ambiguous in his Christological account of temptation: namely, that the devil can tempt human beings *interiorly*.

While Gondreau's approach is commendable, its anthropological foundations are not perfectly secure. Gondreau acknowledges the devil's interior attack but he does so only in a truncated form, speaking only of a demonic "persuasion" that progresses through the imagination and by which the devil "hopes to rouse a [disordered] passion."[36] As I show in chapter 5, however, this persuasion is only one of the two forms of internal attack that Thomas affords the devil in attacking

---

35. Paul Gondreau, *The Passions of Christ's Soul in the Theology of St. Thomas Aquinas* (Scranton, Pa.: University of Scranton Press, 2009), 356.

36. Gondreau, *The Passions of Christ's Soul*, 356.

fallen human beings.[37] Gondreau's error is seen in his use of the word "hope" in the quote above; Thomas is certain that (unless God were to prevent it) the devil can cause a disordered passion in a fallen human subject. Since this power of the devil to cause affective states in human subjects is predicated on the defect of the *fomes peccati*, however, this sort of interior demonic temptation cannot be appropriately attributed to Christ. There is in Thomas's account, therefore, a greater disjunction between the devil's temptation of Christ and that of fallen human beings than Gondreau acknowledges.

Finally, Jean-Pierre Torrell's *Le Christ en ses Mystères: La vie et l'Oeuvre de Jésus selon saint Thomas d'Aquin* provides a valuable and lengthy Thomistic account of Christ's temptation by the devil.[38] Torrell faithfully reproduces the key Thomistic affirmations: Christ was tempted by the devil but not by the flesh.[39] Torrell goes on to acknowledge what Thomas himself neglected: that there is an internal form of the devil's attack. He states that the devil can make "a proposition to the intellect or interior senses.... [A demon] can very well act on one's imagination, whether one be awake or asleep, and that leaves a vast field open to the tempter."[40] Despite this acknowledgement, Torrell's description of the devil's power of internal temptation also does not lay adequate anthropological foundations. Since Torrell wishes to emphasize the likeness between Christ's temptation and that of other human beings, he focuses on the devil's power of imaginative attack while failing to adequately acknowledge the devil's power of appetitive attack against fallen human beings.

Torrell constructs a creative Thomistic account of Christ's temptation, arguing that Christ's temptation in the desert would have

---

37. The *De Malo* avows that there are two forms of attack and not just the one Gondreau acknowledges: the devil acts both as a *persuader* and as a *disposer* (*De Malo* III.4). Thomas Aquinas, *The De Malo of Thomas Aquinas*, trans. Richard Regan (New York: Oxford University Press, 2001).

38. Jean-Pierre Torrell, *Le Christ en ses Mystères: La vie et l'Oeuvre de Jésus selon saint Thomas d'Aquin*, vol. 1 (Paris: Desclée, 1999), 224–42.

39. See Torrell, *Le Christ*, 238, for his denial of the *fomes* from Christ and for the reality of Christ's temptation by the devil.

40. Torrell, *Le Christ*, 239, my translation.

taken place purely inside Christ's mind. Thus, the second and third temptations (at the Temple and on the mountaintop) are, according to Torrell, not physical transportations but images presented internally to Christ's mind. For Torrell, this form of temptation corresponds more closely with our own fallen experience of temptation (without becoming sinful) and is therefore soteriologically valuable when appropriated by Christ. As I will discuss in chapter 6 and in the conclusion, this account is a valuable way forward for the modern Thomistic tradition, yet one must be clear that this account is *not* Thomas's own. Specifically, Thomas's *Commentary on Matthew* takes some pains to argue that the best interpretation of the second and third temptations is physical and not psychological—Thomas prefers to think that Christ was physically transported by the devil to the top of the Temple and mountaintop. Further, Thomas's preference in this regard will have some important consequences for Christ's exemplarity and the *imitatio Christi*. While Torrell's assessment is not that of Thomas, it can still be described as broadly Thomistic and is happily accepted as such.

To date, no account of Christ's temptation has adequately discussed Thomas's anthropological framework for demonic temptation. Consequently, none of the recent studies accurately or adequately frames Christ's own experience of temptation within Thomas's broader understanding of the devil's power to tempt fallen human beings.

This study is arranged in two groups of three chapters, each following the same pattern. Chapter 1 traces post-biblical influences on Maximus's understanding of Christ's temptation: his anthropological and Christological sources. Chapter 2 turns to Maximus's own anthropology. I trace his conception of the original state of humanity in the garden and in the Fall and its consequences, paying particular attention to the interrelationship of demonology and anthropology. Chapter 3 considers the soteriological role of Christ's temptation in Maximus's thought, proceeding from a discussion of Christ's constitution (his human defects and human perfections) to an exposition of his liberating work in his temptation. Chapter 4 is important for the historical trajectory between Maximus and Thomas. It first considers the thin historical link between Maximus and Thomas that is found in the works of John of Damascus and Burgundio of Pisa and, second, traces two pairs of Latin Patristic and medieval sources for Thomas's understanding of Christ's temptation. Parallel to chapters 2 and 3, chapters 5 and 6 proceed through the same anthropological and Christological matters in the thought of Thomas Aquinas.

1

SOURCES FOR MAXIMUS'S PRESENTATION OF CHRIST'S TEMPTATION

The most relevant sources for Maximus's conception of Christ's temptation by the devil can be grouped as *anthropological* and *Christological*. To emphasize the theological challenges with which Maximus grappled, I present these sources topically rather than by author or in a strictly historical order of composition.[1]

Maximus's Anthropological Sources

Because early Christianity was indebted to and bound up with Greek philosophical thought, the following discussion among early Christian authors might be fruitfully framed as an attempt among early Christians to grapple with the Stoic category of "what is up to us" (τὰ ἐφ' ἡμῖν). For the Stoics, as for these early Greek-speaking Christians, this category delimits the extent of praiseworthy action, virtue, and vice since anything that is *not* up to us is beyond the purview of human moral agency.[2] The extent of this category was debated among

---

1. Not all the authors considered in this chapter discuss Christ, temptation, and the demonic together. In contrast, Thomas's sources each reflect on the whole nexus of affectivity, demons, and Christ under consideration in this work. Chapter 4 is arranged to reflect this difference.

2. Christian appropriation of Stoic thought is often traced through its neo-Platonic reception

the Stoics; Christians therefore rightly considered how their own distinctive understanding of the cosmos shapes the landscape of moral perfections. Three topics merit discussion as part of the background to Maximus's understanding of human nature: the structure of the moral act, the origin of the passions, and the nature of demonic temptation. For the first, Nemesius of Emesa's theory of the moral act is undoubtedly the central source for Maximus's own presentation of that matter, and for the second, Gregory of Nyssa's understanding of the origin of the passions foreshadows important difficulties in Maximus's thought. Finally, and crucially, Origen of Alexandria and Evagrius of Ponticus's theories of demonic temptation are important for an adequate understanding of the early ascetic tradition of which Maximus constitutes a later link.

Nemesius of Emesa's Anthropology

For Maximus's general understanding of the human person, there is no source more important than Nemesius of Emesa, who wrote the treatise *On the Nature of Man* around the end of the fourth century.[3] In the following presentation of Nemesius's anthropology, I emphasize the rational faculty's powers of memory, imagination, and thought; the irrational faculty's appetitive powers; and some possible Christological ramifications for Nemesius's approach to the moral act.

In the broadest terms, Nemesius considers the human being to be composed of two substances, a body and a soul. Nemesius affirms that the soul "is not controlled by the body, but itself controls the

---

in figures like Plotinus and not always directly back to the Stoics themselves. For a broader discussion of Stoicism and its reception among neo-Platonists, see Lloyd P. Gerson, "Plotinus and the Platonic Response to Stoicism," in *The Routledge Handbook of the Stoic Tradition*, ed. John Sellars, 44–55 (New York: Routledge, 2016). For more direct links to the Stoics, see Richard Sorabji, *Emotion and Peace of Mind: From Stoic Agitation to Christian Temptation* (Oxford: Oxford University Press, 2003), 343–418.

3. Though Nemesius's anthropology is central to Maximus's own, Nemesius gives scant testimony regarding either demonology or the Fall since Nemesius's own sources were largely non-Christian. For a more comprehensive analysis of Nemesius's anthropology (and a key source for the present summary), see Nemesius of Emesa, *On the Nature of Man*, trans. R. W. Sharples and P. J. Van Der Eijk (Liverpool: Liverpool University Press, 2008), 1–32. Concerning the question of temptation, Nemesius briefly addresses the ways in which external objects are the origin of vicious actions: Nemesius, *Nature of Man*, §30 (96.2–.13). He does not, however, discuss demons in this context. I consider this paragraph below.

body,"[4] and so the body is understood as instrumental, not interfering with the powers of the soul but only carrying out their commands.[5] The various powers or faculties of the soul have their own physical expression in the body. Thus, the body does not have powers of its own, but only carries out the commands given to it by the soul's faculties.

The Aristotelian and Stoic sources from which Nemesius draws divide the soul in differing ways, so Nemesius is forced to try to reconcile these different presentations. Nemesius's harmonization consists of ranked faculties that fit in two broad categories: the rational and irrational. Nemesius's typology indicates the various relationships between the rational and irrational faculties that he investigates: the rational or psychical powers (technically only thought, but in close relationship with imagination, sensation, and memory); the combined powers that share qualities of both rational and irrational faculties (respiration and digestion); the nonrational powers capable of obeying reason (aversion and desire);[6] and the nonrational powers not capable of obeying reason.[7] In the following, I concentrate on the rational powers and the nonrational powers capable of obeying reason.

Three faculties relate to one another in the consideration of the rational power: the imaginative, the thinking, and the remembering faculties, each with its own location in the brain. In the process of imagination, the external sensory organs of the body (according to the five-fold division of the senses) first interact with sensory objects in the outside world. Sensation, secondly, takes note of these interactions. Imagination finally considers the data collected by sensation, interprets it into a mental representation (phantasm) or image (icon), and passes that image to thought for judgment and consideration. In short, imagination collects and organizes particular data from the outside world and passes it on to thought.[8]

---

4. Nemesius, *Nature of Man*, §3 (41.8–.10).
5. Nemesius, *Nature of Man*, §5 (54.2–.5).
6. In the first half of this project, I refer to θυμός as "aversion," whereas in the second half, I will describe the faculty opposite of desire as "irascibility." I justify this choice in relation to Maximus and Thomas in chapter 2, n. 6.
7. Nemesius, *Nature of Man*, §§22–25, 27–28.
8. Nemesius, *Nature of Man*, §6.

Thought, on the other hand, is concerned with the consideration of the data given to it by the imagination, as well as with universal knowledge or ideas that Nemesius calls "natural concepts."[9] As Nemesius explains these concepts, they are truths that exist in everyone without needing to be taught. Such an idea is apparently Platonic in origin, relating to knowledge of the forms.[10] Thought considers these two types of information, judges, agrees to a course of action, and commands movement.[11] Because of this central role, thought is the highest faculty of the soul, the one that rules over all the rest.[12]

When the images or natural concepts no longer need consideration or action, they are passed into memory, where they may be recalled at a later time. Memory, too, passes on images to thought, but it differs from imagination in that the object of the image does not need to be present to the body when it is remembered.[13]

Nemesius further considers the nonrational faculties capable of obeying reason, wherein he discusses the actions of the appetitive faculty of the soul: the passions. Nemesius's morally neutral definition of the passions is significant; other Christians more heavily indebted to the Stoics see passions not as natural faculties but as something contrary to nature. Maximus, in turn, will retain aspects of both usages in his terminology. For Nemesius, the passions are subdivided into desire (ἐπιθυμία) and aversion (θυμός), things that are to be sought and things to be avoided. These appetites are essential to both human and animal life because "without them life cannot be sustained," presumably because a being without desire and drive would quickly deteriorate or be destroyed. For Nemesius, the appetitive faculty also mediates between soul and body when physical movement is involved.[14]

---

9. Nemesius, *Nature of Man*, §13.

10. Nemesius, *Nature of Man*, §13. Nemesius hints at a distinction between διανοητικόν (which would deal with particulars) and νοητικόν (which would deal with universals) but never develops their difference clearly. I treat them as equivalent here.

11. These activities, roughly, are "judgment, assent, avoidance, and impulse," in Nemesius, *Nature of Man*, §12.

12. Nemesius, *Nature of Man*, §6.

13. Nemesius, *Nature of Man*, §13.

14. Nemesius, *Nature of Man*, §16; see also §27. The "impulse [ὁρμή]" Nemesius refers to here should not be confused with the sort of affective desire that Gregory of Nyssa sees in the

TABLE 1-1. Nemesius and Maximus's Affective Categories

	Present Reality	Future Reality
Desire	Pleasure	Desire
Aversion	Distress	Fear

Partly because of this cooperation with the soul in the physical movement of the body, Nemesius argues that the appetitive faculty is capable of obeying reason.[15]

The two major divisions of the appetitive part, desire and aversion, can be further subdivided according to whether the object is currently present or anticipated in the future (see table 1-1). When the desirous part attains what it seeks in the present, it is called "pleasure"; when it anticipates the arrival of the object, it is called "desire." When the repulsive part experiences its object, it is called "distress"; when it anticipates its object, it is called "fear."[16] The relationship of the will to these appetites will be significant in my consideration of Maximus's view of these faculties.[17]

At the close of this material, I call attention to two separate Christological problems concerning what Nemesius believes about virtuous and vicious actions. The first arises from Nemesius's definition of "willful" actions and concerns whether Christ can be said to be ignorant concerning particular facts. The second arises from Nemesius's definition of "choice," "deliberation," and "autonomy" and concerns whether Christ should be said to be impeccable in an absolute sense.

For the first problem, Nemesius defines a willful act as "that which has its origin in the agent who knows the particular fact concerning the action."[18] As such, a willful act is worthy of moral praise or blame.

---

human condition before the Fall (discussed below). Nemesius's sense is that of an action chosen in thought, mediated by appetition, and carried out by the body.

15. Nemesius, *Nature of Man*, §16.
16. Nemesius, *Nature of Man*, §17.
17. Nemesius, *Nature of Man*, §17–21. When considering Christ's demonic temptation, Maximus chooses to organize his presentation according to Nemesius's categories instead of those of Evagrius, discussed below.
18. Nemesius, *Nature of Man*, §32. I render ἑκουσίων as "willful" or willfully and ἀκουσίων

Nemesius sees two ways in which actions become unwillful: either through force or through ignorance of particular facts.[19] Given his apparently Platonic conception of universal truths, he explains that ignorance about universal and general truths is itself willful, an act that might be called "vulnerable" or "vincible" ignorance in modern categories.[20] This vulnerable ignorance follows from the universal accessibility of these truths by the human subject, who must actively avoid knowing them in order to remain ignorant. Because of this fact, any misjudgment or ignorance about universal truths leads to a willful moral evil. However, ignorance of particular truths *can* be unwillful, meaning that the individual did not know and had no legitimate means of knowing a morally relevant fact in a given situation.[21]

Nemesius's approach to this question will require, in chapter 3, an investigation of unwillful ignorance in Christ. First, must all ignorance of universal truths be considered willful? Are Christians thereby bound to a Platonic theory of innate knowledge? Second, on the presumption that some forms of ignorance are constitutive of our current condition, does Christ fittingly identify with that condition? Could Christ unwillfully commit moral evil in the way that Nemesius describes? If unwillful ignorance is denied in Christ, how would this denial not call into question Christ's identification with our condition and his sharing in the current human experience of temptation?

The second Christological problem is associated with Nemesius's

---

as "unwillful" or unwillfully. R. W. Sharples and P. J. van der Eijk prefer to render the terms as "intentional" and "unintentional," respectively, and they reject their translation as "voluntary" and "involuntary." The difficulty of translating this term relates to Nemesius's own apparent equivocation. "Intentional" is accurate in many cases, but in some portions of Nemesius's texts, he denies the need for knowledge of the relevant facts. It makes little sense, however, to say that one "intends" what one does not understand. Since I make reference to those difficult texts below, I avoid the confusing "intentional" rendering. See Nemesius, *Nature of Man*, 168, n. 868, and 176, n. 894. Because of the provenance of this terminology, I follow the same convention of translation when the terms arise in Maximus.

19. Related to the unwillful through force, Nemesius asks whether actions undertaken because of the enticements or provocations of external objects are still considered willful—his examples are a prostitute goading one to licentiousness and an assailant who provokes one to anger. The question is of interest because demonic forces can act for Maximus in a similar way.

20. These terms are not used by Maximus; for their modern sense, see the *Catechism of the Catholic Church*, 2nd ed. (Vatican: Libreria Editrice Vaticana, 2012), §1791 and 1793.

21. Nemesius, *Nature of Man*, §31.

definition of choice, deliberation, and autonomy.[22] To introduce the question, a few of Nemesius's relevant terms require definition. Nemesius at times defines choice more narrowly than an act that he calls willful. For instance, we can willfully do things that we do not choose, as one encounters friends on the street even when such happens unexpectedly and without intent. In essence, if something is surprising but is met favorably, it is *willful* but not *chosen*.[23] Positively, Nemesius defines choice (προαίρεσις) as a collection or combination of appetition, selection, and deliberation. The latter term is most important here; Nemesius states that deliberation "is concerned with things that are still under investigation," meaning that one has yet to decide whether to select them. Nemesius restates that deliberation is not "about what is agreed upon or the impossible" because if something is certain to occur or not to occur, there can be no deliberation about it. Rather, deliberation is concerning the *contingent*, which Nemesius defines as something that is equally likely to happen or not, "for if we could not do both, both it and its opposite, we would not have deliberated."[24]

Autonomy, too, is an essential characteristic of humanity in Nemesius's anthropology. He argues that autonomy is in fact synonymous with rationality; if one wished to blame God for our ability to choose good and evil, one would also have to blame God for creating human beings as rational.[25] Autonomy and rationality stand and fall together. The key observation here, however, is that Nemesius described human beings as autonomous with respect to things that they deliberate: things that can either happen or not happen and the object of which attracts praise or blame.[26] It is with regard to these self-motivated *contingent* things that human beings are considered to be autonomous and therefore rational.

---

22. Nemesius, *Nature of Man*, §29.
23. Nemesius, *Nature of Man*, §33.
24. Nemesius, *Nature of Man*, §34; see also §40: deliberation is "about matters having an equal possibility. What has an equal possibility is that where we are able to do both the thing itself and its opposite."
25. Nemesius, *Nature of Man*, §41.
26. Intention "always attracts praise or blame" (Nemesius, *Nature of Man*, §40); choice is a narrower species within intention; and deliberation is a means to choice. Thus, the object of deliberation also attracts praise or blame.

When addressing Christ's humanity in chapter 3, the essential Christological question in this case will be the precise way in which one should express the impeccability of Christ—the idea that Christ not only *did not* sin but that he was *incapable* of it. If this impeccability were stated in absolute terms within Nemesius's anthropology, it would follow that Christ was incapable of virtue and that he was not autonomous, rational, or fully human. It would also appear that such a person could also not be tempted. Because Nemesius's categories are so important for Maximus, chapter 3 investigates Maximus's navigation of Christ's full humanity, his ability to be tempted, and his impeccability.

The Origin of the Passions in Gregory of Nyssa

Unlike Nemesius, Gregory of Nyssa offers extended commentary on the original state of humanity before the Fall and on sin's effects on that state.[27] Gregory recognizes the moral categories given in Stoic philosophy and modifies the Stoic account for his own ends. Importantly, in Stoic terms, a "passion" denotes an appetitive movement that is irrational and thus contrary to both virtue and human flourishing (εὐδαιμονία).[28] Taken without reference to *eupatheia*, or later Stoic "first movements," such a definition of passion could indicate that *any* appetitive movement or desire in a human being is contrary to human flourishing. In this context, Gregory sets out to affirm the intrinsic nature of human affectivity while acknowledging that this affectivity is altered by sin.

In *On the Soul and the Resurrection*, Gregory of Nyssa devotes a significant portion of his discussion with his sister, Macrina, to the question of the passions: where they come from, their moral quality, and their end.[29] Their understanding of the passions is illustrated through

---

27. I have omitted material on St. Basil of Caesarea because of the highly allegorical nature of his *On the Human Condition*, trans. Nonna Verna Harrison (Crestwood, N.Y.: St. Vladimir's Seminary Press, 2005). There is no direct evidence that Maximus substantively interacted with Basil on this topic.

28. For a brief overview of the tenets of Stoic philosophy, see John Sellars, "Introduction," in *The Routledge Handbook of the Stoic Tradition*, ed. John Sellars, 1–2 (New York: Routledge, 2016).

29. See Lucas Francisco Mateo-Seco and Giulio Maspero, eds., *The Brill Dictionary of Gregory*

an allegorical interpretation of the parable of the tares (Mt 13:24–30). In the eyes of Macrina and Gregory, God is the farmer who establishes within each human individual seeds of natural "impulses [ὁρμή]" or "motions [κινήματα]." These impulses, Macrina explains, are something "sown" in human nature by God from our creation that draw us toward our true good and help us avoid evil. If cultivated and allowed to produce fruit, these motions are the good seed planted in our soul that "would undoubtedly have produced the fruit of virtue for us"[30] and that are "truly good by nature."[31] Thus, from the creation of humankind, these impulses establish the human subject as an affective being, capable of righteous aversion and desire, as long as these impulses were directed toward their proper ends.[32] In the case of desire, this end is a tendency that "raise[s] us toward the union with the heavenly"; for love, it is to join us with the divine; for aversion, the purpose is as a "weapon" against "our adversary."[33] Each of these purposes is so important and deep-set within the constitution of human nature that it would be unthinkable to consider them as extrinsic or as a punitive addition resulting from human sin.

Yet as their allegorical reading of the tares unfolds, human affectivity is revealed to be much more morally ambiguous than indicated

---

of Nyssa (Boston: Brill, 2010), 53 (on dispassion) and 220 (on the passions in human nature). These articles do not discuss significantly the role of the Fall in the origin of the passions. See also the sources cited below concerning the Nyssen's *intellectualist* understanding of the Fall and consequent introduction of passion.

30. Gregory of Nyssa, *On the Soul and the Resurrection*, trans. Catharine P. Roth (Eugene, Ore.: Wipf & Stock, 1992), 58. Greek text is from Patrologia Graeca (PG), 46 (text accessed at https://books.google.com/books?id=fvfuD2TKz_wC).

31. Gregory of Nyssa, *On the Soul*, 59.

32. Gregory of Nyssa, *On the Soul*, 60. Modern scholarship has established that Gregory conceives of desire as a positive part of human nature. See J. Warren Smith, *Passion and Paradise: Human and Divine Emotion in the Thought of Gregory of Nyssa* (New York: Crossroad, 2004), especially 75–103, and the literature indicated by Paul M. Blowers, "The Dialectics and Therapeutics of Desire in Maximus the Confessor," *Vigiliae Christianae* 65, no. 4 (2011): 432, n. 33. Gregory's teaching here is in continuity with a Platonic and Greek patristic tradition concerning the nature of *eros* as both self-interested and selfless, as demonstrated in Catherine Osborne's study of Platonic teaching in Clement, Origen, Gregory of Nyssa, and Evagrius. See Catherine Osborne, *Eros Unveiled: Plato and the God of Love* (Oxford: Oxford University Press, 1994), especially 52–70. One can also point to the discussion of *eros* in Blowers, "Dialectics and Therapeutics," 438, and, sporadically, in John Rist, "On the Platonism of Gregory of Nyssa," *Hermathena* no. 169: 129–151, especially 133.

33. Gregory of Nyssa, *On the Soul*, 59.

thus far. When Macrina explains the sowing of tares by an "enemy" under "cover of darkness," the enemy they have in mind is clearly the devil. But the cover of darkness is required for the devil to accomplish his goal. For Macrina, the primordial sin of Adam and Eve is this darkness. When darkness came, the devil took advantage of the situation: "the judgment of the good has been sown *through sin*."[34] This account involves a mutual interplay between human culpability and demonic intervention; without the sin, the devil would not have found opportunity, and the opportunity led to a further increase in sin. Since the Stoics saw passions to be erroneous judgements, the process of judgement in Macrina and Gregory's account is closely linked to passion.[35] This judgment process, which is in part open to error under the devil's influence, is the root cause of sinful passions.[36] One should note the complexity in comparing the place for judgement in Gregory's account to the place of deliberation in Nemesius's. While both concern the act of moral discernment, Nemesius took deliberation to be a constitutive feature of human rationality, yet judgement, for Gregory and Macrina, is a consequence of human sinfulness.

The discussion of the passions that follows in Gregory and Macrina's discussion is highly indebted to a Stoic account of passion.[37] When choice (προαίρεσις) makes a decision for evil on the basis of an impulse and an incorrect judgment, passion results. On the other hand, when choice makes a decision for good on the basis of an impulse and a correct judgment, virtue results:

---

34. Gregory of Nyssa, *On the Soul*, 58–59, translation modified (PG 46:64C). Roth says, "But since error in the judgment of the good has been sown along with these impulses." In my translation, I follow the discussion of this passage in Mateo-Seco and Maspero, *The Brill Dictionary of Gregory of Nyssa*, 220, so that the *judgment* is the object of the sowing, which is done *through* sin.

35. The secondary literature discusses why Gregory explains the passions after sin in terms of an *intellectual* change. See Smith, *Passion and Paradise*, 75–103, especially 101–3, and Kevin Corrigan, *Evagrius and Gregory: Mind, Soul and Body in the 4th Century* (Burlington, Vt.: Ashgate Publishing Company, 2009), 103–12.

36. The Socratic overtones of this doctrine of sin should be clear, yet the sin does not consist in misjudgment alone but in the wrong use of choice, as discussed next. The implicit demonic aspect of the Nyssen's thought here is not discussed in the secondary literature.

37. At one point (PG 46:61A), Macrina calls motion (κινήματα) a "passion," but her later discussion shows that such a term is in fact inappropriate, as it lacks the judgment of free choice (προαίρεσις). Generally, the distinction drawn in Gregory's discussion is the same as the Platonic and Stoic distinction between impulse and passion; see Smith, *Passion and Paradise*, 90.

We shall declare that these [motions] are neither virtuous nor wicked in themselves, since they are impulses of the soul [κινήματα τῆς ψυχῆς] which lie in the power of the users to serve good or otherwise. When their movement is toward the better, we shall declare that they are material for praise.... If, on the other hand, their inclination is toward the worse, then they become passions and are named accordingly.[38]

For Gregory and Macrina, humans are intrinsically affective beings given impulses toward good and away from evil from their creation. Yet the devil has intervened in a world tainted by human sin so as to warp that affectivity into improper judgments concerning the good, giving rise to forms of affectivity that do not support human flourishing.[39]

The foregoing shows that demonology plays a significant role in Gregory's elaboration of the passions. While ultimately only the human subject can cause a passion in the soul through a free choice, demons helped in the determination of this choice when they introduced judgment concerning the good into human nature. Demons introduced judgment; human subjects create passion. These two interrelated components come together to comprise the moral conditions of fallen humankind. In laying out Gregory's theory, some tensions arise in relation to Nemesius, especially regarding the role of judgment (κρίσις) in the psychology of the moral act. Are judgment and choice punishments for sin or an essential and constitutive part of human nature? If human deliberation is changed by the devil, does the devil thereby change what human beings are—does he become a creator of humanity? If there are different forms of affectivity before and after sin, how does Christ relate to them in order to lift humankind back to a proper vision of our affective life? In all such deliberated acts, how do human beings maintain moral responsibility? Maximus must grapple with these questions in his own articulation of human affective life.

---

38. Gregory, *On the Soul*, 60. The positive use of impulses is parallel to what the Stoics call *eupatheia*. In another important passage, Gregory uses animal imagery to describe the origin of the passions; see Gregory of Nyssa, *On the Soul*, 57.

39. Eschatologically, the foundational affective impulses of human nature remain; humankind remains affective in their heavenly state. Gregory's more strident claims about eschatological dispassion should be read in this light (Gregory of Nyssa, *On the Soul*, 52–53).

Demonic Temptation before Maximus

Two of Maximus's theological predecessors offer important contributions regarding the intersection of anthropology and demonology: Origen of Alexandria and Evagrius of Ponticus.[40] Much work has been done in recent years on early Christian concepts of the devil and the demonic;[41] the present goal is to introduce only those aspects of Origen and Evagrius's thought concerning the demonic that relate to human temptation, especially by means of the passions.

Origen's reflections on the nature and purpose of demonic temptation are some of the earliest and most influential in the Christian tradition. Origen's works reflect early Christian and contemporary Jewish attitudes toward evil desires and, in turn, became the basis of some of Maximus's own reflections on the subject.[42] I discuss four topics in Origen's thought: his understanding of the relationship between demonic beings and human nature; the way demons are related

---

40. On these matters, one might also fruitfully consider both Gregory of Nazianzus and Mark the Monk. Concerning Gregory, see Dayna S. Kalleres, "Demons and Divine Illumination: A Consideration of Eight Prayers by Gregory of Nazianzus," *Vigiliae Christianae* 61, no. 2 (2007): 157–88, especially 184–86. Concerning Mark, see Marcus Plested, "The Ascetic Tradition," in *The Oxford Handbook of Maximus the Confessor*, ed. Pauline Allen and Bronwen Neil, 164–76 (Oxford: Oxford University Press, 2015). Mark's approach to the "giants" corresponds closely with Evagrius's view of the battle lines of ascetic struggle. See Mark the Monk, *Counsels on the Spiritual Life*, trans. Tim Vivian and Augustine Casiday (Crestwood, N.Y.: St. Vladimir's Seminary Press, 2009), 76–78. Some further discussion of the role of the demonic in the moral life of early Christians is seen in David Bradshaw, *Aristotle East and West: Metaphysics and the Division of Christendom* (New York: Cambridge University Press, 2004), 123–24, 127–28, and 135. Bradshaw acknowledges the work of demonic agents inside human beings but is wary of its consequences for human responsibility, thus aiming to downplay the importance of Christian discussion of the topic. The Christian concern for demonic passion appears to have originated in Alexandria and can be found before Origen in Clement of Alexandria (Sorabji, *Emotion and Peace of Mind*, 347–48).

41. See the discussion of the literature in the introduction.

42. For a discussion of Origen's continuity with rabbinic thought on the *yetzer hara*, see Monka Pesthy, "*Logismoi* Origéniens—*Logismoi* Évagriens," in *Origeniana Octava*, vol. II, ed. L. Perrone, 1017–22 (Leuven: Leuven University Press, 2003). For some of Origen's other sources, see Dragos-Andrei Giulean, "The Watchers' Whispers: Athenagoras's *Legatio* 25, 1–3 and the Book of the Watchers," *Vigiliae Christianae* 61 (2007): 258–81. On Origen's contribution to a tradition of internal discernment of spirits, see Henri Crouzel, *Origen*, trans. A. S. Worrall (San Francisco: Harper & Row Publishers, 1989), 133; Dominique Bertrand, "Origène et le Discernement des Esprits," in *Origeniana Octava*, vol. II, 969–75; Pamela Bright, "The Combat of the Demons in Anthony and Origen," in *Origeniana Septima*, ed. W. A. Bienert and U. Kühneweg, 339–43 (Leuven: Leuven University Press, 1999); and Jean Daniélou, *Origen*, trans. Walter Mitchell (New York: Sheed and Ward, 1955), 241–42.

to human vices and passions; the ascetic defeat of demonic powers; and the reasons for which God permits humans to be afflicted with demonic temptation.

For Origen, demons and human beings both originated as equal spiritual natures that fell out of divine contemplation due to satiety. Angels fell the least, humans fell somewhat farther, and demons fell the farthest. Humans have hope of returning to their original spiritual contemplation but demonic forces interfere and attempt to prevent them from doing so. Origen, in his exegesis of battles described in the Old Testament, describes this demonic effort as an organized battle. At the head of this army is Satan, who oversees the various ranks.[43] Within the army, there are others of intermediate rank. Some of these demons are devoted to particular vices, such as fornication, wrath, avarice, and arrogance;[44] others are designated according to the form of sin they attempt to elicit: thoughts, words, or deeds.[45] Origen affirms that the demons assigned to particular vices are in turn the commanders of another, lower rank of demons, which are then assigned to human beings to wage war against them. Normally, an individual would only interact with this lowest rank of demon, and demons from numerous different categories can be engaged with one human being at the same time.

Origen does not always clearly state the relationship between demons and vices in his homilies, due to his diverse and sometimes varying allegorical scriptural interpretations.[46] In one passage, certain "horses" are read alternately as demons, vices, and evil thoughts that must be destroyed, though not in such a way that these readings are considered to be completely interchangeable.[47] For instance, Origen

---

43. Origen, *Homilies on Joshua*, trans. Barbara J. Bruce (Washington, D.C.: The Catholic University of America Press, 2002), homilies 14 and 15.

44. Origen, *Homilies on Joshua*, homily 15.

45. Origen, *Homilies on Genesis and Exodus*, trans. Ronald E. Heine (Washington, D.C.: The Catholic University of America Press, 1982), homily on Exodus 6.3.

46. The association between demons and vices is seen in the above references but also in Origen's *Homilies on Ezekiel*, trans. Thomas P. Scheck (New York: Newman Press, 2010), homily 6, and *Homilies on Judges*, trans. Elizabeth Ann Dively Lauro (Washington, D.C.: The Catholic University of America Press, 2010), homily 9.

47. Origen, *Homilies on Joshua*, homily 15.

indicates that there are passions that do not need to be destroyed as demonic.[48] On the other hand, there is no clear evidence that evil passions exclusively arise from demonic temptation; people appear to be capable of producing evil passions on their own. The formulation that most closely associates demons and vices is the phrase "spirit of *x*," which Origen uses to denote the assignment of demons to particular vices.[49]

The precise activity of these demons is also unclear in Origen: Are they visible apparitions? Do they speak invisibly in one's ear? Do they plant thoughts in one's mind? Can they physically manipulate human bodies? Origen's vocabulary in the relevant passages indicates that he thinks the demons have a largely psychological or mental effect. Origen says that the demons "stir up" sin; that humans are "driven" by them; and that demons reside "within" evildoers, "seduce" people to vice, and "kindle" sins of their assigned type.[50] This vocabulary shows the hidden cunning of demons and externalizes non-normative affective states that humans experience by assigning their source as an outside evil or force. The immediate effect of this explanation is that the Christian is encouraged to fight against these sorts of temptations precisely because they are not constitutive of the human subject but instead form part of a cosmic battle between God and the powers of evil. Notably, by attending to this distinctive feature of his Christian cosmology, Origen has effectively argued for a distinctive Christian limitation of the Stoic category of "what is up to us." Thus, while preserving an affirmation that the human person as created by God is good, his cosmology simultaneously accounts for the experience of inner affective states judged to be immoral.

Origen's exegesis also provides some important reflections on the prospects of success in the battle between demons and human beings.

---

48. Origen, *Homilies on Joshua*, homily 15. It is specifically the "horses of Jabin," that is, the passions of the devil, that are to be "hamstrung," that is, destroyed. This may indicate that there are other horses (not belonging to Jabin) that are not to be hamstrung.

49. For instance, Origen, *Homilies on Joshua*, homily 15.5.

50. Origen, *Homilies on Joshua*, homily 15.5. In another homily, Origen takes the image of a demon "driving" a human being even further; he speaks of the human being as a horse that can be ridden by either Jesus or the devil (Origen, *Homilies on Genesis and Exodus*, homily 6).

Origen conceived of Satan's army as vast, yet ultimately finite. The weight of evidence in Origen's corpus also indicates that the defeat of a particular demon was definitive; a defeated demon would not be allowed to torment anyone else again. With time, Satan's ranks are slowly diminished, if still enormous.[51] Origen could thus envision a social impetus to ascetic combat: defeating a demon could concretely help others in their own battles.[52] On the human side of the battle, Origen believes that baptism is a turning point in the war, decisively turning the tide. Because in Christ the war has already been won, baptism gives the recipient a share in that victory.[53] However, Origen is clear that a full victory will not come until the "consummation of the age."[54] Like a mortally wounded snake, Satan's army continues to represent a threat to humankind in this world, attempting to strike those who are not cautious.

Finally, Origen anticipates criticisms of the strong dualism present in his account by emphasizing that God is always in charge of this battle and that none of it proceeds without God's permission. To explain how an all-loving God could permit these temptations and attacks, Origen articulates a divine pedagogy in which temptation and trial are an important and even *necessary* step toward glory and honor for those striving after virtue.[55] Citing examples such as Job, who wins double honor by his perseverance, and 2 Timothy 2:5, where "an athlete is not crowned unless he competes according to the rules," Origen argues that even powers opposed to God's intentions are good, serving God's ultimate purposes for humanity.[56] In this account, Origen admitted-

---

51. Origen, *Homilies on Joshua*, homily 15, and Origen, *Contra Celsum*, trans. Henry Chadwick (Cambridge: Cambridge University Press, 1965), 8.44. *Homilies on Joshua*, homily 14, speaks of an increase in demonic opposition the more one fights, but the position above is more common. See the editorial note on *Homilies on Joshua*, 148, n. 59.

52. This hidden love for neighbor that exists in the monastic tradition is an important and often overlooked response to the criticism that monasticism seeks to love God to the detriment of love of neighbor.

53. Origen, *Homilies on Joshua*, homily 15.7.

54. Origen, *Homilies on Joshua*, homily 14.

55. Daniélou cites *Homilies on Numbers* 13.7: "God has not deprived the devil of his power over the world, because his collaboration is still necessary for the perfecting of those destined to receive a crown" (Daniélou, *Origen*, 242).

56. Origen, *Homilies on Genesis and Exodus*, homily 1.10. Origen also claims that the devil needs God's permission to tempt in *Homilies on Joshua*, homily 15.

ly shies away from those cases where human beings give in to these temptations. Yet the point for Origen is that opposition is good for the saints "because they can overcome them."[57]

Evagrius of Ponticus is perhaps the clearest and most important influence on Maximus's conception of demonic temptation. Maximus borrows generously from Evagrius's ascetic thought in his writings. I review Evagrius's moral psychology and then move to a discussion of the role of demons within it.[58] Based on these issues, I treat two matters that will recur in my presentation of Maximus: moral responsibility for acts involving demonic temptation and Christ's relationship to the monk's ascetic struggles.

For Evagrius, the human soul is composed of three basic powers: the rational faculty, the faculty of desire, and the faculty of aversion.[59] Evagrius is not particularly concerned, as Gregory was, with the precise origin of the appetitive faculties. What is in any case clear to Evagrius is that each of these faculties as it exists in human beings has a purpose that accords with human nature and is therefore good. Firstly, the rational faculty exists in order to contemplate the world and spiritual realities. Secondly, the faculty of desire exists to guide the subject toward love of God and spiritual realities. Thirdly, the faculty of aversion exists to help the subject spurn evil and reject, with a holy hatred, the advances of demonic powers.[60]

As Evagrius conceives of the matter, if we were composed of only

---

57. Origen, *Homilies on Genesis and Exodus*, homily 1.10.

58. For my summary, I am indebted to Robert E. Sinkewicz, *Evagrius of Pontus: The Greek Ascetic Corpus* (New York: Oxford University Press, 2003), especially his introduction (vii–xl). Sinkewicz's translations are used throughout, though I cite the paragraph number from Evagrius's text and not the page number in Sinkewicz's translation for easier cross-referencing. See also Julia Konstantinovsky, *Evagrius Ponticus: The Making of a Gnostic* (Burlington, Vt.: Ashgate Publishing Company, 2009), 36–45. For Evagrius's Christological reflections, see Rowan Williams, "'Tempted as we are': Christology and the Analysis of the Passions," in *Studia Patristica* XLIV (2010): 391–404, especially 395–399. Though the following do not make sufficient recourse to Evagrius's demonology, see also Michael O'Laughlin, "The Anthropology of Evagrius Ponticus and its Sources," in *Origen of Alexandria: His World and His Legacy*, ed. Charles Kannengiesser and William L. Petersen, 357–73 (Notre Dame, Ind.: University of Notre Dame Press, 1988); Jeremy Driscoll, OSB, *Steps to Spiritual Perfection: Studies on Spiritual Progress in Evagrius Ponticus* (New York: Newman Press, 2005), 66–67; and A. M. Casidy, *Evagrius Ponticus* (New York: Routledge, 2006), 1–38 and 89–91.

59. Evagrius, *On the Practical Life*, §86 and 89.

60. Evagrius, *On Thoughts*, §17.

these three faculties, impassioned sin would not form in us. In addition to these powers of the soul, passionate sin requires the added data made available to the soul by means of the body. For Evagrius, sensory data reaches the soul first by means of images, which Evagrius commonly refers to as "mental representations" that in turn become "thoughts (λογισμοί)" in the soul. Mental representations that an individual has encountered are stored by the mind in memory, which can be recalled at a later time as thoughts.[61] This process of sensation, mental representation, and thought (λογισμός) closely resembles the combination of sense, imagination, and thought (διανόησις) that was seen in Nemesius, but Evagrius does not follow the same distinctions as Nemesius concerning the nonrational parts of the soul capable of obeying reason.

All these processes are natural to the human subject and are not properly the cause of sin in us.[62] Thoughts become morally relevant when they are willfully contemplated and held by the soul in its faculties of desire and aversion in a way that is contrary to nature (πάρα φύσιν). In line with Stoicism, Evagrius sees thoughts that are against nature as "passions." Consequently, for Evagrius, the monk's task is to be completely purged from passion. When one has attained this state, one is perfectly purified from sin. This purification does not mean that the monk somehow ceases to use the faculties from which passion arises; the faculties of aversion and desire both have a function according to nature even in one who has reached perfect impassibility.

For Evagrius, no sin can take its rise from human nature as such. Evagrius admits that evil thoughts can come from within us through a misuse of our *choice*,[63] but he insists that such thought does not derive from our nature, "for we were not created evil from the beginning, if indeed the Lord sowed a good seed in his field."[64] In considering the origin of different kinds of thoughts, Evagrius clarifies that *all* thoughts contrary to nature have an external origin in demonic temptation:

61. Evagrius, *On Thoughts*, §25.
62. Evagrius, *On Thoughts*, §19.
63. Evagrius, *On Thoughts*, §19 and §30.
64. Evagrius, *On Thoughts*, §31.

I am not saying that all memories of such objects [the mental representations present in thoughts] come from the demons—for the mind itself, when it is moved by a human agent, naturally brings forth images of things that exist—but only those memories that bring on aversion or desire contrary to nature.[65]

Thus, the main role that demons play in Evagrius's moral psychology is the presentation of evil or immoral mental representations to the mind of the monk, either through sensible objects or through the evocation of the monk's memories of the past. These demonic attacks against human affectivity (and not human nature as such) are the origin of passion in the soul.

While demons commonly attack by presenting the mind with mental representations that arouse our aversion or desire in a way that is contrary to nature,[66] demons are capable of more crass forms of temptation, physically touching the skin either to induce a sleepy state[67] or to arouse lustful thoughts.[68] In any case, demons do not have complete access to our minds; they remain fundamentally external and must discern the effectiveness of their temptation by means of the outward reactions the monk has to their stimuli. Evagrius affirms that demons "do not know our hearts" and "recognize the many mental representations that are in the heart on the basis of a word that is expressed and the movements of the body."[69]

One might reasonably worry whether the ability of demons to arouse passion within us has not led Evagrius's moral psychology to a moral fatalism. That is, if passion is against nature, and demons inspire passion in us, do not the demons *force* the monk to sin in thought if not in deed? While certainly passion has its origin in demonic activity in the soul, Evagrius clarifies that these passions only become truly culpable with the addition of intentional consideration of the passionate thought. When, for instance, someone has a thought according to

---

65. Evagrius, *On Thoughts*, §2, translation modified.
66. Evagrius, *On Thoughts*, §18.
67. Evagrius, *On Thoughts*, §33.
68. Evagrius, *On Thoughts*, §16.
69. Evagrius, *On Thoughts*, §37.

nature that is subsequently perverted by a demonic suggestion, that suggestion becomes culpable only if the human subject allows the thought to remain. If we cut off the intervening thought against nature, "we will receive the reward only of those thoughts posited first, because," Evagrius explains, "being human and occupied in the fight with the demons, we do not have the strength always to hold onto the right thought intact."[70]

Indeed, certain impassioned thoughts occur suddenly because of the assignment of new demons to a monk after he has nearly defeated a previous opponent:

> When thoughts associated with a particular passion become rare over a long period and there is a sudden boiling up and movement of this passion without our having given any pretext for it out of our negligence, then we know that a demon more formidable than the first has succeeded him and, watching over the place of the one who had fled, has filled it with his own wickedness.[71]

In such a case, Evagrius makes no indication that the renewed attack necessarily results in any culpable act on the part of the monk. Indeed, Evagrius elsewhere makes it clear that there is no compulsion to submit to the thoughts that demons suggest: "it is possible to overthrow all the thoughts inspired by the demons."[72] So while the thoughts themselves may enter against one's will and give rise to the beginning of passion in the soul, it seems that the demons do not *cause* sin in the monk, because there is still freedom of choice in how the monk responds to the thought once it has been suggested. Evagrius, like Origen, has thus limited the range of activities that he would categorize as morally praiseworthy or blameworthy (τὰ ἐφ' ἡμῖν). It is only the willful response to the demonically suggested unnatural thought that constitutes the essence of the moral act regarding demonic temptation.

Evagrius makes an effort to propose Christ as a moral exemplar in this common ascetic struggle. Evagrius's moral theory involves three

---

70. Evagrius, *On Thoughts*, §7.
71. Evagrius, *On Thoughts*, §34.
72. Evagrius, *Practical Life*, §80. This position differs significantly from that of Aquinas. See chapter 5.

fundamental demonic thoughts: gluttony, avarice, and vainglory.[73] These three thoughts are the "front lines" of the monk's spiritual war. Evagrius commonly lists these three alongside five others (fornication, anger, sadness, acedia, and pride) for a total of eight thoughts.[74] These additional thoughts constitute incursions of demons past the front lines of gluttony, avarice, and vainglory, when the monk has had to retreat to a secondary line of defense. For instance, thoughts of fornication represent prior failures of the monk regarding thoughts of gluttony; Evagrius would thus also trace anger, sadness, acedia, and pride back to failures regarding the more fundamental thoughts of avarice and vainglory.

In part, this moral psychology is intended as an aid to the monk who is trying to diagnose his thoughts and failings, yet this psychology also rests on Christological and soteriological footings. Evagrius's reason for tracing all evil thoughts to gluttony, avarice, and vainglory is found in the gospel accounts of Jesus' temptation in the desert. Evagrius writes:

No one can fall into a demon's power, unless he has first been wounded by those in the front line. For this reason the devil introduced these three thoughts to the Savior: first, he exhorted him to turn stones into bread [gluttony]; then, he promised him the whole world if he would fall down and worship him [avarice]; and thirdly, he said that if he would listen to him he would be glorified for having suffered no harm from such a fall [vainglory].[75]

Christ here emerges for Evagrius as the moral exemplar *par excellence* for the monk. But what is implicit in this exemplarity is that Christ has essentially been tested in every way that a morally perfect person can be.[76] By establishing the battle lines of the ascetic confrontation as he

---

73. See Williams, "'Tempted as we are,'" 395–99, for an excellent treatment of this material.

74. Fornication is a failure against gluttony; anger, sadness, and acedia are failures against avarice; and pride is a failure against vainglory. See Evagrius, *Eight Thoughts*. That treatise, however, constitutes an exception in Evagrius's corpus, as it is the only prolonged treatment of the *logismoi* that does not explicitly or commonly pair the thoughts with demons. Other demons appear from time to time; in *On Thoughts*, two additional demons called "vagabond" (§9) and "insensibility" (§11) appear. In *On the Vices Opposed to the Virtues*, he adds a ninth vice called "jealousy" (§8).

75. Evagrius, *On Thoughts*, §1.

76. While Evagrius affirms Christ's exemplarity, it is significant to note that Evagrius does

does, Evagrius has encoded Hebrews 4:15 into his treatise: Christ was tempted like us in every way, yet without sin. Since all evil thoughts can be reduces to gluttony, avarice, and vainglory, any thought of the other five vices is already an indication of a previous moral failure. Thus, since Christ was a perfectly sinless human being, he was only tempted along the original battle lines, having never needed to retreat to the secondary unnatural thoughts that the sinful monk must repel.

Maximus's Christological Sources

A good deal of early soteriological reflection saw Christ as entering into contact with the altered conditions of human life after sin in order to maintain the claim of Hebrews 4:15. Similarly, in considering St. Paul's affirmation that Jesus came "in the likeness of sinful flesh" (Rom 8:3), the Greek and Latin Fathers make varying interpretive judgments about the term "likeness [ὁμοίωμα]."[77] At times, they interpret the verse as indicating Christ's *identity* with fallen humanity, while at other times they view it as indicating Christ's *difference* from other fallen human beings. In turn, recent scholarship has attempted to categorize individual Patristic thinkers or to articulate a consensus among them: did these theologians view Christ's humanity as *fallen* or *unfallen*?[78] In order to demonstrate the complexity in making judgments about this question, I consider some relevant Christological reflections by Gregory of Nyssa and Gregory of Nazianzus, as the ambiguities in these thinkers will in turn constitute matter for Maximus's reflection.[79]

---

not clearly articulate a *causal* connection between Christ's own defeat of the demons and the subsequent battle undertaken by Christ's followers. Maximus takes pains to demonstrate the empowering character of Christ's temptation; see chapter 3.

77. While Maximus lived in Rome and the Christian West for many years, the influence of any given Latin figure on his thought about Christ is difficult to ascertain. For that reason, I address early Latin-speaking Christians on this question in chapter 4.

78. Thomas Weinandy, *In the Likeness of Sinful Flesh: An Essay on the Humanity of Christ* (Edinburgh: T&T Clark, 1993). Weinandy's conclusions are called into question by Ian McFarland, "Fallen or Unfallen? Christ's Human Nature and the Ontology of Human Sinfulness," in *International Journal of Systematic Theology* 10, no. 4 (October 2008): 402–4, especially n. 9.

79. One could also fruitfully include various other significant voices that may have influenced Maximus on this matter. A number of early interpretations of Jesus' temptation by the

Gregory of Nyssa

Gregory of Nyssa at times indicates that Christ shares fully in humankind's fallen condition while at other times interpreting the same scriptural passages to deny this identity.[80] This complex exegetical leg-

---

devil are considered in M. Steiner, *La Tentation de Jésus dans l'Interprétation Patristique de Saint Justin à Origène* (Paris: Librairie Lecoffre, 1962). Irenaeus, Origen, Basil of Caesarea, Ephraim the Syrian, and John Chrysostom would be worthy of consideration as well. For relevant discussion of Irenaeus, see Jan Tjeerd Nielsen, *Adam and Christ in the Theology of Irenaeus of Lyons: An Examination of the Function of the Adam-Christ Typology in the Adversus Haereses of Irenaeus, against the Background of the Gnosticism of his Time* (Assen, Netherlands: Van Gorcum & Company, 1968); the introduction and selections found in Hans Urs von Balthasar, *Scandal of the Incarnation: Irenaeus Against the Heresies*, trans. John Saward (San Francisco: Ignatius Press, 1981), 53–93; M. C. Steenberg, *Irenaeus on Creation: The Cosmic Christ and the Saga of Redemption* (Boston: Brill, 2008), 49–60; Robert M. Grant, *Irenaeus of Lyons* (New York: Routledge, 1997), 50–51; Eric Osborn, *Irenaeus of Lyons* (New York: Cambridge University Press, 2001), 97–142; John Behr, "The Word of God in the Second Century," *Pro Ecclesia* 9, no. 1 (Winter 2000): 85–107, especially 103; Denis Minns, *Irenaeus* (Washington, D.C.: Georgetown University Press, 1994), 83–102; Denis Minns, *Irenaeus: An Introduction* (New York: T & T Clark, 2010), 97–117, especially 108–117; briefly in H. Dressler, "Irenaeus, St." in *New Catholic Encyclopedia: Second Edition*, vol. 7 (New York: Thomson Gale, 2003), 570–72; and at some greater length in E. R. Carroll, "Recapitulation in Christ," in *New Catholic Encyclopedia: Second Edition*, vol. 11 (New York: Thomson Gale, 2003), 952–53. For secondary discussion of Origen's Christology and demonology (though without discussion of Christ's temptation), see Daniélou, *Origen*, 270–73, and Crouzel, *Origen*, 194–96. Richard Sorabji, in *Emotion and Peace of Mind*, 349–50, notes that Origen has some discussion of Christ's temptation in relation to the demonic. For Basil's relevant claims, see St. Basil of Caesarea, *The Letters*, trans. Roy J. Deferrari (Cambridge, Mass.: Harvard University Press, 1961), 80–83. While not likely to have directly influenced Maximus, Ephraim's views of Christ's temptation are considered in T. J. Botha, "An Analysis of Ephrem the Syrian's Views on the Temptation of Christ as Exemplified in his Hymn *De Virginitate* XII," *Acta Patristica et Byzantina* 14 (2003): 39–57, especially 46. For John Chrysostom's claims, see, for instance, Philip Schaff, ed., *Nicene and Post-Nicene Fathers*, vol. IX (New York: Charles Scribner's Sons, 1899), 432; for secondary indication that Maximus may have been influenced by John, see Adam G. Cooper, *The Body in St. Maximus the Confessor: Holy Flesh, Wholly Deified* (New York: Oxford University Press, 2005), 130, and Demetrios Bathrellos, *The Byzantine Christ: Person, Nature, and Will in the Christology of St. Maximus the Confessor* (New York: Oxford University Press, 2004), 92, 136–37, and 144.

80. For secondary discussion on the state of Christ's humanity in Gregory, see Brian Daley, "Divine Transcendence and Human Transformation: Gregory of Nyssa's Anti-Apollonarian Christology," in *Re-thinking Gregory of Nyssa*, ed. Sarah Coakley, 69 (Malden, Mass.: Blackwell Publishing, 2004), where Daley states that "the human nature of Christ ... should gradually lose the mortality, the capacity to change for the worse—and take on the characteristics of the divine nature." The "gradually" implies that this transformation takes place in the course of Christ's human life. In Hans Urs von Balthasar, *Presence and Thought: Essay on the Religious Philosophy of Gregory of Nyssa*, trans. Mark Sebanc (San Francisco: Ignatius Press, 1988), 135–142, the author summarizes Gregory's understanding of human transformation through the incarnation, though the analysis tends to focus on the subjective transformation in Christ's followers and less so on how Christ's own humanity was glorified. *The Brill Dictionary of Gregory of Nyssa* has limited discussion of the state of Christ's humanity. Only the article on the devil, 223–26, addresses Christ's defeat of the devil as a soteriological theme, wherein Christ conquers the devil and despoils him of his "rights" over humanity primarily in his death and resurrection.

acy will inform Maximus's approach to understanding Christ's human nature. As an instance of Gregory's former exegesis, he interprets the Exodus account of Moses' confrontation with Pharaoh's sorcerers in *The Life of Moses* so as to indicate that Christ's human nature is the same as that of humankind's wounded, fallen state:

> the rod's changing into a snake ... seem[s] to me to signify in a figure the mystery of the Lord's incarnation, a manifestation of deity to men which effects the death of the tyrant and sets free those under his power.... For if the father of sin is called a serpent by Holy Scripture and what is born of the serpent is certainly a serpent, it follows that sin is synonymous with the one who begot it. But the apostolic word testifies that the Lord was "made into sin for our sake" [2 Cor 5:21] by being invested with our sinful nature.... For our sake he became a serpent that he might devour and consume the Egyptian serpents produced by the sorcerers.[81]

Gregory claims that Christ was "invested with our sinful nature," without any qualification or hesitation regarding the "likeness" present in Romans 8:3. Of particular interest, though, is the way that Gregory associates Christ's coming in a "sinful nature" with Christ's defeat of the devil. Human salvation rests upon Christ's identity with our morally weakened condition after the Fall.

Similarly, in one of his homilies on Ecclesiastes, Gregory indicates how an affirmation of Christ's human "weakness [ἀσθένεια]" is wholly in accord with God's saving will:

> What is the way back for the wanderer, and the way of escape from evil, and towards good, we learn next. For he *who has had experience like us in all things, without sin,* speaks to us from our own condition. *He took our weaknesses upon him,* and through these very weaknesses of our nature shows us the way out of the reach of evil.[82]

The article's evaluation of Gregory's thinking on the matter is completely negative (225). While I do not wish to evaluate these claims with regard to the Nyssen himself, the article's dismissal of ransom soteriology is made too quickly. A shortcoming of the dictionary lies in the lack of relationship between the articles on Christology (esp. 139–52) and soteriology (694–99) on the one hand and the article on the tunics of hide (768–70) on the other: what do the tunics have to do with Christ? Did *he* put on such a tunic in the incarnation?

81. Gregory of Nyssa, *Life of Moses*, trans. Abraham J. Malherbe and Everett Ferguson (New York: Paulist Press, 1978), 61–62 (PG 44:333, 336).

82. Gregory of Nyssa, *Homilies on Ecclesiastes*, trans. Stuart George Hall and Rachel Moriarty

In this passage as well, Jesus' identity with human nature includes a susceptibility to the weaknesses of our postlapsarian nature. In Gregory's mind, these weaknesses constitute an essential part of Jesus' coming to save humankind, for by identifying with us in our weakness, he joins humankind and leads it into freedom from sin. In such passages, one sees a central soteriological principle at work: Christ must experience the consequences of sin in order to save humanity from them.

However, Gregory uses an opposing exegetical strategy in other passages in which Gregory also alludes to Romans 8:3. In these instances, Christ's "likeness" to sinful flesh indicates the difference between Christ and fallen human beings. The *Life of Moses*—which provided an example of the former strategy—also contains an example of the latter. Gregory, in marked contrast to his above understanding of the serpent and Christ's humanity, uses similar imagery pertaining to the bronze serpent in the desert to indicate Christ's sinlessness.[83] In this passage, Gregory emphasizes that Christ *only* came in the *likeness* of sinful flesh because, unlike other human beings, Christ did not in fact activate his nature in a sinful way. Above, Gregory claimed that Christ became a serpent by being invested with our "sinful nature," but now the snakes in the desert are equated with sinful desires which are wholly absent from Jesus. Whereas Gregory was earlier concerned to show Jesus' *similarity* with other human beings in the constitution of his nature, the emphasis here falls squarely on the moral *difference* between Christ and others, because it is precisely by Jesus' evasion of sinful passion that he plots the course to salvation out of the fallen state.

Using similar images and referring to identical scriptural passages, Gregory can make opposing judgments about Christ's relationship to humanity's "sinful flesh." At times, Gregory affirms that Christ came in our sinful nature. Elsewhere, Christ's identity with fallen humanity is limited by the fact of Christ's sinlessness. Especially in light of the fact

---

(Berlin: Walter de Gruyter, 1993), homily 2 (305.14), 53. The Greek can be found at Gregory of Nyssa, *Homélies sur Ecclésiaste*, trans. Françoise Vinel (Paris: Éditions du Cerf, 1996), 164, 166.

83. Gregory, *Life of Moses*, 124. For further commentary on this passage, see McFarland, "Fallen or Unfallen," 401.

that these opposing readings can appear in the same work, Gregory has provided ample material for Maximus's scrutiny.

Gregory of Nazianzus

As a window into Gregory of Nazianzus's affirmations about Christ, I consider three of his orations. In them, the Nazianzen balances an affirmation of Christ's self-emptying with a recognition of the redemptive purposes of that self-emptying: salvation from the devil. In these terms, Gregory of Nazianzus shares the Nyssan's interest in Christ's similarities to and differences from fallen humankind.

Gregory assigns the devil and his cohort an active role in the Fall of humankind. The demons "drove us away from the tree of life," and "have attacked us in our present weakness, taking captive the mind that should rule us, and opening the door to our passions."[84] Because Adam's sin was at the devil's instigation, God takes pity on humankind; even the "punishment" that Adam receives is already the beginning of the restoration of the human race. Adam "forgot the command that had been given him," so God clothed him with "tunics of skin," our mortal and passible nature.[85] Gregory explains, however, that "even here [Adam] drew a profit of a kind: death, and an interruption to sin; so wickedness did not become immortal, and the *penalty became a sign of love for humanity*."[86]

This initial "punishment" is only the first step of God's plan to restore humankind. Christ, in his incarnation, identifies with our woundedness precisely in order to free us from it. For Gregory, Christ "takes on a share of what is worse"[87] and he "made our thoughtlessness and waywardness his own."[88] This identification is paradoxical, as

---

84. Gregory of Nazianzus, *Oration* 39, §7; throughout, English drawn from Brian E. Daley, *Gregory of Nazianzus* (Oxfordshire: Routledge, 2006), here, page 130. For more on Gregory's view of Christ's defeat of the devil, see Andrew Hofer, *Christ in the Life and Teaching of Gregory of Nazianzus* (Oxford: Oxford University Press, 2013), especially 108–12 and 171.
85. Gregory of Nazianzus, *Oration* 38, §12, in Daley, *Gregory of Nazianzus*, 123.
86. Gregory of Nazianzus, *Oration* 38, §12, in Daley, *Gregory of Nazianzus*, 123.
87. Gregory of Nazianzus, *Oration* 38, §13, in Daley, *Gregory of Nazianzus*, 124.
88. Gregory of Nazianzus, *Oration* 30, §5, in Daley, Gregory of Nazianzus. See also *On God and Christ: The Five Theological Orations and Two Letters to Cledonius*, trans. Frederick Williams and Lionel Wickham (Crestwood, N.Y.: St. Vladimir's Seminary Press, 2002), 97.

Christ thereby both identifies with human weakness and destroys its sources. In a passage that shapes Maximus's thought on this topic, the Nazianzen compares Christ's incarnation to a consuming fire: Christ "bares the whole of me, along with all that is mine, in himself, so that he may consume within himself the meaner element, as fire consumes wax or the Sun ground mist."[89] In this passage, there is both identity with our "meaner element" and liberation from it.

Other analogies used by Gregory include this double aspect. On the one hand, Gregory can affirm that Christ "comes down to the same level as his fellow-slaves;"[90] on the other, Gregory compares Christ to one "leaning, out of kindness, over the pit, in order to rescue the beast who had fallen into it."[91] In the former, Gregory emphasizes that Christ's existential circumstances are those of the people he comes to save, but in the latter, Gregory makes sure that such an identification does not simply "strand" Christ in our same situation.

The above examples speak of human liberation from a generic evil. Other passages in Gregory's texts, though, explicitly recognize Christ as liberating humanity from the power of the devil. Christ's humanity acting as a deceptive bait, the devil "is himself deceived by the screen of [Christ's] flesh, and thinking he was attacking Adam, [the devil] encountered God. In this way the new Adam succeeded in saving the old Adam."[92] Similarly, Christ, the light of the world, allowed himself to be "hunted by the other darkness (the evil one, the tempter)," but whereas Adam and his progeny fell into the power of that darkness, Christ "entirely escaped,"[93] freeing us from that power. In these examples, one sees that the Nazianzen conceives of Christ's incarnation as a ploy to trick the devil and redeem humankind. In order for Christ to serve as effective bait, however, he must appear in the same condition as the rest of humanity that has fallen under the devil's power. Only by appearing as a captive does Christ undo the devil's captivity.

Both Gregorys attempt to accommodate Christ's identity with fall-

---

89. Gregory of Nazianzus, *Oration* 30, §6, in *On God and Christ*, 97.
90. Gregory of Nazianzus, *Oration* 30, §6, in *On God and Christ*, 97.
91. Gregory of Nazianzus, *Oration* 38, §14, in Daley, *Gregory of Nazianzus*, 124–25.
92. Gregory of Nazianzus, *Oration* 39, §13, in Daley, *Gregory of Nazianzus*, 134.
93. Gregory of Nazianzus, *Oration* 30, §6, in *On God and Christ*, 97.

en humanity and Christ's unique and differentiating sinlessness. The relationship between these two claims in these Cappadocians, however, is not entirely clear. The Nyssan offers two exegetical strategies of a single verse that point in opposite directions and the Nazianzen uses imagery of rescue and release that similarly places Christ in differing positions *vis-à-vis* fallen humanity. When later authors attempt to systematize these "fallen" and "unfallen" characteristics of Christ's human existence, they will be assembled as what I will call a Christological synecdoche, a pattern of Christological reflection that will occupy thinkers from Maximus the Confessor to Thomas Aquinas.

2

MAXIMUS'S ANTHROPOLOGY OF TEMPTATION

Maximus was an ascetic, and as such, his thought frequently had in view the spiritual development of the reader in light of the transformative work of Christ. For Maximus, Christ is an empowering exemplar for the ascetic's journey. In his overcoming of temptation, Christ provides a particularly powerful example that, by means of liturgical and ascetic practice, enables the monk to follow and become like Christ. The monothelite controversy helped to sharpen Maximus's articulation of Christ's relationship to the ascetic, yet the essential components of this articulation can be found in Maximus's earlier corpus as well.

Harkening back to the Apollinarian and monophysite controversies, Maximus came to see in the monothelite position an abrogation of Christ's full humanity, which was assumed in order to redeem the entirety of human nature. To say that Christ had only one will, as Maximus conceived the problem, was to deny will as an essential component of human nature. The force of Maximus's position, however, arguably made him susceptible to accusations of the contrary heresy of Nestorianism. If Christ has both human and divine wills, after all, how does Christ not become two beings, willing contrary things as human and as God? In this way, Maximus had to articulate carefully his conception of the natural human will so as not to render it intrinsically opposed to the divine will. To sufficiently articulate his developed orthodox dyothelitism, Maximus had to argue for the mutual compatibility of these two wills.

Maximus's attempt to thread this needle occupied much of his intellectual efforts in his later years, yet the ascetic tradition that he inherited also deeply and constantly shaped his understanding of the spiritual life, including the Evagrian tradition of demonic thought imbedded deeply in the human experience of temptation. In practice, this tradition appears to risk the integrity of Maximus's developed dyothelite Christology since it places the deepest spiritual warfare inside the human being, specifically inside the human being's appetitive faculties. To say that Christ (as a human being) experienced this warfare might appear to invite the accusations of his theological opponents, who already feared that Maximus placed Christ's humanity at war with his divinity. I argue in this chapter that Maximus's recognition that this warfare is ultimately external—arising from demonic intervention in the human mind—preserves the goodness of human nature without downplaying the severity of the temptation involved in such experiences. Maximus's early writings embed demons in human affectivity, while his later dyothelite writings argue for the fundamental goodness of human affectivity. Rather than argue that Maximus abandoned the first ascetic claim in his later period, I argue that these two anthropological claims can remain compatible. In so doing, I hope to respond simultaneously to Maximus's monothelite opponents, who would see in Maximus's position a version of neo-Nestorianism and demonstrate the consistency of Maximus's writings regarding human affectivity throughout his career. While explicit reference to the monothelite controversy in this chapter is sparse, the theological connections to that controversy are never far from reach.

As for the anthropological focus of this chapter, Maximus conceives of human nature as proceeding through a number of historical stages. For my purposes, it will suffice to keep three of these stages in mind: God's original constitution of humankind; the ways that humanity was changed by Adam's sin; and the way that humanity will be restored at the end of time. The first two stages explain how humanity got where it is and establish the terms of Maximus's Christology in the next chapter; the first and the third explain in different ways how it will be in the eschatological life; and the second clarifies the particular challenges set before the monk in making progress toward the goal. This overarching cosmic and chronological approach will structure my overview of Maximus's anthropology, considering in turn the three general steps of humanity's *exitus* and *reditus*. Because my goal is a close consideration of Christ's demonic temptation in the next chapter, I consider in particular detail the way in which temptation functions in Maximus's anthropology, including its source, progress, purpose (according to both God and the devil), and God's permission to allow it.

Adam's Created State and Fall

In his modification of Origen's thought, Maximus outlines three major stages in human salvation: its creation (*genesis*), movement (*kinesis*), and rest (*stasis*). For this reason, I treat the characteristics of humanity in its *genesis* and consider the mutability, or *kinesis*, present in Adam and Eve that was the basis of both the Fall and of the *stasis* found in the final deified state. My primary concern is the ways in which human nature was affected by Adam's transgression, attending especially to demonic components of this fallen condition. I will provide a systematic presentation of human nature, its faculties, and the structure of the moral act later, as this articulation will fit more easily into the description of the fallen state in the second part of this chapter.

Adam's Created State

In the beginning, Adam was created in a good, though not unchangeable, state.[1] His constitution, with all its natural faculties, was orient-

---

1. Maximus generally argues that this state had no chronological duration, as Adam is taken to have sinned at the moment of his creation. However, the logical (even if not chronological) existence of this state is undoubtedly important to Maximus and at other times he is willing

ed and directed toward God; nothing natural in Adam resisted God.[2] In continuity with a Platonic patristic tradition of reflection on *eros*, Maximus believes that Adam experienced a "spiritual pleasure"[3] that drew him toward the divine, a desire that is innate in human nature.[4] Indeed, because of the greatness of God and the smallness of the human subject, Adam was also constituted with a natural fear of God that respects and falls reverently before God's greatness.[5] These two acts constituted the original functions of human affectivity as intended by God and were rooted in the appetitive faculties of desire and aversion.[6] At that time, Adam's spiritual gaze was fixed on God and,

---

to consider that it may have had some duration; see *Ambigua ad Iohannem* (hereafter, *Amb. Io.*) 45 (PG 91:1353A-B). A discussion of Adam's created state can also be found in Joshua Lollar, *"To See into the Life of Things": The Contemplation of Nature in Maximus the Confessor's "Ambigua to John"* (unpublished diss., University of Notre Dame, 2011), 298–306, and Joshua Lollar, "Christ and the Contemplation of Nature in Maximus the Confessor's *Amibigua to John*," in *A Saint for East and West: Maximus the Confessor's Contribution to Eastern and Western Christian Theology*, ed. Daniel Haynes, 252 (Eugene, Ore.: Cascade Books, 2019).

2. *Theological and Polemical Opuscula* (hereafter, *TPO*) 7 (PG 91:80A) in Andrew Louth, *Maximus the Confessor* (New York: Routledge, 2006), 185; *TPO* 3 (PG 91:45B-48A) in Louth, *Maximus*, 193. Jean-Claude Larchet argues the same in *Questions à Thalassios* (hereafter, *QT*), 3 vols., trans. Françoise Vinel (Paris: Éditions du Cerf, 2010), vol. 1, 33.

3. *QT* 61 (PG 90:625D-628B; CCSG 22:85–87) in Maximus, *On the Cosmic Mystery of Jesus Christ*, trans. Paul M. Blowers and Robert L. Wilken (Crestwood, N.Y.: St. Vladimir's Seminary Press, 2003), 131. Short in-line translations are made either in consultation with available English translations or, when the French is noted, from the Greek in consultation with the French.

4. See chapter 1, n. 4, concerning Gregory of Nyssa on this point. As for Maximus's relationship with this tradition of reflection on *eros*, see Paul M. Blowers, "The Dialectics and Therapeutics of Desire in Maximus the Confessor," *Vigiliae Christianae* 65, no. 4 (2011): 434–41, especially 438. Blowers argues that for Maximus, *eros* opens the creature to an ever-growing union with God, as a way of articulating the process of deification.

5. *QT* 49 (PG 90:449A-C; CCSG 7:355) in *Questions à Thalassios*, vol. 2, 98–99; Maximus the Confessor, *On Difficulties in Sacred Scripture: The Responses to Thalassios*, trans. Fr. Maximos Constas (Washington, D.C.: The Catholic University of America Press, 2018), 282 (after the Greek editions in parentheses, I first cite the French edition that I consulted, and I then note the newly available English translation at the end; I follow this convention whenever an English edition has recently been published).

6. In *QT* 43 (PG 90:412D; CCSG 7:295) in *Questions à Thalassios*, vol. 2, 32–33, and *On Difficulties in Sacred Scripture*, 247, the faculties are described by their actions: pleasure (ἡδονή) and pain (ὀδύνη). It should be noted that the second of these faculties (θυμός) is sometimes translated as "aversion," "temper," "fervor," or "irascibility" (see Blowers, "Dialectics and Therapeutics of Desire," 431, and Blowers, *Maximus the Confessor*, 123, 208). For consistency, I render it as "aversion" since this term often conveys an important part of Maximus's sense, especially when he is concerned with describing the action of these faculties (pleasure and pain). I refrain from translating as "irascibility" (as I will with Aquinas in the second half) because the respective terms are not used by Thomas and Maximus interchangeably. For Maximus, desire and aversion are often related simply as attraction and repulsion, whereas for Thomas, desire and irascibility are related as an attraction to a good and a difficult striving for that same good (see *Summa Theologica* [hereafter, *ST*] I-II 23.1, response). For Aquinas, the irascible passions are all

though he was created with appetitive faculties that would enable him to be naturally drawn to God, he did not experience desire or fear with regard to the created order.[7] He enjoyed a balance in his nature, even though his intellectual faculties and sensitive faculties naturally consider different objects.[8] He had the ability to continue in this relationship with God and with the world indefinitely, enjoying a "natural virtue" and knowledge of God.[9]

Since Adam was in motion from his creation, there was a certain mutability concerning Adam's state of being, yet to specify the nature of this mutability requires an explanation of a distinction in Maximus's thought between the *logos* (λόγος) and *tropos* (τρόπος) of human nature. Maximus believes that nothing that pertains to human nature as such is changeable; the *logos* of Adam's humanity is immutable. To admit a change of nature would be to say that Adam had become a different being, thus ceasing to be human.[10] The nature of human mutability, then, does not pertain strictly to *what* human beings are. Instead, Maximus speaks of different "laws" active in human nature in different periods of human history. As humanity passes from one of these laws to another, the way (τρόπος) in which human beings acti-

---

reducible to concupiscible ones (*ST* I-II 25.1 and *ST* I-II 82.3, ad. 2), but there is no parallel sense in Maximus that aversion is related to desire in this way. Finally, the difference can be seen in the different virtues that they assign to the faculty. Thomas believes that irascibility is governed by fortitude (aimed at the difficult good), whereas for Maximus, aversion is governed by patience (resisting an ongoing evil).

7. *QT* 1 (PG 90:268D-269D; CCSG 7:47–49) in Blowers and Wilken, *Cosmic Mystery*, 97–98. See also *Amb. Io.* 7 (PG 91:1073B) in *On Difficulties in Sacred Scriptures*, 87: this affectivity "by nature coexists with beings."

8. *QT* 58 (PG 90:596D; CCSG 22:33) in *Questions à Thalassios*, vol. 3, 45; *On Difficulties in Sacred Scripture*, 406. See also *QD* 48 (CCSG 10:40–2) in *Questions and Doubts* (hereafter, *QD*), trans. Despina D. Prassas (DeKalb: Northern Illinois University Press, 2010), 71. Maximus's formulation of this matter begs the question of how high an end the sensitive faculties were designed to reach (and thereby of the relationship of nature and supernature); given their protological and eschatological forms, however, Maximus often expresses that they can reach quite high.

9. *Dispute with Pyrrhus* (PG 91:309B) in *Dispute de Maxime le Confesseur avec Pyrrhus: Introduction, Texte Critique, Traduction et Notes*, vol. 2, trans. Marcel Doucet (unpublished diss., Institut d'Études Médiévales at the University of Montréal, 1972), 566 (French on 648). See also Larchet's introduction to *QT*, vol. 1, 134–35.

10. *Amb. Io.* 42 (PG 91:1345B; Latin trans. in CCSG 18:207–8) in Blowers and Wilken, *Cosmic Mystery*, 92. Maximus makes this claim in part to protect the distinction between the Creator and the creature, so that deification does not make Adam ontologically divine.

vate their humanity changes.¹¹ Most importantly, for instance, when Adam fell, a new law was introduced by God and, in a different sense, also by the devil.¹² These means of activation and laws are the aspect of the human being that are subject to change in the process of deification.

Adam's original *tropos*, then, was not completely fixed and had the ability to transform itself into another *tropos*; Adam was self-governing, self-determining, and free.¹³ God created him in this way so that he could choose the good freely and thereby be rewarded with an immutable *tropos* fixed in its orientation toward God—even in his created state, Adam was destined for a higher and more perfect condition.¹⁴ However, his freedom also contained the possibility of a misuse of human nature, which would lead to a different *tropos* of human nature. Even in his created state, Maximus affirms that there was in Adam an imaginative appetite called wish (βούλησις)—an ability to seek specific ends that arise from thought—whereby he inclined toward things that appeared desirable.¹⁵ While Adam was created with a natural desire for and knowledge of God, it was possible for that desire to be diverted toward other objects and for that knowledge to be corrupted.¹⁶ This diversion and corruption constitute the Fall, an

---

11. For further discussion of the distinction between *logos* and *tropos*, see Jean-Claude Larchet, "The Mode of Deification," in *The Oxford Handbook of Maximus the Confessor*, ed. Pauline Allen and Bronwen Neil, 341–47 (Oxford: Oxford University Press, 2015).

12. See, for example, *QT* 61 (PG 90:625D-641B; CCSG 22:85–105) in Blowers and Wilken, *Cosmic Mystery*, 137, which speaks of the devil as the cause for the introduction of the law of pleasure and pain in human nature; see also the discussion of providence later in this chapter.

13. *QD* III 1 (CCSG 10:170) in *Questions and Doubts*, 156–57.

14. This movement is expressed in Maximus's correction of Origenistic cosmology. Maximus argues that the individual moves from creation (*genesis*) through movement (*kinesis*) into stability (*stasis*) or, similarly, from being to well-being to eternal well-being.

15. *QT* 40 (PG 90:396A-B; CCSG 7:267) in *Questions à Thalassios*, vol. 1, 404–5; *On Difficulties in Sacred Scripture*, 230. Maximus does not give a precise definition of this appetite here but he does in *TPO* 1 (PG 91:13B-16A) in Maximus the Confessor, *Opuscules Théologiques et Polémiques*, trans. Emmanuel Ponsoye (Paris: Éditions du Cerf, 1998), 113–14. As the *QT* passage is not as technical as the later *TPO* text, it is possible that Maximus is using it interchangeably with "deliberation [βούλευσις]," which makes decisions about means to an end that is within our power (whereas wish is more spontaneous and also seeks things that are not within one's power to attain). The context indicates that wish was responsible for rendering void knowledge of the human ability to achieve the good. I return to the meaning and moral character of wish below. Christological matters become connected to the definition of wish and deliberation because the latter, but not the former, is eventually denied by Maximus to be in Christ.

16. *QT* Introduction (PG 90:253A-B; CCSG 7:29–31) in *Questions à Thalassios*, vol. 1,

event that Maximus believes to have taken place at the time of Adam's creation.[17]

The Fall

Since the *logos* of Adam's nature is immutable, the changes to humanity that arose from the Fall concern consequences for the *tropos* of his nature that were implicit in Adam's free choice to transgress God's law.[18] There was an unbalancing of Adam's nature bound up with the activity of Satan, so that the original equilibrium of Adam's faculties was offset.[19]

That these consequences are introduced and maintained both through divine and demonic intention is significant. Maximus describes the devil as both bringing about our fallen condition *and* ensuring that this condition results in sinful activation of our nature. Concerning the original introduction of this new law of nature, Maximus variously states that Adam's transgression introduced the "deadly venom" of the "cruel beast";[20] the devil introduced the "crookedness of sin" to human nature;[21] and human nature was killed by a "diabolical fever."[22] Most importantly, the addition of pleasure and pain to human sensibility was "devised" by the devil as a means of human enslavement.[23] When Maximus lists the unintended consequences

---

134–35; *On Difficulties in Sacred Scripture*, 82–83. Precisely *how* Adam's choice and knowledge became diverted from their natural object is beyond my purview. Maximus may have held that, in a hypothetical sense at least, there was a certain "natural weakness (φυσικῆς ἀσθενείας)" in human nature apart from divine grace, though such a situation did not attain, in any case, before the Fall. See *QT* 52 (PG 90:496A; CCSG 7:421) in *Questions à Thalassios*, vol. 2, 172–73, and *On Difficulties in Sacred Scripture*, 321.

17. I noted above that the logical distinction between an unfallen and fallen state is important for Maximus's Christology. In chapter 3, I show that Maximus sees Christ's incarnation as enfolding aspects of both conditions; see *QT* 62 (PG 90:653C-656D) in *Questions à Thalassios*, vol. 3, 138–141, and *On Difficulties in Sacred Scripture*, 457–58.

18. *QT* 42 (PG 90:405B-D; CCSG 7:285) in Blowers and Wilken, *Cosmic Mystery*, 119. Larchet argues that these are summarized by Maximus as the "law of sin." See text and notes on *QT* 49, in *Questions à Thalassios*, vol. 2, 113–15.

19. *QD* 48 (CCSG 10:40–42) in *Questions and Doubts*, 71.

20. *Amb. Io.* 10 (PG 91:1156C-1157A) in Maximus the Confessor, *Ambigua*, trans. Emmanuel Ponsoye, Paris: Éditions de l'Ancre, 1995, 189; Maximus the Confessor, *On Difficulties in the Church Fathers: The Ambigua*, vol. 2, trans. Nicholas Constas (Cambridge, Mass.: Harvard University Press, 2014), 247–49.

21. *QD* 9 (CCSG 10:8–9) in *Questions and Doubts*, 46–7.

22. *QD* 11 (CCSG 10:9–10), in *Questions and Doubts*, 48.

23. *QT* 61 (PG 90:633B; CCSG 22:95) in Blowers and Wilken, *Cosmic Mystery*, 137. *Amb. Io.* 10 (PG 91:1156C-D) also implicates the "serpent" in the corruption of the senses.

of Adam's sin, they are most commonly categorized as *corruptibility, mortality,* and *passibility*.[24]

Corruptibility is a susceptibility to change and an inclination toward earthly realities. Corruption is associated with the physical mode of human conception after Adam's sin. Thenceforth, human beings come into being in the same way as the irrational animals, in a mode that is perhaps not altogether becoming for the rational creatures that human beings are.[25] Similarly, mortality entered human nature as a consequence of Adam's transgression. If Adam had obeyed God and eaten only of the permitted trees, "he would not have lost immortality."[26] In this way, Adam unwillfully gave up the "divine life" that was his in the garden and put on a way of life that was like that of "irrational being," giving nature over to death.[27]

The third of these consequences (passibility) involves a diversion of the natural affective faculties of desire and aversion from their natural, spiritual objects toward physical realities. One must take particular care to explain the concomitant action of demonic power in passibility. When Adam chose to incline his will, desires, and knowledge toward earthly realities instead of God, the natural balance between human intellect and sensibility was upset, in part through the evil intentions of the devil. Adam's intellect chose to listen to sensibility instead of leading it, and thereafter, the sensible power, the "most irrational part of nature," was infiltrated by evil spirits and happily suggested worldly objects of investigation to the intellect that further distracted it from its original divine object.[28] What was once territory thoroughly in Adam's power now becomes a contested battleground. Maximus says that demons make use of this new arrangement of human pas-

---

24. See, for instance, *QT* 42 (PG 90:405B-409A; CCSG 7:285-89) in Blowers and Wilken, *Cosmic Mystery*, 119-22.
25. *Amb. Io.* 31 (PG 91:1273D-1276D) in *Ambigua*, 272; *On Difficulties in the Church Fathers*, vol. 2, 39-43.
26. *Amb. Io.* 10 (PG 91:1156C-1157A) in *Ambigua*, 189; *On Difficulties in the Church Fathers*, vol. 1, 247-49.
27. *Amb. Io.* 10 (PG 91:1156C-1157A) in *Ambigua*, 190; *On Difficulties in the Church Fathers*, vol. 1, 247-49.
28. *QT* 1 (PG 90:268D-269D; CCSG 7:47-49) in Blowers and Wilken, *Cosmic Mystery*, 97-98.

sibility in an attempt to elicit sin.²⁹ The object of sensibility in this newly unbalanced condition is bodily pleasure, and the main thing that it avoids is bodily pain. When kept under the control of reason, these natural faculties, even in their fallen state, have the ability to be activated according to nature (κἄτα φύσιν), that is, in a way that promotes the physical and spiritual wellbeing of the subject.³⁰ Because of the possibility of this natural activation, these faculties are still an intrinsic and good part of human nature.

Maximus spells out how this introduction of passibility took place. After the Fall, the natural sensibility of humanity is instead used by the devil to drive the human subject into unnatural passions:

> For in this passibility, through natural finitude, [nature] had an increase of sin, suffering the opposing power of the principalities and powers according to the sin born out of our passibility, by the burial of the energies of the natural passions beneath the unnatural passions. Through the energy of the natural passions, all evil powers are at work, driving the deliberative will, according to the passibility of nature, into the corruption of the unnatural passions through the natural ones.³¹

Notice that the energies of the natural passions are still present; Maximus thereby indicates the perduring goodness of human nature itself. These energies, are buried or, more literally, hidden within the unnatural passions solicited by demonic powers. It is, however, precisely in the natural passions that the evil demonic powers work.³²

---

29. *QT* Introduction (PG 90:249A-B ; CCSG 7:23) in *Questions à Thalassios*, vol. 1, 126–27; *On Difficulties in Sacred Scripture*, 78.

30. *QT* 55 (PG 90:541A; CCSG 7:487) in *Questions à Thalassios*, vol. 2, 240–43; *On Difficulties in Sacred Scripture*, 360; *QT* 1 (PG 90:268D-269D; CCSG 7:47–49) in Blowers and Wilken, *Cosmic Mystery*, 97–98.

31. *QT* 21 (PG 90:313A-B; CCSG 7:127) in Blowers and Wilken, *Cosmic Mystery*, 110; *Questions à Thalassios*, vol. 2, 252–53. Block quotations from Maximus are my own translations, made from the Greek in consultation with the French and, when available, the English. As mentioned above, shorter in-line translations are made either in consultation with available English translations or, when the French is noted, from the Greek in consultation with the French.

32. Maximus affirms that these natural passions are the only way that unnatural passions arise in the soul. *QT* 55 (PG 90:541A; CCSG 7:487) in *Questions à Thalassios*, vol. 2, 242–43: "the reprehensible and unnatural passions ... have no other origin in us than the movement of natural passions"; *On Difficulties in Sacred Scripture*, 360, differs, but I take Vinel's rendering, in conjunction with the affirmation of *QT* 21, as more accurate. Together, these texts indicate that the devil must work with what is natural in humanity in order to solicit activity contrary to its own nature.

Human passibility, therefore, undergoes a two-fold corruption after Adam's sin, expressed by Maximus in *QT* 62 through an analogy of a home. First, the devil constructs a home out of Adam's sinfulness. The beams of the home are human desires rising out of the faculty of desire. The stones of the home are appetitive movements of aversion rising from the corresponding faculty. Second, once this home is constructed in and through the Fall, the devil is able to use this home to his advantage, continuing his attacks against the rest of humankind from within their own God-given appetites. The home is constructed through Adam's sin, and the continued attacks from within it take place among humankind after Adam's transgression.[33] These continued attacks—and the anthropology implicit in them—are the focus of the next section.[34]

Human Nature and Demonic Temptation after the Fall
An Account of Maximus's Anthropology in the Fallen State

Maximus's view of the fallen condition is influenced by many of the figures considered in chapter 1, so the following treatment traces Maximus's navigation of Platonic, Stoic, Evagrian, and Nemesian

---

33. *QT* 62 (PG 90:653C-656D) in *Questions à Thalassios*, vol. 3, 138–41; *On Difficulties in Sacred Scripture*, 457–58.

34. Since Maximus's views will be placed in conversation with Latin traditions in the second half, certain objections to his way of proceeding should receive some attention at this juncture. First, despite Maximus's theoretical optimism regarding human triumph over these forces, he still affirms fallen humanity's universal sinfulness. In QD 118 (CCSG 10:86–87) in *Questions and Doubts*, 104, Maximus states that "no one dies without faults and [everyone] is crushed by sin, but only the Lord died intact and without any sin." Universal sinfulness is bound closely to the matter of the *gnomic* will (γνώμη), a topic of importance in Maximus's Christology. In Maximus's later works (which I follow on this matter), the *gnomic* will is the *tropos* of the human will, according to which human beings vacillate or deliberate with regard to the good. Second, Maximus's view of the *necessity* of sin in the fallen state requires careful articulation with regard to the *gnomic* will. Maximus's developed position is that it does not pertain to the *logos* of human nature but rather is a sinful *tropos* of its activation. Because the *logos* of human nature remains good even when covered by an evil activation, Maximus may consequently affirm a sort of theoretical possibility (though not the actuality) of a natural avoidance of sin. This difficulty is by no means unique to Maximus's way of speaking. When articulating his view of the *non posse non peccare*, Augustine attributes enough to the human will that it is still responsible for its sins (see *The Spirit and the Letter*). Augustine does not mean to say in an absolute way that human beings are constitutionally required to sin, as he would acknowledge that such an act would no longer be subjectively culpable.

thought.[35] First, I consider humanity's composition as a combination of body and soul, including the faculties of reason and sensation. To explain their relationship to one another, I outline Maximus's view of the passions and indicate some of the ambiguities that surround Maximus's use of the term. Second, I treat the role of imagination, thought, and memory in Maximus's anthropology, where Maximus's indebtedness to Evagrius is quite clear. Third, I consider the structure of the moral act as Maximus presents it, defining and relating important categories such as deliberation, choice, ignorance, and judgment that bear a distinctly Nemesian character. The account of human nature in this section concerns both the *logos* of human nature and the concrete *tropos* of its activation after Adam's sin, but this account of the moral conditions of fallen humanity will remain incomplete without the investigation in the following section concerning the way demons are active in this nature after the Fall.[36] Fourth, in anticipation of Latin distinctions between "internal" and "external" temptation, I address Maximus's categories of ignorance and the willful on the way to a clarification of how Maximus conceives of temptations that come from "within" and "without."

35. For Maximus's interaction with Aristotelian thought, see Marius Portaru, "Classical Philosophical Influences: Aristotle and Platonism," in *The Oxford Handbook of Maximus the Confessor*, ed. Pauline Allen and Bronwen Neil, 127–47 (Oxford: Oxford University Press, 2015), as well as Christophe Erismann, "A Logician for East and West," in *A Saint for East and West*, 50–65. Erismann implies that Maximus consciously appropriated Aristotle's thought and may have had explicitly philosophical training (Erismann, "Logician," 53). This argument overstates Maximus's position as a "philosopher," not because he is not one but because Maximus would not recognize "philosophy" as an area of study that could be distinguished from theology (see Lollar, "Christ and the Contemplation of Nature," 245–59). I agree with Portaru, who indicates that Nemesius is likely the major conduit of Aristotle to Maximus. Furthermore, Nemesius, as a Christian, would constitute a clearer authority than a pagan like Aristotle would have. For a detailed account of authority in early monasticism, see Philip Rousseau, *Ascetics, Authority, and the Church of Jerome and Cassian*, Second Edition (Notre Dame, Ind.: University of Notre Dame Press, 2010), especially 127. Maximus himself indicates as much in the way that he speaks about the "outside philosophers" when he is explicitly aware of them from Nemesius. See *Amb. Io.* 10.42 (PG 90:1189C) in *On Difficulties in the Church Fathers*, vol. 1, 312–13. For these reasons, I generally refer to Maximus's most proximate interlocutors rather than their original non-Christian sources.

36. By dividing my presentation in this way, I follow a common structure of Maximus's own presentation, whereby what appears at the outset of his discourse to be merely a matter of anthropology slowly morphs into a much broader discussion of cosmology and spiritual warfare. See *Amb. Io.* 10.4–9 (PG 91:1117A-20A) in *On Difficulties in the Church Fathers*, vol. 1, 171–9, and *Amb. Io.* 10.21–22a (PG 91:1145C-48C) in *On Difficulties in the Church Fathers*, vol. 1, 229–31, for two places where the seemingly anthropological gradually emerges as demonological.

Body and Soul. Because of the spiritual nature of the soul and the physical nature of the body, there is a natural tension between the two, though when the spiritual leads the physical as it is supposed to, they remain in harmony.[37] At the level of the *logos* of human nature, no contradiction exists between mind and sense. However, when activated by the *tropos* of a vacillating or *gnomic* will (γνώμη), the two operations become disordered, with the spiritual following the sensible instead of the other way around. When sensation has been turned to sensible reality, for instance, Maximus describes the objects of these two components of human nature as opposed to one another: "The intellect (νοῦς) and sensibility (αἴσθησις) have operations that are naturally opposed to one another through the supreme variance and otherness of those [things] subjected to them."[38] When such disorder occurs, Maximus can even describe the body as the enemy of the soul, though the essential goodness of the nature itself must be kept in mind.[39]

Closely associated with the distinction between mind and body is that between reason and sensibility, the latter in turn being subdivided into desire (ἐπιθυμία) and aversion (θυμός).[40] This three-fold Platonic distinction of human faculties was seen in both Nemesius and in Gregory of Nyssa in the previous chapter. For Maximus, the "power

---

37. Maximus's description of body and soul as an integrally combined reality can be found in *Amb. Io.* 7 (PG 91:1100B-1101C) in *On Difficulties in the Church Fathers*, vol. 1, 137–41; *Amb. Io.* 15 (PG 91:1220A-1221B) in *On Difficulties in the Church Fathers*, vol. 1, 371–77; and *Amb. Io.* 42 (PG 91:1321D-1341C) in *On Difficulties in the Church Fathers*, vol. 2, 137–73. The fallen condition of this relationship can be seen in *Amb. Io.* 10.2a (PG 91:1112A-D) in *On Difficulties in the Church Fathers*, vol. 1, 159–61. A description of a deified (and possibly prelapsarian) version of this relationship appears to follow in *Amb. Io.* 10 (PG 91:1112D-1116D) in *On Difficulties in the Church Fathers*, vol. 1, 163–71.

38. *QT* 58 (PG 90:596D; CCSG 22:33) in *Questions à Thalassios*, vol. 3, 45; *On Difficulties in Sacred Scripture*, 406. Maximus acknowledges, even in a natural activation, the joining of two different functions that are conjoined in the spiritual and somatic reality of the human being. The variance between these functions may imply, as noted above, a distinction between the natural and supernatural that does not easily settle with Maximus's sometimes very high estimation of the goal of affectivity.

39. *QD* I 27 (CCSG 10:146) in *Questions and Doubts*, 145.

40. *QT* 49 (PG 90:447B449A; CCSG 7:353) in *Questions à Thalassios*, vol. 2, 96–97; *On Difficulties in Sacred Scripture*, 281–82; *QD* 41 (CCSG 10:34–5) in *Questions and Doubts*, 66. For the subdivision of sensibility into desire and aversion, see *QT* 43 (PG 90:412D; CCSG 7:295) in *Questions à Thalassios*, vol. 2, 32–33, and *On Difficulties in Sacred Scripture*, 247.

of sin" has been "mingled" into these latter two faculties in connection with demonic powers.[41]

As for passion, Maximus defines the term variously in conversation with the preceding strands of the tradition outlined in the previous chapter. He is clearly aware of the Stoic view that a passion is by definition disordered and unnatural. Indeed, Maximus at times sides explicitly with this view, as when he states that a passion is what happens when nature is diverted from its natural activity.[42] This definition tends toward assigning moral blame to the individual who undergoes such passion. Perhaps reflecting his reading of Dionysius, however, Maximus diverges sharply at times from this Stoic inheritance, as when he states that only a *blameworthy* passion is "an impulse of the soul contrary to nature,"[43] or when he distinguishes in a later work between dishonorable passions (morally blameworthy) and the punitive passions (not blameworthy).[44] One can also recognize this neutral sense of passion when he presents it as the threefold combination of a sense object, a sensation, and a natural power.[45] In such cases, Maximus implies that a passion is most closely equivalent to

---

41. QT Prologue (PG 90:264C-D; CCSG 7:11) in *Questions à Thalassios*, vol. 1, 112–13; *On Difficulties in Sacred Scripture*, 71. Later in the same paragraph, Maximus equates the "power of sin" with the "law of sin (ὁ νόμος τῆς ἁμαρτίας)"; Larchet argues that this law of sin is the corruptibility, mortality, and passibility of the body introduced by Adam's transgression (see his notes on QT 49 in *Questions à Thalassios*, vol. 2, 113–15). I argue at greater length for the association of passions with demonic powers below.

42. QT 16 (PG 90:301C-D; CCSG 7:109) in *Questions à Thalassios*, vol. 1, 228–29; *On Difficulties in Sacred Scripture*, 132–33. This Stoic definition can also be found in *Centuries on Love* (hereafter, CL) II 16 (PG 90:988D-989A) in *The Philokalia*, vol. 2, trans. and ed. G. E. H. Palmer, Philip Sherrard, and Kalistos Ware (New York: Faber and Faber, 1981), 67, where a passion is "an impulse of the soul contrary to nature."

43. CL I 35 (PG 90:968A) in *Philokalia*, vol. 2, 56. For some indication of how Dionysius may have helped direct Maximus away from this Stoic reading of passion, see Kalistos Ware, "Imitation of Christ according to Saint Maximus the Confessor," in *A Saint for East and West*, 82.

44. The relevant terms are ἐπιτιμία (dishonorable) and ἀτιμία (punitive). I will discuss this distinction again at more length in chapter 3. For the dating of Maximus's works and the methodological problems with such dating, see Marek Jankowiak and Phil Booth, "A New Date-List of the Works of Maximus the Confessor," in *The Oxford Handbook of Maximus the Confessor*, ed. Pauline Allen and Bronwen Neil, 19–83 (Oxford: Oxford University Press, 2015). Their list makes some modifications to the older date-list in Polycarp Sherwood, OSB, "An Annotated Date-List of the Works of St. Maximus the Confessor," *Studia Anselmiana*, vol. 29 (Rome: Pontificium Institutum S. Anselmi, 1952).

45. QT 16 (PG 90:301C-D; CCSG 7:109) in *Questions à Thalassios*, vol. 1, 228–29; *On Difficulties in Sacred Scripture*, 132–33.

what Gregory of Nyssa called an affective "impulse." Since Maximus uses the term passion in this morally neutral sense in the most important Christological passages, I generally avoid using the term with its negative Stoic connotations.[46]

Maximus's categorization of the passions is not identical to that of Evagrius, though there are important similarities. Most notably, both figures hoped to align Christ's experience of temptation with that of other human beings. Further, both used Christ's temptations in the desert as an important source for reflection on the matter. Evagrius, however, restricted his Christological reflection to the desert temptations against Christ's faculty of desire, whereas Maximus extended these temptations to include temptations against both of the faculties in human sensibility and, at some points, prolonged the chronological duration of these temptations throughout Christ's public ministry.

The three basic Evagrian passions were vainglory, avarice, and gluttony. Christ, in turn, experienced these three in the desert temptation scenes.[47] For Maximus, however, these temptations tell only half the story. Maximus places these three temptations toward pleasure alongside a second group of temptations to flee from pain or that attempt to arouse a disordered anger in Christ.[48] By showing that Christ was tempted through both desire and aversion, Maximus attempts to affirm that Christ purifies the entirety of human possibility by assuming the experiences that come with all parts of it. In a more anthropological mode, Christ's assumption of both desire and aversion likewise

---

46. See *QT* 21 (PG 90:312B-316D; CCSG 7:127-33) in Blowers and Wilken, *Cosmic Mystery*, 109–113. In this way, Maximus diverges from the tradition in some Patristic authors of using the term 'propassion' to describe Christ's affectivity. For discussion of the origin of the tradition of propassions in Origen and Didymus the Blind, see Richard A. Layton, "Propatheia: Origen and Didymus on the Origin of the Passions," in *Vigiliae Christianae* 54 (2000): 262–82. The use of this term implies an acceptance of the Stoic definition and results in the idea that the presence of a *full* passion in Christ would amount to the presence of sin in Christ; thus, Christ must merely experience the *beginning* of a passion. The theory of propassions heavily influences medieval Christology but does not affect Maximus's way of speaking about Christ's affectivity.

47. These three are found unaltered in Maximus's early articulation of the passions: *QD* 37 (CCSG 10:30–31) in *Questions and Doubts*, 63–64, and *QD* 194 (CCSG 10:136) in *Questions and Doubts*, 140.

48. *QT* 21 (PG 90:312B-316D; CCSG 7:127-33) in Blowers and Wilken, *Cosmic Mystery*, 109–13; for the chronological extension of this temptation, see *AL* 10–13 (PG 90:920C-21C) in Maximus, *The Ascetic Life and the Four Centuries on Charity*, trans. Polycarp Sherwood (New York: Newman Press, 1955), 109–11.

demonstrates the enduring and essential quality of these faculties in human nature.

Imagination, Thoughts, and Memories. The function of imagination, thoughts, and memories is parallel to the psychological structure of a passion noted above. An imagination is composed of a subject, an object, a faculty, and the action of that faculty. Specifically, for imagination, there is an imaginer, an external object that is imagined, imagination, and a mental image of the external object in the imagination.[49] The word for this final component varies in different texts; it is sometimes called an "image,"[50] or "memory,"[51] and, in some places, it goes by the same word that Evagrius uses for these "mental representations."[52] Maximus also occasionally uses it interchangeably with "thought (λογισμός)," but because it is associated with the activity of a human faculty, such a thought is not intrinsically disordered or demonic—though as discussed below it still has the ability to become such.[53] Couched in this anthropological context, imagination creates images of things currently present and recalls objects experienced in the past.[54] Because of the wide range of terms used for this mental process and because it involves mental functions such as memory that are not ascribed to sensation, imagination is best understood as a faculty distinct from sensation that belongs to the rational part of the soul (νοῦς, the intellect) and that considers, reflects on, and stores images of external objects.[55] The ways in which demons exploit imagination will be considered in the next subsection.

---

49. *Amb. Io.* 19 (PG 91:1236A) in *Ambigua*, 244; *On Difficulties in the Church Fathers*, vol. 1, 405.

50. *QT* 49 (PG 90:449B-C; CCSG 7:355–57) in *Questions à Thalassios*, vol. 2, 100–101; *On Difficulties in Sacred Scripture*, 283.

51. *CL* III 42 (PG 90:1029A-B) in *Philokalia*, vol. 2, 89.

52. See, for instance, the *CL* III 52–3 (PG 90:1032C-D) in *Philokalia*, vol. 2, 91.

53. See *CL* III 67 (PG 90:1037A-B) in *Philokalia*, vol. 2, 93; *QT* 49 (PG 90:453A-C; CCSG 7:359–61) in *Questions à Thalassios*, vol. 2, 104–5; and *On Difficulties in Sacred Scripture*, 285–86.

54. *Amb. Io.* 19 (PG 91:1236A) in *Ambigua*, 244; *On Difficulties in the Church Fathers*, vol. 1, 405.

55. As mentioned above, sensation generally appears more "physical" than imagination, as sensation involves the "most irrational part of the soul." See *QT* 1 (PG 90:268D-269D; CCSG 7:47–49) in Blowers and Wilken, *Cosmic Mystery*, 97–98.

The Progression of the Moral Act. The final anthropological structure to consider here is the progression of the moral act, which largely follows the presentation of Nemesius in the previous chapter. Maximus provides numerous considerations of this subject in his works, but perhaps the most developed (and also the most Nemesian) is that found in *TPO* 1, which presentation I follow here.[56] After mapping this basic structure, I work toward Maximus's understanding of temptation that comes from "within" and "without" since these words bear a superficial similarity to the Latin distinction between "internal" and "external" temptation.

The basis in the *logos* of human nature for all moral activity is a "natural desire" called the "will (θέλησις)." This desire pertains to the *logos* of human nature and is therefore wholly good, seeking what is good for the subject. Thanks to this natural will, human beings "stretch out toward" objects that realize its "full natural being." It is an appetite (ὄρεξις) that is in no way up to us—it only depend on what is natural to humanity.[57] It is, in short, the seat of positive, healthy desire in human nature, the acts of which are the fodder for all moral behavior.

This definition of will is central to Maximus's Christological dyothelitism, as it grounds will in the essence of human nature and in the goodness of our being. Contrarily, when Maximus, in his later writings, denies the presence of the deliberative, *gnomic* will (γνώμη) in Christ, he does so insofar as he understands the *gnomic* will as neither essential to human nature nor characteristically oriented toward the good of nature. The debates concerning Christ's will(s) in Maximus's time were drawn precisely concerning how to affirm Christ's unity with God, both morally and ontologically; Maximus's position affirming a human *thelesis* in Christ was potentially open to the criticism of rupturing this union in Christ. Thus, a construal of the natural

---

56. One can also find a helpful diagram of the structure of this act in Blowers, *Maximus the Confessor*, 161. In the structure of this diagram, Blowers indicates that the *gnomic* will is best understood as a stage of this process. I have excluded it here for the reasons described above.

57. *TPO* 1 (PG 91:12C-13A) in *Opuscula*, 112–13. For another discussion of the term "appetite," see Christoph Schoenborn, "Plaisir et Douleur dans l'Analyse de S. Maxime, d'après les Quaestiones ad Thalassium," in *Maximus Confessor*, ed. Felix Heinzer and Christoph Schoenborn, 273–84 (Fribourg: Éditions Universitaires Fribourg Suisse, 1982).

will of human nature in a morally negative way would be taken, in those debates, as evidence against the orthodoxy of Maximus's solution. While the natural will is fundamentally in accord with human nature, however, Maximus argues that the natural will is capable of being influenced through the intervention of demonic agency. In short, Maximus's developed position allows that Christ's lack of a *gnomic* will does not preclude his being tempted through his desires. A close investigation of the anthropological form of this temptation appears in the next section.

On the basis of *thelesis*, there is another source of "appetite (ὄρεξις)" in the human subject called "wish (βούλησις)," which I mentioned in the first part of this chapter. It concerns both things that are up to us, on the one hand, and things that are not up to us and do not come to be through us, on the other.[58] It excludes "rational deliberation" and seeks only ends. Maximus's examples of these ends are important, as John of Damascus's reception of his theory diverges somewhat from his presentation. His examples are things that pertain to earthly life and are thus not absolutely good, yet that might generally be agreed to be desirable (whether or not a particular individual is able to attain them): health, wealth, and immortality. The ends that wish has in mind, then, are not spiritual ends, but physical, this-worldly ones.[59] Given that Maximus also associates wish with the imagination, it can also be directed toward past and present mental images that enter the mind through memory and from external, physical objects. The objects of wish, in short, are this-worldly realities that are remembered or physically present and accepted as desirable without deliberation.

58. *TPO* 1 (PG 91:12C-13A) in *Opuscula*, 112–13. Will [θέλησις] and wish [βούλησις] are also considered at PG 91:317B-320A. His definition of the latter is different there, but I take his presentation in *TPO* 1 as definitive. Thunberg and Doucet are not in agreement about how Maximus understands wish. Thunberg argues that wish is already a part of the *gnomic* deliberative process that would therefore be absent in Christ (see Thunberg, *Microcosm and Mediator*, 218–19). However, Doucet argues—I believe convincingly—that wish is prior to choice and is a necessary component of human nature (Doucet, *Dispute avec Pyrrhus*, vol. 1, 357, 360). For this reason, I list βούλησις here as a proper element of the human moral act.

59. The "this-worldliness" of wish is significant in considering the fear that Christ demonstrates in the Garden of Gethsemane, as I discuss in chapter 3. However, I avoid the debates concerning humanity's natural and/or supernatural end(s) that have appeared in recent decades. I address this issue briefly again in chapter 3.

These natural and imaginative appetites are the beginning of the process of choice (προαίρεσις), which is a combined activity composed of appetite (ὄρεξις), deliberation (βούλευσις), and judgment (κρίσις).[60] *Proairesis*, choice, combines these three in this order, moving from either a natural or imaginative appetite (which seeks an end directly), to deliberation about the means for the attainment of that end, to a judgment about the course of action to be pursued, which ends in a choice. Having considered appetite, deliberation and judgment can also be briefly explained.

Maximus defines deliberation and its object in precisely the same way as Nemesius.[61] Unlike a wish (βούλησις), deliberation concerns only things that are up to us, that take place through our action, and the end of which is unseen. Two clarifications of these features are in order. Firstly, while one can *wish for* something outside of one's power, one cannot *choose* or *deliberate* such a thing; therefore, deliberation only concerns what is up to us and takes place through us. Elsewhere, Maximus echoes Nemesius, saying "we deliberate only those things the accomplishment of which in action is equally possible."[62] Secondly, deliberation requires that the end of the action be unseen, meaning that there is some uncertainty or lack of knowledge about whether the considered action will accomplish one's natural ends. One must

---

60. TPO 1 (PG 91:16B-C) in *Opuscula*, 114. My decision to consider choice as an innate faculty of human rationality is related to the Christological resolution I offer in the next chapter. I have decided to place choice in my consideration of the *logos* of human nature because (1) no purely anthropological passage in Maximus's corpus contradicts this placement, and (2) such a reading is consistent with Maximus's own anthropological source material. For various positions (either implicit or explicit) regarding the place of choice in Maximus's anthropology, see Ian A. McFarland, "'Naturally and by Grace': Maximus the Confessor on the operation of the will," *Scottish Journal of Theology* 58, no. 4 (2005): 410–33; Adam G. Cooper, *The Body in St. Maximus the Confessor Holy Flesh, Wholly Diefied* (New York: Oxford University Press, 2005), 214; Philipp Gabriel Renczes, *Agir de Dieu et Liberté de l'Homme: Récherches sur l'Anthropologie Théologique de Saint Maxime le Confesseur* (Paris: Éditions du Cerf, 2003), 269–272; Marcel Doucet, "Vues Récentes sur les 'Metamorphoses' de la Pensée de Saint Maxime le Confesseur," *Science et Esprit* 31, no. 3 (1979): 300; Hans Urs von Balthasar, *Cosmic Liturgy: The Universe According to Maximus the Confessor* (San Francisco: Ignatius Press, 1988), 260–71; Jean-Claude Larchet, *Maxime le Confesseur*, 89 and 114; Larchet, *La Divinisation de l'Homme*, 241; Jean-Miguel Garrigues, *Le Dessein Divin d'Adoption*, 131–40; and Demetrios Bathrellos, *The Byzantine Christ: Person, Nature, and Will in the Christology of St. Maximus the Confessor* (New York: Oxford University Press, 2004), 153, 156, and 191.

61. See chapter 1.

62. See TPO 1 (PG 91:16D-17B) in *Opuscula*, 115.

speak of the *telos* envisioned here in a qualified way; Maximus is clear that deliberation does not consider ends themselves, but rather only the means to an end. Thus, deliberation is still subordinate to wish, which establishes those ends in itself. It is not that wish (βούλησις) is sure about its goal and deliberation (βούλευσις) is unsure about that same goal; rather, the former formulates a goal or goals, the accomplishment of which the latter considers as its indeterminate, subordinate end. Finally, judgment is simply the end of the deliberative act, which results in a decision of which means to pursue. Free will is that by which human beings act out their appetites and choices, thereby attracting praise or blame depending on the use made of them.

One important point of comparison between Maximus and Nemesius arises in this material. When Maximus earlier considers these questions in the *Dispute with Pyrrhus*, he defines human rationality by its ability to search, deliberate, judge, and make a choice (just like Nemesius). In *Dispute with Pyrrhus*, these activities are said to take place in the *will* (θέλησις), whereas in the later *TPO*, they are said to take place as part of *choice* (προαίρεσις).[63] That Maximus would shift these activities into choice in the *TPO* is significant. As discussed in chapter 1, Nemesius implicitly encounters a Christological impasse because of his definition of rationality in terms of deliberation. For Nemesius, Christ's full humanity came into direct conflict with his absolute impeccability, because if Christ were fully human (and therefore rational), he deliberated; if he deliberated, there were actions that were indeterminate for him, whose outcomes were unknown and in need of investigation, with the possibility to form incorrect judgements; and if Christ can form incorrect judgements, he is not impeccable.

This same problem would appear to recur in Maximus's articulation in *Dispute with Pyrrhus*. In *TPO* 1, however, the problem takes a slightly different form because Maximus redirects the most problematic aspects of human deliberation away from the contested natural will (θέλησις) and places them instead in the category of choice, which was not central to the contested issues of the day. This shift allows

---

63. See *Dispute with Pyrrhus* (PG 91:293B-D) in *Dispute with Pyrrhus*, 549 (French on 628).

Maximus to more easily argue against the monothelites for Christ's human natural will, since its presence would no longer imply that Christ vacillated in regard to God's will. Nevertheless, this deflection leaves yet another portion of the human moral act in serious jeopardy. Maximus's anthropological texts understand choice as an intrinsic part of the moral act, yet Maximus has rendered its presence in Christ difficult to affirm. The consequences of this shift and the adequacy of this solution to these problems in Nemesius's anthropology will be considered further in chapter 3.

Temptations from Within and Without. Finally, the comparison of Maximus with Latin thought on temptation requires a clarification of what Maximus means by temptations that come from "within" and "without." In order to pursue that clarification, I must first explain how ignorance and the willful relate to Maximus's account of an individual's culpability. For Maximus, as for the Christian tradition as a whole, moral evil arises from bad choice and free will (*akrasia*), not simply because one is ignorant of the correct course of action or thought. Maximus defines moral evil in the soul as the "irrational movement of natural faculties according to an erroneous judgment (κατ' ἐσφαλμένην κρίσιν) toward something other than its end."[64] Thus, moral evil arises out of the deliberative process of choice described above.

At certain junctures of Maximus's presentation, it appears that ignorance takes a key role in this erroneous judgment. Ignorance "blinded humanity's intellect" and connected this intellect with sensibility.[65] Ignorance removed knowledge of God and filled the human subject with "passionate knowledge of sensible realities."[66] Despite the important role that ignorance plays in human sinfulness, however, Maximus introduces moral distinctions into ignorance that place the core moral

---

64. QT Introduction (PG 90:253A-B; CCSG 7:29) in *Questions à Thalassios*, vol. 1, 132–35; *On Difficulties in Sacred Scripture*, 82. One might note the similarity to Gregory of Nyssa on this point.
65. QT Introduction (PG 90:2257A; CCSG 7:35) in *Questions à Thalassios*, vol. 1, 140–41; *On Difficulties in Sacred Scripture*, 85.
66. QT Introduction (PG 90:2257A; CCSG 7:35) in *Questions à Thalassios*, vol. 1, 140–41; *On Difficulties in Sacred Scripture*, 85.

issue back in the use or misuse of free will. Maximus distinguishes between ignorance that is in some sense *chosen* and another kind that is not willful. In the earlier *Questions and Doubts*, Maximus argues that there is one kind of ignorance that is up to us—that is, we could have known, but do not—and another kind that is not up to us—it was not in our power to have known. In this way, the root of an error can be differentiated: ignorance is sometimes unwillful, but in other cases, ignorance is a product of choice. The latter is "reproachable" and the former is "irreproachable": we could know the latter, but do not; we want to know the former, but cannot.[67] Subjective culpability is determined by the presence of a prior decision of free will not to seek knowledge.

If willful acts are the ones that attract moral praise and blame, Maximus's association of passion with the categories of the "willful (ἑκουσίων)" and "unwillful (ἀκουσίων)" also deserves some commentary. While these terms are often translated as "voluntary" and "involuntary" (respectively), the Nemesian roots of Maximus's usage may not fully support this translation.[68] As explained in the preceding chapter, Nemesius defines the willful (ἑκουσίων) as a larger category than voluntary choice. For example, if one stumbles upon a treasure while digging a grave, such an action is willful but not chosen because the finding of the treasure was not up to the one who found it. This arrangement can work to one's moral detriment. If one accidentally kills a man who is one's enemy (and whose death is met with joy), Nemesius considers such an action to be *willful* (ἑκουσίων). On the other hand, when a result of an action is met with sadness and is accompanied by ignorance of relevant facts, that result is *unwillful* (ἀκουσίων). Thus, Nemesius describes a son who accidentally kills a father with an arrow while hunting: Nemesius concludes that the son neither chose the death nor willfully caused it.

When these categories are applied to passions by Maximus, willful passions are usually associated with pleasure (ἡδονή) and unwillful

---

67. QD I 67 (CCSG 10:155) in *Questions and Doubts*, 148–49.
68. Most translations of Maximus's works renders these terms as "voluntary" and "involuntary," but there are times when this translation does not convey Maximus's meaning. In my translation, I follow the advice of R. W. Sharples and P. J. Van Der Eijk in their translation of Nemesius. See Nemesius of Emesa, *On the Nature of Man* (Liverpool: Liverpool University Press, 2008), 168, n. 868, a decision I justified in n. 19 in chapter 1.

TABLE 2-1. The Individual Who Lacks Virtue

	Bodily Response	Spiritual Response
Pleasure	Willful	Willful
Pain	Unwillful	Unwillful

passions are usually associated with pain (ὀδύνη).[69] The reason for this association is fairly clear. Generally speaking, pleasure is something sought and pain something to be avoided, so even if one does not *choose* to experience pleasure in a given circumstance, such a result would usually be willful, precisely because it is met with approval. Similarly, even if one does not *choose* to experience pain, that experience can still be called "unwillful" because it is met with disapproval. These nuances of meaning are obscured when ἑκουσίων is rendered as "voluntary" and ἀκουσίων as "involuntary," as these English terms seems to imply that the experience is chosen or rejected in deliberation, which Maximus would deny.

Maximus normally associates the terms "willful" and "unwillful" with respect to how a passion is received by the body: happily or with disapproval, respectively. Yet Maximus at times acknowledges that the willful and unwillful passions have spiritual parallels, thereby producing four different kinds in all. Following the natural opposition between body and soul, willful passions are pleasurable to the body but, often in reality, spiritually painful (since they tend to attach the soul to material bodies instead of to their true end) and unwillful passions are painful for the body but, often in reality, spiritually pleasurable (since they tend to provoke the soul to separate itself from attachment to worldly realities).[70] When one's passions control reason, the soul perceives these passions in the same way as the body, even though this perception is objectively wrong (see table 2-1).

---

69. See, for instance, *QT* 26 (PG 90:341D; CCSG 7:173–75) in *Questions à Thalassios*, vol. 1, 304–5, and *On Difficulties in Sacred Scripture*, 173.

70. *QT* 58 (PG 90:592C-596D; CCSG 22:27–33) in *Questions à Thalassios*, vol. 3, 38–45; *On Difficulties in Sacred Scripture*, 403–5.

TABLE 2-2. The Virtuous Individual

	Bodily Response	Spiritual Response
Pleasure	Willful	Unwillful
Pain	Unwillful	Willful

However, when one's soul has taken its rightful place of governance over the body through temperance and patience, the soul ceases to consider the experience of the body: spiritual joy then arises from unchosen physical pain, and spiritual pain can arise from unchosen physical pleasure.[71] There is, then, a sense in which virtue reverses the meaning of "willful" and "unwillful" passions, responding to pain with joy and to pleasure with disapproval—though not in a way that could be confused as masochistic (see table 2-2).[72]

Maximus also occasionally describes these willful and unwillful passions as coming, respectively, from "within (ἔνδοθεν)" and "without (ἔξωθεν)." Given the way that the Latin tradition in the second half of this project will differentiate between "internal" and "external" temptations, it is important to explain Maximus's distinct meaning in his use of these terms.[73] On the one hand, it means that willful passion

---

71. QT 58 (PG 90:596D-597B; CCSG 22:33–35) in *Questions à Thalassios*, vol. 3, 44–45; *On Difficulties in Sacred Scripture*, 405–6.

72. Maximus considers a category of "willful pain" that arises through patience. The virtue of patience, thus, has the role of *reversing* the normal associations of willfulness and passion. Certainly, one can choose to seek pleasure or avoid pain, but when these befall one unexpectedly, temperance and patience make these pleasures and pains *unwillful* and *willful*, respectively. Patience is seen as the remedy for pain at QD 163 (CCSG 10:114) in *Questions and Doubts*, 124; QT 26 (PG 90:344B-C; CCSG 7:177) in *On Difficulties in Sacred Scripture*, 174–75; and *Questions à Thalassios*, vol. 1, 306–7 (esp. Larchet's notes). Both are associated at Amb. Io. 10 (PG 91:1204C-1205B) in *Ambigua*, 223, and *On Difficulties in the Church Fathers*, vol. 1, 339–43; see also QT 49 (PG 90:452B-D; CCSG 7:357–59) in *Questions à Thalassios*, vol. 2, 102–3, and *On Difficulties in Sacred Scripture*, 284–85. That is, one who is patient meets unexpected bodily pains with a certain approval, and, presumably (though Maximus does not state this explicitly), one who is temperate meets unexpected pleasure with a certain disapproval. In neither case is this pain or pleasure *chosen*, since in neither case is the pleasure or pain in the power of the one undergoing the experience; what makes it willful or not is the attitude with which the passion is met. The translation of the relevant terms as voluntary and involuntary has serious negative consequences here, as they would seem to imply a masochistic seeking of pain. In order to preserve Maximus's position from such a charge of masochism, the distinction between willfulness and choice/volition is essential.

73. See QD 153 (CCSG 10:107) in *Questions and Doubts*, 120, and QD 163 (CCSG 10:114) in *Questions and Doubts*, 124.

(pleasure) arises in human nature on the basis of ends conceived by appetites of either nature or thought; coming from "within" thus refers to a spontaneous, nondeliberative movement toward the object. Similarly, it means that unwillful passion (pain) comes to the subject as something to be avoided; coming from "without" simply means that it is a passion that the appetite of aversion spontaneously avoids. On the other hand, coming from "within" does not mean that these unsavory desires originate in human nature in the manner of a Latin conception of concupiscence or the *fomes peccati*. In fact, Maximus avows that *external* forces can influence these appetites coming from "within." Similarly, coming from "without" does *not* mean that the attack can leave the faculties of the individual involved utterly unperturbed. With these unwillful passions, there is a corresponding reaction from the faculty of aversion; an attack from "without" still corresponds to an internal response from the sensitive faculty.[74] This clarification is important, by way of anticipation, when comparing Maximus's articulation to the Latin distinction between "internal" and "external" temptation. It will become apparent that Maximus's way of thinking does not correspond perfectly with the predominant Latin way. More proximately, this clarification is also important to Maximus's vision of the activity of demons in bringing about human temptation.

Demonic Temptation in Human Nature

Maximus's view of demonic temptation reflects the tradition that he inherited, yet his account is also creative. He diagnoses temptation because he ultimately wants to prescribe a solution for it that is both spiritually engaging and Christologically oriented. This discussion of his view of temptation, then, is essential to the purpose of the next chapter, for one must understand how human beings are tempted if one is to consider how Christ was "tempted like us in all things, yet without sin" (Heb 4:15). In the preceding section, my concern was to elaborate the psychological structures of Maximus's thought along the same anthropological lines as previous studies of Maximus and as

---

74. *QD* 163 (CCSG 10:114) in *Questions and Doubts*, 124.

Maximus often does in his own writings before transposing into demonological categories. In this section, however, I show how previous studies fall short of a full description of Maximian psychology due to a lack of attention to his demonology.

There will always remain something mysterious about the way in which human beings turn from their final end. For Maximus, however, the human experience of temptation is regularly and even systematically related to the activity of demonic forces in and through the psychological structures laid out in the previous section. If there is something mysterious in human sin, it is not, for Maximus, an ambiguity about the goodness of human nature but rather how something fundamentally good is, through the devil's prodding, misused. No matter the human agent involved, the devil is an indispensable component of moral theology, throwing up obstacles against the most trained moral athlete and, crucially, against Christ himself.[75]

On the way to this Christological investigation, I address Maximus's general anthropology of demonic temptation in four sections: a review of how human nature was rendered susceptible to demonic temptation by Adam's transgression; a consideration of how demons interact with human passibility to elicit sin; an account of how Maximus relates demons with thoughts and memories; and an argument that Maximus's theory maintains human autonomy and responsibility.

Postlapsarian Susceptibility to Demonic Temptation. Maximus often indicates that demons are especially active in the natural faculties of human nature after the Fall. While Maximus at times appears to render the consequences of human sin in a wholly anthropological or psychological register, a closer reading of these passages in Maximus's work draws out the demonological associations of these concepts. Maximus's own way of speaking makes this demonology hard to recognize; he will often begin a discussion in the anthropological terms of passion yet

---

75. Maximus also considers the case of those who cooperate with the devil's instigations, though such a case is not of interest in this study. Maximus states that the scribes and Pharisees are "energized" (which, Sherwood points out, is the root of the Latin word for possession) by the devil. See *AL* 12 (PG 90:921A-B) in *Ascetic Life*, 110. I agree with Sherwood's argument that what Maximus describes here is not to be confused with possession (242, n. 35).

slowly transpose his analysis into an elaboration of demonology. One prominent example is Maximus's understanding of the "deception" of human beings. In *Ambigua to John*, Maximus on occasion describes the senses and bodies as "deceptive."[76] In these cases, however, the deceptive quality of the passions does not tell the whole story. Tellingly, in other junctures of *Ambigua to John*, Maximus associates such bodily deception with the work of the devil.[77]

There are a number of other passages in *Ambigua to John* which more clearly demonstrate a close association between the Fall and increased demonic activity against humanity through its natural appetitive faculties.[78] In two of the lengthiest examples, Maximus begins a discussion of a passionate temptation that appears to take place in only anthropological categories. Yet as Maximus expounds the situation, he draws the reader's attention to the devil's work inside the human agent. This transposition from the apparently anthropological into the explicitly demonological can be seen in the movement from *Ambigua to John* 10:21 to *Amb. Io.* 10:22a, and again at even greater length in

---

76. *Amb. Io.* 10.4 (PG 91:1117A-B) in *On Difficulties in the Church Fathers*, vol. 1, 171; *Amb. Io.* 10.21 and 22b (PG 91:1145B and 1149A) in *On Difficulties in the Church Fathers*, vol. 1, 229, 235; and *Amb. Io.* 47 (PG 91:1360B) in *On Difficulties in the Church Fathers*, vol. 2, 209. Although the word "deceptive" is not present, the same sentiment can be found at *Amb. Io.* 8 (PG 91:1101D-1104A) in *On Difficulties in the Church Fathers*, vol. 1, 143.

77. *Amb. Io.* 7.32 (PG 91:1092D) in *On Difficulties in the Church Fathers*, vol. 1, 121; *Amb. Io.* 38 (PG 91:1301A) in *On Difficulties in the Church Fathers*, vol. 2, 95; *Amb. Io.* 50 (PG 91:1369A-B) in *On Difficulties in the Church Fathers*, vol. 2, 229; and *Amb. Io.* 54 (PG 91:1376C-D) in *On Difficulties in the Church Fathers*, vol. 2, 243-45. See also *AL* 16 (PG 90:924C-D) in *Ascetic Life*, 112. Louth, "Introduction," xxiii, notes this deception but does not trace it to its demonological roots.

78. Some major examples are in the main text; other more minor examples follow here: *Letter 2* (PG 91:396D-397B) in *Lettres*, trans. Emmanuel Ponsoye (Paris: Éditions du Cerf, 1998), 84; *QD* 9 (CCSG 10:8-9) in *Questions and Doubts*, 46-47; *QT* 61 (PG 90:625D-641B; CCSG 22:85-105) in Blowers and Wilken, *Cosmic Mystery*, 137; *QT* 62 (PG 90:653C-656D) in *Questions à Thalassios*, vol. 3, 138-41; *On Difficulties in Sacred Scripture*, 457-58); *AL* 5 (PG 90:913D-916B) in *Ascetic Life*, 105-6; *AL* 32-33 (PG 90:937B-940A) in *Ascetic Life*, 122-23; *Amb. Io.* 10.13 (PG 91:1124C) in *On Difficulties in the Church Fathers*, vol. 1, 185-87; *Amb. Io.* 10.18 (PG 91:1132A) in *On Difficulties in the Church Fathers*, vol. 1, 199 ("the law of the flesh in no way differs from the Antichrist"); *Amb. Io.* 10.22b (PG 91:1149C) in *On Difficulties in the Church Fathers*, vol. 1, 237; *Amb. Io.* 10.28 (PG 91:1156C) in *On Difficulties in the Church Fathers*, vol. 1, 247; *Amb. Io.* 55 (PG 91:1377C) in *On Difficulties in the Church Fathers*, vol. 2, 249, where Maximus is indifferent regarding the interpretation of his text as "the assaults of the passions" on the one hand or "the assaults of the demons" on the other; *Amb. Io.* 56 (PG 91:1377D-80B) in *On Difficulties in the Church Fathers*, vol. 2, 249-51; and *Amb. Io.* 67 (PG 91:1404A) in *On Difficulties in the Church Fathers*, vol. 2, 301.

the extended exegesis found in *Ambigua to John* 10:4–9.⁷⁹ In this latter case, the first three contemplations speak anthropologically, but *Ambigua to John* 10:7–9 slowly transitions into demonology. Christ's exemplary defeat of passion (a struggle initially presented as psychological) comes through Christ's confrontation with evil powers and the devil (now no longer merely psychological but essentially demonological). As the Christological solution takes the form of reflection on demonology, it follows that the problem itself must also be conceived in these same terms. *Ambigua to John* 10:51 raises the association and "embedding" of demons in passability to the level of a general anthropological principle. First, Maximus explains how the demons arouse passion in fallen humanity: "The demon, who arouses the passions, ... casts the mind into the fire of anger and the water of desire, seeking to drown it, and will not cease from this until the Word of God appears and drives away the wicked, material spirit ... and so frees the possessed man from the evil tyranny."⁸⁰ Maximus then states that this way of experiencing temptation is universal, even among the saints: "It was in this manner that all the saints, having genuinely received the divine and unerring Word, passed through this present age, without their souls leaving so much as a footprint in any of its pleasures."⁸¹

Other examples appear in *QT*. In Maximus's exegesis of the story of the prophet Jonah, Jonah's being cast into the sea becomes a metaphor for the Fall. In this wounded condition, nature is swallowed by the devil and carried by the devil through the "water" of temptation and attachment to material objects. Similarly, it has also been driven by evil powers into ignorance.⁸² This analogy draws out the active role that demons have taken in bringing about the fallen state of human nature. Through this double-submersion into evil and ignorance, demonic power attacks both the sensible and rational faculties of human nature. Much of what constitutes the imbalance of human nature

---

79. PG 91:1145C-9C, in *On Difficulties in the Church Fathers*, vol. 1, 229–31; PG 91:1117A-20D, in *On Difficulties in the Church Fathers*, vol. 1, 231–33, respectively.
80. *Amb. Io.* 10.51 (PG 91:1204C-5B) in *On Difficulties in the Church Fathers*, vol. 1, 339–41.
81. *Amb. Io.* 10.51 (PG 91:1204C-5B) in *On Difficulties in the Church Fathers*, vol. 1, 339–41.
82. *QT* 64 (PG 90:696D-697C; CCSG 22:191–93) in Blowers and Wilken, *Cosmic Mystery*, 148–49.

after the Fall is reason's inability to guide sensibility; Maximus attributes this imbalance to the devil actively (symbolized by the fish) but to human nature only passively (as Jonah, subject to the fish's movement).

Similarly, throughout QT 21, there is a chiastic structure regarding Adam's Fall into the power of demonic forces and Christ's redemption from those forces.[83] Maximus's emphasis in that text falls on the latter half of this structure, but Maximus's argument is predicated on the existence of a Fall *into* the grasp of demonic powers that are associated with human passibility.

In a final example interpreting the "filling of the valleys and leveling of the mountains" proclaimed by John the Baptist, Maximus again shows the close association between humanity's fallen condition and demonic temptation. In his exegesis, the valleys are human flesh "cleft by a great stream of passions" as well as the soul when it is "hollowed out by the great storm of ignorance."[84] Maximus then notes that valleys are most often "set together" with mountains.[85] These mountains represent the "spirits of false knowledge and of evil" and the "demons trading in unnatural ignorance and evil."[86] Given their close geographical placement, the relationship that Maximus sees between the two is intimate, even intrinsic.[87] Indeed, Maximus states that the "leveling" of these mountains is simultaneously "the complete restoration of the natural powers of the body and soul."[88] Thus, the end of demonic activity itself restores the natural functioning of human faculties.

---

83. QT 21 (PG 90:316B-D; CCSG 7:131–33) in Blowers and Wilken, *Cosmic Mystery*, 112. On the discussion of the *cheirograph* in QT 21, note Michael E. Stone, *Adam's Contract with Satan: The Legend of the Cheirograph of Adam* (Bloomington: Indiana University Press, 2002). Maximus does not state that the *cheirograph* was with Satan, but Stone has shown that Christian authors after the year 200 viewed the cheirograph in this way (104); the weight of contextual evidence indicates that Maximus did as well.

84. QT 47 (PG 90:425A-D; CCSG 7:319–21) in *Questions à Thalassios*, vol. 2, 58–61; *On Difficulties in Sacred Scripture*, 260–61.

85. QT 47 (PG 90:425A-D; CCSG 7:319–21) in *Questions à Thalassios*, vol. 2, 60; *On Difficulties in Sacred Scripture*, 261.

86. QT 47 (PG 90:425A-D; CCSG 7:319–21) in *Questions à Thalassios*, vol. 2, 60; *On Difficulties in Sacred Scripture*, 173, 261. The term for "trading" indicates that it is the demons' habitual trade or business to concern themselves with ignorance and evil.

87. The word for the relationship can be used to denote a marriage.

88. QT 47 (PG 90:425A-D; CCSG 7:319–21) in *Questions à Thalassios*, vol. 2, 60, 64–65; *On Difficulties in Sacred Scripture*, 261.

Demons and Passibility. If demonic temptation is among the consequences of Adam's sin, what are demons permitted to do to humankind? Maximus provides at least two different lists of this activity. One list includes demonic activity in the three faculties of human nature: reason (τὸ λογιστικὸν), desire (τὸ ἐπιθυμητικὸν), and aversion (τὸ θυμικὸν);[89] another list includes other attacks that come from memory and thoughts.[90] These latter temptations from memory and thoughts include both recollections of material realities (attacking the sensitive faculties) and the suggestion of vice to the mind (attacking the reasoning faculty).[91] Similar to Evagrius, Maximus associates different demons with different temptations, though he does not provide a rigorous catalog of temptations with the associated demons.[92]

Every demonic temptation has as its basis a natural faculty of human nature.[93] Since these faculties are intrinsically good and oriented toward the natural flourishing of humankind, the demon's job is to attempt to elicit an activation of those faculties that goes against nature.[94] Maximus argues in *TPO* 7 that while human beings are responsible for the perversion of nature, "According to this [perversion], we became inclined to evil by the originally evil snake, but according to that [original creation], we came into existence formed by God and as a valued creature by nature."[95] In the construction of this sentence,

---

89. *CL* II 12 (PG 90:988A) in *Philokalia*, vol. 2, 66–67. The inclusion of reason in this list requires further consideration not possible in the present work; if the devil also inhabits the highest faculties of the soul, it is unclear what ground the monk has from which to mount a counter-attack.

90. *QD* 85 (CCSG 10:67) in *Questions and Doubts*, 90.

91. More precisely, Maximus has in mind the distinction between the enemies of the "left" and "right." To the left are evil things, such as evil thoughts; to the right are good things, like askesis and good thoughts that, if reflected on in the wrong way, still lead one to vainglory and pride. Thus, even good things can be used by the devil to elicit vice. See *Questions à Thalassios*, vol. 2, 86–87, n. 1.

92. *QT* 26 (PG 90:345D-348A; CCSG 7:181) in *Questions à Thalassios*, vol. 1, 312–13; *On Difficulties in Sacred Scripture*, 177.

93. Again, see *QT* 55 (PG 90:541A; CCSG 7:487) in *Questions à Thalassios*, vol. 2, 242–43. As mentioned above, in *QT* 21 (PG 90:312B-316D; CCSG 7:127–33) in Blowers and Wilken, *Cosmic Mystery*, 109–13, Maximus states that "Through the energy of the natural passions, all evil powers are at work, driving deliberation, according to the possibility of nature, into the corruption of the unnatural passions through the natural ones."

94. See, for instance, the exegesis of David and Goliath in *QT* 53 (PG 90:501C-D; CCSG 7:431–33) in *Questions à Thalassios*, vol. 2, 184–85, and *On Difficulties in Sacred Scripture*, 326–27.

95. *TPO* 7 (PG 91:80B) in Louth, *Maximus*, 185.

the "snake" and "nature" play the same structural role in each clause. In our perversion, the "snake" takes the place of nature by perverting it, replacing or at least covering its natural functions with its own activities. While natural desires of attraction remain directed toward one's natural good, the devil can use them for his own purposes, prodding the human subject on to something significantly different. The devil, for instance, attempts to excite the faculty of desire with an "appetite contrary to nature."[96] In another place, the devil "yokes" the natural operation of the soul into what is against nature through "undisciplined impulses" of desire and aversion.[97] In yet another text, the devil produces "confusion, impiety, and ignorance," which in turn bring forth "evil, error, and atheism" in the one they attack.[98] Similarly,

> Scripture thus calls "powerful" the evil demon who presses on toward desire and inflames it toward an unseemly appetite for shameful pleasures; for nothing is more powerful [δυνατώτερον] or more violent [βιαιότερον] than a natural appetite.[99]

The same is the case for the faculty of aversion and the faculty of reason, each of which has a demon assigned to it.[100] The "natural appetite" in this quotation is important, for it indicates that the desires involved are not intrinsically or culpably sinful but that they are incited by the devil in a certain, even "violent," way so that they might become sinful.

Demons use different passions in different ways. Recall that Maximus says that willful passions arise from "within" and unwillful pas-

96. *QT* 50 (PG 90:472B; CCSG 7:387) in *Questions à Thalassios*, vol. 2, 134–35; *On Difficulties in Sacred Scripture*, 301.
97. *Letter* 4 (PG 91:413A-B), in *Lettres*, 93. See also *Letter* 8 (PG 91:440C-445B) in *Lettres*, 108–11, where wolves (the demons) feast on the flesh (human appetitive desires), and *Letter* 33 (PG 91:628B-C) in *Lettres*, 220–21.
98. *QT* 25 (PG 90:336B-C; CCSG 7:167) in *Questions à Thalassios*, vol. 1, 296–97; *On Difficulties in Sacred Scripture*, 168.
99. *QT* 50 (PG 90:472C-D; CCSG 7:387–89) in *Questions à Thalassios*, vol. 2, 136–37; *On Difficulties in Sacred Scripture*, 302. The otherwise excellent discussion of pleasure and pain in Schoenborn, "Plaisir et Douleur dans l'Analyse de S. Maxime, d'après les Quaestiones ad Thalassium," falls short because it fails to take into consideration the devil's intentions for these phenomena.
100. *QT* 50 (PG 90:472C-D; CCSG 7:387–89) in *Questions à Thalassios*, vol. 2, 136–37; *On Difficulties in Sacred Scripture*, 302: "And [Scripture] names 'warrior' the demon who sits in the faculty of aversion and unceasingly prepares [it] to fight for pleasure."

sions arise from "without." In both cases, though, Maximus affirms that demons are involved in bringing them about.[101] Willful passions are put to use by demonic powers by convincing the human subject to seek and prefer physical realities over eternal goods.[102] Their goal is to cause the rational faculty to divert its activity from natural contemplation to a consideration of physical realities with a view to passion. On the other hand, demons also have their own purpose in eliciting unwillful passions, with which the demons hope to drive the human subject to lose "hope in God ... under the great weight of painful misfortunes," attempting to elicit atheism.[103] In both cases, though, the human act of subjecting one's rational faculties to the sensible faculties renders them culpably sinful.

These temptations overlap with the broader psychology of appetite described in the previous section. An appetite, whether pertaining to the natural will, wish, or imagination, is an unsolicited desire that is not subject to deliberation. When arising from the natural will (θέλησις), such an appetite is, by Maximus's definition, according to nature; it reaches out to God and seeks spiritual realities. How demons can elicit "unseemly appetites"[104] or even appetites "against nature"[105] (as Maximus sometimes indicates) in this faculty is difficult to understand. Maximus's language is somewhat imprecise.[106] Perhaps the best way to understand his claim is to say that by making natural desires violent, demons bring them to the brink of being unnat-

101. This is seen at QD 163 (CCSG 10:114) in *Questions and Doubts*, 124.
102. See QT 26 (PG 90:341A-D; CCSG 7:173–75) in *Questions à Thalassios*, vol. 1, 302–5; *On Difficulties in Sacred Scripture*, 172–73.
103. QT 26 (PG 90:341A-D; CCSG 7:173–75) in *Questions à Thalassios*, vol. 1, 304–5; *On Difficulties in Sacred Scripture*, 173.
104. QT 50 (PG 90:472C; CCSG 7:387) in *Questions à Thalassios*, vol. 2, 136–37; *On Difficulties in Sacred Scripture*, 302.
105. QT 50 (PG 90:472B; CCSG 7:387) in *Questions à Thalassios*, vol. 2, 134–35; *On Difficulties in Sacred Scripture*, 301.
106. Given that Maximus's fully developed account of "appetite" was not complete until the TPO, I am inclined to think that the phrase "appetite against nature" should not be taken too literally. In his later thought, an "appetite contrary to nature" would be a contradiction in terms, as appetites arise naturally and without deliberation from the *logos* of human nature. In another passage, Maximus refers to a "love potion [φίλτρον]" that lies in nature concerning things near at hand. See TPO 19 (PG 91:224C) in *Opuscula*, 237. While not explicitly demonic, the analogy does associate a desire for material reality with a magical spell or charm that, presumably, is cast on the subject from an external source.

ural or disobedient to reason. From this violent state, it only takes a slight miscalculation on the part of the human subject in order for such a natural appetite to become an unnatural passion. If temptation through *thelesis* poses particular challenges (since it aims at humanity's highest good), the two other appetites of wish and imagination aim at more proximate ends of human flourishing and thereby introduce more room for external manipulation by demonic force. In these cases, Maximus may have in mind an Evagrian mechanism to explain the insertion of an "unseemly appetite," that is, it may be possible for the devil to insert a spontaneous appetite in the imagination that would not necessarily be in accord with the true human flourishing of a particular individual in certain circumstances. In the case of wish, even though its ends are broadly natural, it would not be difficult to see how an external agent could introduce a desire regarding health or wealth (examples that Maximus gives of wish) that would be sinful in a particular circumstance.

Demons and Thoughts. Maximus reflects his Evagrian heritage most strongly in his association of demons with thoughts and memories. For Maximus, this component of demonic attack is important because thoughts involving passion are commonly the origin of an unnatural passion.[107] In order to arouse unnatural passion within the soul, demons are most commonly able to use external objects as a way of forming thoughts about sensible realities. These sensible realities are the habitual means by which the devil attacks human beings,[108] though people who have separated themselves from society are not as easily attacked in this way. In these circumstances, the devil turns to somewhat extraordinary measures, calling to mind "material representations" which attack the soul with "appearances and forms of sensible realities."[109] Demons call these representations to mind by means of

---

107. Larchet argues that *all* sin has an evil representation or thought at its origin (see *Questions à Thalassios*, vol. 1, 225, n. 3).

108. *QT* 49 (PG 90:453A-C; CCSG 7:359–61) in *Questions à Thalassios*, vol. 2, 104–5; *On Difficulties in Sacred Scripture*, 285.

109. *QT* 49 (PG 90:453A-C; CCSG 7:359–61) in *Questions à Thalassios*, vol. 2, 104–5. See also *QT* 49 (PG 90:453A-C; CCSG 7:359–61) in *Questions à Thalassios*, vol. 2, 100–101, and *On*

the recollection of evil thoughts.[110] When sensibility perceives these appearances, it often becomes the devil's tool because its natural function is to react to these objects.[111]

Because wish (βούλησις) is a natural appetite (ὄρεξις) of created humanity in a way similar to the natural will (θέλησις), a demonic attack through thoughts may be described by Maximus as somewhat parallel to the way demons attempt to elicit unnatural passions. As discussed above, wish is a natural appetite that seeks a natural *telos* regardless of whether it is attainable or not. Indeed, given that this appetite seeks more proximate ends than *thelesis*, the goodness of the ends that it seeks may be more contingent on an individual's vocation or circumstances than are the ends of *thelesis*. Thus, it would be possible for the devil to elicit or implant thoughts of these natural ends (good in themselves) in people or in circumstances where that end is not something that ought to be pursued.[112] In this way, a demonic attack against wish might bring the appetite to seek ends that require some discernment regarding the pursuit of the end envisioned. The monk, for instance, might spontaneously recognize wealth as something desirable, but the monk is not thereby compelled to seek wealth through deliberation, nor is he compelled to dwell on that thought. Such an understanding of these natural desires would at least fit with what Maximus affirms about wish and the workings of demonic powers in and through natural appetites.

Human Responsibility and Demonic Temptation. Maximus certainly does not intend automatically to exculpate the human agent who ex-

---

Difficulties in Sacred Scripture, 284–86. It is unclear whether these appearances are meant to be physical manifestations of sensible objects that are not truly or currently present or if they are mental representations of these objects in the monk's mind.

110. *CL* III 20 (PG 90:1021B-C) in *Philokalia*, vol. 2, 85–86. Here, anger is stirred up by memories of those who have offended the monk. More explicitly, however, *QD* 85 (CCSG 10:67) in *Questions and Doubts*, 90, shows that demons "stir up the memory through the recollections of evil thoughts." Demons are invoked almost interchangeably with thoughts in *AL* 18 and 41 (PG 90:925B-C and PG 90:952A-953A) in *Ascetic Life*, 113, 132.

111. *QT* 49 (PG 90:453A-C; CCSG 7:359–61) in *Questions à Thalassios*, vol. 2, 104–5; *On Difficulties in Sacred Scripture*, 286.

112. Such a scenario may be what Maximus believes to occur for Christ in the desert and in Gethsemane; see chapter 3 below.

periences a temptation from a demonic source. Nevertheless, he uses rather striking language to describe the devil's power over fallen humanity.[113] Two forms of demonic attack merit consideration: attacks against sensibility and attacks through deception directed against the intellect. Maximus protects against a demonic "cause" of sin in passibility by means of the distinctions he draws about what constitutes sin. Attacks against the intellect, however, are less easily explained and require separate, somewhat speculative treatment.

When demonic attack comes through sensibility, Maximus delineates the boundary between what is culpable and what is natural or, equivalently, not in our power. In the QD, Maximus considers four stages in the development of sinful actions: the attack, the desire, the consent, and the act. In his exegesis, only the final two categories are culpable; the attack and the desire are not in our power and therefore do not attract praise or blame.[114] While his terminology here is not perfectly clear, the attack appears to be a reference to a demonic attack, and the desire corresponds most closely with the natural appetite that the attack attempts to elicit in an unnatural way. If this reading is accurate, Maximus is clear that the natural desires roused by demons do not result in an activity in the genus of sin; these actions of the sensible faculty, being stimulated from without, are not within the power of reason to prevent (and thus not within τὰ ἐφ' ἡμῖν). Only when the intellect offers consent does the desire become culpable. As will be noted in chapter 4, the culpability of desires prior to consent will be treated much differently among Latin Christian readers of the texts of Gregory the Great.[115]

---

113. QT 21 (PG 90:312B-316D; CCSG 7:127–33) in Blowers and Wilken, *Cosmic Mystery*, 109–113, for instance, says that demons "drive" humanity to unnatural passion; QD 85 (CCSG 10:67) in *Questions and Doubts*, 90, says that demons can use passion to "force open [the soul] as with a crowbar (ἐκμοχλεύω)."

114. QD I 31 (CCSG 10:149) in *Questions and Doubts*, 146; see also QD I 33 (CCSG 10:150) in *Questions and Doubts*, 146–47.

115. Since this phenomenon involves demonic manipulation of a human's body, it should be carefully distinguished from possession. Arguably, an adequate definition of possession requires two components (which are helpfully distinguished by Aquinas [see chapter 5] but not explicitly indicated by Maximus): (1) the one possessed is unable to exercise their reason and will in the domain of the body, and (2) their body is overtaken by other forces in order to produce objectively immoral actions. In the scenarios Maximus outlines, the first criterion is possibly met, though Maximus seems to indicate that human beings, even apart from demonic temptation,

When it comes to demonic deception of the intellect, Maximus is less clear how human culpability is maintained. As discussed above, the devil's first act against Adam was to inspire ignorance of God; trickery or deception is at the root of many sins with demonic origin.[116] Can the devil, due to intellectual deception, cause a human being to do something objectively evil without the consent of the will? Maximus seems to answer affirmatively. He speaks in the QD of three kinds of "involuntary (ἀδιάθετος)" sin: sin through "tyrannical constraint," through deception, and through ignorance.[117] When such an attack occurs, the monk is to make a hasty retreat so that the passion involved does not cause him to sin "of his own volition"; he does not recommend repentance but rather ascetic discipline. Both of these facts indicate that he does not believe the human subject to have incurred moral guilt through such an involuntary sin; one might detect here a distinction between an objectively incorrect action and the subjective guilt it may or may not incur.[118]

As discussed above, Maximus acknowledges that within the category of actions performed through ignorance there are some actions where the ignorance itself was preceded by a decision not to seek the appropriate knowledge of the situation. In such a case, the involuntary sin could still be called willful indirectly, and the subject could thereby incur guilt for the ignorance if not for the act. Regardless, there are also scenarios where one does not know the correct course of action and where one simultaneously has no recourse to investigate the mat-

---

do not have voluntary control over these functions in the first place. Thus, the devil would not be taking "control" of something normally under the complete direction of the human agent. The second criterion, however, is not met. Since the thoughts and passions suggested by the devil are essentially still in accord with the natural functioning of those faculties, the devil is not causing anything in the human subject in the genus of sin.

116. QT Introduction (PG 90:254B; CCSG 7:31) in *Questions à Thalassios*, vol. 1, 134–35; *On Difficulties in Sacred Scripture*, 82–83.

117. QD 29 (CCSG 10:24) in *Questions and Doubts*, 58–59: "tyrannical constraint" is Prassas's translation; it could also be the "exercise of tyranny." Maximus may have in mind the sort of constraint that one person has over another, as when one forces another to do an action under pain of death. However, there is no immediate reason to constrain Maximus to this narrow anthropological reading of tyranny; the other two causes, at least, are both commonly associated with the devil.

118. Unlike temptation through sensibility, then, this kind of deception of the intellect is more akin to possession since it produces an act in the genus of sin for which the human subject is not considered responsible.

ter properly. In these circumstances, the above considerations indicate that Maximus would assign no subjective guilt to one so deceived or ignorant.

By considering the action of demonic agency in and through the faculties of human nature, Maximus offers a way for human beings to reflect on their own mental and emotional states that does not call their fundamental goodness into question. Still, Maximus indicates that these emotional states require careful moral discernment. The experience of such temptation—a universal characteristic of humankind's postlapsarian *tropos*, or law—feeds into the sort of moral vacillation described by the *gnomic* will (γνώμη). Yet, divergent from his treatment of the *gnomic* will, Maximus indicates that the experience of demonic temptation can be carried over from his anthropology to his Christology. The literature to date has shown that an approach focused on the *gnomic* will ultimately requires a divergence between the moral experience of fallen humankind and of Christ. In contrast, this demonological approach to the anthropological problem of human sinfulness renders the soteriological problem of Christ's temptation soluble. This solution is considered in the next chapter.

Goals and Means of Monastic Life

If demonic powers are capable of tempting human beings from within, some discussion of the ascetic life that combats these powers should follow. I consider the goal of the monk's efforts, the means through which they defeat the demons, and the monk's expectations for progress toward—but not perfect attainment of—that goal in this life.

Most succinctly, Maximus envisions the goal of the monastic life as knowledge and dispassion (an instance of one of Maximus's more Stoic moments). One who "does not give himself to bodily pleasure and does not fear pain at all" has become dispassionate; by putting self-love to death, such a monk also destroys "ignorance which is, above all, the origin of evils."[119] Maximus elsewhere provides a sub-division of dispassion in four stages: restraint from evil action; lack of assent

---

119. *QT* Introduction (PG 90:260D-261A; CCSG 7:41) in *Questions à Thalassios*, vol. 1, 146–47; *On Difficulties in Sacred Scripture*, 89.

to evil thoughts; the "immobility" of desire; and the total purification from phantasms of the passions.[120] The first two correspond closely to the fourth and third "generations" of sin Maximus described in the *Questions and Doubts*: restraint from evil action reverses the fourth generation and lack of assent to evil thoughts undoes the third generation. Thus, these two forms of dispassion are required for one to avoid culpability in sin. The latter two may further attempt to reverse the first two "generations" of sin, though it is unclear whether this reversal could take place before the eschaton.[121]

The means by which this goal is attained include the Christological core to be addressed in the next chapter, since Christ ultimately enables the monastic to pursue and attain knowledge and virtue. Speaking more proximately to the monk, however, there are two important means by which Christ's power and, thereby, knowledge and dispassion are accessed: sacramental participation and the monastic disciplines of praxis and contemplation. Since the devil is involved in the origin of ignorance and passion, the means of overcoming them also involve one's defeat of powers opposed to God. I consider the Eucharist and monastic discipline as they relate to the defeat of demonic powers.[122]

Maximus's most extensive discussion of the sacraments is in the *Mystagogy*, where he explains the spiritual meaning of various components of the liturgy. Since the devil must be rejected prior to the central Eucharistic part of the liturgy, Maximus's reflection on the

---

120. *QT* 55 (PG 90:544C-D; CCSG 7:493) in *Questions à Thalassios*, vol. 2, 246–49; *On Difficulties in Sacred Scripture*, 363. It is interesting to note that, though Maximus does not discuss Christ in this context, Christ himself does not meet the latter two definitions of dispassion, as Christ certainly demonstrates fear in the garden. Since Maximus's claims are bound to the exegesis of a particular text, one might question whether, in the context of his thought, he truly accepts the latter two stages of dispassion, which might be characterized as perhaps more Stoic than many elements of Maximus's thought seen above.

121. *QD* I 31 (CCSG 10:149) in *Questions and Doubts*, 146. It is possible that the third and fourth impassibility correspond inversely to the second and first "generations." The third impassibility concerns desire, as does the second "generation" of sin; the fourth impassibility (lack of thoughts about passions) may somehow correspond to the "attack" Maximus mentions in the first generation.

122. Regarding another sacrament not addressed in the main text, Maximus also attributes the defeat of the devil to baptism: the "'face' of the adversary" vanishes in the "first sea" of baptism. See *QD* 187 (CCSG 10:127–28) in *Questions and Doubts*, 184.

devil concerns events relatively early in the liturgy: the sign of peace and the readings from scripture. In the sign of peace (between readings), the aid of the angels comes to the believer and God calls off the "invisible struggle" against "hostile powers." When the battle has been called off, God gives an opportunity for the believer to strengthen the powers of the soul to "disperse the armies of the evil spirits" as members of Christ's army who "scatters the sharp and wily machinations of the devil."[123] In the readings themselves, the believers are armed with virtue to "set themselves bravely and unshakenly against the devil's wiles."[124] The consecration and distribution of the Eucharist takes place without reference to the devil, in part because the rejection of the devil took place earlier in the liturgy. The Christological center of the Eucharist is revealed in the distribution of the sacrament, which "transforms [those who worthily share in it] and renders [them] similar to the causal good by grace and participation."[125]

Maximus also reflects on the transformative power of monastic discipline. There are three components of this discipline that reach out toward dispassion and knowledge: praxis, natural contemplation, and theological contemplation.[126] While praxis in a sense precedes the other two stages, these disciplines should not be considered as completely separate steps through which one successively and temporally passes toward spiritual perfection; each of these disciplines has a place as one continues to progress toward perfection.[127] For the moment, I focus on the first two of these components. The practical life consists of the various ascetic activities undertaken by the monastic whose goal is to dry up the passions and cut off the attacks of demons

---

123. *Mystagogy* 12 (PG 91:690D-691A; CCSG 69:40–41) in Maximus the Confessor, *Selected Writings*, trans. George C. Berthold (Toronto: Paulist Press, 1985), 199–200.
124. *Mystagogy* 24 (PG 91:705D; CCSG 69:61) in *Selected Writings*, 208.
125. *Mystagogy* 21 (PG 91:696D-697A; CCSG 69:48–49) in *Selected Writings*, 203.
126. *QT* 46 (PG 90:420B-D; CCSG 7:309) in *Questions à Thalassios*, vol. 2, 48–51; *On Difficulties in Sacred Scripture*, 255–56.
127. *QT* 45 (PG 90:417C-420A; CCSG 7:305) in *Questions à Thalassios*, vol. 2, 47, n. 2. Larchet argues (*Questions*, vol. 2, 50–51) that praxis and contemplation cannot be separated strictly into two periods of one's life. Some degree of dispassion is likely a prerequisite to the stages of contemplation, but praxis never fades from view entirely. See Lollar, "Christ and the Contemplation of Nature," 248, and Adrian Guiu, "Eriugena's Appropriation of Maximus Confessor's Anthropology," in *A Saint for East and West*, 17–18.

that attempt to inflame them.¹²⁸ Natural contemplation, on the other hand, seeks to separate thoughts from passion by entering into consideration of the nature of things in themselves. This separation also requires one to struggle against demonic forces, who seek to infiltrate the intellect by means of sensation.¹²⁹

Different demonic attacks require different responses from the monk. On the one hand, while Maximus considers contemplation to be the better part of the monastic life, in QT 49, he admits that demonic temptation can often require the monastic to have recourse from natural contemplation to askesis. When one is engaged in natural contemplation, the devil can assault the soul with images and phantasms of sensible realities that natural contemplation alone cannot defeat. Maximus affirms that it is by means of representations of sensible realities that the devil usually "forges" passions relating to the appearances of visible realities.¹³⁰ In those circumstances, Maximus suggests the following: "Let us put an end to natural contemplation and advance by prayer alone and by the affliction of the body ... so that the Evil One might not treacherously and unwittingly attack."¹³¹ Here, where the monastic is in danger of falling into passionate attachment to the objects of contemplation, the response is to cease such contemplation and turn to discipline of the body that helps separate thought from passion.

On the other hand, askesis itself can become a source of temptation. The devil attacks the intellect by means of the "realities of the right," meaning that monastic askesis can become a source of vainglory and pride through demonic thoughts of one's goodness.¹³² In such

---

128. QD 97 (CCSG 10:74) in *Questions and Doubts*, 94–95); for the demonic component, see *Amb. Io.* 6 (PG 91:1068B-C) in *Ambigua*, 127, and *On Difficulties in the Church Fathers*, vol. 1, 73–75.

129. QT 48 (PG 90:441A; CCSG 7:341) in *Questions à Thalassios*, vol. 2, 84–85; *On Difficulties in Sacred Scripture*, 274–75.

130. QT 49 (PG 90:449D-4452B; CCSG 7:355–57) in *Questions à Thalassios*, vol. 2, 100–101; *On Difficulties in Sacred Scripture*, 283–84.

131. QT 49 (PG 90:449D-4452B; CCSG 7:355–57) in *Questions à Thalassios*, vol. 2, 100–101; *On Difficulties in Sacred Scripture*, 283–84. The same can be seen in QT 49 (PG 90:456D-457B; CCSG 7:365–67) in *Questions à Thalassios*, vol. 2, 110–11, and *On Difficulties in Sacred Scripture*, 289–90, where he also suggests retreat from natural contemplation to bodily discipline.

132. QT 49 (PG 90:453A-C; CCSG 7:359–61) in *Questions à Thalassios*, vol. 2, 104–5; *On Difficulties in Sacred Scripture*, 86–87, 285–86.

cases, Maximus suggests that one turn to humility and moderation so that one not become vainglorious.[133] At other times, the monk may not need to turn to askesis to defeat demonic thoughts. The monastic can also defeat them by turning those very thoughts to contemplative use, thereby making the thoughts good.[134] When a natural desire is suggested by a demon, at times the monk can consider that desire closely so as to preserve the desire as wholly natural.[135] Since the desires in themselves are not evil, they instead require close examination to determine what in them is necessary and what in them would give rise to unnatural passion. All successful responses to these attacks are made possible by God's gifts to the monastic.[136]

Because the demons are constantly trying new tactics to bring forth sinful thoughts and actions, there is always a heuristic quality to Maximus's suggestions to the monk. Sometimes, it is best to retreat from contemplation to askesis; at other times, it is best to cut off askesis and return to natural contemplation. While he has ideas about when each of these will be most effective against the devil, his advice is aphoristic and *ad hoc*, leaving room for discernment by the individual monastic and the broader community.

Since Maximus wanted to give sound advice in the evasion of temptation and sin, he also gave his reader a sense of what can realistically be accomplished in this life. Such advice is important not only for his monastic reader but also for this study since Maximus's articulation of what is possible differs significantly from Aquinas's. In his reflection on inner demonic temptation, Maximus is largely optimistic about the possibility (if not always the reality) of successful struggle.[137] Yet the nature of his optimism requires a distinct approach

---

133. QT 48 (PG 90:441B-D; CCSG 7:343) in *Questions à Thalassios*, vol. 2, 86–87; *On Difficulties in Sacred Scripture*, 275.
134. QT 49 (PG 90:453C-456A; CCSG 7:361–63) in *Questions à Thalassios*, vol. 2, 106–7; *On Difficulties in Sacred Scripture*, 286–87.
135. QD 89 (CCSG 10:69) in *Questions and Doubts*, 91.
136. QT 54 (PG 90:516B-C; CCSG 7:453) in *Questions à Thalassios*, vol. 2, 204–5; *On Difficulties in Sacred Scripture*, 339.
137. This optimism can at least in part be explained by Maximus's desire not to make moral stumbling a normative part of the process of sanctification; he does not want monks to fall into a state of mind where impassioned thoughts are simply taken for granted. See Maximus, *Centuries on Theology* (hereafter, CT), II 41–2 (PG 90:1144B-C) in *Philokalia*, vol. 2, 147–48; see also

to the relationship between virtue and inner temptation, with which Aquinas disagrees. Both contemplation and askesis are seen, in their own places and circumstances, to lead to successful struggle. In one's askesis, the practice of the virtues is key, especially the central Maximian virtues of humility (driving away vainglory), temperance (against pleasurable things), and patience (against painful things).[138] On the basis of these practices, Maximus states that the monk is able to stop the passions entirely and also "to expel the demons who rouse them up."[139] The monk can completely destroy each attack of the devil and free the soul from slavery to passion;[140] he can even become "perfect" by healing the soul's sickness and driving out demons.[141]

Despite this optimism, Maximus gives indications that the devil's attacks cannot be completely prevented; thus, there will always be some form of inner temptation in this life. In the *QD*, for instance, he states that temptations can be crushed and sent away unsuccessful, but he does not speak of an absolute *prevention* of demonic temptation.[142] Since it is not in human power to prevent, however, Maximus holds that such inner temptation does not detract from one's personal virtue.[143] In *QT* 52, he speaks of a virtuous lover of God who is still

---

Paul Blowers, "Gentiles of the Soul: Maximus the Confessor on the Substructure and Transformation of Human Passions," *Journal of Early Christian Studies* 4, no. 1 (Spring 1996): 74–75.

138. *QT* 49 (PG 90:452B-D; CCSG 7:357–59) (temperance and patience) in *Questions à Thalassios*, vol. 2, 102–3; *On Difficulties in Sacred Scripture*, 285; see also *QT* 48 (PG 90:441B-D; CCSG 7:343) in *Questions à Thalassios*, vol. 2, 86–87; *On Difficulties in Sacred Scripture*, 275. Note that these correspond to the three faculties of the soul (intellect, desire, and aversion) as well as to the three fundamental vices (vainglory, gluttony, and anger).

139. *QD* 109 (CCSG 10:81) in *Questions and Doubts*, 100.

140. *QT* 54 (PG 90:516B-C; CCSG 7:453) in *Questions à Thalassios*, vol. 2, 204–5; *On Difficulties in Sacred Scripture*, 339.

141. *QD* 5 (CCSG 10:5) in *Questions and Doubts*, 44–45. See also *Amb. Io*. 38 (PG 91:1297C-1301A) in *Ambigua*, 290; *On Difficulties in the Church Fathers*, vol. 2, 89–95; *CL* II 85 (PG 90:1012B-C) in *Philokalia*, vol. 2, 79–80; *CT* I 15 (PG 90:1088D-1089A) in *Philokalia*, vol. 2, 117; *CT* I 16 (PG 90:1089A) in *Philokalia*, vol. 2, 117; *CT* II 94 (PG 90:1169B-C) in *Philokalia*, vol. 2, 161–62; and Maximus, *Centuries on Various Texts*, II 65 (PG 90:1244C-D), II 79 (PG 90:1249B-C), and II 82 (PG 90:1252B-C) in *Philokalia*, vol. 2, 201, 204, and 205, respectively. Finally, see *Centuries on Various Texts* III 96 (PG 90:1301C) in *Philokalia*, vol. 2, 233–34, where Maximus holds in common with Origen that perfection actually *requires* one to have undergone temptation: "A perfect man is one who with the power of his intelligence has struggled against the pleasure and pain of the flesh and has overcome them."

142. *QD* 64 (CCSG 10:50–51) in *Questions and Doubts*, 78.

143. For more on Maximus's concept of human moral dispositions and habits (virtues and vices), see Philipp Gabriel Renczes, *Agir de Dieu et Liberté de l'Homme: Récherches sur*

assailed invisibly in his intellect by evil spirits.¹⁴⁴ In *QT* 47, Isaac is said to maintain a "state of virtue and knowledge" and a total absence of evil passions "even when he was attacked by the evil spirits."¹⁴⁵ In *Ambigua to John* 10, Maximus speaks of virtuous saints who remain beyond the grasp of "troubling temptations," but continues in the passage to speak of them being "assailed" by temptations attributed to demonic activity. They are not "vanquished" by these temptations, but neither are the temptations wholly prevented.¹⁴⁶ In each case, one sees a person assailed internally by temptation yet held up as a model of virtue.

In order to maintain this balance between temptation and virtue—as well as the correspondence between Christ's temptation and that of the monk—Maximus holds a *noneschatological* conception of affective virtue that is *extrinsic* and *historically realized*. It is noneschatological because it can apply fully in this life to both the virtuous monk and Christ, who experience interior temptation through the passions from the demons throughout this life.¹⁴⁷ Virtue is extrinsic in the sense that it must reside outside the territory currently occupied by the demons. That is, if demons can directly attack, inflame, and occupy the affective faculties of desire and aversion, those faculties cannot themselves be the habitual bulwark against the devil. To experience persistent and unceasing temptation in and through those faculties is to say that

---

l'Anthropologie Théologique de Saint Maxime le Confesseur (Paris: Éditions du Cerf, 2003). Renczes addresses the question of human disposition in Maximus's thought at great length, yet his purpose in that text is to describe the relationship of human action and divine action—not Maximus's theory of virtue itself.

144. *QT* 52 (PG 90:497B; CCSG 7:425) in *Questions à Thalassios*, vol. 2, 176–77; *On Difficulties in Sacred Scripture*, 323. In the rest of the passage, Maximus accuses this individual of pride, which renders him less than perfectly virtuous. In the set-up of the problem, however, there is no indication that the person in question is in any other way morally deficient before the demonic attack.

145. *QT* 47 (PG 90:421C-D; CCSG 7:313–15) in *Questions à Thalassios*, vol. 2, 54–55; *On Difficulties in Sacred Scripture*, 258.

146. *Amb. Io.* 10 (PG 91:1204C-1205B) in *Ambigua*, 223; *On Difficulties in the Church Fathers*, vol. 1, 339–43. The attribution of the temptations to the devil comes at the beginning of the passage (*Ambigua*, 222). As a final example, see the final two reasons God allows temptation in *CL* II 67 (PG 90:1005B-C) in *Philokalia*, vol. 2, 76. Neither of these imply that the one subjected to temptation is morally deficient.

147. I discuss below Maximus's reserved approach to the description of the eschatological condition. By refusing to articulate exactly what that eschatological condition looks like, he confines his discussion of virtue to the forms that it takes in this life.

those faculties are not themselves the seat of virtue. Instead, the virtues that govern those faculties—temperance and patience—must be somewhat extrinsic to the faculties themselves, at least in this life. In turn, one might question what it means to call someone "temperate" and "patient" whose desires themselves are not wholly transformed by their service at reason's command. This conception of virtue, finally, is historically realized because Christ's example of struggle against the demons can be fully imitated by the ascetic even in this life. These characteristic features of the relationship of virtue and temptation differ significantly from Thomas Aquinas's conception of these matters.

Providence and Affectivity in an Eschatological Perspective

While Maximus sees demonic temptation as perduring throughout earthly existence, he also speaks of a complete eschatological cessation of demonic temptation. In *Centuries on Theology*, a certain "rest" from any phantasms associated with passions takes place on the "Sabbath," the seventh day that exists only at "the limit of the flow of temporal existence."[148] The first "generations" of sin—the demonic attack and desire—are definitively put off at the end of earthly life. In order to explain this arrangement of moral struggle against the demonic, the final section of this chapter considers God's providential action in temptation as well as the devil's own purposes for it. I close with a brief exposition of Maximus's understanding of desire and aversion in the eschaton.

Providence and Temptation

As has been pointed out by Panayiotis Nellas, there is an ambiguity to the qualities added to humanity after the Fall. He helpfully describes the garments of skin in Orthodox thought as "biform," like the "duck-rabbit" popularized by Ludwig Wittgenstein in his *Philosophical Investigations*: a single image that can appear in two different ways

---

148. *CT* I 53 (PG 90:1101D-1104A) in *Philokalia*, vol. 2, 124–25, but see also the preliminary explanation in *CT* I 51 (PG 90:1101C) in *Philokalia*, vol. 2, 124.

without any physical change in the image.¹⁴⁹ I would argue that Maximus's thought concerning demonic temptation is much the same. When viewed the way the devil wants humanity to view temptations, they are inevitable traps that lead the believer inextricably to sin; when viewed the way God would have the believer view such temptations, they are reminders of human finitude, tests to prove and strengthen moral resolve, and the means by which we may be crowned with glory (2 Tm 2:5).¹⁵⁰

I have noted that Maximus at times attributes the very existence of material pleasure and pain in human nature to the devil; for instance, the arrangement of human nature after the Fall (including the introduction of pleasure and mortality) is described in *QT* 61 as having been "contrived by the sower of sin and father of evil, the wicked Devil, who ... in his envy both toward us and toward God, banished Adam from paradise in the attempt to destroy God's handiwork."¹⁵¹ This description itself may be an example of the negative character of these consequences. The changes to human nature that occurred after the Fall can be described, on the one hand, as the devil's corruption of humanity; but they can also be understood more fundamentally as God's providential arrangement in anticipation of God's saving, economic work in the incarnation.¹⁵²

Focusing directly on demonic temptation, a similar dual interpretation is given in *QT* 26, which states that the devil "is simultaneously the enemy and vindicator (ἐκδικητής) of God."¹⁵³ First, the devil is God's *enemy* because he attempts to persuade human beings to move their natural faculties contrary to nature. Through pleasure, the devil entices the believer's faculty of desire to abandon love of God in ex-

---

149. Panayiotis Nellas, *Deification in Christ: Orthodox Perspectives on the Nature of the Human Person* (Crestwood, N.Y.: St. Vladimir's Seminary Press, 1987), 63.

150. To admit this kind of perspectivalism is not to say there is no *correct* way of looking at temptation; in fact, the devil's interpretation of temptation may itself be part of the devil's deception, driving one to despair in God's providence.

151. *QT* 61 (PG 90:633B; CCSG 22:95) in Blowers and Wilken, *Cosmic Mystery*, 137.

152. As I describe in the paragraphs that follow, this corruption of human nature by the devil should most likely be categorized as God's economic will, aiming toward its ultimate restoration and glorification.

153. *QT* 26 (PG 90:341A-B; CCSG 7:173) in *Questions à Thalassios*, vol. 1, 302–3; *On Difficulties in Sacred Scripture*, 172.

change for ephemeral realities.[154] The devil can also be seen as God's enemy when he inflicts human beings with pain, thereby inflaming the faculty of aversion. Maximus explains that the devil's intention in this punishment is to make us lose hope in God and fall into atheism.[155] The intellectual faculties, finally, are attacked when the devil suggests to the monk that he should consider his goodness, thereby eliciting vainglory. Despite these evil intentions, God's intentions for allowing this temptation are opposed to the devil's goals; in this second way, the devil serves as God's *vindicator*.

Before explaining God's intentions for demonic temptation, I must first explain the three ways in which Maximus holds that God intends or wills different activities: by good pleasure, by divine economy, and by permission.[156] The first of these wills concerns things that God does completely gratuitously, such as creation and the election of Israel. The second "economic" will concerns apparently unfortunate or even evil circumstances that take place so that God might bring about some greater good from it. Maximus's recurring example of God's economic will is Joseph's enslavement in Egypt; it is a real evil perpetrated by his brothers (and others) that God allows so that God might eventually bring his people out of that land with power.[157] Even more than Joseph, however, the central example of this will is Christ's incarnation, a condescension into human nature whose ultimate purpose renders it worthwhile. Finally, God's permissive will concerns intentional sin that results immediately in evil, such as the devil's affliction in the case of Job. Maximus may not define the latter two categories as clearly as he could have; after all, God brings good out of Job's suffering, yet the devil's actions in that instance are categorized by Maximus

---

154. QT 26 (PG 90:341A-B; CCSG 7:173) in *Questions à Thalassios*, vol. 1, 302–3; *On Difficulties in Sacred Scripture*, 172.

155. QT 26 (PG 90:341B-D; CCSG 7:173–75) in *Questions à Thalassios*, vol. 1, 304–5; *On Difficulties in Sacred Scripture*, 173.

156. These three wills are explained carefully in two passages in the *Questions and Doubts*: QD 83 (CCSG 10:65–66) 89, and QD 161 (CCSG 10:112–13) 123.

157. Joseph is mentioned both in QD 83 (CCSG 10:65–66) in *Questions and Doubts*, 89; QT 26 (PG 90:345B-D; CCSG 7:181) in *Questions à Thalassios*, vol. 1, 310–11; and in *On Difficulties in Sacred Scripture*, 177, as an example of the divine economy and, in the latter case, typologically in relationship with Christ.

as permissive, not economic. Similarly, the immediate consequence of the decision of Joseph's brothers is Joseph's slavery, something that should be categorized as permissive but is considered by Maximus as "economic." Perhaps the best way to explain the difference between these latter two is that when Maximus is able to articulate the positive end toward which an action takes place, it is economic; when Maximus cannot or does not discern the good that comes from an evil, he categorizes it as permissive.

When Maximus states that the devil is God's *vindicator* and God's servant, he is dealing exclusively with the final two categories of will. It is never God's good pleasure that creatures fall from God, yet God permits it for a variety of reasons. Some of these reasons are best characterized economically, others only permissively.[158] As just mentioned, there will always be some instability to any categorization, as the proper category for these temptations is partly determined by one's ability to determine the reason for which the temptation takes place. For instance, Maximus is able to give a clear redemptive purpose for demonic infliction of temptation through the faculty of aversion: suffering "scrapes the venom of pleasure" from our souls.[159] God hopes to encourage the one tempted to return to virtue and give up the unending search for pleasure. In a slightly different sense, a similar divine purpose is seen when demons tempt the monk to vainglory; from God's perspective, such temptation hopes to inspire humility and gratitude to God as the ultimate cause of the monk's virtue and success in contemplation.[160]

When considered in isolation, the form of temptation that is most easily understood by Maximus as merely permissive or even punitive is demonic temptation to pleasure. In the normal course of things, the believer is tempted to pleasure only when the individual has already

---

158. Since in *QT* 26 Maximus is concerned with showing how the devil is ultimately subservient to God, he does not invoke the distinction between the two "permissive" wills of God.

159. *QT* 26 (PG 90:341B-D; CCSG 7:173–75) in *Questions*, vol. 1, 304–5; *On Difficulties in Sacred Scripture*, 173. See also *Centuries on Various Texts* I 83 (PG 90:1213C-D) in *Philokalia*, vol. 2, 183–84, and *Centuries on Various Texts* I 81 (PG 90:1213B-C) in *Philokalia*, vol. 2, 183.

160. *QT* 52 (PG 90:497B; CCSG 7:425) in *Questions à Thalassios*, vol. 2, 176–77; *On Difficulties in Sacred Scripture*, 323.

submitted to the devil by taking on the devil's disposition toward God's will. Indeed, the seeking of material pleasure as an end in itself shows God's permissive will precisely because such seeking is itself the act that constitutes Adam's fall, the primordial example of God's permissive will. Maximus describes it as fitting and just that those who have willingly given in to the devil's evil council should be further punished by the devil with other temptations toward pleasure.[161] There is, when considered in isolation, no clearly positive, didactic, or pedagogical outcome of this permission.[162] Yet material pleasure, too, can take on a biform character when considered in connection with the broader nexus of human temptations.

Considered more holistically, temptation toward material pleasure can most adequately be considered as part of God's economic will for humankind when it is placed in connection with pain. Indeed, this is Maximus's most common way of articulating the relationship of material pain and pleasure: they come into existence with Adam's Fall as intrinsically linked poles of a single redemptive reality. The seeking of pleasure always results in and is bound to an experience of pain. God's positive will for material pleasure is thus seen precisely in its connection to pain, which leads one to look beyond the material realities that pleasure seeks.[163] When viewed in this second way, pleasure is part of God's broader economic will for humankind. This way, in turn, is linked to God's broader providential action in Christ.

Cumulatively, and in light of divine providence, Maximus articu-

---

161. *QT* 26 (PG 90:341B-D; CCSG 7:173–75) in *Questions à Thalassios*, vol. 1, 304–5; *On Difficulties in Sacred Scripture*, 173.

162. Two speculative readings are possible in identifying an economic will for pleasure. First, it is possible to explain temptation toward pleasure in terms of development in temperance, but Maximus only rarely invokes this explanation. See *QT* 49 (PG 90:452B-D; CCSG 7:357–59) in *Questions à Thalassios*, vol. 2, 102–3, and *On Difficulties in Sacred Scripture*, 285. Second, it is possible to explain sensory attraction to physical realities by saying that pleasure itself can spur the creature on toward self-preservation and continued bodily existence. For instance, Maximus describes the passions as existing "for the present life." See *QT* 55 (PG 90:541A; CCSG 7:487) in *Questions à Thalassios*, vol. 2, 242–43, and *On Difficulties in Sacred Scripture*, 360–61, which indicates the passions have a concrete purpose in our earthly existence. His lists of the natural and blameless passions (such as hunger and thirst) also describe things necessary for our bodily survival in the fallen world.

163. *QT* Introduction (PG 90:256A; CCSG 7:33) in *Questions à Thalassios*, vol. 1, 136–37; *On Difficulties in Sacred Scripture*, 83–84.

lates an optimistic and pedagogical vision for human temptation as a whole. Maximus recognizes punitive elements in fallen human temptation but maintains that God has a bigger picture in mind even in these punishments. Thomas Aquinas, by contrast, will more heavily emphasize the role of fallen temptation as a punishment for human sin.

Affectivity in Humanity's Final State

Maximus describes the goal of the monastic life as "dispassion," yet this term gives the misleading impression that humanity's final state will put off the affective life entirely. When Maximus articulates the goal of the monk as "dispassion," one should not understand him in a Stoic sense of excluding the affective life from the eschatological condition. Insofar as these faculties are part of the *logos* of human nature, Maximus would recognize that their eradication would be the destruction—not the glorification—of our nature.[164] Instead of reading "dispassion" as a Stoic denial, the term should instead be understood as an apophatic denial that our bodily conditions now are at all like those of the eschaton. Maximus perceives these faculties to be transformed—not eradicated—in the final law of human nature, their resurrected glory.

Maximus consistently holds to this apophatic approach to the eschatological condition of humanity. This reticence is theologically motivated by our current conditions: we "know partially and prophesy partially" (1 Cor 13:9), as Maximus admits.[165] He is also hesitant because he believes that too much concern for our resurrection condition can in fact arise from demonic thoughts. The devil asks questions

---

164. *Amb. Io.* 42 (PG 91:1345B, Latin trans. in CCSG 18:207–8) in Blowers and Wilken, *Cosmic Mystery*, 92. Admittedly, in one of his Stoic moments, Maximus argues that the passions are not a permanent fixture of human nature and thus that they will be removed at the end of time. Following Gregory of Nyssa, Maximus explains that because the passions were not part of human nature in the beginning, they also will not exist in our final state. See *QT* 55 (PG 90:541A; CCSG 7:487) in *Questions à Thalassios*, vol. 2, 242–43, and *On Difficulties in Sacred Scripture*, 360–61. However, just as Gregory ultimately affirmed the permanent status of human affective appetites in other terms, Maximus should also be understood, on the whole, to maintain the enduring place of human affectivity in the eschaton, despite the different bodily conditions of that state.

165. *QT* 9 (PG 90:285B-288A; CCSG 7:79–81) *Questions à Thalassios*, vol. 1, 192–93; *On Difficulties in Sacred Scripture*, 114–15.

to inspire us to doubt the resurrection; he attempts to convince us that if human nature is anything like it has been in any of its previous states, life will still be "vain and useless," still uncleansed of past evils and susceptible to future change.[166] Indeed, such speculation "clearly introduces [mere] chance and casts Providence from reality."[167]

In response, Maximus speaks generally of the "incorruptibility" of human nature in its resurrected state, itself an apophatic locution.[168] God renders the body and soul similar to God though the life-giving human existence of Christ.[169] What exactly that transformation looks like remains intentionally unclear. Maximus denies that our final state will be like any of the earlier laws of human nature but reassures that Christ himself guarantees the worthiness of this final condition.[170]

Still, demonic struggle is an important part of this transformation. Referring to 2 Timothy 2:5, Maximus explains that those who "competed according to the rules" are rewarded with the gift of God's salvation. In context, these rules are the passible conditions of humanity along with "bearing the divine combat" with the enemies of God.[171] As affirmed also by Origen, only through struggle with the demonic do the virtues come to their full stature for the monk and reach their final perfection in heaven. The final state of incorruptible dispassion that Maximus anticipates succinctly summarizes the final and definitive conquest of the devil. In his exegesis of Joel 2:20, the "law of sin" and the devil both come to their demise at the resurrection of the

---

166. QT 38 (PG 90:389C-392A; CCSG 7:255–57) in *Questions à Thalassios*, vol. 1, 394–95; *On Difficulties in Sacred Scripture*, 225. This concern may be a response to the objections raised against the resurrection by Gregory of Nyssa; see Gregory of Nyssa, *On the Soul and the Resurrection*, trans. Catherine P. Roth (Eugene, Ore.: Wipf & Stock, 1992), chapter 10, 103–21.

167. QT 38 (PG 90:389C-392A; CCSG 7:255–57) in *Questions à Thalassios*, vol. 1, 394–95; *On Difficulties in Sacred Scripture*, 225.

168. QT 38 (PG 90:389C-392A; CCSG 7:255–57) in *Questions à Thalassios*, vol. 1, 394–95; *On Difficulties in Sacred Scripture*, 225; see also QD 190 (CCSG 10:131–32) in *Questions and Doubts*, 137.

169. *Amb. Io.* 21 (PG 91:1249C-D) in *Ambigua*, 254; *On Difficulties in the Church Fathers*, vol. 1, 435–37; QT 41 (PG 90:404C-405D; CCSG 7:281) in *Questions à Thalassios*, vol. 2, 16–17; and *On Difficulties in Sacred Scripture*, 239–40.

170. QT 38 (PG 90:389C-392A; CCSG 7:255–57) in *Questions à Thalassios*, vol. 1, 394–95; *On Difficulties in Sacred Scripture*, 225. This claim is distinct from Gregory of Nyssa's view, who argues that our final condition will be like our first (*On the Soul and the Resurrection*, 103–21).

171. QT 47 (PG 90:428A-B; CCSG 7:323) in *Questions à Thalassios*, vol. 2, 64–65; *On Difficulties in Sacred Scripture*, 262–63.

body. In that exegesis, the "'face' of the adversary" vanishes in the "first sea" of baptism—the devil's defeat draws near—but the "back parts of the enemy" are not defeated until the "last sea" of the resurrection. It is only then that "our nature completely puts aside the law of sin that was placed in us through the transgression,"[172] and through the devil's intervention. At that time, human desire and aversion will return to their original purpose in a new mode. Operating in a definitive *tropos* of stability (*stasis*), desire and aversion seek and adore the all-desirable and all-glorious Creator.

※

In this chapter, I have traced the role that the devil plays in the origin of sinful actions after the Fall. Maximus takes great interest in this subject because he and his intended audience are greatly concerned with how the monk might adequately respond to the various demonic ruses they encounter in their ascetic discipline. Though Maximus is optimistic about the monk's theoretical ability (with God's help) to overcome the devil, there are limits on what one can expect in this life; the devil does not give up the battle until the war comes to an end in the monk's death and resurrection. In the preceding, I have emphasized the general anthropological struggle of the individual monk in interior combat with the devil. I turn in the next chapter to the Christological center of Maximus's thought on demonic temptation in order to demonstrate how Maximus sees that Christ empowers the monk by being "tempted like us in every way" (Heb 4:15).

---

172. *QD* 187 (CCSG 10:127–28) in *Questions and Doubts*, 184.

3

MAXIMUS'S VIEW OF CHRIST'S
TEMPTATION

Maximus's ascetic theology attends closely to the devil's activity in the monk's mind, stirring up desires for material realities and implanting impassioned thoughts. Maximus held that spiritual progress and purity of virtue are no obstacles to this temptation. In this context, Maximus sees no obstacle to proposing just such a temptation of Christ; indeed, Christ's salvific mission, his perfection in virtue, and his empowering exemplarity positively call for Christ to confront the demonic in this way. In Christ's temptation by the devil, Maximus sees the depths of Christ's identification with the fallen human condition, as well as the ultimate defeat of the powers and principalities opposed to God's will. Maximus considers Christ's temptation as salvific because it exorcises from human nature the demonic powers that had been active in it from the moment of Adam and Eve's Fall.

The first matter for consideration is Maximus's affirmation of Christ's identity with the fallen condition, since Christ is capable of providing a meaningful example and efficacious aid on the basis of a humanity that is conditioned by the existential circumstances of fallen human beings. Second, it is necessary to consider abstractly how Christ's condescension into human passibility and demonic temptation is compatible with the sorts of perfections Maximus also affirms in Christ, especially his perfection of virtue, knowledge, and sinlessness or impeccability. In the third portion of the chapter, I consider how, for Maximus, Christ's human temptation constitutes a defeat of the devil and an empowering example for the monk seeking to imitate Christ.

Christ's Humanity, Human Fallenness, and the Devil

For Maximus, Christ's relationship with fallen human nature renders him susceptible to temptation and demonic attack as experienced after Adam's Fall. To make sense of this claim, Maximus first distinguishes between Christ's *essential* and *relational* appropriations of human nature. Second, he sees in Christ's essential appropriation of human nature a "double descent" into characteristic features of both unfallen and fallen human beings. After outlining these distinctions, I explore some key terms that Maximus uses to indicate Christ's essential appropriation of fallen human nature to show how this appropriation enables Christ to experience temptation in a mode parallel to that of fallen humanity.

Following from an affirmation of Christ's sinlessness, Maximus recognizes that there are some aspects of fallen human existence that Christ cannot experience. If Christ's moral life were perfectly identical to that of others since Adam, he would no longer be a savior; he would be engulfed by sin like everyone else. Yet, Christ's experience must make sufficient contact with the fallen conditions of humankind to render the affirmation of Hebrews 4:15 meaningful. How is Christ "tempted like us in all things, yet without sin?" To differentiate between the grounds of temptation and the beginnings of sin, Maximus distinguishes between Christ's *essential* and *relational* appropriation, or "taking on," of human nature.[1] According to the former appropri-

---

1. *TPO* 19 (PG 91:220B) in *Opuscules Theologiques et Polemiques*, trans. Emmanuel Ponsoye (Paris: Editions du Cerf, 1998), 234. Hans Urs von Balthasar also draws attention to this distinction in *Cosmic Liturgy: The Universe According to Maximus the Confessor* (San Francisco: Ignatius Press, 1988), 266–67.

ation, Christ assumes what is an intrinsic aspect of the *logos* of human nature; according to the second, Christ takes on, out of love of humanity, what belongs to others "without suffering or doing it himself."[2] By his essential appropriation, Christ becomes everything that other humans are by nature. On the other hand, what Christ appropriates *relationally*—what he does not experience—is truly sinful, a "falsification of nature."[3] Thus, Christ's relational appropriation is the way in which Christ relates to the evil activation of human nature; he does not himself do it, but, by his essential appropriation of human nature, he understands the nexus out of which it arises.

Within Christ's essential appropriation of human nature, Maximus further articulates Christ's double-descent into human existence. Maximus argues that Christ's descent into human nature has two moments: a "self-emptying" and a "condescension."[4] The distinction, while logical and not temporal, expresses two aspects of Christ's essential appropriation of humanity. By his self-emptying, Christ entered into human nature as constituted prior to sin, and by his condescension, he further entered into contact with the corruptibility, mortality, and passibility that mark the fallen human condition, existing as a "man passible by nature."[5] This double-descent serves several distinct soteriological purposes in Maximus's thought.

In the first descent, Christ's assumption of a passionless birth (i.e., the Virgin birth) served to break the cycle of material and passionate pleasure and pain that ruled after Adam's sin. The Virgin birth thus

---

2. See *Dispute with Pyrrhus* (PG 91:304A-B), in *Dispute de Maxime le Confesseur avec Pyrrhus: Introduction, Texte Critique, Traduction et Notes*, trans. Marcel Doucet, vol. 2 (unpublished diss., Institut d'Études Médiévales at the University of Montréal, 1972), 559–60 (French translation on 640).

3. *TPO* 20 (PG 91:237B-C) in *Opuscules*, 245. In the same passage, he calls these passions "opposition" and "revolt," also stating that these things "are culpable in us."

4. *Ambigua to Thomas* (hereafter, *Amb. Thom.*) 4 (PG 91:1041D; CCSG 48:13–9) in *On Difficulties in the Church Fathers*, vol. 1, 22–25; see also *Ambigua Iohannem* (hereafter, *Amb. Io.*) 42 (PG 91:1317A-C) in *On Difficulties in the Church Fathers: The Ambigua*, vol. 2, trans. Nicholas Constas (Cambridge, Mass.: Harvard University Press, 2014), 124–29. Maximus consistently uses "condescension" and "self-emptying" to describe these two stages, but his use of each term appears to be inverted between the passages above. In the main text, I follow his usage in the later *Amb. Thom.* 4.

5. *Amb. Thom.* 4 (PG 91:1041D; CCSG 48:13–9) in *On Difficulties in the Church Fathers*, vol. 1, 24–25.

asserts Christ's sovereignty over passion, and so he was not naturally bound to take on these characteristics of human nature consequent to the Fall.[6] Simultaneously, by being born in this way, Christ shared in the mode of birth of the first human beings. By this first descent, Christ further shared with Adam a freedom from the sinfulness that came after Adam's sin.[7] This similarity with Adam's original state serves Christ's saving mission by affirming Christ's familiarity with that original *tropos* of human nature.

Despite Christ's natural freedom from the consequences of Adam's sin, Maximus argues that Christ, through his condescension, entered into deeper contact with those consequences. Christ *willingly* took on a passible, corruptible, and mortal body in order to heal each of these aspects of human life. Similarly, Christ suffers "out of weakness" precisely in order to save those equally weak and sinful human beings striving after Christ's example; for this reason, Christ assumed a human nature that included the consequences of Adam's sin.[8] Thus, while in an absolute sense he did not need to, he willingly bore in his humanity the punishment of Adam, in particular the passibility, corruptibility, and mortality that all other human beings experience.[9]

---

6. See Jean-Claude Larchet's note to *QT* 21 in *Questions à Thalassios*, vol. 1, trans. Françoise Vinel, 250–51 (Paris: Editions du Cerf, 2010).

7. *Amb. Io.* 42 (PG 91:1317A-C) in *On Difficulties in the Church Fathers*, vol. 2, 124–29. Maximus does not commonly use the word "sinfulness" to describe the fallen condition, and its use could appear to endorse a more Augustinian approach to fallen humanity. There are reasons, however, to doubt this reading. Maximus links an opposing term, impeccability (ἀναμάρτητον), to the hypostatic union (*TPO* 20 [PG 91:236D], in *Opuscules*, 244). Impeccability, though, is not what Adam shared in the original condition, since Adam was clearly capable of sin. For that reason, the contrast is not between Adam's unfallen and fallen conditions. Instead, this denial of "sinfulness" in Christ may harken back to the distinction between essential and relational appropriation, so that Christ only relationally appropriates this "sinfulness," or "peccability" (a *tropos* of human existence) much like Maximus will claim of the *gnomic* will in his later writings. For this reason, I take the Virgin birth as the clearest, most significant feature of Christ's sharing in the unfallen condition.

8. *CT* II 27 (PG 90:1137A-B) in *The Philokalia*, vol. 2, trans. G. E. H. Palmer, Philip Sherrard, and Kallistos Ware (New York: Faber and Faber, 1981, 144. See also Kallistos Ware, "The Imitation of Christ according to Saint Maximus the Confessor," in *A Saint for East and West: Maximus the Confessor's Contribution to Eastern and Western Christian Theology*, ed. Daniel Haynes, 78 (Eugene, Ore.: Cascade Books, 2019).

9. See *QT* 21 (PG 90:311B-317A; CCSG 7:127–33) in *On the Cosmic Mystery of Jesus Christ: Select Writings from St. Maximus the Confessor*, ed. Paul M. Blowers and Robert Louis Wilken, (Crestwood, N.Y.: St. Vladimir's Seminary Press), 109–113, and *QT* 61 (PG 90: 632D-633B; CCSG 22:93) in Blowers and Wilken, *Cosmic Mystery*, 136.

Maximus's combination of unfallen and fallen characteristics in Christ harkens back to the Christological reflection of his theological forebears, who also inchoately recognized in Christ similarities to and differences from fallen human existence. In Maximus's thought, however, these similarities and differences are arranged coherently into a Christological synecdoche, a term I introduced at the close of chapter 1.[10] By combining features of different historical stages of human existence in Christ's own life, Maximus attempts to relate Christ's saving mission to each of them. First and foremost, Maximus's Christological synecdoche asserts the universal saving significance of Christ's human nature and his consubstantiality with the entire human race in each of its historical stages. Christ empties himself into Adam's original constitution, and he condescends into the fallen condition. Thereby, Christ raises these different stages to their final glory, raising each above their original stature. Christ's sharing in certain fallen characteristics, however, is the origin of his natural susceptibility to passibility. This deepest association of Christ with the fallen condition in human passibility is what enables Christ to experience human temptation in a way similar to other fallen human beings. Since (as shown in chapter 2) demonic activity is concomitant with fallen human passibility, this affective nexus carries over into Maximus's Christological reflection as well.

Maximus indicates that the reason for Christ's condescension into passibility pertains to Christ's salvific defeat of the devil. For instance, Christ "became a slave for my sake, who am a slave by nature, so that he might make me lord over the one ... who through deception despotically lorded it over me."[11] Christ enters into human passibility in order to free humanity from demonic tyranny.[12] In the depths of

---

10. See Marilyn McCord Adams, *What Sort of Human Nature? Medieval Philosophy and the Systematics of Christology* (Milwaukee, Wis.: Marquette University Press, 1999), 67, where Adams refers to what I have dubbed Christological synecdoche as "telescoping." Adams identified Boethius as the earliest example of this kind of telescoping. Maximus may be the earliest explicit Greek example of this Christological arrangement.

11. *Amb. Thom.* 4 (PG 91:1044C; CCSG 48:13–9) in *On Difficulties in the Church Fathers*, vol. 1, 26–7.

12. In a similar vein, at the end of *Ambigua* 4, Maximus marvels at the mystery of Christ's salvific condescension by quoting without commentary Gregory of Nazianzus's *Fourth Theological Oration*: "it is a more wonderful thing that [Christ] should have been chased [by the evil one and the tempter] than that we should have been captured" (translation taken from Edward

Christ's condescension into the human condition, he encounters the weakest aspect of human nature: human passibility and its susceptibility to demonic attack. Two terms in Maximus's thought demonstrate how Christ relates himself to the moral challenges of fallen humanity: "weakness (ἀσθένεια)" and "confusion (σύγχυσις)." His use of these terms illuminates the soteriological significance of Christ's descent into human passibility and demonic temptation.

As for Christ's weakness, *TPO* 7 discusses Christ's human will in the Garden of Gethsemane, arguing that Christ's refusal of the cup manifests "the weakness of his own flesh."[13] He reiterates a similar claim shortly thereafter in an explanation of a passage from Athanasius: Christ's human will, "because of the weakness of the flesh, seeks to avoid the passion; the divine will is *eager*."[14] In both of these passages (as in others), Maximus indicates that the weakness of Christ's flesh helps Christ to demonstrate the *logos* of his humanity.[15] But, as I consider in greater depth in the third part of this chapter, one cannot forget that Maximus also believes there to be a demonic component to Christ's temptation in the Garden. The "weakness" that Christ demonstrates there certainly pertains to his human passibility, but it also bears a close relationship to the powers and principalities that rise up to tempt Christ to sin through that passibility.

Maximus also trades heavily on the idea of *confusion* to describe the limit of Christ's identification with postlapsarian human nature. This confusion has strongly negative associations for Maximus relative to our lived experience. One sees in his early *Questions and Doubts* that the one who enters the "confusion of life" becomes a temple to the devil;[16] in the *QT*, the "seed of confusion" is captivity to the

---

Rochie Hardy, ed., *The Christology of the Later Fathers* [Louisville, Ky.: Westminster John Knox Press, 1954], 181). Christ's passibility is an essential condition for his having been chased.

13. *TPO* 7 (PG 91:80C-D) in Andrew Louth, *Maximus the Confessor* (New York: Routledge, 2006), 186.

14. *TPO* 7 (PG 91:81B-C) in Louth, *Maximus*, 187.

15. *QT* 42 (PG 90:405B-409A; CCSG 7:285–289) in Blowers and Wilken, *Cosmic Mystery*, 119–22. This text ends with a reference to the salvific possibilities of a "weakness of nature [φυσικὴν ἀσθένειαν]"; see *QT* 42 (PG 90:409A; CCSG 7:289) in Blowers and Wilken, *Cosmic Mystery*, 122.

16. *QD* 20 (CCSG 10:18–9) in *Questions and Doubts*, trans. Despina D. Prassas (DeKalb: Northern Illinois University Press, 2010), 54.

passions,[17] and the world is the devil's "residence of corruption and perpetual confusion."[18] Despite these negative associations, Christ's entrance into this confusion is emphasized in several passages with a soteriological focus. In *Questions and Doubts*, Christ goes down into the "sea of life," which is the "confusion of the passions," to draw out human nature and dissolve the passions from it.[19] In *QT*, Christ enters the devil's residence of "perpetual confusion" in order to bind him.[20] In another passage of *QT*, Christ was

> conceived, born, and entered the world in the confusion of our nature [ἐν τῇ συγχύσει τῆς φύσεως ἡμῶν] and he became human according to nature to return nature to [humanity] after having separated it from confusion. He was not born captive with us and he was not exiled into the confusion of the passions, for he did not commit sin and no treachery was found in his mouth; but in the midst of us who were captive he was born captive and was counted among us who were lawless.[21]

In all of these passages, confusion functions as a limit-concept of Christ's identity with fallen humankind. Christ came into human existence in the confusion of our nature, but he was not exiled into the confusion of the passions. Did Christ "suffer" this confusion? In one sense, yes; he was born into it and lived in its midst. In another sense, no; he did not live it out and was not personally deceived by it. In the course of his own life, Christ was in the process of separating out this confusion from human nature. He experiences the passions (and, through them, demonic temptation) by an essential appropriation, but he does not live out those conditions as does every other human being. The confusion and weakness of Christ's humanity thus mark the very limit of Christ's identity with fallen humanity in passibility and demonic temptation.

17. *QT* 54 (PG 90:508D-509B; CCSG 7:443) in *Questions à Thalassios*, vol. 2, 194–95; *On Difficulties in Sacred Scripture*, 333–34.
18. *QT* 62 (PG 90: PG 90:653A-B; CCSG 22:125–27) in *Questions à Thalassios*, vol. 3, 136–39; *On Difficulties in Sacred Scripture*, 456.
19. *QD* 45 (CCSG 10:38) in *Questions and Doubts*, 69.
20. *QT* 62 (PG 90:653B; CCSG 22:125–27) in *Questions à Thalassios*, vol. 3, 136–39; and *On Difficulties in Sacred Scripture*, 456.
21. *QT* 54 (PG 90:517A-B; CCSG 7:455) in *Questions à Thalassios*, vol. 2, 206–7; *On Difficulties in Sacred Scripture*, 340–41.

The psychological and soteriological reasons for this particular association of passibility with Satan rise out of the previous chapter; Maximus affirms this same association when he considers the particular case of Christ. Psychologically, the association of demons with natural appetites creates, for the virtuous soul, the border and brink of an unnatural passion. Maximus can call such appetites both "powerful" and "violent."[22] Soteriologically, this association is necessary in order for Christ to experience the particular forms of temptation that are unique to the fallen condition. Maximus would deny, for instance, that the appetites of the natural will on their own could *tempt* the subject to sin. If Christ were to experience only the natural will and wish as such, he could not be said to be tempted. Thus, the association of these appetites with demonic agency is central to the soteriological claim of Christ's association with fallen human temptation.[23] The demons incite even Christ through these natural and imaginative appetites, though they fail to arouse in him any desire contrary to nature since he maintains his activation of the "natural and blameless passions."[24] Nevertheless, the nexus of Christ's experience of this temptation is identical to that of other human beings, for whom even the slightest "push" of these appetites in the wrong direction would render them contrary to nature and culpably sinful.

Through the above distinctions, Maximus draws near to the mystery of Christ's entry into solidarity with the fallen human condition. Christ's relational appropriation sets the negative boundary: Christ does not sin. Yet, within Christ's essential appropriation, his double-descent approaches that boundary from the positive side. Maximus's

---

22. QT 50 (PG 90:472C-D; CCSG 7:387–89) in *Questions à Thalassios*, vol. 2, 136–37; *On Difficulties in Sacred Scripture*, 301–2.

23. See QT 61 (PG 90:633B-C; CCSG 22:93–95) in Blowers and Wilken, *Cosmic Mystery*, 137: "the evil devil ... banished Adam from paradise to hide the work of God and to dissolve what was put together at creation."

24. QT 21 (PG 90:311B-317A; CCSG 7:127–33) in Blowers and Wilken, *Cosmic Mystery*, 109–13. The phrase "natural and blameless passions" is not particularly common in Maximus's corpus; see, for instance, QT 55 (PG 90:541A; CCSG 7:487) in *Questions à Thalassios*, vol. 2, 240–43; *On Difficulties in Sacred Scripture*, 360; or *Amb. Thom.* 4 (PG 91:1041C-1044A; CCSG 48:13–9) in *On Difficulties in the Church Fathers*, vol. 1, 22–25). I note this phrase, however, because it becomes formulaic in John of Damascus's work and again in the thought of Thomas Aquinas; see chapters 4 and 6.

consideration of weakness and confusion in Christ draws ever closer to that line. The natural appetites involved in Christ's weakness pertain to the *logos* of nature and thus to an ontological or essential appropriation when assumed by Christ. The intensity and aggressiveness with which demonic powers incite these appetites does not contradict the *logos* of nature, but they render the experience of desire and fear to be truly tempting for the one experiencing them, requiring discernment and careful attentiveness. Because this subjection to demonic temptation and the passions is not strictly unnatural, they pertain to Christ's essential appropriation of and double-decent into fallen human nature. These appetites constitute a deep point of fragility in human nature and the deepest aspect of Christ's identification with the fallen human condition.

The Perfections of Christ's Humanity and His Temptation

If these appetites express Christ's solidarity with the fallen condition, their compatibility with Christ's human perfections remains to be seen. Arguably, three perfections of Christ's humanity could conflict with this temptation: his perfect virtue, knowledge, and impeccability. Since the Maximian resources that aid in the resolution of the first two matters have been articulated at some length in the preceding chapters, I address them here relatively briefly. The compatibility of Christ's temptation and impeccability requires a more lengthy consideration.

Christ's Perfect Virtue

The compatibility of temptation with perfection in virtue is not perfectly obvious, though the outline of this compatibility appears in the last chapter.[25] Given that Aquinas's resolution of this matter differs from Maximus's, some further comment is in order. For Thomas, perfection in virtue—temperance, for instance—precludes any in-

---

25. One sees an affirmation of Christ's perfect virtue in QT 53 (PG 90:504D; CCSG 7:435) in *Questions à Thalassios*, vol. 2, 188–89, and *On Difficulties in Sacred Scripture*, 330. His unique sinlessness is affirmed at QD 118 (CCSG 10:86–87) in *Questions and Doubts*, 104.

ner movement toward excessive stimulation or satiety. If Christ can be violently and powerfully driven through his natural desires toward things that would be unnatural and culpably sinful if activated incorrectly, does that imply for Maximus that Christ is not perfectly virtuous? Or, contrariwise, would not his perfect virtue preclude the kind of temptation that was just discussed in the previous section?

The key consideration in a Maximian response is that the real source of these temptations is not one's own humanity, as if Christ were not in control of his desires. Rather, the source is the movement of evil forces within that naturally good humanity attempting to corrupt it with the consent of free will. As discussed in chapter 2, Maximus believes that it may be possible to expel demons for a time,[26] but the devil is overcome progressively through life and definitively expelled only at the resurrection.[27] The presence of these demonic impulses is thus not a matter of a lack of virtue.[28] For human beings, demonic temptation is not something that is dealt with once and then left behind. It is not within human power to prevent it. That temptation continues throughout one's earthly life, even with the attainment of virtue, is simply a sign that demonic forces will be at work throughout the present age. So long as human nature remains under the current law, it will have a fundamental susceptibility to demonic temptation. Maximus affirms that Christ himself experienced this inner temptation from the devil all the way to the end of his life, but Maximus surely does not mean to indicate thereby that Christ was somehow lacking in virtue before that defeat.[29]

---

26. See *QD* 109 (CCSG 10:81) in *Questions and Doubts*, 100.

27. *Amb. Io.* 38 (PG 91:1297C-1301A) in *Ambigua*, 290; *On Difficulties in the Church Fathers*, vol. 2, 89–95. See also *QD* 187 (CCSG 10:127–28) in *Questions and Doubts*, 134, on the two "seas" of baptism and the resurrection that overcome the "adversary," as well as *QT* 55 (PG 90:541B; CCSG 7: 360–1, 489) in *Questions à Thalassios*, vol. 2, 242–43, and *On Difficulties in Sacred Scripture*, 360–1.

28. Hezekiah is put forward as an example of temptation in an apparent state of virtue at *QT* 52 (PG 90:497B; CCSG 7: 360–1, 425) in *Questions à Thalassios*, vol. 2, 176–77, and *On Difficulties in Sacred Scripture*, 322–24. Isaac is such an example at *QT* 47 (PG 90:421C-D; CCSG 7:313–15) in *Questions à Thalassios*, vol. 2, 54–55, and in *On Difficulties in Sacred Scripture*, 258.

29. *QT* 21 (PG 90:311B-317A; CCSG 7:127–33) in Blowers and Wilken, *Cosmic Mystery*, 109–13. Even Christ did not attain the impassibility described by Maximus as "a complete lack of fear before pain." See *QT* Introduction (PG 90:260D-261A, CCSG 7:41) in *Questions à Thalassios*,

There remains a tension in the way that Maximus speaks of Christ's "taking off" of the powers and principalities: Was Christ's victory singular and succinct, or was it prolonged throughout his human life? At some junctures, Maximus reflects Origen's belief that when a demon is defeated, it is definitively prevented from again attacking another human being. This tendency is seen in *QT* 21, where Christ experiences each temptation exactly *once* and then sets it aside for good. In that text, the demons of pleasure rise up against him in the desert, and he defeats them with no further battle against them. The demons of pain rise up against him at the time of his death, and he defeats them once and for all in his voluntary death. In this text, it seems that Maximus is worried that if Christ were to allow the same demon to attack him twice, it might undermine an affirmation of Christ's perfectly virtuous victory over these powers.

At other junctures, however, Maximus sees soteriological significance in the *ongoing* quality of the demons' attack. Thus, in *The Ascetic Life*, Maximus extends Christ's temptation throughout his public ministry so that he experiences similar temptations over and over.[30] In this case, the soteriological emphasis falls on the similarity in duration and persistence between the monk's experience of temptation and that of Christ. To perfectly attain and demonstrate the virtue of patience, in other words, requires that one persist in the face of adversity for a significant length of time; Maximus thus sees it fitting that Christ himself should demonstrate such persistence over a long period of time. One might resolve this tension between Jesus' succinct and prolonged temptation by reference to Origen's understanding of the devil's army. Accordingly, each demon may only attack Christ once, but the various combinations of "specialties" in temptation allows Christ to experience a number of distinct "shades" of temptation within the same genus over an extended period of time.[31]

---

vol. 1, 146–47. The consistency of this position is dependent on Maximus's definition of virtue, discussed in chapter 2.

30. *AL* 10–13 (PG 90:920C-21C) in *The Ascetic Life and the Four Centuries on Charity*, trans. Polycarp Sherwood (New York: Newman Press, 1955), 109–11.

31. Further, since a number of demons have exactly the same role, Christ could arguably experience the exact same temptation more than once without having to defeat the same

Christ's Knowledge

In chapter 2, it became clear that ignorance was a key component of the devil's attack against Adam, Eve, and their progeny. Deception and trickery, in part, led Adam and Eve to choose to disobey the commandment, and ignorance of God continued to drive them and their descendants to sin into the present age. Since deception and ignorance are key components of the devil's tools in human temptation, does Christ's temptation "like us in every way" require that he in some way share in the common experience of deception, demonic trickery, and ignorance?

To provide an adequate response to this question, one must pay close attention to Maximus's categories of knowledge, ignorance, and culpability identified in the previous chapter. At the heart of a properly Christian theory of sin and culpability is the idea that one can choose to do something that one knows to be wrong, an affirmation of the existence of open-eyed *akrasia*.[32] Knowledge and ignorance are morally relevant in these theories, but in the end they are not the *source* or *origin* of moral evil. While ignorance can be the source of other objective evils, an ignorance that has no foundation in a previous, morally reprehensible choice cannot be categorized as a *moral* evil. Such a distinction is found in Maximus's own thought, which recognizes two kinds of ignorance: *willful* and *unwillful* ignorance.[33] The former kind ultimately traces its source back to the will. In that case, one *should* have known or had good reason to have known that something is wrong or right but decided not to investigate the action properly. In that case, this kind of ignorance would properly be called morally culpable. On the other hand, when an ignorance is truly *un-*

---

demon twice. If this resolution suffices, the accounts of Christ's temptations present in the Gospels would be understood as emblematic and not exhaustive. Such a resolution would be compatible with Maximus's reflection, but I find no evidence that Maximus explicitly supports it.

32. In Christian scripture, this claim is usually traced to St. Paul's psychological dilemma described in Romans 7. See Troels Engberg-Pedersen, "Stoicism in Early Christianity: The Apostle Paul and the Evangelist John as Stoics," in *The Routledge Handbook of the Stoic Tradition*, ed. John Sellars, 29–43 (New York: Routledge, 2016). This Stoic view stands against Socratic theories that all evil is ultimately rooted in ignorance.

33. *QD* I 67 (CCSG 10:155) in *Questions and Doubts*, 148–49.

willful (not in our power to have known or sought to know), such ignorance does not fall into the realm of morally relevant actions. While one might perform an action that is objectively evil in such a state, in those particular circumstances, the action does not add to or subtract from one's virtue or moral integrity.

It is on these foundations, in part, that one must understand Maximus's denial of ignorance in Christ.[34] On the one hand, Christ's sinlessness is a sufficient explanation for his lack of willful ignorance. Since responsibility for that ignorance redounds to the subject's moral praise or blame, it would be a straightforward denial of Christ's sinlessness to say that he was willfully ignorant. That part of the problem of demonically inspired ignorance is still a *moral* problem, since the problem lies fundamentally not in the ignorance itself but in the way in which the ignorance came about: namely, though a decision of the will. Given a robust conception of the *communicatio idiomatum*, this denial of willful ignorance may suffice to explain Christ's omniscience; since the *Logos* has (or is) perfect knowledge in the divine nature, it is possible that the category of *unwillful* ignorance would be null in Christ's case.[35] The unity of the subject of Christ would thereby be sufficient to show that Christ could have sought to know any morally relevant data, and therefore did. It is also possible that the only kinds of ignorance that the devil could induce would be this kind of willful ignorance.

On the other hand, even if one were to argue for a weaker conception of the *communicatio idiomatum* and a more robust conception of demonic ignorance, the above distinction shows that any action performed in those circumstances would not morally redound to Christ. One could use this fact to argue that Christ was unwillfully ignorant, but the grounds for this argument would *not* be that Christ lived a

---

34. QD I 67 (CCSG 10:155) in *Questions and Doubts*, 148–49. As I discuss in a moment, the ultimate reason for Christ's fullness of knowledge in Maximus's account is the hypostatic union. In contrast to that "top-down" reasoning (Christ's ontological constitution resulting in human properties), I proceed in the following paragraph with a "bottom-up" reasoning (Maximus's moral categories that carry ramifications into the divine economy of the incarnation). I use this bottom-up justification to avoid the implication that the hypostatic union renders Christ's moral life categorically different than other human beings.

35. Maximus indicates this reasoning in QD I 67 (CCSG 10:155) in *Questions and Doubts*, 148–49.

sinless life from the same moral circumstances as other human beings. In other words, even if such a case were demonically inspired, true unwillful ignorance could not be categorized as a *temptation*, because temptation in a Christian sense implies an ability to do otherwise, whereas one cannot choose to be unwillfully ignorant. Consequently, no argument about Christ's being "tempted like us in every way yet without sin" could be made relative to the presence of unwillful ignorance in Christ. The conclusion follows not because the resulting action would not be culpable sin (which, technically, it would not be) but because it would not be *temptation*. In this way, Christ's being "tempted like us in every way" has nothing to do with whether he was unwillfully ignorant of morally relevant information.

Whether this ignorance would be present in Christ is ultimately only related to which other non-moral characteristics one expects to find in the God-man. Maximus speaks of other divinely inspired messengers as the standard here.[36] If other prophets were granted extraordinary knowledge of the world as part of their mission to God's people, how much more would Christ have access to such knowledge? As united as the prophets were to God, the hypostatic union guarantees that Christ—the divine *Logos*—enjoys perfect knowledge in the divine nature.

In short, an affirmation of ignorance in Christ would come in one of two forms: willful or unwillful ignorance. If one were to say that Christ were willfully ignorant, Christ's sinlessness would thereby be contradicted. If one were to say that Christ were unwillfully ignorant, one could not so argue on the basis of Christ's identity with fallen temptation. Since unwillful ignorance bears no direct relationship to the question of Christ's human temptations, one needs grounds other than Hebrews 4:15 to argue in its favor. But because Christ's mission involves the revelation of the knowledge of God as well as his perfect moral virtue, Maximus can argue on those grounds that Christ would in fact have knowledge where others might remain blamelessly ignorant.

---

36. QD I 67 (CCSG 10:155) in *Questions and Doubts*, 148–49.

Maximus's denial of ignorance in Christ also has a corollary for Christ's moral psychology, albeit only implicitly. Maximus defines deliberation and choice as concerning matters of action that are indeterminate—things that are possible and of which the end is unknown.[37] The affirmation of Christ's perfect knowledge, then, is one of the roots of Maximus's claim that Christ did not deliberate or choose. Using Nemesius's definition of human rationality, however, this Christological affirmation would mean, problematically, that Christ was not a rational human being. Moreover, Maximus also holds that a straightforward affirmation of choice in Christ would substantially conflict with an affirmation of Christ's impeccability. A discussion of choice, impeccability, and temptation is therefore in order.

Christ's Impeccability and Temptation

In his late polemical texts against the monothelites, Maximus repeatedly affirms not only Christ's sinlessness but also his impeccability, the idea that Christ is completely *incapable* of sinful action. The problem here can be stated briefly: What could it possibly mean to say that one who *cannot* sin is *tempted* to sin? Are they not contrary terms? That is, does Maximus's affirmation of Christ's impeccability mean that Christ was incapable of experiencing temptation in a meaningful way? If Christ is impeccable, how does Christ's human nature have any capacity for decision-making and free will?

In the following, I first explain how Christ's impeccability is related to the hypostatic union and to human choice in Maximus's thought. These topics represent, respectively, the Christological and anthropological principles that come into tension in Maximus's thought. In the remainder of this section, I show that the way that Maximus resolves the conflict is crucial to understanding Christ's temptation. I argue that in Maximus's thought, impeccability and temptation are compatible in Christ in exactly the same way that impeccability and choice are compatible in him.[38]

---

37. See *TPO* 1 (PG 91:16D-17B) in *Opuscules*, 115.
38. My usage of "temptation" here considers the matter from the center of Christ's rational

Before considering the compatibility of these two terms in Maximus's thought, the precise basis for Maximus's affirmation of Christ's impeccability requires clarification. In his late *TPO*, Maximus twice explains Christ's impeccability. In *TPO* 1, Maximus's argument for Christ's impeccability begins as a criticism of monothelitism.[39] Arguing a *reductio ad absurdum* on the basis of monothelite assumptions, Maximus criticizes:

> And if the choice of Christ was according to nature, not only do we accuse them of audaciously and arbitrarily creating another nature of the divine Christ, but we laugh at their foolishness of saying that [Christ is] naturally [capable] of opposing things by choice, as a bare human being in the way Nestorius makes Christ capable of experiencing.[40]

Maximus argues that the monothelite position falls into the error of Nestorius, who divided Christ in two and made the humanity independent of the divinity. What, precisely, did Nestorius make Christ capable of experiencing that Maximus must reject? As Maximus explains, a Nestorian Christology implies that Christ's humanity was equally capable of either following or not following nature, as if the two options were, in an absolute sense, equally possible for Christ, and as if Christ's humanity were really a separate subject from his divinity.[41] Maximus here uses Nemesius's definition of choice: the equal possibility of two acts, seeming to imply a certain indifference toward humanity's final end. For that reason, Christ, who is always oriented toward that final end, cannot choose like other human beings.

---

and volitional characteristics as a human being. For Maximus, the passions rest somewhat farther from that center than they will for Thomas Aquinas. For Thomas, to be tempted by one's own passions is to be divided against oneself, at war with one's own body. For Maximus, to be tempted by the passions requires that one also be assailed by external forces, thus placing the center of the moral agent outside those passions themselves. In that sense, Thomas would equate the question "Did Christ's passions assail him?" with "Did Christ's humanity tempt him?" whereas Maximus would allow different answers to those questions. I should note that my effort to find an affirmation of choice in Christ is in part motivated by my concern to find compatibilities with Thomas, who affirms choice in Christ at *ST* III 18.4, opposing the Damascene's exposition of Maximus in an objection.

39. *TPO* 1 (PG 91: 29B) in *Opuscules*, 121–24.
40. *TPO* 1 (PG 91: 29B) in *Opuscules*, 121–24.
41. As seen in chapters 1 and 2, the idea that choice (προαίρεσις) concerns things that are "equally possible" comes from Nemesius.

In this text, for Christ to choose—to be equally capable of doing good or evil—would be to fall into Nestorianism.

In a second text, *TPO* 20, Maximus explains that Christ's orientation toward humanity's final end is a consequence of his "highest union" with God:

> For the human will [θέλειν] of the Savior, even if it was natural [φυσικὸν], was not bare like ours, no more than was his humanity, as [it was] above us and deified with the highest union, upon which, properly speaking, [his] impeccability [ἀναμάρτητον] hangs.[42]

While a "bare" human, like the Nestorian Christ in the previous example, would be capable of activating his natural will in a way that is contrary to nature, Maximus believes that the hypostatic union of the divine and human natures in Christ precludes such an activation of his humanity. Similarly, in *TPO* 1, one reads

> For the humanity of God was not moved according to choice [κατὰ προαίρεσιν] as we are, working through deliberation and judgment the discernment of opposites; in order that [his] nature might not practice a liability to be turned according to choice, but taking [his] being at the moment of its union with God the Word, he undoubtedly had a stable motion according to natural appetite [κατ' ὄρεξιν φυσικὴν], that is, truly a will.[43]

Choice, again, is the essential point of contention, and Maximus again uses Nemesius's definition when he denies its presence in Christ. Using this definition, a humanity activated through choice would not be directed perfectly according to natural appetite but would instead consider both the natural and the unnatural indifferently.[44] In all this material, Maximus follows Nemesius's understanding and definition of choice, which leads Maximus to strongly qualify any sense of choice in Christ's humanity.[45]

---

42. *TPO* 20 (PG 91:236D) in *Opuscules*, 244.
43. *TPO* 1 (PG 91:32A-B) in *Opuscules*, 121–24.
44. The definition of choice and deliberation as regarding things that are "equally possible" is significant both Christologically and anthropologically. If understood in this Nemesian fashion, the fundamental orientation of the creature toward its final end may be called into question.
45. Blowers and Wilken state that Maximus "retracts" choice from Christ in *TPO* 1 (see Blowers and Wilken, *Cosmic Mystery*, 120, n. 1), but as has been pointed out by others, what Maximus says in *TPO* 1 does not outright contradict what he said earlier in *QT*. Balthasar, for

Maximus's qualification of choice in Christ is problematic in light of Maximus's affirmation in his anthropological texts (also following Nemesius of Emesa) that choice is essential to the nature of created, rational nature. I have made this point in chapters 1 and 2 above, but I briefly review the relevant aspects of that claim here. Maximus avows in principle that Christ's human *logos* is identical to that of other human beings: everything that pertains to the *logos* of human nature is present in Christ.[46] Further, Maximus at times indicates that choice is part of that *logos*, writing, for instance, "Certainly, the human being, having by nature a living rationality, is endowed with appetite, and reason, and desire, and the ability to search and to examine, and choice [προαιρετικὸς], and motion, and realization."[47] If one takes a statement like this perfectly seriously, there is a clear contradiction: something that pertains to the *logos* of human nature as such is denied in Christ.[48]

There are two ways of resolving the conflict between choice and impeccability: one can either (1) deny that choice is essential to the *logos* of human nature or (2) change the definition of choice so that it is not necessarily opposed to impeccability. In the first option, one can argue that choice, being an aspect of our humanity that leaves us indifferent to God, is not something that constitutes human nature as such. If choice is not natural, it does not need to be taken on by Christ in order to redeem humankind. In the second option, one could attempt to redefine choice so that it does not imply an indifference or vacillation with regard to the final end of humankind. In that case, one who is impeccable could still be affirmed as having choice. Maximus seems to recognize this conflict between these statements and, rather surprisingly, attempts at different times to resolve the problem in *both* ways.

---

one, argues for a certain affirmation of choice in Christ (see Balthasar, *Cosmic Liturgy*, 268). I return to this debate below.

46. *TPO* 20 (PG 91:237A) in *Opuscules*, 244–55; see also *TPO* 1 (PG 91:36A-B) in *Opuscules*, 126.

47. *TPO* 1 (PG 91:21D-24B) in *Opuscules*, 119. As seen in chapter 1, Nemesius believes that choice is *essential* to the definition of human rationality. Maximus almost surely follows Nemesius's definitions in passages such as these.

48. The context shows that other human properties would encounter the same problem; see *TPO* 1 (PG 91:21D-24B) in *Opuscules*, 119.

In some passages, Maximus offers a solution along the lines of the first option by clarifying that choice is not necessary for humanity in an absolute sense. Maximus argues that when the truth concerning material realities is clear, judgment and choice recede, since the correct course of action recommends itself:

> Therefore, since ambiguity concerns deliberation, judgment, and choice about what is up to us, whenever there is no ambiguity, truth brilliantly showing its *hypostasis* to all, then there is no [need for] choice among intermediate things and things that can be accomplished by our action. Wherefore there is [also] no judgment, making a determination between opposites—which one of them we consider to be taken as higher [better] than the other. But if according to the law now holding sway in nature, there is no [need for] choice, all ambiguity of beings having been taken away, the active appetite will be intellectual alone in those animated by appetite in this way according to nature.[49]

Since the immediate context of this passage concerns the resurrection, there is some lack of clarity here about whether Maximus is referring to a condition that currently obtains in human nature or whether he is referring to humanity's resurrected condition. Either way, the passage is clear: choice is not essential to the *logos* of humanity because even in mere human beings, it does not occur in cases where there is full knowledge of what is under investigation. If mere human beings will be able to exist without choice, then so too can Christ.

In another passage, however, Maximus offers a solution along the lines of the second option, where he discusses the relationship between his earlier texts in which he acknowledged choice in Christ and what he later meant by denying this choice in Christ. As he explains, Christ's essential and relational assumptions of human nature bring about a new stability of human nature that includes a transformed, stabilized choice:

> In considering this [matter] extremely closely, your servant and disciple spoke of choice in [my] exposition to my most holy lord and teacher Thalassius, concerning difficulties in the holy Scriptures. If indeed for us the mak-

---

49. *TPO* 1 (PG 91:24B-C) in *Opuscules*, 119–20.

er of humanity became human, then the unchangeable creator clearly set straight for us the immutability of choice. He freely accepted the passions of punishment through his experience by essential assumption and accepted the dishonorable passions by relational assumption and out of love of humanity. By the passions taken relationally, he made a beginning for the [human] race in choice without passion; and by the ones taken by experience, he gave to the faithful the first fruits of incorruptibility that naturally follow.[50]

In this passage, Maximus decides to redefine choice rather than exclude it from human nature; he does not deny choice in Christ as he did above. Instead, he argues that Christ brought about a new form of choice, "immutable" and "without passion." Because he did not himself experience the sinful "dishonorable" passions, he shows that "choice without passion" is possible and, in fact, brings about choice in this new mode. The force of this argument is that choice *does* pertain to human nature as such. If it did not, there would be no reason to try to affirm it in Christ in any form. Indeed, it would otherwise pertain to the falsifying "dishonorable" passions that Christ only assumes relationally. The new form of choice present in Christ, however, differs from the Nemesian definition; as immutable and without passion, it does not look on two possible actions equally or indifferently.[51]

Why would Maximus resolve the tension in both directions? After all, only one solution is necessary to remove the contradiction. It seems that the two solutions should be understood as coordinated and even interrelated. As argued in the previous chapter, Maximus conceived of human nature as existing in different, concrete historical stages, most importantly a created state, a fallen state, and (ultimately) a perfectly deified state. The first transition between these stages is effected by the sin of Adam and Eve, but in the question of Christ's choice, Maximus is dealing with the minutiae of the transition from the fallen condition to a renewed and, eventually, resurrected condition. In this way, both of the options explored by Maximus above are true. Choice, as it exists now, is not absolutely essential to human

50. *TPO* 1 (PG 91:29C-32A) in *Opuscules*, 123–24.
51. On Christ's assumption of choice without passion, see *Amb. Io.* 7 (PG 91:1076A-C), as well as the note on this text in *On Difficulties in the Church Fathers*, vol. 1, 480, n. 16.

nature, and, as will be seen in the resurrection state, this choice will be eradicated. That state only comes about, however, because of the stabilization of our choice effected by Christ's human life, in which choice exists not as an indifference to humanity's final end but as a dispassionate resting in a disposition toward that end.

There are two ways this arrangement impacts a consideration of Christ's temptation. The first is the way that Christ's temptation can be considered in parallel with Christ's choice. Secondly, the way Maximus speaks of the hypostatic union has consequences for an affirmation of Christ's temptation. Concerning the first, a few last words on the relationship of impeccability and choice are in order because their relationship sheds light on the relationship of impeccability and temptation. There is no short and straightforward answer in Maximus's corpus to the question of whether Christ had choice. Insofar as choice is a deliberation between two equally attractive possibilities and a fundamental neutrality with regard to what is according to nature, Christ did not have it. But insofar as choice can be activated as an immutable resting in "a stable motion according to natural appetite,"[52] one may be able to answer affirmatively.[53] The point is that Christ accepts choice only to make it immutable and, therefore, to no longer have choice as it formerly existed. One might speak of Christ's humanity as having or effecting an oxymoronic immutable choice. Even when demonic forces are at work attempting to arouse a natural appetite against nature, Christ's immutability of choice remains firmly within natural bounds and fundamentally oriented to what is according to nature, never considering that what is against nature is equally possible.

Much the same can be said, in turn, of the relationship between Christ's impeccability and temptation. Was Christ tempted like others in all things? If temptation means that Christ would have to look on the natural and unnatural indifferently as though both were equally

---

52. *TPO* 1 (PG 91:32A).

53. The caveat, of course, is that a choice that is immutable is, according to the original definition of choice, no longer a choice at all. Balthasar makes a similar assessment in *Cosmic Liturgy*, 268 and 270–71. On this point, Maximus may reflect his general reticence to describe the eschatological condition as I discussed in chapter 2. By refusing to describe choice in its eschatological form, he is left with a purely apophatic description: it will not be like it is now.

attractive, then Christ cannot be tempted in this way because his humanity was always inclined naturally and willingly toward what was according to nature. To say otherwise would impinge on Christ's impeccability and his stabilization of our choice.[54] If temptation means, on the other hand, that demons were active in Christ's passibility, affecting his natural appetites in ways that make them violent and strong and consequently requiring a certain discernment of spirits concerning how they must be properly activated, then Christ may be said to have been tempted. The point is that Christ accepts temptation by the devil precisely in order to heal human nature from the insinuation of demonic powers that made such temptation possible in the first place. One might speak of Christ having or effecting an unassailable temptation; the one who, as God, is incapable of disobeying God's will can be and is, as human, tempted by the devil to disobey God. Through the experience of allowing the devil to approach him through his passibility, he essentially and definitively overcomes the experience of temptation that other human beings encounter throughout their life, thereby concretely inaugurating a state of human nature that can be irrevocably free from demonic perturbation.[55]

Secondly and finally, Maximus's conception of the hypostatic union also stands in some tension with Christ's temptation. Because of Maximus's Christological protections against Nestorianism, Maximus's method most commonly precludes an examination of Christ's humanity alone. For instance, he denies ignorance in Christ on the ground that one must divide Christ in order for ignorance to make sense.[56] From an exegetical standpoint, Maximus is able to avoid an impasse concerning ignorance because, while scripture sometimes makes Christ *appear*

---

54. One might further add that even in other human beings, this sort of indifference toward the good might already be considered sin and not temptation.

55. For an argument that supports my reading of Maximus on both choice and temptation, see Torstein T. Tollefsen, "The Metaphysics of Maximus: Becoming One with God," in *A Saint for East and West*, in which he argues that union with the divine entails "an expansion of human nature and activity beyond the present limits and properties" and "even transforms [human nature] into a new mode of being beyond itself" (see 229–30). A similar resolution appears to be commended in Blowers, *Maximus the Confessor*, 246: in its eschatological mode, "human choice would not endure as a selection between alternatives ... but would embrace the *multiple goods* of God in the form of the *logoi*."

56. *TPO* 19 (PG 91:218B-224B) in *Opuscules*, 233–36.

ignorant, it arguably never *says* that he is.⁵⁷ That God is omniscient and that Christ appears not to be can be reconciled with reference to Christ's relational appropriation of human nature: he was able to speak *as if* he were ignorant even though he was not. The scriptural evidence regarding temptation does not allow for a parallel solution, however. Scripture is clear, on the one hand, that God cannot be tempted to evil, but scripture is also clear, on the other, that Christ most certainly is tempted.⁵⁸ If Maximus were to attempt to resolve the question of Christ's temptation as he resolves the question of Christ's apparent ignorance, he would end up denying that Christ was really tempted and arguing that Christ only acted *as if* he were. Temptation, perhaps more than any other Christological concern, strains the affirmation of Christ's unity and veers all too easily into Nestorianism. On this question, Maximus has no ready solution. Nevertheless, Maximus remains faithful to the affirmation of the scriptural texts and rightly takes the scriptural affirmation of Christ's temptation perfectly seriously.

Salvation through Temptation: Christ's Victory over the Devil

Maximus views Christ's temptation as a central moment of Christ's defeat of the devil, who had formerly ruled over humanity by means of the corruptibility, mortality, and passibility that had entered humanity through the Fall. By defeating the devil, Christ undoes these consequences and saves humanity from the demonic tyranny that was formerly active through them. I have discussed how Maximus believes Christ to have been naturally free from these consequences yet bearing them willingly (not from necessity) out of love of humanity. He makes this argument, in part, in order to serve as an appropriate exemplar for those who strive after perfection.⁵⁹ While one should

---

57. Matthew 24:36 is the strongest indication of ignorance in Christ. This verse, however, is often read as indicating Christ's unwillingness to share that information. Given Maximus's affirmation of Christ's omniscience, he would seem to endorse this reading.

58. See James 1:13 and Hebrews 4:15.

59. For example, *QT* 21 (PG 90:312B-313A; CCSG 7:127) in Blowers and Wilken, *Cosmic Mystery*, 109–10.

not speak of a progressive deification of Christ's humanity, Christ's human experiences accompany the believer in the various practical and contemplative moments of the spiritual journey.[60] Christ is adaptable, appearing in different forms for different believers, becoming "all things to all."[61] Again, as mentioned earlier, Christ suffers "out of weakness" precisely in order to save those in each part of the spiritual journey,[62] and for this soteriological reason, Christ assumed a human nature with the consequences of Adam's sin. Thus, even if Christ's coming in corruptibility, mortality, and passibility is not necessary *per se*, it was soteriologically fitting for him to enter into these consequences in such a way that they are reversed and healed.

I have argued that, for Maximus, all three of these consequences are related to demonic activity. Passibility is centrally important for Maximus's treatment of Christ's temptation, but since they all bear relevance to Christ's defeat of the devil, I discuss all three in the order in which Christ confronted them in his own life: corruptibility, passibility, and mortality.

For Maximus, one comes under the reign of the three consequences of the Fall (and under their instigator, the devil) through the bodily and impassioned mode of birth introduced after Adam's sin.[63] For

---

60. Larchet argues against Riou, Léthel, and Garrigues, who claim that Maximus sees a "progressive" character in Christ's deification (see Jean-Claude Larchet, *La Divinisation de l'Homme*, 275–78). Another voice supporting the "progressive" deification of Christ is found in Luis Granados, "The Action of the Holy Spirit in Christ, according to Saint Maximus the Confessor," in *A Saint for East and West*, 116, 126, and 129. When considered from the perspective of a bald progress *toward* virtue, Larchet is correct to object to a "progressive" deification of Christ. However, Maximus indicates that there is in Christ a progressive "putting off" of temptation by demonic forces through the passions, even if it is on the basis of a wholly deified human nature. Indeed, *AL* 10–13 (PG 90:920C-21C) in *The Ascetic Life*, 109–11, indicates that this "putting off" takes place throughout the duration of Christ's public ministry. In any case, the specific sort of accompaniment of the monk intended in the text is not seen by Maximus as "progressive." As noted in chapter 2, Larchet is correct to insist that *praxis* and contemplation are not distinct chronological stages of deification (see *Questions à Thalassios*, vol. 2, 50–51, n. 1). See also the conclusion.

61. One sees this idea at *CT* II 27 (PG 90:1137A-B) in *The Philokalia*, vol. 2, , 144; *CT* I 13 (PG 90:1088B-C) in *Philokalia*, vol. 2, 140; and *CT* II 31 (PG 90:1139A) in *Philokalia*, vol. 2, 145. Perhaps most eloquently, Maximus expresses this "adaptability" of the *Logos* in an extended analogy concerning the Israelites' manna in the desert in *CT* I 100 (PG 90:1123C-D) in *Philokalia*, 135–36.

62. *CT* II 27 (PG 90:1137A-B) in *Philokalia*, vol. 2, 144.

63. *Amb. Io.* 31 (PG 91:1273D-1276D) in *Ambigua*, 272–73; *On Difficulties in the Church Fathers*, vol. 2, 39–43, speaks of Christ's undoing of our natural origin through his incorruptible

human nature up until Christ, the consequences propagated themselves cyclically, pleasure giving rise to corruptible bodily birth and corruptible bodily birth giving rise to pleasure in one's progeny. Thus, in the concrete pattern of human life after Adam, corruptible and impassioned birth lies at the origin of the devil's tyranny. In order to undo this tyranny, Maximus believes that Christ's human existence has to break this cycle at its beginning. Since Christ's birth was in no way preceded by pleasure, he heals humanity's origin by restoring it to a new mode of origin. Herein lies the importance for Maximus of the Virgin birth. By breaking the cycle of corruptible and impassioned birth in our origin, Christ begins to undo the curse of the devil who planted pleasure in nature "justly" as a consequence of Adam's transgression.[64] By his mode of origin, Christ had already brought an end to the essential and necessary corruption humanity experiences.

Christ also freely came in a passible body and, by taking on this quality, enters into a salutary and reconciling war against the enemies and adversaries of human nature. Christ's temptation thereby becomes a salvific and empowering event.[65] In a number of passages, Maximus speaks of the way in which Christ's passibility constitutes the reversal of the devil's power over humanity in pleasure and pain.[66] A typical example of this defeat is found in *QT* 47, where Maximus

---

and dispassionate birth. See also *QT* 61 (PG 90:628C-629B; CCSG 22:7) in Blowers and Wilken, *Cosmic Mystery*, 133; in this passage, Maximus explicitly refers to pleasure (related to passibility), death, and (later in the passage) to birth and corruptibility. The devil is explicit somewhat later (*QT* 61 [PG 90:628C-629B; CCSG 22:7]; Blowers and Wilken, *Cosmic Mystery*, 137).

64. *QT* 61 (PG 90:628C-629B; CCSG 22:7) in Blowers and Wilken, *Cosmic Mystery*, 133.

65. See *QD* 22 (CCSG 10:20) in *Questions and Doubts*, 55, and *QD* 33 (CCSG 10:27–28) in *Questions and Doubts*, 61. To a lesser extent (since the devil is not named), one could also reference *QD* 18 (CCSG 10:16–17) in *Questions and Doubts*, 53, for the restoration of human nature by the removal of sinful passion.

66. For clarity of presentation, I focus on *QT* 47 and *QT* 21 in the main text. Christ's simultaneous destruction of passions and condemnation of demons appears in *QT* 54 (PG 90:525A-C; CCSG 7:465) in *Questions à Thalassios*, vol. 2, 218–19, and *On Difficulties in Sacred Scripture*, 347. One could add Maximus's consideration of the "house" of passibility in which the devil resides until Christ casts him out and destroys the house, found in *QT* 62 (PG 90:653C-656D) in *Questions à Thalassios*, vol. 3, 138–41, and *On Difficulties in Sacred Scripture*, 456–58. Finally, *Amb. Io.* 10.4–9 outlines the anthropological problem of passionate temptation and culminates in the following resolution, which is both Christological and demonological: Christ, "destroyer of the evil powers ... *smote* [sin's] *king* the devil ... and He *destroyed all that breathed* in it, that is, the passions that are in us, along with the shameful and evil thoughts that they create," See *Amb. Io.* 10.8 (PG 91:1120C-D) in *On Difficulties in the Church Fathers*, vol. 1, 179.

allegorically explains how the "valleys are filled and the mountains made low." The valleys, he explains, are the evil passions and ignorance that enter human nature through the transgression. They represent the corruption of the natural powers of human nature. The mountains, on the other hand, represent evil and demonic powers that are closely associated with these valleys. Both the valleys and mountains are simultaneously destroyed by the coming of Christ:

And every mountain and hill will be made low. Valleys, it seems, are most frequently set together with mountains and hills. The mountain is every lofty power that raises up against the knowledge of God and the hill [is] every evil that takes a stand against virtue. If the mountains are every spirit working for ignorance and the hills those who produce evil, supposing that as said before every valley, that is, the flesh and soul that prepared, as I was saying, the way of the Lord and made straight his pathways, will be filled with knowledge and virtue through the coming of the Word that moves about in them through the commandments of God, then all the spirits of false knowledge and of evil will be lowered, the Word tramples them under foot, places [them] under [him], overthrows the evil powers that rise up against human nature, and, as one tearing down the greatness and height of mountains and hills and bringing them to the valleys, he fills [them] up. For, in reality, if one were to understand by the power of the Word that, as greatly as the demons take hold against [human] nature, working (as their profession) toward [ἐδημιούργησαν] ignorance against nature and evil, in no way whatsoever does he support the heights of ignorance and evil, just as there would be neither mountain nor hill of visible sensation if someone were able to devise a means to bring down mountains and hills and fill up valleys. Certainly, the toppling of the perceptible and evil mountains and hills is the complete restoration [ἀποκατάστασις] of the natural powers of the body and soul to themselves.[67]

Maximus argues that the destruction and defeat of the devil is *coterminous* with the restoration of the natural functioning of human nature. When Christ battles and defeats the devil on the field of human passibility, he thereby brings about the end of evil activation of human

67. QT 47 (PG 90:425B-D; CCSG 7:319–21) in *Questions à Thalassios*, vol. 2, 60–61; *On Difficulties in Sacred Scripture*, 260–61; Constas has omitted "For, in reality … fill up valleys," but it is unclear whether this omission is for critical reasons.

nature, not for himself (as he never activated it in this way), but for the rest of humanity.

One further aspect of this passage is noteworthy. Because of the way that evil passion, ignorance, and the demonic are considered in *QT* 47, Maximus also indicates that human nature itself does not resist God: only the devil incites nature and tries to drive it against God. This distinction between the natural and the demonic requires that one take Maximus's demonology realistically; any reductive psychologization of the demons would undercut the essential anthropological point of Maximus's argument and in turn jeopardize the consistency of his dyothelite affirmation. If the natural will itself is what separates one from the divine, the monothelites would be right to reject its presence in Christ.

Further, the distinction makes clear where the monastic must mount his or her own battle against evil. On the one hand, the devil and his evil suggestions must be rooted out wherever they are found. As a part of this battle against the demonic, Maximus seems to require a discernment of spirits even within one's natural desires to determine which are to be acted on and which are not. This inner discernment of spirits would appear to be a necessary component of a Maximian moral theology. On the other hand, the natural passions themselves are neither evil nor to be resisted in themselves; when the devil is removed from influencing them, they are restored to their "natural functioning." On this basis, Maximus would still argue that human nature itself is good, even if demonic forces are active within it.

QT 47 does not exposit fully the way in which Christ defeats the devil in his temptation. Rather, it outlines how Christ's victory over the devil results in the healing of human passibility. The means of this defeat itself are seen most clearly in *QT* 21.[68] In this passage, Maximus

---

68. Maximus presents a different outline for Christ's temptations in *AL* 10–13 (PG 90:920C-21C) in *The Ascetic Life*, 109–11, where his temptations are categorized as those against love of God (in the desert) and against love of neighbor (in the scribes and Pharisees). This arrangement would give a greater temporal extension to the period of Christ's temptations (i.e., throughout the public ministry), but the temptations still correspond to the passible faculties: desiring things of the world above God and expressing hatred toward other human beings (thus pertaining to aversion).

explains how Christ's temptation occurred and how it had salutary consequences for the rest of humanity. Christ "puts on" the activities of evil powers and principalities at the incarnation, wherein Christ assumes human passibility and with it the activity of evil spirits working through the natural passions in an attempt to elicit unnatural passion. This assumption parallels the anthropological process of temptation explained in the previous chapter. Maximus appears to treat these temptations in the order that Christ experienced them in his own life: the temptation toward pleasure in the desert and the temptation to flee from pain at the time of Christ's death.[69] This latter temptation is the focus of Maximus's energy throughout the monothelite controversy, and modern secondary literature has addressed this aspect of his thought in great detail. In light of the extensive literature concerning this temptation, my concern will be to draw out the demonological characteristics of that temptation while arguing for the compatibility of that demonological reading with his broader dyothelite Christology that drew his attention and energy toward the end of his life.

In the desert, Christ allows the devil to approach him and tempt him with attractive things, thus proceeding against Christ's faculty of desire. Given Maximus's understanding of natural appetites, each of the three temptations considers something *naturally* desirable, possibly taking their rise from wish (βούλησις). In the first case, the particular desire is clear: Christ is tempted on the basis of his natural hunger. In the second and third instances, the natural desire involved is less clear. One might speculate in the Temple temptation about a natural desire to know God's care for oneself and, in the temptation to rule the nations, a natural desire for proper ordering of the world. Articulated in this way, these sorts of desires would be compatible with Maximus's understanding of the object of wish, thereby grounding these desires in the positive, natural appetency of human nature. Yet these desires are stirred up by the devil in a way that would attempt to render them

69. This same pairing is also seen in the earlier *QD* 194 (CCSG 10:136) in *Questions and Doubts*, 140. For ignorance as a passion, see *TPO* 19 (PG 91:220B-224B) in *Opuscules*, 234–36, and Larchet's commentary on it in *Opuscules*, 70–71. As above, the chronological duration of the temptation regarding aversion is expanded to the length of Jesus' public ministry in *AL* 10–13 (PG 90:920C-21C) in *The Ascetic Life*, 109–11.

unnatural. In that way, they became an object of discernment in Christ's inner affective life. Christ is victorious over the prodding of demons because he constantly discerns these desires appropriately, rejecting the demons' suggestion to activate his desires unnaturally and remaining oriented toward humanity's final end. He thereby stabilized the natural human faculty of desire, "eliminating [the demonic powers] from human nature."[70] This stabilization has effects for the rest of humanity, who comes to share in it through sacramental and ascetic practice (as outlined in chapter 2). This stabilization, further, concretely moves human nature from one historical state or stage to another. By overcoming temptation to pleasure, Christ reestablished the natural functioning of human desire, leveling the mountains and filling the valleys discussed in *QT* 47. By removing the powers and principalities from the faculty of desire, desire is restored to its natural condition.

The second half of Maximus's interpretation of Christ's temptation concerns later periods of Christ's earthly ministry. *AL* stretches this second temptation over the course of Jesus' public ministry, but *QT* considers the crucial locus of the period around Jesus' death, from Christ's agony in the garden until his death on the cross.[71] Maximus frames this series of events as a battle against the demonic within Christ's faculty of aversion in order to restore the natural functioning of that faculty to itself. Christ overcomes this second kind of temptation at "the time of [his] death," when he showed fear in the Garden of Gethsemane and accepted death on the cross:

> Since, therefore, by his first experience according to pleasure the Lord destroyed the strength of the principalities and powers, so a second time, he allowed them to provoke him through the tempting experience of being forsaken, through pain and suffering, in order to empty completely in himself

---

70. *QT* 21 (PG 90:313B-D; CCSG 7:129) in Blowers and Wilken, *Cosmic Mystery*, 111.

71. Few authors note the inclusion of Gethsemane in Christ's victory over fearful temptations, though none argue for its exclusion. Adam G. Cooper, *The Body in St. Maximus the Confessor: Holy Flesh, Wholly Deified* (New York: Oxford University Press, 2005), 227, concurs with my argument. It can also be noted in Marcel Doucet, "La Volonté Humaine du Christ, Spécialement en son Agonie. Maxime le Confesseur, Interprète de l'Écriture," *Science et Esprit* 37, no. 2 (1985): 142.

the corrupting poison of their [the demons'] evil, as a fire burns, absolutely, utterly destroying [them] in nature. He took off the principalities and powers at the time of his death on the cross, remaining unconquered by suffering, and moreover exhibiting fear of death, saving nature from the passions of fear.[72]

Like the temptation toward pleasure in the desert, Maximus considers the demonic temptation to be based in a natural passion, this time a function of the natural faculty of aversion: namely, a natural fear of suffering, pain, and death. This desire also would appear to be founded in Christ's imaginative appetite of wish.[73] Just like the demons of desire in the desert, these demons of fear also attempt to divert Christ from God's will by means of his internal affective life.

Given the significance of the scene in Gethsemane to modern discussion of Maximus's dyothelitism, some further comments on this interpretation of the scene are in order. The secondary literature, especially when dealing with the monothelite controversy, has frequently and consistently pointed out that Maximus views Christ's fear in these events as a *natural* fear, morally blameless even if it is in some sense a consequence of the Fall.[74] While this account is accurate to a point, it fails to consider that Maximus at times avows that someone is actively working against God's purposes in Christ's fear. In Gethsemane, demonic powers are at work in Christ's humanity driving his nondeliberative appetite to avoid death into a "powerful" and "violent" state.[75] While Christ's elicited human will is to do the will of the Father, the "not my will" comes from a combination of an unelicited appetite of Christ's human nature along with demonic forces that present it in a particularly acute form and at an extremely poignant moment.

---

72. *QT* 21 (PG 90:316A-B; CCSG 7:129–31) in Blowers and Wilken, *Cosmic Mystery*, 112.

73. I avoid addressing whether the natural will and wish are oriented toward different ends (supernatural and natural, respectively), as this perennial difficulty would significantly complicate my presentation. Maximus, for his part, does not identify the number of humankind's ends and seems to indicate that wish, at least, offers no resistance to the highest supernatural end of humanity. Whether Christ's humanity has one end or two, Maximus holds that Christ's fear has a constitutional foundation in his humanity. That constitutional foundation, whatever it may be, is what the devil exploits in Gethsemane.

74. See the discussion of this literature in the introduction.

75. *QT* 50 (PG 90:472C-D; CCSG 7:387–9) in *Questions à Thalassios*, vol. 2, 136–37, and *On Difficulties in Sacred Scripture*, 302.

These affirmations coincide with the first two "blameless" stages of sin in Maximus's account of the moral act: the attack and the desire that are not in our power. As Maximus states, only the consent and the act (both absent from Christ) are morally culpable. Thus, while the demons' ability to stir up these natural thoughts and desires is so great that Christ can even describe their temptations as "my will," he at no point consents to their goading and thereby remains blameless throughout their attack.

This interpretation expands significantly on the reading of Christ's agony in Gethsemane that would later predominate in Maximus's writings responding to monothelitism.[76] While this reading has a different focus, it is not incompatible with (and in fact bolsters) the developed dyothelite solution Maximus later offers. By framing the garden temptation as primarily from the devil, Maximus maintained the ultimate goodness of the natural will and shows the importance of Christ's essential appropriation of this will if Christ is to heal the entire *logos* of human nature. At the same time, this demonological reading did not "divide" Christ by placing his humanity at war with his divinity; the battle lines ultimately cast human nature on the same side as the divine and against the devil. In this way, Maximus precluded his opponents' accusation of Nestorianism in his account. In the midst of the monothelite controversy, it is not surprising that Maximus did not further complicate the debate with these demonological considerations. Yet one should not view his relative silence on this matter to indicate that Maximus had changed his mind about his demonology. Such a consideration would have simply distracted from the focus of that later controversy.

There are two components of Maximus's conception of the salvific meaning of Christ's temptation. On the one hand, Christ functions as the perfect, exemplary ascetic who goes into spiritual warfare against the powers and principalities. As an exemplary figure, Christ

---

76. The challenge of monothelitism required an emphasis on how Christ's wills were in agreement. The complex consideration of demonic temptation in Christ did not lend itself to the clear affirmation that, in Christ, the divine and human wills were in perfect accord. Thus, it is not that Maximus changes his mind; rather, he simply concentrated his energy on the stability of Christ's natural human will.

"despoiled" the powers in his death; he "triumphed" over them on the cross.[77] This theme indicates how Maximus relates Christ's life to the life of the monk. The monk is encouraged to strive after Christ's example in moral combat with demonically inspired pleasure and pain. Just as Christ attained a perfect victory over the devil in his spiritual combat, so too the monk shares in Christ's victory through askesis and sacramental participation. This victory is possible, however, only because of the second theme of Christ's *empowerment* of human nature.

On the other hand, Maximus portrays Christ as a doctor and a liberator who heals humanity's wounds and frees it from slavery and imprisonment. In these terms, Christ is more than an exemplar; he is also an empowering figure who "freed our human nature from the evil which had insinuated itself therein through the liability to passions."[78] He removes the "deadly poison" of demonic wickedness from human passibility.[79] He heals human nature of the evil passions associated with pleasure and pain. In other texts, Christ, by his fasting in the desert, frees humanity from the bondage to sin in all its forms: action, consent in thought, and even the mental representation of sinful actions.[80] Christ's human weakness becomes the means through which he destroys the power of the one who held human nature captive;[81] the words of the devil that "resonate" in nature are destroyed by Christ's accepting our "mortally wounded" humanity;[82] and Christ, as the first and only to undergo death voluntarily, destroys the third and final consequence of Adam's transgression: human mortality.[83] Desire and aversion do not themselves constitute the sickness of human nature, nor are the natural faculties of human nature out of which plea-

---

77. *QT* 21 (PG 90:316B-D; CCSG 7:131–33) in Blowers and Wilken, *Cosmic Mystery*, 109–13.
78. *QT* 21 (PG 90:311B-317A; CCSG 7:127–33) in Blowers and Wilken, *Cosmic Mystery*, 113.
79. *QT* 21 (PG 90:311B-317A; CCSG 7:127–33) in Blowers and Wilken, *Cosmic Mystery*, 113. One can also see a parallel between Christ's defeat of demonic powers and the ascetic's battle against passion in *QD* 68 (CCSG 10:52–53) in *Questions and Doubts*, 79.
80. *QD* 193 (CCSG 10:135–36) in *Questions and Doubts*, 140.
81. *QT* 64 (PG 90:712D-713B, CCSG 22:217–19) in Blowers and Wilken, *Cosmic Mystery*, 160.
82. *QT* 54 (PG 90:520B-C; CCSG 7:459) in *Questions à Thalassios*, vol. 2, 210–11; *On Difficulties in Sacred Scripture*, 343. Later in this text, the deceit of the devil is replaced with true knowledge by Christ, who "teaches the soul, condemns the flesh, punishes the passions, and condemns the demons." See *QT* 54 (PG 90:525A-C; CCSG 7:465) in *Questions à Thalassios*, vol. 2, 218–19; *On Difficulties in Sacred Scripture*, 346.
83. *QD* 118 (CCSG 10:86–87) in *Questions and Doubts*, 104.

sure and pain rise the oppressive forces of slavery and imprisonment that hold humanity captive. The devil and his minions alone cause this sickness and slavery. Passibility itself is not destroyed by Christ. Rather, the powers and principalities are subjugated—albeit eschatologically—to the passibility over which they had formerly ruled. In place of the demonic enslavement of humanity through passion, Christ's victory over the devil puts the devil under the rule of even the lowest faculties of human nature.

Christ's victory over the devil is empowering to others because it concretely effects the transition of human nature from a stage in which it is dominated by the "law of sin" to a renewed condition—a transition that others enjoy by means of ascetic practice and sacramental participation.[84] Only by drawing the devil out to fight in the field where he had originally conquered humanity could Christ fittingly undo the tyranny of the devil and restore human nature to itself. In the language of QT 47, by destroying the power of the devil over human nature, Christ restores human nature to its natural functioning, oriented toward its final end in God. Desire and aversion will no longer constitute (even potentially) an obstacle to human salvation; they instead become a tool that draws humanity to its Creator and helps it to ascend toward that supernatural destiny.

⁘

Two closing remarks are in order. The first is primarily Christological and bears on the way that demonic temptation affords a particularly fruitful avenue for the exploration of Christ's identity with the fallen human condition. The second remark is anthropological and, more specifically, relates to certain ramifications of this study in the realm of moral theology.

First, the question of Christ's temptation requires a precise analysis of the genesis of sinful action in the individual's soul. In presenting Maximus, I have indicated that the fallen human *tropos* with its *gnomic* will, while indeed an important way of articulating human moral

---

84. Even in these practices, it is still Christ performing the transition; Christification is not Pelagian.

fragility, may not be the proper place on which to focus when considering Christ's rectification of that fragility. Rather, I have argued that the *gnomic* will should be considered as symptomatic and descriptive, whereas demonic temptation should be seen as a root cause of that wounded *tropos*. Such a view of human fallenness, while certainly leaning on the dualistic aspects of Christian cosmology, may provide for a deeper and more penetrating framework for incarnational theology than would a heavy dependence on the *gnomic* will. As Maximus considers it, demonic temptation is a weakness of human nature that is redeemable—and able to be taken on by Christ—in a way that an inner division like the *gnomic* will never could be.

Second, future explanations of Maximian moral theology will also have to take account of the demonology uncovered in the preceding two chapters. In so doing, important questions related to virtue and vice remain for this demonology. The theory of demonic temptation I have presented emphasizes the concrete decisions that must be made in specific circumstances in order to discern the devil's temptation. In this presentation, it has not been clear what place remains for virtue and vice—habitual inclinations to or against the good—in the faculties of desire and aversion. Maximus certainly cares about vice, yet the structural neglect of this nexus of moral questions in the preceding chapters has been due to my orientation toward a presentation of what kinds of temptation are possible for one *without* vicious habits. Maximus's demonological approach to temptation shapes his understanding of virtue in a way that will differ significantly from Thomas's understanding in the second half.

4

SOURCES FOR THOMAS'S PRESENTATION OF CHRIST'S TEMPTATION

Among the sources that impact Thomas Aquinas's view of Christ's temptation, the comparative focus of this work necessitates a particular emphasis on the connections between the thought of Maximus and Thomas. In addition to this unifying material, the latter two sections of this chapter concentrate on Latin patristic sources and Latin medieval sources that treat Christ's defeat of the devil.[1] These sections cannot be comprehensive; instead, I have selected two figures from both the Patristic period (Augustine and Gregory the Great) and the Medieval period (Peter the Lombard and Alexander of Hales) because of their individual reflections on Christ's humanity and on his temptation by the devil.

---

1. As mentioned in chapter 1, n. 1, Thomas benefits from an array of sources that directly and explicitly consider the specific nexus of Christology and demonology essential to my central argument. For that reason, and in contrast to chapter 1, I treat each thinker as a whole rather than subject by subject. I do not need to address at length Aquinas's sources for his theory of the human passions since this work has already been commendably performed by Paul Gondreau in his study on Christ's passions. See Paul Gondreau, *The Passions of Christ's Soul in the Theology of St. Thomas Aquinas* (Scranton, Pa.: University of Scranton Press, 2009), chapters 1 and 2, especially 67–68, 84–85, and 130–31.

John of Damascus as the Historical Link between Maximus and Thomas

The historical relationship between Maximus and Thomas is indirect; Thomas Aquinas never substantively read the works of Maximus the Confessor.[2] However, one need not show that Thomas read Maximus's works directly in order to demonstrate the Confessor's influence on the Angelic Doctor. A two-stage transmission process bridges the thought of Maximus and Thomas: first, the *De Fide Orthodoxa* (hereafter, *DFO*) by John of Damascus, and second, the translation of this work into Latin by Burgundio of Pisa, sometime between 1148 and 1158. Burgundio's version of *DFO* was widespread; it was used by Peter the Lombard[3] and, for linguistic reasons seen below, Thomas almost certainly used it as well.[4] In what follows, I trace notable points of continuity and discontinuity in this transmission, looking back to Maximus from time to time and glimpsing forward to Thomas when necessary. Since the *DFO* is the main and concrete link between Maximus and Thomas, I do not treat John's thought holistically but will focus on the connections to each thinker found in that text. I consider John's view of Christ's temptation by the devil in two familiar sections: his anthropology and his Christology.

Anthropology of the Passions in John of Damascus

Within John's anthropology, there are three aspects worth noting: John's theory of the moral act; the goodness of the passions; and demonic activity inside human beings consequent to the Fall.[5] On the first point, R.-A. Gauthier has demonstrated to a great extent the way

---

2. See the discussion of the literature in the introduction.
3. John of Damascus, *De Fide Orthodoxa: Versions of Burgundio and Cerbanus*, ed. Eligius M. Buytaert (Louvain, Belgium: E. Nauwelaerts, 1955), ix–xv.
4. R.-A. Gauthier, "Saint Maxime le Confesseur et la Psychologie de l'acte humain," *Recherches de Théologie Ancienne et Médiévale* 21, no. 1 (1954): 82, presumes the same, taking Burgundio's translation for granted as the basis of Aquinas's reading of John.
5. References to the Greek in this section will be from John's Greek text from the Patrologia Graeca (hereafter PG) and the Sources Chrétiennes edition, Jean Damascène, *La Foi Orthodoxe*, 2 vols. (Paris: Éditions du Cerf, 2010 and 2011); however, I include references to Burgundio's translation of these passages in the footnotes.

in which Maximus's explanation of the moral act finds its way into the *Summa Theologica*.⁶ On the second, Paul Gondreau has executed fine work showing much of the Damascene's relationship to Thomas on the valuation of the passions. In the coming discussion of Gondreau's findings, I emphasize aspects of particular importance for this study and discuss one point where Gondreau's analysis is, on the basis of *DFO*, deficient as an understanding of John's thought. Third, in relation to the above deficiency, I discuss John's psychological demonology as presented in key texts of *DFO*.

John's psychology of the moral act closely follows that recounted by Maximus, reproducing and perhaps even overemphasizing terms from Maximus's account that were originally less than technical.⁷ My goal here is not to trace every stage of the moral act through John of Damascus; rather, I focus on three aspects of Maximus's and John's accounts: will (θέλησις or *voluntas*), wish (βούλησις or *voluntas*), and choice (προαίρεσις or *electio*). While these terms themselves stretch from Maximus to Thomas, John and Burgundio change a few relevant details along the way.

John accurately summarizes Maximus's thought concerning *thelesis*, calling it an "an innate force [in the soul] appetitive of what is natural to the soul and embracing all those things which pertain to its nature essentially" and as "a rational and vital appetite attached solely to natural things."⁸ This appetite is expressive only of natural desires and is not, in itself, the origin of anything contrary to nature. Even in their fallen form, John sees such appetitive movements as, at worst, morally neutral, referring to them as the natural and blameless pas-

---

6. Gauthier, "Saint Maxime," 51–100.

7. Gauthier's work intends to inculpate Maximus for certain confusions in the progression of the moral act so as to arrive at a clearer Thomistic usage of consent, command, and use (see Gauthier, "Saint Maxime," 98). Gauthier finds particularly problematic the second "appetite" that occurs after the choice of the will. I agree that the terminology used prior to Thomas could have been clearer, but the second appetite he is concerned about does not affect my own argument, since my interest lies in the former desire that is shaped prior to the assent of free will by θέλησις and Βούλησις.

8. *DFO* II 22 (PG 94:944B) in John of Damascus, *Writings*, trans. Frederic H. Chase, Jr. (Washington, D.C.: The Catholic University of America Press, 1958), 248. For the most part, John's thought will be considered in the main text and matters of Burgundio's translation will be placed in the notes.

sions (a phrase borrowed from Maximus). This understanding of the natural will accurately reflects Maximus's dyothelite views. The power of *thelesis* is directed toward humanity's true end and seeks to draw the individual to that end.

John's account of wish (βούλησις), on the other hand, is different than Maximus's and, in turn, calls into question John's continuity with Maximus's account of natural appetites.[9] Given my argument in chapter 3 that Maximus sees Christ's temptations as based upon the natural activity of wish, the stakes of this change are especially high. John indicates that wish is the specification of *thelesis* with regard to a particular worldly object, and that it seeks an end alone: wish is "a sort of natural willing, that is to say, a natural and rational appetite for some thing" that "concerns the end, and not the means to the end."[10] With respect to these ends, however, John provides a misleading example that shows that he is willing to part ways with Maximus's view of wish and of the broader category of natural appetite. Among John's accurate and helpful examples of wish (health, being king, sleep, and exercising self-control), John includes a sinful desire as its object:

> We speak of wishing both in respect to things which are in our power and in respect to things which are not; in other words, in respect to possible and impossible things. Thus, oftentimes we may wish to fornicate [Βουλόμεθα γὰρ πολλάκις πορνεῦσαι] or to exercise self-control, or to sleep, or some other such thing.[11]

Since wish is (for Maximus) a natural appetite directed toward a particular worldly end, John parts ways with Maximus when he inserts a sinful action like fornication into this list of objects of wish. As seen in chapter 2, Maximus includes no corresponding evil examples; rather, he listed apparent, this-worldly goods that would not have been con-

---

9. Burgundio's translation creates a certain amount of confusion about the difference between will and wish; while he transliterates both Greek terms into Latin, he translates both them parenthetically as "voluntas," which appears to render them equivalent terms. See Burgundio, *DFO* II 22: "thelima [id est voluntas]" and "[b]ulisis [id est voluntas]."

10. *DFO* II 22 (PG 94:944C) in *Writings*, 249.

11. *DFO* II 22 (PG 94:944C) in *Writings*, 249. The contrast with self-control demonstrates the negative connotation.

sidered necessarily sinful.¹² The reader of John's text, on the other hand, is led to the conclusion that the natural appetite of wish could seek both natural and unnatural objects, which (in Maximus's language) would mean that nature can tend away from God. In this way, John significantly parts ways with Maximus's sense and renders the natural appetites upon which the moral act is based indifferent to the final end of humankind. For Maximus, nature tends to God; for John (insofar as this example indicates), nature can tend toward *or away* from God.

A final point that will return when I consider John's Christology is the role of *choice* in the moral act. John's description indicates a structured process that constitutes and governs the moral act as the moral faculties move the subject into concrete action. Unlike Maximus, John does not explicitly define the rationality of the human being by the presence of this process, yet it is clear that John sees this process as fully *natural*, pertaining to all human beings' free will as a condition of action in this world.¹³ I have no intention of analyzing this process in detail here;¹⁴ I merely want to point out that choice is an essential part of this process. The primary definition given by John states that choice is "the choosing and picking out of this one rather than the other of two things proposed."¹⁵

In his later Christological reflection, however, John provides the further explanation that choice implies ignorance and a search after knowledge that involves deliberation and judgment.¹⁶ This fact thereby indicates that choice has a particularly close relationship with humanity's fallen condition—an ambiguity that was also found in Maximus's texts. With respect to the strictly anthropological presen-

---

12. See chapter 2. One might contest the example of wealth, but one detects no judgmental attitude in Maximus's discussion of it. In taking the example from Nemesius, Maximus apparently understands some rightful concern for worldly provision.

13. In this respect, John is aware of the *logos/tropos* distinction from Maximus; see *DFO* III 14 (PG 94:1046B) in *Writings*, 247.

14. The interested reader can see Gauthier, "Saint Maxime," 51–100.

15. *DFO* II 22 (PG 94:945B) in *Writings*, 249. John includes γνώμη as a distinct stage in this process, which also constitutes a significant flattening of Maximus's complex shifts with regard to γνώμη throughout his writings.

16. *DFO* III 14 (PG 94:1044B-1045A) in *Writings*, 302. *DFO* II 22 (PG 94:945C-D) in *Writings*, 249, shows the connection of choice to deliberation.

tation of choice, then, John accurately summarizes and passes on what Maximus argued on this subject. In continuity with Nemesius, neither Maximus nor John consider demonology directly in their accounts of the moral act, but for neither of them does this exclusion mean that the devil plays no role in the development of evil desires. John considers the genesis of immoral action (including the action of the devil) elsewhere; I address this subject in the following material.

As Paul Gondreau has commented in his work on the passions in Aquinas's thought, the *DFO* draws heavily on Nemesius of Emesa for its theory of the passions. In this respect, Gondreau concludes that John recognizes that "all aspects of human nature, including the passions, are expressive of God's will in creation" and that Nemesius and John consequently have a "positive appraisal of human affectivity."[17] In Gondreau's estimation, this positive appraisal is seen most clearly in John's text from Christ's assumption of affectivity in the incarnation.[18] Gondreau mentions in passing the role that Maximus plays in John's theory of Christ's passions,[19] but he does not consider any broader anthropological influence that Maximus had on John.

In his effort to portray the Damascene's thought on the passions as largely positive (and thus distance John's position from that of the Stoics), Gondreau is forced to equivocate at times concerning the role assigned by John for the passions in the moral life. On the one hand, Gondreau states that the passions are, for John, "an essential feature of human nature" that are an expression of God's will in creation.[20] On the other hand, Gondreau recognizes the Damascene's hesitancy on this question, for instance, John's exclusion of passion from Adam and Eve's created state. Gondreau further argues that John sees in all human beings other than Christ a "'spirit/flesh' conflict ... [that] arises from the naturally rebellious propensity of the lower appetitive pow-

---

17. Paul Gondreau, *The Passions of Christ's Soul in the Theology of St. Thomas Aquinas* (Scranton, Pa.: University of Scranton Press, 2009), 122.
18. Gondreau, *Passions of Christ's Soul*, 60–66; this positive assessment stands in contrast to potentially troubling passages found in Hilary of Poitiers that seems to deny this affectivity. Gondreau's treatment of Hilary is at 48–51.
19. Gondreau, *Passions of Christ's Soul*, 61.
20. Gondreau, *Passions of Christ's Soul*, 63.

ers."[21] Concerning the first hesitancy, it is curious, if not contradictory, for an "essential" characteristic of human nature to be rejected from Adam and Eve's original condition; in this way Gondreau, overestimates the positive (or at least enduring) role that John—apparently reflecting a Stoic definition at this juncture—assigns to the passions in the human moral life. As for the second hesitancy, if such is an accurate representation of the Damascene's thought, John would appear to be in conflict with Maximus, who would not say that human nature itself is responsible for impulses that separate us from God. In this way, Gondreau appears, in fact, to overestimate the negative role that John assigns to (fallen) human nature in the moral life.

While John certainly sees that the passions *can* have a positive role in the moral life, there is a deeper ambivalence in John's thought than Gondreau allows. Gondreau is right to argue that this ambivalence should not be located in human nature itself. Nevertheless, by ignoring the way in which John connects the negative role of the passions with demonic suggestion, Gondreau is forced to explain John's thought in categories that are not his own.[22]

Gondreau's oversight here, while minimal in the context of his own task and goals, has significant ramifications for this study. For Maximus, it is theologically dangerous to claim that human nature itself has a "naturally rebellious propensity." In Maximian terms, such would be tantamount to saying that nature resists God—something that Maximus would deny. Indeed, the *DFO* does not explain human sinful impulses purely by reference to the "flesh" or its "rebellion" against God; rather, John's careful expressions on the matter place these impulses in connection to *both* the devil and human bodiliness. In a consideration of the divinely providential power of the devil over humankind, John states that demons

---

21. Gondreau, *Passions of Christ's Soul*, 64.
22. The "disordered interior movements" Gondreau describes (64) are not native to John's terminology; nor is the distinction between "enfeebled" affectivity (affirmed in Christ) and "disordered, and, hence, sinful experiences" (denied in Christ) that Gondreau invokes to distinguish Christ's moral life from that of others (63). Such categories may be helpful in clarifying John's (admittedly) less clear claims (as, certainly, Aquinas will do with precisely the terms Gondreau introduces), but they do not demonstrate the categories with which John himself worked.

have no power or strength against anyone, unless this be permitted them by the dispensation of God, as in the case of Job and as has been written in the Gospel about the swine. If God does give them permission, they have strength and change and transform themselves into whatever apparent form they may desire.... All evil and the impure passions [κακία ... καὶ τὰ ἀκάθαρτα πάθη] have been conceived by them and they have been permitted to visit attacks upon man. But they are unable to force anyone, for it is in our power either to accept the attack or not."²³

This explanation of the origin of evil and impure passion accounts simultaneously for the providential purpose of such temptation and for the goodness of human nature. John does not ascribe the origin of evil passion to a natural resistance to God, but rather to demonic powers permitted to attack through divine providence. One should note that for John, the "attack"²⁴ occurs prior to the consent of the will. In any case, the suggestion of evil passion by the devil (whatever form it takes) does not appear here as a purely "internal" suggestion of the flesh.

Similarly, in a description of how the functioning of human free will can be hampered, John explains:

With men, however, it [free will] is such that the inclination precedes the execution in point of time. This is because, though man is free and has this freedom of will naturally, he also has the assault of the Devil to contend with and the motion of the body. Consequently, because of this assault and the burden of the body, the execution comes after the inclination.²⁵

Undoubtedly, the body appears as a component of the chronological separation of inclination and act, but it is placed—as John habitually does—in conjunction with demonic "interference." While the sentiment expressed here is in its own way Maximian, this passage is partic-

---

23. *DFO* II 4 (PG 94:877A-B) in *Writings*, 209–10 (translation modified). Burgundio's version of this passage is found in *Fide*, 76–77.
24. This is the same term used by Maximus to describe the first generation of sin that does not incur guilt; see Maximus, *QD* I 31 (CCSG 10:149); see also chapter 2 and the discussion of the four "generations" of sin in Maximus's thought. See *Questions and Doubts*, trans. Despina D. Prassas (DeKalb: Northern Illinois University Press, 2010).
25. *DFO* III 14 (PG 94:1041C) in *Writings*, 301, translation modified. The key part of Burgundio's version of *DFO* III 14 is found in *Fide*, 223.

ularly significant because the text from Maximus upon which this passage is based is not concerned with obstacles to the moral act.[26] This view, then, is not something that John merely passively hands on from Maximus; rather, John is able to interject creatively and independently a theory of demonic interference in the human exercise of free will.

One final example from *DFO* shows the interdependence of the body and the devil in the origin of evil desires. This instance is perhaps the most important, since it contains John's reflections on Romans 7 and its application to the fallen human condition. In this passage, John discusses the "law of the mind" and the "law of the flesh" that conflict with one another in humanity's fallen state. John does not frame this conflict as one between the interior aspects of "spirit" and "flesh" in human nature; rather, the conflict, as John sees it, is between the individual's conscience and the suggestion of the devil. While the law of the mind is the "commandment" of God and our "conscience," the law of the flesh is described as follows:

> Sin results from the Devil's suggestion [τοῦ διαβόλου προσβολῆς] and our own unconstrained and free acceptance of it. And this, too, is called a law.
> The suggestion of the evil one [ἡ προσβολὴ ... τοῦ πονηροῦ], or the law of sin, also acts upon the members of our flesh and through it attacks us. For, once we succumbed to the suggestion of the evil one and freely violated the law of God, we allowed it [this suggestion] to gain entrance and sold ourselves to sin. For this reason our body is easily brought to sin. Hence, the odor and sense of sin which is inherent in our body, that is to say, the desire and pleasure of the body, is also called a law in the members of our flesh."[27]

Again, the body plays an essential role in the law of sin, yet John's affirmation is that the primary referent for the "law of sin" is not the body

---

26. The passage appears to be based on Maximus, *Dispute with Pyrrhus* (PG 91:293C), in *Dispute de Maxime le Confesseur avec Pyrrhus: Introduction, Texte Critique, Traduction et Notes*, vol. 2, trans. Marrcel Doucet (unpublished diss. at Institut d'Études Médiévales, University of Montréal, 1972). In that passage, Maximus is dealing with a technical distinction between "habit" and "energy" that seems to be lost on John. This distinction is treated in Philipp Gabriel Renczes, *Agir de Dieu et Liberté de l'Homme: Récherches sur l'Anthropologie Théologique de Saint Maxime le Confesseur* (Paris: Éditions du Cerf, 2003), especially 267–80. Since John does not know the distinction between "habit" and "energy," he uses the opportunity to insert another explanation that happens to reflect another Maximian theme.

27. *DFO* IV 22 (PG 94:1197C-1200B) in *Writings*, 388–89, translation modified.

or its desires, but *the devil's suggestion*, repeated as the "suggestion of the evil one." The rest of the passage quoted above describes how Adam's sin brought about this dominion of the devil in the human body. Whereas prior to the Fall the devil's suggestion was exterior, after the Fall, the devil's suggestion "gains entrance" into our body and becomes as if interior. This intimate relationship between the passions and the devil is overlooked in Gondreau's assessment of the passions in John's work.

It is worth noting, as a concluding observation, that this passage is somewhat weakened in Burgundio's translation. While Burgundio maintains "τοῦ διαβόλου προσβολῆς" as "*diaboli immissionem*," the strong overtones of personification in "ἡ προσβολὴ τοῦ πονηροῦ" are weakened to "*immissio perniciosi*" at the moment this suggestion is identified with the law of sin.[28] Thus, the law of sin in Burgundio's translation is not as quickly or as easily identifiable with the suggestion of the devil as it is in John's text. While this change is perhaps small in itself, it is indicative of how later Latin readers of John's text will interpret this law of sin.

John of Damascus on Christ's Temptation by the Devil through the Passions

I consider next how John relates this preceding anthropology of demonic temptation to Christ's moral life. First, I address John's denial of choice in Christ; second, I consider John's soteriological claims about Christ's natural and blameless passions and their relationship with demonic activity.

Despite the fact that John recognizes choice as an essential characteristic of human nature, John's Christological reflections on this

---

28. Burgundio's version of *DFO* IV 22 is found in *Fide*, 358–59. Burgundio uses forms of "pernicious" to refer to the devil elsewhere, so the close reader would understand the demonic overtones of the phrase. Without this careful reading of Burgundio's use of "pernicious," the reader could easily be misled to understand that this suggestion originates *within* the subject without any relationship to demonic activity, whereas John's text more closely identifies the source of the suggestion as exterior. The editors of Burgundio's version place "perniciosi" in quotation marks to indicate a quotation of another source, but none of the Vulgate verses that are cited use this word. I have been unable to locate a clear reason why this word is identified as a quotation by the editors.

subject deny such choice in Christ. John precedes this denial with a reflection on the denial of choice in God:

> While we speak of wishing in God, in the strict sense we do not speak of choice. For God does not deliberate, because deliberation is due to ignorance. No one deliberates about what he knows. But, if deliberation is due to ignorance, then choice, too, is most certainly so. Hence, since God knows all things absolutely, He does not deliberate.[29]

John's reasoning connects a lack of choice with a fullness of knowledge; one deliberates only about unknown things. For precisely this same reason, John denies choice in Christ:

> Neither do we speak of deliberation or choice in the soul of the Lord, because He did not suffer from ignorance. Even though He did have such a nature as was ignorant of future events, nevertheless, in so far as this nature was hypostatically united to God the Word, it did have knowledge of all things—not by grace, but, as has been said, by virtue of the hypostatic union. Thus He was Himself both God and man, and therefore did not have a will based upon opinion. He did have a will that was natural and simple and such as is to be found in all human persons, but His sacred soul held no opinion, that is to say, willed nothing contrary to His divine will, nor did it have a will in opposition to His divine will.[30]

While John's account of choice in Christ reflects some strains of Maximus's account, John's version flattens Maximus's account. Maximus, too, links his strong qualification of choice in Christ to Christ's fullness of knowledge, but Maximus remains willing to speak of an "immutable choice" in Christ in the midst of this qualification. In this way, I argued in chapter 3 for a transformative assumption of choice that renders something intrinsically unstable into something absolutely immutable—that is, Christ institutes a new (and oxymoronic) mode of choice. Maximus maintained this apophatic approach in part to avoid speculation about humanity's eschatological condition. Most notably, though, such an account keeps Maximus's distinction be-

---

29. *DFO* II 22 (PG 94:945C-D) in *Writings*, 250. Burgundio's version is found in *Fide*, 139.
30. *DFO* II 22 (PG 94:948A) in *Writings*, 250. Burgundio's version is found in *Fide*, 139. One can also find this denial at *DFO* III 14 (PG 94:1044B-1045A) in *Writings*, 302.

tween *logos* (λόγος) and *tropos* (τρόπος) intact by affirming the essential constitutional elements of human nature in Christ while allowing for their inner transformation in the incarnation.

John's complete denial of choice in Christ resolves the issue in a different way than Maximus had. On the one hand, John recognizes in his anthropological material that choice is an intrinsic component of the human moral act in this life; on the other hand, John feels compelled to deny this otherwise essential human capacity in Christ. Such a combination potentially commits an Apollinarian error, denying Christ's full and consubstantial humanity. If one interprets John so as to avoid such a conclusion, however, John's resolution appears to require that choice *not* pertain to the essence of human nature and that Christ shows humankind how it will exist in the next life, not how it is now.[31] Any resolution here must be reconstructed out of John's claims; neither in his anthropological material nor in his Christological material does John attempt to address this apparent difference between the humanity of Christ and that of every other human being.

In the remaining consideration of John's thought, I examine the way John relates the demonic to passibility in Christ's experience in the key text of *DFO* III 20. First, I outline John's Christological synecdoche and, second, turn to the importance for John of Christ's *voluntary* experience of the passions.

John's reflections on Christ's humanity in *DFO* III 20 echo Maximus's affirmation that Christ took on parts of the prelapsarian and postlapsarian conditions of human nature, so that Christ might redeem each of those states or conditions. For John, as for Maximus, the aspects of each condition present in Christ act by synecdoche, making each condition virtually present in Christ through the presence of some part of each. Notably, however, John modifies Maximus's arrangement of the content of the representative elements of each condition. For John, the postlapsarian condition is made present through the presence of the "natural and blameless passions" in Christ (through which the devil attacks him), whereas the prelapsarian con-

---

31. Thomas may in fact be closer to Maximus's claims regarding choice than he is to John's. See *Summa Theologica* (*ST*) III 18.4.

dition is made present by Christ's immunity to demonic thoughts.

As already established, John believes that the sin of Adam introduced a new state of life, characterized both by the demonic "law of sin" as well as the "natural and blameless passions" through which the devil seeks to arouse sin. When discussing the moral conditions of Christ's life, John affirms these fallen conditions to have been Christ's own: "Moreover, we confess that He assumed all the natural and blameless passions of man."[32] These natural and blameless passions are not some prelapsarian form of affectivity: they "are not under our control and have come into man's life as a result of the condemnation occasioned by his fall."[33] I show in a moment that these passions in Christ are closely associated with the activity of the devil.

On the other hand, John makes the prelapsarian state present in Christ when he denies that one aspect of the moral conditions of the fallen state is present in Christ. John argues that Christ identifies with the unfallen Adam by taking on an imperviousness to temptation through demonic thoughts:

[Christ] assumed all that He might sanctify all. He was put to the test and He conquered that He might gain for us the victory and give to our nature the power to conquer the Adversary, so that through the very assaults by which the nature had been conquered of old it might conquer its former victor.

Now, the Evil One attacked [Christ] from the outside, just as he had with Adam, and not through thoughts [λογισμῶν]—for it was not through thoughts that he attacked Adam, but through the serpent. The Lord, however, repelled the attack and it vanished like smoke, so that the passions [πάθη] which had assailed Him and were conquered might become easy for us to conquer and the new Adam thus restore the old.[34]

---

32. *DFO* III 20 (PG 94:1081A-B) in *Writings*, 323, translation modified.

33. *DFO* III 20 (PG 94:1081B) in *Writings*, 323. Burgundio's version here reads: "Naturales autem et indetractibiles passiones sunt, quae non in nobis quaecumque ex ea quae per transgressionem condemnatione in humanam devenere vitam" (*Fide*, 259). "Indetractible" maintains the sense of the morally blameless quality of these passions yet has a semantic range that affects its reception by Aquinas, who interprets the term as "unable to be taken away" instead of "not blameworthy." See chapter 6 below.

34. *DFO* III 20 (PG 94:1081C) in *Writings*, 324, translation modified. Burgundio's version is found in *Fide*, 260.

In order to sort out the synecdoche of this passage carefully, the relationship between "thoughts" and "passions" requires clarification. John contrasts thoughts with "external" temptations and equally denies the demonic use of thoughts in Christ's temptation, which by contrast would be "internal" temptations. In denying demonic thoughts, Christ's temptation was extrinsic for John, and insofar as thoughts are a foundation of the devil's attack after the Fall, John argues that Christ's temptation conforms to a decidedly prelapsarian condition.

Yet John describes Christ's passions as "attacking" him, in conjunction with the devil's attack. Given John's insistence that the law of sin in human beings *is* the devil's attack (and not merely an anthropological disorder), the attack of the passions is coordinated through the devil's intervention. In that way, John views the passions as sufficiently extrinsic to the human moral life that they can blamelessly "attack" Christ as instruments of the devil. This affirmation sits well with Maximus's approach to Christ's temptation. One should note, however, that the way John describes thoughts has no apparent parallel in Maximus's approach. Maximus makes no such distinction between passion and thought when discussing the assault of the devil against Christ.

In this respect, Gondreau's assessment that, in the Damascene, Christ's "psychological strengths precluded any kind of temptation arising from disordered interior movements" is misleading.[35] Most notably, it is unlikely that Gondreau's analysis can account for John's affirmation that Christ was *attacked* by or through the passions. John's reasoning hinges on the proper arrangement of unfallen and fallen aspects of Christ's temptation and not, per se, on an affirmation that "no such rebellious conflict assailed Jesus' interior life."[36]

Relative to Maximus, John's distinction between passions and thoughts grants a larger place to the unfallen state in Christ's humanity. Conversely, Christ's contact with the postlapsarian conditions of

---

35. Gondreau, *Passions of Christ's Soul*, 64. The difficulty in Gondreau's claim is simply that "disordered interior movements" is not native to John's thought; the claim is misleading insofar as it confuses John's categories with Aquinas's. What for Aquinas is "interior" (the passions) is for John an "exterior" attack.

36. Gondreau, *Passions of Christ's Soul*, 64.

temptation is necessarily more limited. As this distinction will continue to be drawn out by John's medieval Latin commentators (especially Peter the Lombard), one will see an ongoing the attempt to negotiate what aspects of Christ's humanity fittingly share the fallen condition and which do not. The later medieval tendency will be to reduce further Christ's synecdochal contact with the fallen condition.

Concerning the voluntary character of Christ's passions, *DFO* III 20 develops a point of particular importance because of the impact it has on later medieval thought. In continuity with some of Maximus's reflections on Christ's assumption of passibility, John takes care to clarify that Christ's experience of passibility was not one *forced* on him as it is with other human beings:

> For with Him nothing is found to be done under compulsion [ἠναγκασμένον]; on the contrary, everything was done freely [πάντα ἑκούσια]. Thus, it was by willing that He hungered and by willing that He thirsted, by willing that He was afraid and by willing that He died.[37]

To deny Christ's *voluntary* experience of human nature in its entirety would simultaneously risk the absolute freedom of the divine will and the perfect obedience of the human will in the incarnation. In the two chapters of *DFO* preceding the one under investigation here, John had spent significant time elaborating the relationship between the human and divine will in Christ. It is surprising, in light of this previous context, that John does not provide greater clarity about what is proper to each will—human and divine—in this voluntary experience of passion. In *DFO* III 20, it makes the most sense that John was speaking primarily of the *human* will of Christ, yet his earlier discussion of dyothelitism makes this interpretation less likely. One finds in John's previous discussion of Christ's wills that

> since the same one was both God and man, He willed according to His divine and His human will.... For His divine will was without beginning and all-creating and having the corresponding power, and it was impassible. But

---

37. *DFO* III 20 (PG 94:1084A) in *Writings*, 324. Gondreau is correct to insist on this aspect of the Damascene's thought; it is an important and original addition to later reflections on Christ.

his human will had a beginning in time and *was itself subject to natural and blameless passions* [τὰ φυσικὰ καὶ ἀδιάβλητα πάθη].[38]

Thus, while the divine and human wills cooperate in Christ and agree in all things, each has properties that are distinct to each, affecting the way in which each will acts. Thus, John states that Christ's *human* will experiences a sort of submission to the natural passions, which indicates that, even if the submission is still voluntary in a sense, the natural passions are logically prior to the command of the will. John again distinguishes between the two wills, saying:

> When the flesh is acting, the divine nature is associated with it because the flesh is being permitted by the good pleasure of the divine will [διὰ τὸ εὐδοκίᾳ τῆς θείας θελήσεως παραχωρεῖσθαι] to suffer and do what is proper to it.[39]

Here, indeed, it appears that absolute preeminence over the passions is reserved to the "good pleasure" of the divine will—not, in an absolute sense, to the human will of Christ. In light of these statements, what John says in *DFO* III 20 requires more precision: Does John mean to say that Jesus has an absolute authority as human over his passions? For instance, could Jesus, as human, simply turn off the natural and blameless passions? Or is the absolute freedom over the passions more appropriately assigned primarily to the divine will, considered from the eternal decision to take on flesh and thus logically prior to the incarnation? Later scholastic reflection, including that of Thomas, will continue to dwell on the voluntary quality of Christ's human passions.

✣

Four significant results rise out of this consideration of the *DFO*. First, John reproduces the structure of the moral act recounted by Maximus. This structure is, by and large, accurately conveyed by both John and Burgundio, though John modifies what was for Maximus the *natural* quality of wish, rendering it apparently indifferent to humanity's final end. Second, John hands on Maximus's association between the

---

38. *DFO* III 18 (PG 94:1076D-1077A) in *Writings*, 321.
39. *DFO* III 19 (PG 94:1080B) in *Writings*, 322.

devil and the passions in his anthropological consideration of the "law of sin," though this association is somewhat weakened in Burgundio's translation. For John, the deepest moral ambiguity of the passions is seen in the suggestion of the devil that occurs through them; for Burgundio, a more purely anthropological reading of this passage in his Latin text is possible. Third, John somewhat flattens Maximus's understanding of choice in Christ. Maximus, for his part, was highly ambivalent on this point, and it comes as no surprise that John felt the need to resolve this ambivalence. In so doing, John rules out the possibility of a transformed mode of choice that Maximus's own account leaves on the table. Fourth and finally, while John himself largely understood the synecdochal character of Maximus's reflection on the Fall and incarnation, John rearranges the aspects of Christ's experience that represent the fallen and unfallen conditions, somewhat reducing Christ's contact with the fallen experience of temptation. This modification, in turn, affects the way that his readers would think about the experience of temptation that Christ would have undergone.

Western Patristic Thought on Christ's Temptation by the Devil

In this section, I consider matters relevant to Christ's demonic temptation in the writings of Augustine of Hippo and Gregory the Great. In each of these authors, the influence on Thomas Aquinas is explicit; they are by far the two most commonly-cited sources in Aquinas's theory of demonic temptation.[40] I treat them in historical order and consider their respective relevant anthropological and Christological claims.

---

40. Since the subject of this study is demonic temptation, I cannot include consideration of Thomas's broader demonology in its cosmological aspects. Another source—Hilary of Poitiers—could also be added here. While his thought is relevant in certain respects, Hilary has already received adequate treatment in other recent works. Essentially, Hilary's anti-Arian polemics led him to certain troubling Christological affirmations that tended to deny Christ's experience of the passions. Stoic articulations of Christ's affectivity throughout the medieval Latin world are often indebted to Hilary's general rejection of passion from Christ. See Gondreau, *Passions of Christ's Soul*, 48–51, and Nicholas E. Lombardo, *The Logic of Desire: Aquinas on Emotion* (Washington, D.C.: The Catholic University of America Press, 2011), 201–2.

Augustine of Hippo

No Christian source is more important for Aquinas's account of demonic temptation than Augustine, who far exceeds other such sources in the sheer number of Thomas's references in questions that treat the devil. Further, Aquinas's discussion of demons in *De Malo* is largely shaped by questions raised and answered in Augustine's works. Many of those questions do not directly impact the subject of this study, yet some of them merit discussion here. In what follows, I review how Augustine believes humankind fell into the power of the devil; what power the devil is understood to hold "within" the human subject; whether the elect (those destined for heaven) are also subject to this internal temptation; and what Augustine believed concerning Christ's temptation by the devil in relation to the temptation experienced by other humans after the Fall.

First, Augustine understands that the sin of Adam entails certain consequences for the rest of humankind. Beyond Augustine's well-known development and refinement of the concept of original sin and its concomitant disordered concupiscence, he also articulates consequences of Adam's sin that lie strictly in the realm of demonology.[41] Augustine most commonly speaks of the postlapsarian dominion of the devil as entailing human death, but in some passages, he considers new methods of demonic temptation that arose specifically after the Fall. With Adam's sin, the devil had

as it were acquired full property rights over [man], and being himself liable to no corruption of flesh and blood had held [man] in thrall in his weakness and poverty and the frailness of this mortal body.[42]

---

41. For some of the relevant secondary literature, see J. Patout Burns, "Augustine on the Origin and Progress of Evil," *Journal of Religious Ethics* 16, no. 1 (1988): 9–27 (for a discussion of the condition of the repentability of Adam's sin); Francois Vandenbroucke, "Démon," in *Dictionnaire de Spiritualité*, vol. 3, ed. Charles Baumgartner, 218–19 (Paris: Beauchesne, 1957); E. Mangenot, "Démon," in *Dictionnaire de Théologie Catholique*, vol. 4, ed. E. Amann, 379–80 (Paris: Librairie Letouzey et Ané, 1908); Joseph F. Kelly, "The Devil in Augustine's Genesis Commentaries," *Studia Patristica* 33 (1997): 119–24; and David Scott-Macnab, "St. Augustine and the Devil's 'Mousetrap,'" *Vigiliae Christianae* 68 (2014): 409–15.

42. Augustine, *De Trinitate*, IV 3.17, in Augustine, *The Trinity*, trans. Edmund Hill (Brooklyn, N.Y.: New City Press, 1991), 165.

In addition to the connection of demonic powers with mortality, the devil is also seen here as responsible for humanity's "weakness" and "poverty."[43] Thus, the devil's influence extends beyond the rule of death over humanity and extends in some way into the inner workings of human nature.

Augustine specifies in various passages the nature of that dominion. Concerning what demons are able to produce in the human mind, Augustine's view of demonic influence bears some similarity to forms encountered in chapter 1. Spirits can impress sensory data onto human minds that are intended to lead to sin:

> But sometimes ... some interference by another spirit, whether a bad or a good one, will impress the images of bodily realities on the spirit as strongly as if the bodies themselves were being presented to the senses of the body, full consciousness still remaining in these same senses; and then the images of bodies being produced in the spirit are being seen just like the bodies themselves seen through the body.[44]

A pseudo-Augustinian text (in fact written by Gennadius) called the *Liber Ecclesiasticorum Dogmatum* pronounces on the ubiquity of demonic activity in the mind. Aquinas cites this text as authentically Augustinian, so I briefly mention Gennadius's view here.[45] One finds that

> Not all of our evil thoughts are [always] excited by the influence of the devil, but sometimes emerge from the movement of our free will: but good thoughts are always from God.[46]

---

43. This relationship is sometimes quite remote, meaning that the devil only brings about human inclination toward evil by his original temptation of Adam. See Augustine, *Earlier Writings*, trans. John H. S. Burleigh (Philadelphia: Westminster Press, 1953), 205, and in a similar vein, Augustine, *De Trinitate* IV 15 in *Trinity*, 163. Beyond mortality, then, the devil is, for Augustine, remotely responsible for reducing humanity to a "state of misery" that is described as "burdensome duties" and as "difficulty of well-doing."

44. Augustine, *Literal Commentary on Genesis* XII 25, in Augustine, *On Genesis*, trans. Edmund Hill (Hyde Park, N.Y.: New City Press, 2002), 476–77. See also *Book of 83 Questions* XII, in Augustine, *Responses to Miscellaneous Questions*, trans. Boniface Ramsey (Hyde Park, N.Y.: New City Press, 2008), 35.

45. Aquinas cites this text at ST I-II 80.4.

46. Gennadius, "Liber Ecclesiasticorum Dogmatum," §48–49, *Journal of Theological Studies* 7 (October 1905): 78–99, my translation. Gennadius's view of the origin of evil thoughts, if perhaps not formally in contradiction with Evagrius, certainly emphasizes a different understanding of thoughts than that seen in the early Greek ascetic literature (see chapter 1). Gennadius, for his part, considers that evil thoughts *can* come from the devil, but he does not consider demons to have an exclusive role in their origin.

While this text cannot be relevant to Augustine's own mind on the question, the practical consequences of this pseudo-Augustinian text for medieval accounts of demonic temptation are significant. If evil thoughts come from the devil (as for Evagrius, for instance), one's proper response is resistance and struggle, but if they arise from the will, the appropriate response also includes repentance and contrition. This need for contrition is further expanded by Augustine's articulation of disordered concupiscence, which will be described in the later medieval period as the *fomes peccati*. Articulated in entirely anthropological categories, Augustine's internally divisive view of disordered concupiscence inculpates the person who experiences this desire and puts the individual in direct conflict with their own desires. Such an arrangement draws the boundaries of spiritual conflict in significantly different ways than the ascetic spirituality of the first half of this project. Thus, the Augustinian tradition inherited by the medieval scholastics implies a different spiritual pedagogy of internal spiritual struggle than the early Greek monastic traditions. While the devil's interior action is affirmed in Augustine, this tradition comes to recognize that an individual can be (and, indeed, is usually) directly responsible for evil thoughts so that internal division and guilt become bound to the experience of such thoughts.

A more characteristic interest in Augustine's authentic works on demonic temptation is how demons become aware of humanity's own inner states, as it is only by carefully assessing our own mental states that the devil is able to suggest the appropriate temptations.[47] In his earlier writings, Augustine believes he understands this process well, but in his *Retractions* he admits that the means of this knowledge are obscure and difficult for humans to know. Somewhere between his most confident and most reserved statements on the subject, Augustine says in his *Literal Commentary on Genesis* that

---

47. In chapter 1, Evagrius also showed interest in the question of the means by which demons know human thought. Augustine, for his part, spends much more time on it. The relationship between demons and magicians (seen, for instance, in the *Book of 83 Questions* LXXIX and in *De Trinitate* III 2) is a theme that Evagrius did not consider at all. However, it is a theme that features prominently in Aquinas's demonology, especially in the *De Malo*.

It is difficult to find out and explain how these spiritual likenesses of bodily realities in our spirits become known even to unclean spirits, or what kind of obstacle our souls experience from these earthly bodies, so that we are unable in our turn to see them in our own spirits. These [coming examples] have, all the same, been the most definite and certain indications to establish that what people have been thinking has been made public by demons.[48]

In his earliest writings, his best guess is that demons are able to extrapolate from very fine movements of our bodies what our mental state might be. The temperature of our skin and other bodily effects that are imperceptible to human beings are within the grasp of the demons. That information gives them an indication of their victim's mental state.[49] While in the later *Retractions* Augustine remains confident that demons *can* learn of our interior states of mind, he becomes fairly agnostic about the means by which this knowledge is possible.[50]

These sorts of temptation apply particularly to the conditions of humanity after the Fall. Moreover, Augustine indicates that not everyone necessarily suffers the worst of these temptations. For instance, while God sometimes allows the devil to afflict the good or elect for a time,[51] God prevents the devil from afflicting the elect from within:

> The Omnipotent did not debar him [the Devil] altogether from putting the saints to the test; but he threw out the Devil from their inner man, the seat of belief in God, so that they might profit from his outward assault.[52]

Similarly, in the *De Trinitate*, Augustine speaks of Christ's role in this prevention:

---

48. *Book of 83 Questions* XII, in Augustine, *Responses*, 35. He expresses a little more hesitancy on this question in another early work, his *Literal Commentary on Genesis* XII 34, in Augustine, *On Genesis*, 482.
49. See, for instance, *Demonic Divination*, §7, 9, and 10, in Augustine, *On Christian Belief*, trans. Matthew O'Connell (Hyde Park, N.Y.: New City Press, 2005), 211, as well as his *Literal Commentary on Genesis* XII 25, in Augustine, *On Genesis*, 476–77.
50. Augustine, *Retractions*, §56, in Augustine, *The Retractions*, trans. Mary Inez Bogan (Washington, D.C.: The Catholic University of America Press, 1968), 180–83.
51. Augustine, *Book of 83 Questions* LXXIX 5, in Augustine, *Responses*, 147.
52. Augustine, *City of God* XX 8, in Augustine, *Concerning the City of God against the Pagans*, trans. Henry Bettenson (Harmondsworth: Penguin Books, 1972), 910–14.

the true mediator of life ... has cast that dead spirit and mediator of death out of the spirits of those who believe in him, so now that one no longer reigns inside them, but only attacks them from the outside without being able to overthrow them.⁵³

Both of these passages indicate an exemption of the elect from a particular consequence of sin. The instances of demonic assault against the elect that *are* permitted are pedagogical and external; only those who are not elect are punitively attacked by the devil. Thus, Augustine holds that if one is elect, the devil is withheld from his most interior forms of attack. This distinction between "interior" and "exterior" attack—and its correlation to the reprobate and elect—is significantly different than the temptations from "within" and "without" that I described in chapter 2.

Augustine elsewhere considers the Christological and soteriological basis for the freedom of the elect from inner demonic temptation.⁵⁴ Immediately following the passage just quoted, Augustine elaborates the Christological consequences of that distinction in different forms of temptation: the "true one," Christ,

also allowed himself to be tempted by him, in order to be a mediator for overcoming his temptations by way of example as well as by way of assistance. For when the devil was driven off after attempting to insinuate himself by every entry into the inner citadel of Christ, after the one dead in spirit had completed every seductive temptation in the desert after the baptism, and had failed

---

53. Augustine, *De Trinitate*, IV 3.17, in *Trinity*, 164. For another angle, see *De Trinitate* III 14, 136.

54. Some recent scholars have emphasized the relative scarcity of Augustine's explicitly Christological writings; Augustine was not himself embroiled in Christological controversy as were many of his Greek-speaking contemporaries. For various discussions of Augustine's Christology, see Brian E. Daley, "A Humble Mediator: The Distinctive Elements in Saint Augustine's Christology," in *Word and Spirit: A Monastic Review* 9 (1987): 100–117; Walter H. Principe, "Some Examples of Augustine's Influence on Medieval Christology," in *Collectanea Augustiniana* (Leuven: Leuven University Press, 1990), 955–74; David R. Maxwell, "What Was 'Wrong' with Augustine: The Sixth-Century Reception (or Lack Thereof) of Augustine's Christology," in *In the Shadow of the Incarnation: Essays on Jesus Christ in the Early Church in Honor of Brian E. Daley*, ed. Peter W. Martens, 212–27 (Notre Dame, Ind.: University of Notre Dame Press, 2008); Rowan Douglass Williams, "Augustine's Christology: Its Spirituality and Rhetoric," in *In the Shadow of the Incarnation*, 176–89; and Lewis Ayres, "Christology as Contemplative Practice: Understanding the Union of Natures in Augustine's Letter 137," in *In the Shadow of the Incarnation*, 190–211.

to force an entry into the living spirit, being avid for human death in any shape or form he turned his attention to procuring the only death which he was able and permitted to, the death of that mortal element which the living mediator had received from us. And precisely there, where he was able really to do something, was he well and truly routed; and *by his receiving the exterior authority to strike down the Lord's flesh, the interior authority by which he held us captive was itself struck down.*[55]

The last line is a striking aspect of Augustine's soteriology that stands in contrast to Maximus's Christology. For Augustine, in order to undo the sort of temptations from within that constitute the *inner* authority of the devil over human beings after the Fall, Christ needed only to submit to an *exterior* authority of the devil over his human flesh in his mortality. The particular sovereignty by which the devil had bound (non-elect) humanity did not bind Christ.[56] Christ's temptation is not itself held to reverse the devil's power; Augustine treats only Christ's death (wherein the devil is granted an 'external' authority over Christ's body) as destroying the devil's dominion. Further, Christ's temptation, while certainly like that of Adam and the elect, did not take the particular interior and punitive form that it takes for those who are not elect. Thus, for Augustine, the affirmation of Christ's "being tempted like us in all things" depends on the identity of the "us" under consideration. Since some forms of demonic temptation are only punitively assigned to the reprobate, Christ did not need to experience them.[57]

Gregory the Great

Gregory the Great is also among Aquinas's explicit citations in his questions on demonic temptation.[58] While perhaps not as structur-

---

55. Augustine, *De Trinitate* IV 3.17, in *Trinity*, 164–65, emphasis added.

56. This arrangement is discussed in Gert Partoens and Dominic Dupont, "*Sed de quo peccato?* Augustine's exegesis of Rom 8:3 in *sermo* 152, 9–11," in *Vigiliae Christianae* 66 (2012): 190–212, and Dominic Keech, *The Anti-Pelagian Christology of Augustine of Hippo 396–430* (Oxford: Oxford University Press, 2012). The latter work argues that the tensions in Augustine's Christology between "fallenness" and "unfallenness" are never satisfactorily resolved.

57. Perhaps, in this sense, the Synod of Dort correctly understood Augustine: Christ's life only shares in and atones for that form of life experienced by the elect. In this soteriological matter, Augustine's theory of atonement is accurately described as limited.

58. For a close and sustained consideration of Gregory the Great's demonology, see Charlotte

ally significant for Aquinas as Augustine, Gregory's thought on the devil's attack certainly shapes later medieval reflection on temptation. Gregory's thought about demons, found in greatest density in his *Morals on Job*, reflects themes from Augustine while differing on details of the devil's temptation of the elect. I discuss Gregory's theory of the stages of sin, demonic temptations of the elect and of the reprobate, the moral psychology implicit in Gregory's account of demonic temptation, and some soteriological aspects of his position.

Gregory's theory of the "stages" of sin—inherited from Augustine—is highly influential on medieval moral psychology.[59] Gregory explains this theory in a number of works, including the *Morals on Job*, the *Pastoral Rule*, and the *Gospel Homilies*. There are three constant components in his presentation of the progress of a sinful act: suggestion, pleasure, and consent. Gregory often couches this terminology in an exegesis of Genesis 3, where the serpent, Eve, and Adam respectively represent each of the three stages.[60] The purpose of the theory, ostensibly, is ascetic, helping the reader to recognize and cut off sin as early as possible before it has the chance to gain power over the soul.[61] Curiously, Gregory uses the term *peccatum* to denote each of these three stages, but this use should not be understood as denoting that an individual is morally responsible or culpable for all three stages.[62] Gregory certainly never means to assign moral blame in the

---

Emily Kingston, *The Devil in the Writings and Thought of Pope Gregory the Great (590–604)* (Unpublished diss., University of York, Department of History, 2011), especially 79–89

59. For the dependency of Gregory on Augustine for his understanding of temptation, see Carole Straw, "Gregory's Moral Theology," in *A Companion to Gregory the Great*, ed. Bronwen Neil and Matthew J. Dal Santo, 188 (Boston: Brill Publishers, 2013). See also André Godin, "Tentation," in *Dictionnaire de Spiritualité*, vol. 15, ed. A. Derville, P. Lamarche and A. Solignac, 235 (Paris: Beauchesne, 1991) and with the article on Gregory in *Dictionnaire de Spiritualité*, vol. 6, ed. A. Derville, P. Lamarche, and A. Solignac, 888–90 (Paris: Beauchesne, 1991).

60. See Gregory's *Moralia* IV 49 (CCSL 143:193) in Gregory the Great, *Morals on the Book of Job*, vol. 1 (3 vols.) (London: John Henry Parker, 1844–1850), 215, and *Pastoral Rule* III 29, in Gregory the Great, *The Book of the Pastoral Rule*, trans. George E. Demacopoulos (Crestwood, N.Y.: St. Vladimir's Seminary Press, 2007), 179–83. The Latin of the *Moralia* is found in CCSL 143b. Gregory occasionally adds a fourth stage that is not relevant to my present concerns; it is called the "boldness to defend."

61. See also Straw, "Gregory's Moral Theology," 198, for the pedagogical purpose of Gregory's distinctions.

62. Gregory, *Moralia* IV 49 (CCSL 143:193) in Gregory, *Morals*, vol. 1, 215, where he states that sin "is committed by the suggestion, the pleasure, the consent, and the boldness to defend"; see also *Pastoral Rule* III 29, in Gregory, *Rule*, 179–83.

first stage to the one tempted. In the case of this suggestion, the "sin" is metaphorical, external, and in no sense culpable. The third stage is equally clear in the opposite direction; when Adam consented to eat, the spiritual sin is completed and is clearly culpable. However, an ambiguity enters in the middle stage—that of pleasure—because Gregory is unclear about where the conscious ability to prevent such pleasure enters and, equivalently, about when culpability becomes possible.[63] Particularly important is the question of the devil's relationship to pleasure in the soul. While Gregory is clear that (after the Fall) pleasure resides in the flesh, a further distinction is needed in order to understand how Gregory thinks demons might directly elicit the second stage of pleasure.[64]

Augustine, as seen earlier, argues that the elect are providentially protected by God from certain forms of temptation by the devil, so that the devil is permitted to attack them only from the outside. Gregory modifies this arrangement, allowing some form of "inner" attack of the devil to take place against both the reprobate and the elect. Concerning the reprobate, Gregory's moral interpretation of a certain "beast" (understood as the devil or Antichrist) reaches the conclusion that the devil "abides [*possidet*]" in the mind of the wicked, since they welcome his evil suggestions. The reprobate become the "den" of the devil because the attacks that are permitted lead the reprobate happily into the commission of sin:

For he doubtless abides in and occupies the minds of those, whom he possesses as his own den: because he first leads on their thoughts to wicked desires [*prius in eis cogitationes usque ad iniqua desideria ... perducit*], and afterwards leads their wicked desires even to the commission of most sinful deeds. For the reprobate do not endeavour to repel, with the upright hand of judgment, the suggestions of him, to whose wishes they desire to yield, by submissive delight. And when any evil thought arises in their hearts, it

63. For a not completely satisfying account of human culpability for the three stages, see F. Homes Dudden, *Gregory the Great: His Place in History and Thought* (New York: Russell & Russell, 1905), 385. Two other works also ignore Gregory's affirmations in the *Moralia* about the devil's power to elicit passion: Vanderbroucke, "Démon" in *Dictionnaire de Spiritualité*, vol. 3, 219, and Mangenot, "Démon" in *Dictionnaire de Théologie Catholique*, vol. 4, 381.
64. Dudden, *Gregory the Great*, 379–84, does not satisfactorily address this question.

is cherished at once by the eagerness of delight; and when no resistance is made to him, he is strengthened immediately by consent, and consent is instantly carried into outward act, but outward act is also made worse by habit.[65]

The three stages are present in this arrangement; Gregory here uses "thoughts" and "suggestions" from the devil interchangeably. However, the true extent of the devil's power is somewhat obscured in the case of those who openly cooperate with his suggestions.

The elect, therefore, become important for Gregory's conception of the devil's power in relation to thoughts, suggestions, and desires. Gregory's language indicates that the elect are not immune from the devil's inner attack. Unlike Augustine, Gregory argues that God does not categorically prevent the devil from attacking the good as he does the wicked. Rather, the key difference between the elect and reprobate for Gregory is that the devil is not allowed to "abide" in the elect:

> But I think it ought to be specially observed, that this beast is said, not only to enter his den, but to abide therein. For he sometimes enters even the minds of the good, he suggests unlawful thoughts, he wearies them with temptations, he endeavours to turn aside the uprightness of the spirit to the pleasure of the flesh; he also strives to carry out delight as far as to consent [*delectationem quoque ad consensum perducere nititur*]: but yet he is kept from prevailing by the opposition of aid from on high. He can enter therefore into the minds of the good [*Intrare ergo in mentes bonorum potest*], but cannot abide therein, because the heart of the righteous is not the den of this beast.[66]

Certainly, God (and perhaps the angelic hosts) comes to the aid of the elect in allowing them to succeed over these demonic attacks, but the fact remains that the devil can and does attack even the good by entering into their minds.[67] The morally relevant difference between

---

65. *Moralia*, Book XXVII 50 (CCSL 143B:1370) in Gregory, *Morals*, vol. 3.1, 237–39. The lot of the reprobate is discussed in the preceding paragraph, *Moralia* XXVII 49 (CCSL 143B:1369) in Gregory, *Morals*, vol. 3.1, 236–37.

66. Gregory, *Moralia* XXVII 50 (CCSL 143B:1370) in Gregory, *Morals*, vol. 3.1, 237–39. See also *Moralia* XIV 46 (CCSL 143A:725–27) in Gregory, *Morals*, vol. 2, 147; text quoted in Alexander of Hales, *Summa* II.II.II 1.1.3.2, in Alexander of Hales, *Summa Theologica*, vol. 3, ed. P. Bonaventurae Marrani (Florentiae: Typographia Collegii S. Bonaventurae, 1930), 181.

67. Gregory's views on this matter may be in continuity with Eastern Origenistic demonology,

the elect and the reprobate does not appear to pertain to the *means* or "depth" of temptation that the devil uses against them. Rather, it is the response that they have to these various forms of temptation (whereby the devil either is cast out or remains) that redounds to their moral praise or blame.

Accordingly, Gregory does not always assign blame to the *temporary* internal attack of the devil when perpetrated against the elect. Much like what was seen in Maximus in chapter 2, Gregory does not see the attack of the devil as intrinsically morally culpable. He assigns to the devil an ability to place evil thoughts in the elect, but there is some lack of clarity about whether *desires* or pleasures are also placed in the mind by the devil.[68] At times, Gregory appears to argue that the devil cannot do so. Gregory, referring to the three stages, states that

since sin is admitted in three ways, namely, when it is perpetrated by the suggestion of the serpent, with the pleasure of the flesh, with the consent of the spirit; [therefore] this Behemoth first puts forth his tongue suggesting unlawful thoughts, afterwards alluring to delight, he infixes his tooth, but lastly, gaining possession by consent, he clenches his tail.[69]

From the context, this second "delight" is only possible when the one attacked has "carelessly allowed" the first suggestion to gain strength, indicating that there is some minor fault involved.[70] This vein of Gregory's thought is repeated by many voices in the medieval tradition (such as Alexander of Hales, below), who in turn argue that the devil can *only* independently suggest thoughts of evil, not evil desires.

---

thanks in part to John Cassian. See Vandenbroucke, "Démon" in *Dictionnaire de Spiritualité*, vol. 3, 208–10, and Straw, "Gregory's Moral Theology," 199–200, and 199, n. 139.

68. For another passage that could be read as both anthropological/subjective and demonological/objective, see *Moralia* VIII 8 (CCSL 143:385–86) in Gregory, *Morals*, vol. 1, 418–19. For secondary discussion of the relationship of subjective and objective evils (though taking opposing positions on the matter), see Gerard G. Carluccio, *The Seven Steps to Spiritual Perfection according to St. Gregory the Great* (Ottawa: University of Ottawa Press, 1949), 116–18 and 128–34; Bernard Green, "The Theology of Gregory the Great: Christ, Salvation, and the Church," in *A Companion to Gregory the Great*, ed. Bronwen Neil and Matthew Dal Santo, 153 (Boston: Brill, 2013); and Straw, "Gregory's Moral Theology, 199–200.

69. Gregory, *Moralia* XXXII 19.33 (CCSL 143B:1643) in Gregory, *Morals*, vol. 3.2, 536–37.

70. Gregory, *Moralia* XXXII 19.33 (CCSL 143B:1643) in Gregory, *Morals*, vol. 3.2, 536–37. A prior fault is fairly clearly implied by the separation between the first suggestion and the later assaults; the later assaults are a sort of punishment for letting in the devil in the first place.

In this reading, as soon as desire appears, one has begun to cooperate in the suggestion and is somewhat culpable for that cooperation.

Gregory, however, does not always speak of the devil's suggestion in this way. In the quote below, for instance, the devil uses "sudden suggestions" to sneak past the "threshold" (the suggestion itself) and into the "first vestibule" (desire). Gregory does not blame the one who is assailed in this way, either for the suggestion or for the desire:

> For He does not blame for their [the thoughts/demons] coming, but for their remaining there. And unlawful thoughts come even unto good hearts, but they are forbidden to remain; because the righteous, in order to keep the house of conscience from being taken, drive away the enemy from the very threshold of the heart. And if he has ever secretly crept [*subripuerit*] by sudden suggestions to the first vestibule [desire], yet he does not reach to the gate of consent.[71]

The "threshold" is the devil's suggestion and the first vestibule is the desire, both of which are clandestinely accomplished by the devil (even against the will of the one tempted). Gregory thereby indicates that in these circumstances, only the *consent* to the first two is blameworthy. What is essential in Gregory's account here—and that upon which the consistency of his presentation hangs—is the length of time the devil's suggestion is allowed to remain. In the previous examples, the person involved allowed the devil through carelessness to take up residence in the heart. Here, however, the devil's movement is *sudden* and even if the demon quickly proceeds into movements of desire, one who withholds consent would appear blameless: God "does not blame for their coming, but for their remaining."[72] Thus, the second

---

71. Gregory, *Moralia* XXVII 50 (CCSL 143B:1370) in Gregory, *Morals*, vol. 3.1, 237–39, translation modified. Other examples of demonic suggestion transitioning immediately into appetitive states can be found in the *Moralia*. See *Moralia* II 72–76 (CCSL 143:101–6) in Gregory, *Morals*, vol. 1, 113–19; *Moralia* II 75–79 (CCSL 143:103–9) in Gregory, *Morals*, vol. 1, 116–23; *Moralia* II 32 (CCSL 143:79–80) in Gregory, *Morals*, vol. 1, 90–91; *Moralia* XIII 19 (CCSL 143A:679–80) in Gregory, *Morals*, vol. 1, 377; *Moralia* XIV 20 (CCSL 143A:709) in Gregory, *Morals*, vol. 2, 129; *Moralia* XV 19 (CCSL 143A:759–60) in Gregory, *Morals*, vol. 2, 183–84; *Moralia* XXI 7 (CCSL 143A:1068–69) in Gregory, *Morals*, vol. 2, 519–20; *Moralia* XXI 12 (CCSL 143A:1074) in Gregory, *Morals*, vol. 2, 525; and *Moralia* XXVIII 43 and 45 (CCSL 143B:1429–30 and 1431–32) in Gregory, *Morals*, vol. 3.1, 297–99.

72. Gregory, *Moralia* XXVII 50 (CCSL 143B:1370) in Gregory, *Morals*, vol. 3.1, 237–39; see

stage of Gregory's moral psychology is not always sinful: it becomes so only if it is met without resistance and allowed to take up residence in the soul.

If such inner demonic temptation is not culpably sinful, the sole evidence of Hebrews 4:15 would indicate that it *should* be present in Christ. However, Gregory follows Augustine in arguing that Christ would not have been tempted from within by the devil. In a general denial of illicit thoughts in Christ, Gregory states that Christ could experience evil suggestions only externally. Christ could never experience evil desires within or consent to them:

> God, who became human in the womb of the Virgin, and came into the world without sin to take to himself a body, endured no inconsistency within himself. He could therefore be tempted by suggestion, but no delight in sin took hold of his heart. This whole diabolic temptation then took place from without, not from within.[73]

Of course, the lack of desire could simply indicate that Gregory denied that Christ ever cooperated with the devil's suggestion, but Gregory gives other indications that the devil never independently aroused desire for sin in Christ.

At least two passages from *Morals on Job* provide further evidence of the purely external temptation of Christ. Gregory denies that the devil could "wound [Christ's] mind": "And because [the devil] could not reach so far in his temptation, as to wound the mind of our Redeemer [ad *lacerationem mentis*], he was eager for His death in the flesh."[74] This reasoning is almost identical to that in Augustine, who, as demonstrated above, also saw a connection between Christ's insusceptibility to internal attack and the devil's attempt to seek Christ's

---

also Gregory, *Moralia* XXXIII 6 (CCSL 143B:1674–75) in Gregory, *Morals*, vol. 3.2, 558–59, for the brevity of the devil's penetration into the soul of the elect.

73. Gregory, *Gospel Homilies* 16, numbered according to PL 76:1135, in Gregory the Great, *Forty Gospel Homilies*, trans. Dom David Hurst (Kalamazoo, Mich.: Cistercian Publications, 1990), 102. For some relevant secondary discussion of Gregory's soteriology (which does not resolve the point currently at issue), see Rodrigue Bélanger, "La dialectique Parole-Chair dans la christologie de Grégoire le Grand," in *Gregory the Great: A Symposium*, ed. John Cavadini, 82–90 (Notre Dame, Ind.: University of Notre Dame Press, 1995) and Carluccio, *The Seven Steps to Spiritual Perfection*, 36–37.

74. *Moralia* XXVII 49 (CCSL 143B:1369) in Gregory, *Morals*, vol. 3.1, 236–37.

bodily death. In another passage, Gregory clarifies the soteriological significance of Christ's immunity to interior demonic attack:

> Never ... was the soul of your Redeemer disordered by [temptation's] urgency.... [The devil] has no power to shake by temptation the mind of the Mediator betwixt God and man. For He so condescended to take all this upon Himself externally, that His mind, being still inwardly established in His Divine Nature, should remain unshaken ... while Satan is let loose to smite the Redeemer's flesh, he is debarred the soul, forasmuch as at the same time that he obtains His Body to inflict upon it the Passion, he loses the Elect from the claims of his power. And while That One's flesh suffers death by the Cross, the mind of these is established against assaults.[75]

Like a biting dog who is distracted by a bone, the devil releases the elect when he seeks the destruction of Christ's body. Similar to Augustine, Gregory believes that Christ did not need to accept or assume inner demonic temptation in order to free (elect) humankind from these torments. For Gregory, Christ's external death suffices for driving the devil out of the hearts of the elect and protecting them from future attack.[76] Gregory indicates that Christ heals humanity not by experiencing their interior temptations but precisely by being free from them. Gregory has opened a further experiential gap between Christ and the elect that was absent in Augustine, since for Gregory even the elect experience some forms of internal temptation, yet Christ does not. Christ's death alone—and not his temptation—suffices to heal humanity's slavery to the devil.

Considering Augustine and Gregory together, an important Christological distinction developed in the West that, through them, passed into Latin reflection on Christ's temptation: in order to free other human beings from the tyranny of the devil both without and within, Christ does not need to experience every kind of demonic temptation to which other human beings (even the good or elect) are

---

75. *Moralia* III 30 (CCSL 143:134–35) in Gregory *Morals*, vol. 1, 151–52. For a possible Christological explanation of this passage, see Green, "The Theology of Gregory the Great," 144–45. See also *Moralia* XVII 46–47 (CCSL 143A:877–79) in Gregory, *Morals*, vol. 2, 308–10.

76. See also *Moralia* XXVII 49 (CCSL 143B:1369–70) in Gregory, *Morals*, vol. 1, 236–37. On Christ's rule in the hearts of the elect, see *Moralia* XX 11–12 (CCSL 143A:1009–10) in Gregory, *Morals*, vol. 2, 453–54.

susceptible after the Fall. Certainly, Augustine and Gregory are not the only sources of this idea; for his own reasons, John of Damascus also bars the devil from tempting Christ in some of the interior ways characteristic of fallen humanity. Subsequent Latin thinkers continue to follow this distinction, refusing to consider an *interior* temptation of Christ by the devil as soteriologically fitting.

High Medieval Sources on Christ's Temptation by the Devil

Peter the Lombard and Alexander of Hales provide some of the most immediate theological background to Thomas Aquinas's own writings on this subject.[77] In this section, I consider significant anthropological and Christological claims in each of these figures in their historical order.

Peter the Lombard

Peter the Lombard's influence on Thomas Aquinas needs no demonstration; Aquinas's first major work is a commentary on Peter's *Sentences*. In what follows, I examine the Lombard's thought on temptation in general and demonic temptation in particular, followed by some reference to his understanding of Christ in relation to these two things. Even though Peter does not reflect on Christ's temptation, there are other ways of gleaning what he has to say on the subject—not least of which is Paul Gondreau's substantive work on Thomas's sources. At various points, I connect Peter back to sources that preceded him, but my goal is to explain some of the fundamental points that will pave the way for the later commentatorial tradition on the *Sentences*, including that of Thomas. In this capacity, I discuss the forms

---

77. Bonaventure could also fruitfully be included. Some of Bonaventure's most relevant claims on this subject are found at Bonaventure, *Sent. Comm.* II 21.2. q. 1, in Bonaventure, *Opera Omnia*, vol. 3, ed. Adolphe Charles Peltier (Paris: Vivès, 1845), 100–104. For secondary discussion of Bonaventure's Christology, see Zachary Hayes, *The Hidden Center: Spirituality and Speculative Christology in St. Bonaventure* (New York: Paulist Press, 1981), 126–27, 142, 146–87; for some minor discussion of Bonaventure's demonology, see Christopher M Cullen, *Bonaventure* (New York: Oxford University Press, 2006), 135, 147–48.

of temptation that Peter recognizes, try to discern the source or origin of disordered concupiscence as Peter understands it, and finally look at Peter's relevant Christological reflections.

Concerning Peter's thought on human temptation, he follows Augustine, Gregory, the Damascene, and Hugh of St. Victor in their basic distinction between two general kinds of temptation: inner and outer.[78] Peter's account of this distinction, however, differs from that of his predecessors.[79] Peter identified three morally distinct forms of temptation: exterior, demonic interior, and fleshly interior.[80] Peter defines exterior temptation as when

> an evil extrinsic to us is visibly suggested to us by some word or sign [*verbo vel signo aliquo*], so that the one to whom the suggestion is made may bend to consent to sin. And such a temptation is done only by the adversary.[81]

Two comments regarding this definition are in order. First, Peter states that the adversary—the devil—is the sole source of exterior temptation. Peter does not discuss whether God can be said to tempt or whether human beings incline each other to evil (as the later scholastic tradition will affirm). Second, Peter limits exterior temptation to temptation that is visible through "some word or sign." Whereas for

---

78. Marcia L. Colish, *Peter Lombard*, 2 vols. (New York: E. J. Brill, 1994) provides a summary of other notable positions in the twelfth century on the question of temptation, particularly in Adam and Eve's Fall (vol. 1, 372, 377–78). Colish does not provide a detailed account of the Lombard's definition or explanation of human temptation in general; she takes for granted the easy separability of inner and outer temptation that is under investigation here.

79. Hugh of St. Victor stands at an important juncture in Western Christian theology. Much could be said about his role in the development of medieval typologies of temptation, but there is little evidence that Hugh directly influenced Aquinas's view. Rather, his influence was mediated through later scholastic thinkers. For the relevant passages, see Hugh of St. Victor, *De Sacramentis* 1.7.9, in Hugh of St. Victor, *On the Sacraments of the Christian Faith*, trans. Roy J. Deferrari (Eugene, Ore.: Wipf & Stock Publishers, 1951), 124, and Rainer Berndt, SJ, ed., *Hugonis de Sancto Victore: De Sacramentis Christiane Fidei* (Aschendorff: Monasterii Westfalorum, 2008), 172–73). Hugh indicates that there are two different kinds of exterior temptation, one "visible" and one "invisible." As seen below, Peter the Lombard categorizes this latter "invisible" temptation as interior.

80. Lombard, *Sentences* II 21.6: On the Double Kind of Temptation. Citations to the *Sentences* drawn from Peter Lombard, *The Sentences*, 4 vols., trans. Giulio Silano (Toronto: Pontifical Institute of Mediaeval Studies, 2007–10).

81. Lombard, *Sentences* II 21.6. Latin text in Peter the Lombard, *Sententiae in IV Libris Distinctae*, vol. 1.2 (3 vols.) (Grottaferrata: Editiones Collegii S. Bonaventurae Ad Claras Aquas, 1971), 437.

Peter's predecessors it was in some cases possible to call an invisible demonic temptation "exterior," the only way in which the devil can tempt from without in Peter's categorization is through explicit suggestions accessible to the external senses. Peter's distribution thereby renders invisible forms of demonic attack categorically "internal."

On the other hand, internal temptation, broadly speaking, occurs when "an evil intrinsic to us is suggested invisibly."[82] Such temptation comes in two forms, one demonic and the other from the "corruption of the flesh." As seen above, the conceptual basis for this second internal movement—the *fomes peccati*, or concupiscence—rises out of Augustine's thought.[83] Now, Peter elsewhere argues that the first movement of the sensible faculty—a disordered affective movement prior to rational deliberation—is venially sinful,[84] but here Peter qualifies that claim so that such movement is sinful only when it comes from within:

> Indeed, both the devil invisibly suggests evil, and an unlawful motion and depraved titillation arises from the corruption of the flesh [*ex carnis corruptione*]. And for that reason the temptation which is from the flesh does not occur without sin [*non fit sine peccato*]; however, the one which is from the enemy, unless consent is extended to it, does not cause sin but is matter for the practice of virtue [*non habet peccatum, sed est materia exercendae virtutis*].[85]

When inner temptation has its origin from the flesh, it is sinful; when it has its origin from the devil, it is *materia exercendae virtutis*. Three

---

82. Lombard, *Sentences* II 21.6.

83. This articulation of human disorder takes shape within Latin anthropological reflection. In part because the concept is nearly strictly anthropological in character, the inner divisions that it introduces into postlapsarian humankind affect the way that later Latin theology will relate this concept to Christ. Lest Christ appear internally divided, Western Christian thinkers until the twentieth century universally denied its presence in Christ. See Gondreau, *Passions of Christ's Soul*, chapters 1 and 2, especially 67–68, 84–85, and 130–31.

84. Peter's exposition of the sensitive appetite is presented in *Sentences* II 24. In this distinction, Peter borrows a tripartite understanding of human nature from St. Augustine's *De Trinitate*, which is itself based on a reading of Genesis 3. See Augustine, *On the Trinity: Books 8–15*, ed. Gareth B. Matthews, trans. Stephen McKenna (Cambridge: Cambridge University Press, 2002), XII 12. Peter's passage adopts this analogy, but he draws moral conclusions from the analogy that are uniquely his own. See Odon Lottin, *Psychologie et Morale aux XIIe et XIIIe Siècles*, vol. 2.1 (Louvain: Abbaye du Mont César, 1948), 494–95, and Peter the Lombard, *Sentences* II 24.9 (Latin in Lombard, *Sententiae*, vol. 1.2, 457); *Sentences* II 24.12; *Sentences* II 23.6–11; and *Sentences* II 24.11.

85. Lombard, *Sentences* II 21.6, translation modified.

comments should be made about this explanation of interior temptation: one about Peter's definition of temptation, a second about the origin of concupiscence, or the *fomes peccati*, and a third about the blamelessness of interior temptation.

First, this distinction indicates that a category of inner temptation—that arising from concupiscence—is culpably sinful. Such a category thus combines sin and temptation in a single act. Peter explains this category by arguing that the rational faculty has the ability to prevent the movement of the sensible faculty in any given instance. In common usage, one might expect temptation and sin to be related as necessary (but not sufficient) cause and effect; in this instance, though, one culpable sin is also a temptation toward another. The clarification of the relationship between temptation and sin in the *fomes* is left to the later commentatorial tradition to resolve; Aquinas himself will provide a distinctive solution in the coming chapter.

Second, Peter speaks somewhat inaccurately when he categorizes concupiscence as a purely interior disorder between the rational and lower appetitive powers. Even if concupiscence is experienced as coming from within, Peter acknowledges that disordered concupiscence has at least in part an *exterior* cause. Peter considers the origin of concupiscence in Book II, Distinction 32.3, where he argues that concupiscence has two origins according to its two major defining characteristics: *poena* and *culpa*, punishment and fault. He explains, "Insofar as it is a punishment, it has God as its author, but insofar as it is a fault, it has the devil or man as its author."[86] As just stated, the concupiscence, or "fleshly corruption," discussed above (in Book II, Distinction 21) has this second character, that of culpable fault. One should note the tension in this arrangement: in Distinction 32, when concupiscence is considered as fault (sin), its origin is at least in part the devil, but in Distinction 21, if an interior temptation has the devil as its origin, it is not intrinsically sin. This contradiction is uncomfort-

---

86. Lombard, *Sentences* II 32.3 (Latin in Lombard, *Sententiae*, vol. 1.2, 514–15). In other passages, Peter speaks of concupiscence without any reference to the devil; see *Sentences* II 31.3 and 5, where the "law of sin" has to do with concupiscence but nothing is said of any role the devil might take in its origin.

able at best. I only wish to suggest, however, that even in Peter's own account, fleshly and demonic temptations are not as easy to separate as he indicates in Book II, Distinction 21. Later attempts to resolve this tension in the Lombard will be seen in the work of Alexander of Hales and Thomas Aquinas.

Third and last, this distinction also makes clear that there are kinds of inner temptation that are *not* intrinsically sinful. But nowhere does Peter explain whether this internal temptation from the devil could be experienced by Christ. As an attempt to extrapolate, Peter's Christology likely continues the trajectory of the Christological synecdoche noted in the work of John of Damascus above: a tendency to reduce Christ's contact with the fallen condition. In Distinction XVI 2, Peter gives a soteriological account of why Christ took on only *some* defects of fallen humanity. He argues that

> Christ, who came to save all, took something from each of the states of man. There are four states of man: first before sin, second after sin and before grace, third under grace, forth in glory. From the first state, he took immunity from sin.... But he took the punishment and other defects from the second state; from the third, he took the fullness of grace; from the forth, he took the inability to sin and the perfect contemplation of God. Indeed, he took simultaneously some of the goods of the wayfarer and some of the goods of the fatherland, as he took also some of the evils of the wayfarer.[87]

The soteriological principle seen in Peter's text is the same as that seen in both Maximus and John of Damascus. However, the Christological synecdoche that Peter constructs out of this principle is composed differently than that of Maximus and John.[88] Instead of the two states of human nature they consider, Peter argues for four. More importantly, however, he more explicitly limits Christ's contact with the fallen conditions of temptation. This limitation can be seen in other texts.

Peter states in Distinction XV 1 that Christ took "the defects of punishment, but not those of fault; and yet not all the defects of punishment, but all those which it was suitable for him as man to assume

---

87. Lombard, *Sentences* III 16.2 (Latin in Lombard, *Sententiae*, vol. 1.2).
88. One also sees this synecdoche in *Sentences* III 15.1 (Latin in Lombard, *Sententiae*, vol. 1.2).

(*eos omnes quos homini eum assumere expediebat*) and which did not derogate from his dignity."[89] Peter provides contrasting evidence for what constitutes an "expedient [*expediebat*]" defect in Christ's temptation. On one hand, Peter denies in Christ any ignorance, even of an invincible, and thus blameless, kind, as well as a "difficulty to will and do the good (*difficultatem volendi vel faciendi bonum*)," a recognizable articulation of disordered concupiscence or the *fomes peccati*. Both of these defects, as the Lombard explains, are not sin, yet are not to be considered in Christ.[90] The latter defect, a "weakness by which one cannot restrain oneself from evil" pertains "to our misery," and for that reason, Peter states, Christ "did not take on all the defects of our infirmity apart from sin."[91] From these considerations, it is therefore likely that Peter would deny an "inner" temptation of Christ by the devil.

On the other hand, Peter provides soteriological reflections later in this same question that could point to a different understanding of Christ's inner demonic temptation. Peter explains that Christ took human defects

> either to demonstrate his true humanity: such as fear and sadness; or to fulfill the work for which he had come [*ad impletionem operis ad quod venerat*]: such as the capacity to suffer and die; or to raise our hope from our despair of immortality: such as death.[92]

Surely, the overcoming of demonic temptation would "fulfill the work for which he had come." One could argue on those grounds that internal demonic temptation would be fitting for Christ to assume. Yet this reasoning is purely speculative. No explicit soteriological statement about Christ's temptation by the devil is to be found in Book III; the chapters that Peter devotes to Christ's defeat of the devil treat only Christ's death as the means of humanity's liberation from the devil.[93]

---

89. Lombard, *Sentences* III 15.1.3 (Latin in Lombard, *Sententiae*, vol. 2, 94).
90. Lombard, *Sentences* III 15.1.6 (Latin in Lombard, *Sententiae*, vol. 2, 94).
91. Lombard, *Sentences* III 15.1.5 (Latin in Lombard, *Sententiae*, vol. 2, 94).
92. Lombard, *Sentences* III 15.1.7 (Latin in Lombard, *Sententiae*, vol. 2, 94).
93. Lombard, *Sentences* III 19.1, III 20.3, and II 20.4. In these chapters, Peter follows Augustine and Gregory before him and does not associate this victory with Christ's temptation. Lombard, *Sentences* III 16.1, discusses Christ's natural defects, among which Peter could have included (but did not explicitly include) his temptation.

In balance, the Lombard provides very little consideration of the soteriological significance of Christ's temptation, thereby leaving little room for any contact between the postlapsarian experience of temptation and that of Christ.

One final aspect of Peter's Christology appears to reflect the then-newly translated *DFO* of John of Damascus. Peter affirms that Christ *willingly* accepted the appropriate defects of human nature—that is, that Christ did not take them by natural necessity as one under the rule of original sin.[94] The purpose of this qualification, as it was for John, is to safeguard the liberty and sovereignty of God by avoiding God's entanglement in sin; Peter states that "he could have taken it without any infirmity" but did not do so "from the will of his compassion."[95] However, as was also the case with John, Peter does not specify how each of Christ's wills—human and divine—cooperate in their object.[96] While it is appropriate to argue that Christ *freely* accepted the consequences of fallen human nature, dyothelite Christology would seem to require that one explain in more detail what kind of freedom was appropriate to Christ as God and as human in this freely chosen act. Did this freedom pertain to Christ's human will *during* the incarnation? Could Christ have chosen, as human and during the incarnation, to cease from an activation of his passible faculty entirely? As in John's thought, this question is left unresolved.

Alexander of Hales

Alexander of Hales inherits the ambiguities left by the Lombard in his treatment of Christ's temptation by the devil. In contrast to Peter, though, Alexander writes at great length about Christ's temptation by the devil. Alexander dedicates significant space in his *Summa Theologica* to questions on temptation, both regarding its general form and regarding the specific form of temptation experienced by Christ. Alexander, as a *Sentences* commentator, agrees in most substantive ways

---

94. Lombard, *Sentences* III 15.1.8.

95. Lombard, *Sentences* III 15.1.8 (Latin in Lombard, *Sententiae*, vol. 2, 94).

96. Peter's language may indicate that he is speaking primarily of the *divine* will: he "*could have* assumed [*assumere potuit*]" human nature without those defects.

with the explicit affirmations of Peter. The depth of his investigation of controversial aspects of Peter's teaching, however, makes its place among Thomas's sources particularly significant. I consider Alexander's account of the culpability of fleshly and demonic temptation; the devil's powers regarding human imagination and intellect; and Alexander's application of these ideas to Christ's temptation.

Following Peter the Lombard, Alexander divides human temptation into three categories: an external demonic temptation, an internal fleshly temptation, and an internal demonic temptation.[97] Alexander follows the Lombard in arguing that external temptation occurs by some "word or sign." He further clarifies that while hearing and sight play a privileged role in one's temptation, words and signs are not limited to hearing and sight; rather "sign" is understood as any sensible object that appeals to one of the senses.[98] In what follows, then, internal temptation will be distinguished in part by the lack of a sensible external object presented to the one tempted.

Culpability for Internal Temptation from the Devil and the Flesh. Both the internal temptation from the flesh and that from the devil are species of this "internal" temptation. What makes them distinct from exterior temptation is that these forms act on an interior power of the soul without external stimuli. The internal powers susceptible to this interior attack are the intellectual and affective powers.[99] The attack against the affective power is also referred to as "from the motive rational part, which draws near to sensuality [*ex parte motivae rationis, quae appropinquat sensualitati*]."[100] As a final distinction, the intellectual temptation, sometimes called temptation against the cognitive part, is subdivided into that which is against the imagination and that which is through thoughts. The distinction between the cognitive (intellectu-

---

97. Alexander of Hales, *Summa Theologica* II.II.II 1.1 Cap. 7 [*quo modo fiat unaquaeque tentation*], in Alexander, *Summa Theologica* 173ff.; my translations throughout this section.
98. Alexander of Hales, *Summa Theologica* II.II.II 1.1 Cap. 6.4, in Alexander, *Summa*, vol. 3, 168–69.
99. Alexander of Hales, *Summa Theologica* II.II.II 1.1 Cap. 6.4, in Alexander, *Summa*, vol. 3, 168–69.
100. Alexander of Hales, *Summa Theologica* II.II.II 1.1 Cap. 6.4, in Alexander, *Summa*, vol. 3, 168–69.

al) part and the motive (sensual) part is essential to the moral distinctions that Alexander draws between demonic and fleshly temptations.

Corresponding with each of these kinds of internal attack, there are two forces responsible for internal temptation: the devil and the flesh. Like the Lombard, Alexander acknowledges that in a sense, fleshly temptation comes from demonic temptation. Insofar as one is concerned with the proximate cause of a particular temptation, however, he maintains that it is appropriate to distinguish between the two forms:

> For when this division is given, something about the proximate cause of temptation is understood. But it may happen that the flesh, that is carnal concupiscence, is the principle of temptation of reason itself. And thus nothing prevents (although all evil is originally from the devil) that a certain one is from the devil as from the proximate cause, but another from carnal concupiscence.[101]

Nothing here strays significantly from the Lombard's presentation, though Alexander is somewhat clearer about the relationship between the two sources of temptation.

By far the most significant anthropological innovation that Alexander introduces is an explanation of the moral distinction between demonic and fleshly temptation. For Peter, interior demonic temptation was not intrinsically culpably sinful, yet fleshly temptation was. Alexander is able to provide an explanation for this difference by correlating two parts of the soul (the cognitive and appetitive) with the two kinds of temptation (demonic temptation and fleshly temptation), respectively. That is, Alexander argues that the devil is solely responsible for *intellectual* attacks and the flesh is solely responsible for *affective* attacks. One sees the moral relevance of this distinction in Alexander's questions on the sinfulness of each form. In his explanation of the culpable sinfulness of fleshly temptation, Alexander argues that

> the case of this [fleshly] temptation is not similar to that of the others. For the other two [internal and external demonic attacks] are from the part of

---

101. Alexander of Hales, *Summa Theologica* II.II.II 1.1 Cap. 6.3, in Alexander, *Summa*, vol. 3, 168–69.

cognitive power, but this is from the part of the motive power, in which there is sin by reason of affection.[102]

He explains further in his treatment of internal demonic temptation of the imaginative power:

> This temptation is not necessarily with sin. For this temptation has its origin in the cognitive part, but that [other has it] in the motive part, which is from the flesh; and thus that [fleshly temptation] is necessarily said [to be] with venial sin because of the corruption of motion from the *fomes*. But if the corruption is in itself cognitive, it is only said to be a certain obscurity [*obscuratio quaedam*], and this corruption is not called sin.[103]

Throughout his treatment of the different internal temptations, the only reason Alexander suggests for this moral distinction is the different faculties they tempt.[104] Alexander thus indicates that if the devil were able to tempt the motive power of sensation, the devil would cause an act in the genus of sin, which would perhaps be more akin to possession than temptation.

If this distinction accurately represents Alexander's intention, it must however be acknowledged that Alexander is not perfectly consistent in keeping these two faculties and temptations (respectively) separate. In at least two places, Alexander argues that demonic temptation, like fleshly temptation, can be against the sensitive or animal part of humanity.[105] He concedes in one place that inner demonic temptation "is similarly from the movement of sensuality [*licet communiter fiat ex motibus in sensualitate*],"[106] though he continues to maintain that it "is not in itself a cause of sin [*non tamen est per se causa*

---

102. Alexander of Hales, *Summa Theologica* II.II.II 1.1 Cap. 7.2, in Alexander, *Summa*, vol. 3, 178.

103. Alexander of Hales, *Summa Theologica* II.II.II 1.1 Cap. 7.3, in Alexander, *Summa*, vol. 3, 179–80.

104. This use of the distinction between cognitive and affective temptation is particularly significant in light of Thomas's later rejection of the distinction; for Thomas, the devil is capable of eliciting a fully appetitive movement in fallen humankind. See chapter 5.

105. The two clear instances are explained in the text. In a third location, Alexander grants the devil a significant role in the intellectual aspect of the tinder of sin, though his speculation on this point ends on a relatively apophatic note. See Alexander of Hales, *Summa Theologica* II.II.II 1.1 Cap. 7.3, prob. 2, in Alexander, *Summa*, vol. 3, 180–84.

106. Alexander of Hales, *Summa Theologica* II.II.II 1.1 Cap. 6.3, in Alexander, *Summa*, vol. 3, 166–68.

peccati]." His explanation is that fleshly temptation is sinful because its movement of sensuality is "illicit" or unlawful.[107] It is unclear whether the demonic temptation of sensuality would, on the contrary, be called "licit" or lawful, but such may be the implication. In the other instance, Alexander grapples with Augustine's claim that the devil tempted us *only* through our animal part, which Alexander interprets as sensibility. There, Alexander also concedes that the devil tempts not only "though the sensible part, but [also] by the intelligible part; nevertheless the greater aptitude is through temptation from the sensible part."[108] These instances show the difficulty Alexander faced in maintaining the culpable sinfulness of internal fleshly temptation and the relative blamelessness of internal demonic temptation.[109] Despite these points of hesitation, his overall position is clear: fleshly temptation is venially sinful from the movement of the *fomes* and internal demonic temptation, being only cognitive, is not sinful in itself.

The Devil's Temptation of Imagination and Intellect.

Given that the devil's internal temptation is to be understood as strictly cognitive and not

---

107. Alexander of Hales, *Summa Theologica* II.II.II 1.1 Cap. 6.3, in Alexander, *Summa*, vol. 3, 166–68. Alexander defines illicit desire in opposition to a "natural" desire at Alexander of Hales, *Summa Theologica* II.II.II 1.1 Cap. 7.1, in Alexander, *Summa*, vol. 3, 173–75. It seems likely that any movement the devil would stir up would meet one of these criteria for an "illicit" desire as well but Alexander generally tries to avoid the conclusion that the devil could perform this sort of movement; see the treatment of the devil's movement of the imagination below.

108. Alexander of Hales, *Summa Theologica* II.II.II 1.1 Cap. 8, in Alexander, *Summa*, vol. 3, 184–85. Alexander does not mention the devil as the source of the temptation in his response even though the title of the question is explicitly the devil's temptation. One can sense his hesitancy to ascribe sensible temptation to the devil and in his reply to the first objection he tries to mitigate that sense of Augustine's words. See Alexander of Hales, *Summa Theologica* II.II.II 1.1 Cap. 8, in Alexander, *Summa*, vol. 3, 184–85). For another instance where Alexander equates the sensual and the sensible faculties, see Alexander of Hales, *Summa Theologica* II.II.II 1.1 Cap. 7.3, in Alexander, *Summa*, vol. 3, 178–84.

109. Structurally, Alexander avoids this problem in the most important questions on internal demonic temptation by only addressing demonic temptations against the cognitive powers. In another instance, Alexander conversely wavers on the venial sinfulness of fleshly temptation. When discussing the positive spiritual value of temptation from the flesh, he argues that "the one who guards himself from venial sin [*Qui enim custodit se a peccato veniali*], directs himself to the use of power and consequently to salvation, and thus temptation in this way (i.e., from the flesh) is material for the exercise of virtue." See Alexander of Hales, *Summa Theologica* II.II.II 1.1 Cap. 6.3, in Alexander, *Summa*, vol. 3, 166–68. Strongly implied in this reasoning is that fleshly temptation provides an opportunity to protect against venial sin, but Alexander generally does not hold this prophylactic use of concupiscence to be possible; see what Alexander says about Paul's temptation at Alexander of Hales, *Summa Theologica,* II.II.II 1.1 Cap. 7.2, in Alexander, *Summa*, vol. 3, 178.

affective, Alexander considers two forms of internal demonic temptation: against the imagination and through thoughts. The first requires further commentary in order to distinguish it from fleshly temptation. The second needs careful consideration because of its substantive disagreement with an Evagrian (and in turn Maximian) tradition of demonic thought.

Fleshly temptation comes from the conjunction of the sensual part with the body.[110] Demonic temptation, however, arises from the insertion of "likenesses (*similitudines*)" into the imagination of the one tempted:

> the devil, as Augustine says, represents likenesses by way of prosperity [and] by way of adversity, from which representation the soul negotiates according to the imaginative part, and consequently inclines or disposes the intellect itself to that inclination.[111]

The difference hangs on the distinction between sensuality (where fleshly temptation rises) and sensitivity (where demonic temptation rises).[112] Alexander likely envisions a distinction between a power of perception in sensitivity and a power of appetition in sensuality. Granting such a distinction would help render coherent the idea that inner demonic temptation is somewhat more "exterior" than fleshly temptation. Whereas the latter implies the presence of a desire (in sensuality), the former implies only an image that is "determined to one [way], as to the apparently desirable or to the apparently sad" as it approaches sensitivity.[113] The devil does not force the one tempted to desire the thing, but merely represents a thing that is apparently attractive or apparently to be avoided and leaves it to the mind to decide whether to pursue or avoid it.

The devil's imaginative attack, then, does not directly move human

---

110. Alexander of Hales, *Summa Theologica* II.II.II 1.1 Cap. 7.2, in Alexander, *Summa*, vol. 3, 175–78, especially 176.

111. Alexander of Hales, *Summa Theologica* II.II.II 1.1 Cap. 7.3, in Alexander, *Summa*, vol. 3, 178–84.

112. The two, however, are equated at Alexander of Hales, *Summa Theologica* II.II.II 1.1 Cap. 7.3, in Alexander, *Summa*, vol. 3, 178–84.

113. Alexander of Hales, *Summa Theologica* II.II.II 1.1 Cap. 7.3, in Alexander, *Summa*, vol. 3, 178–84.

affectivity. But when considering the second form of demonic attack concerning thoughts, Alexander also denies that this attack can directly affect human thoughts. Alexander's denial of this power rests upon his understanding of the *imago Dei*. That is, Alexander hopes to protect the innermost part of the human soul—the intellect—from the devil's attack, because in that highest part, "the image of God shines naturally."[114] For this reason, the devil cannot be called a "sender of evil thoughts [*immissor malarum cogitationum*]."[115] The primary sense of this term is as one who makes or creates such thoughts, so for the devil to insert them in the intellect, he must occupy the space that is properly God's image in the soul. Instead, Alexander argues that "evil thoughts, insofar as they are evil, are from man himself."[116] This particular affirmation stands in significant tension with the monastic tradition traced in the first half of this study and marks perhaps the sharpest departure from it in the high medieval period.[117] For Alexander, the devil can send thoughts only in the lesser sense of one who disposes "to that which is done ... as if from outside."[118] Even in the *internal* temptation of the devil, Alexander renders the devil's action *exterior*.

Since the devil is not properly the "sender" of evil thoughts, Alexander asks next whether the devil can be called their "inflamer." He argues that, for the devil, "to inflame is to move so as to choose what should not be chosen, and consequently to desire,"[119] but his explanation of that movement toward desire mitigates a strong interpretation of the "inflaming" the devil performs. Alexander states that "man is said to inflame as the one who provides kindling for the fire [*ut qui*

---

114. Alexander of Hales, *Summa Theologica* II.II.II 1.1 Cap. 7.3, in Alexander, *Summa*, vol. 3, 178–84.

115. Alexander of Hales, *Summa Theologica* II.II.II 1.1 Cap. 7.3, in Alexander, *Summa*, vol. 3, 181–82.

116. Alexander of Hales, *Summa Theologica* II.II.II 1.1 Cap. 7.3, in Alexander, *Summa*, vol. 3, 181–82.

117. Alexander does not distinguish in this instance between an "objectively" evil thought (insofar as it is evil because the devil intends evil by it) and a "subjectively" evil thought (which would include the human being's consent to the evil act). Were this claim construed objectively, it would be explicitly at odds with Evagrius's view.

118. Alexander of Hales, *Summa Theologica* II.II.II 1.1 Cap. 7.3, in Alexander, *Summa*, vol. 3, 181–82.

119. Alexander of Hales, *Summa Theologica* II.II.II 1.1 Cap. 7.3, in Alexander, *Summa*, vol. 3, 182–83.

praebet pabulum igni], but the devil as assistant [*ut coadiutor*]." He explains his analogy:

> For when he [the devil] sees that we are prone to some kind of sin, he manages to place those desirable things before [us], so that from those the intellect [might be] led to thought of those in an illicit manner, and in this way he is an assistant.[120]

The role of the devil here is remote and material at best; the devil adds nothing that is not already present in the one tempted. Before the devil tempts in this way, the one tempted is already "prone [*pronos*]" to the sin that the devil assists in committing.[121] When I address Thomas on this question in the next chapter, it will be clear that his understanding grants significantly more to the devil in his role of providing "kindling" to the fire. For now, I note that the analogy of a fire and kindling (*fomes*) is an important one (for both Alexander and Thomas) and that the details of this analogy matter a great deal when determining moral culpability. For Alexander, the human agent provides all that is essential for the temptation, and the devil's involvement is quite remote.

Christ's Temptations. Alexander's consideration of the relevant Christological material includes two important details: whether Christ was tempted in the Garden of Gethsemane and whether Christ was tempted from within.

When Alexander evaluates the scene of Christ in the Garden, he considers two ways in which the flesh might be said to have tempted Christ. In the first way, Christ experienced a natural fear, "not desiring the dividing of the soul from the body according to nature," though in this way, Christ was not said to be *tempted* by fear (or, consequently, by the flesh). Alexander allows, however, that there may have been something of temptation in the propassion of fear that Christ took on in his condescension, and that the devil may have had something to do with it:

---

120. Alexander of Hales, *Summa Theologica* II.II.II 1.1 Cap. 7.3, in Alexander, *Summa*, vol. 3, 183–84.

121. Alexander of Hales, *Summa Theologica* II.II.II 1.1 Cap. 7.3, in Alexander, *Summa*, vol. 3, 183–84. In the same question, Alexander also denies two other senses in which the devil is the inflamer of evil thoughts: the devil cannot provide fuel for concupiscence, and the devil cannot be said to blow on that fire.

There is another fear, which is called a *propassion*, I do not mean a passion that is a disturbance of the mind. For this kind [a passion] could not be applied to Christ, but [only] a propassion, and in this way he assumed our infirmities that were appropriate for our redemption. And a sudden motion on the part of his sensuality is said to exist, but not on the part of his deiform rationality, to which nothing was sudden. And in this way there could be a temptation from fear, [though] not because the devil had power to stir up this kind of fear, except in so far as the Son of God himself was willing both according to his Divinity and according to his humanity.[122]

Despite Alexander's qualifications about the omnipotence and freedom of Christ, Alexander admits that the devil may have had a hand in Christ's fear at the end of his life. This interpretation is amenable in important ways to Maximus's reading of the Garden scene: it admits that the devil's temptations did not end in the desert, and it affirms that Christ's fear is both real and in a sense plays into the devil's plot to defeat Christ. This convergence with Maximus is limited, however, by Alexander's distinction between passion and propassion, which requires Alexander to accept a Stoic definition of passion as a disordered or irrational movement of the soul. Maximus, preferring the term "natural passion," does not use the term propassion in describing Christ's temptations, thereby indicating a closer relationship between Christ's experience and the fallen experience of passion.

While Alexander mentions the devil with respect to Christ's fear, he stops short of affirming that the devil tempted Christ from within. Alexander first denies that Christ was tempted from within by fleshly temptation, as Christ was free from the *fomes peccati* that bind humanity after the Fall. In this respect, Christ must be said to have been tempted exteriorly because "the temptation that is from the enemy is called exterior."[123] Then, anticipating the three-fold division of temptation discussed above, Alexander concedes that "there is nevertheless something interior from the enemy." He concludes that

---

122. Alexander, *Summa Theologica* II.II.II 1.1 Cap. 3.3, in Alexander, *Summa*, vol. 3, 153–54. For a broader discussion of the concept of *propassion*, see Gondreau, *Passions of Christ's Soul*, chapters 1 and 2.

123. Alexander, *Summa Theologica* II.II.II 1.1 Cap. 3.3, in Alexander, *Summa*, vol. 3, 154.

Christ was not tempted by that temptation. For temptation is in three gradations, just as B. Gregory says that the devil strikes on the exterior, touches the interior, and draws to consent: the strike is without sin, the touching with venial [sin], and the drawing with mortal [sin]. The first gradation alone concerned Christ, namely the knocking, the other two truly were not fitting nor could they be fitting.[124]

In his anthropological distinctions, *no* form of demonic temptation is intrinsically culpably sinful, but in his Christological discussion, he concludes on the basis of a flattened reading of Gregory the Great that any demonic "touching" of Christ's interior or drawing on toward consent would be culpably sinful and thus must be denied of Christ. The gulf between Christ's experience of temptation and that of fallen humanity widens; Christ's contact with the fallen circumstances of temptation has entirely disappeared.

⁜

In this overview of material that bridges the historical period between Thomas Aquinas and Maximus the Confessor, I have shown some of the major trends that characterize Latin Christian thought about Christ's temptation in that period. Two summative comments are in order.

First, one can see a successive tendency to place distance between Christ's moral life and that of fallen human beings. In an effort to maintain Christ's perfect sinlessness, each link in this chain corrects their predecessor by further diminishing Christ's experience of fallen human temptation. The synecdochal character of Christ's identity with the prelapsarian condition grows while the synecdoche regarding the fallen condition shrinks. Maximus had seen the prelapsarian synecdoche in Christ's mode of birth, yet Maximus's vision of Christ's affective life conforms wholly to his understanding of the postlapsarian conditions of temptation. For John of Damascus, this prelapsarian synecdoche expanded to include Christ's insusceptibility to demonic thoughts, though leaving room for Christ to experience a postlapsarian "attack"

---

124. Alexander, *Summa Theologica* II.II.II 1.1 Cap. 3.3, in Alexander, *Summa*, vol. 3, 154. Alexander flattens the robust complexities of Gregory's account of the devil's inner workings noted earlier in this chapter.

by passion and demon. As later Latin figures like Peter the Lombard and Alexander of Hales reflected on the Augustinian anthropological category of concupiscence, or the *fomes peccati*, this internal inclination to moral disorder became a further way in which Christ must share the prelapsarian condition. Though Peter and Alexander recognized that the devil's power over fallen human beings experientially overlaps with this disordered internal movement (yet in a way that each recognizes as morally blameless), this experience is still denied in the case of Christ, so that whatever postlapsarian synecdoche remains in their writings has nothing in particular to do with Christ's temptation.

Second, in this period, the categories for anthropological reflection shift, thereby changing in significant ways the geography of Christian anthropological reflection. Looking back to Evagrius and Maximus, the goodness of human nature was conditioned by the threat of the devil in and through one's thoughts and feelings. Gregory the Great, via John Cassian, preserves much of this teaching, synthesizing it with an Augustinian conception of original sin. This latter Augustinian tradition of human fallenness, however, conditions human goodness in significantly different ways than the monastic tradition had. The dominance of this tradition in early scholastic reflection on human temptation is equally important.

This gradual shift has advantages for the Christian West that should not be ignored. First, the minimization of the devil's role in the Fall renders its account of human sinfulness less cosmically dualistic than the early Origenist tradition because it assigns less disordering activity to the devil in the (mis)shaping and later (mis)activation of fallen human nature. Second, it appears less anthropologically "superstitious" since it refuses to let the moral agent shift the blame for one's "inner demons" onto real ones. Yet the drawbacks of the increasingly anthropological approach are most apparent in the Christological matters outlined in this chapter. As the inner moral rectitude of Christ takes shape in an anthropological context shaped increasingly by disordered concupiscence, Christ's role as a moral exemplar living out of the same moral circumstances becomes harder and harder to maintain.

5

THOMAS'S ANTHROPOLOGY OF TEMPTATION

Thomas Aquinas was a university professor. As such, the form of his exposition—especially in his systematic treatises—tends to prioritize the flow of his own argument and concepts more than did Maximus's corpus. Maximus critically engaged with various philosophical schools and positions, but Thomas more consciously writes with the broad goal of assimilating Aristotelian philosophy into his Christian worldview. Thomas's position and times lent themselves to a particularly clear and precise style of argumentation that results in an exposition of demonic temptation that is unrivaled by Maximus. On the other hand, his status and training affect his audience and the content of his thought about the devil. Thomas's theory of demonic temptation synthesizes Aristotelian philosophical categories with the views of temptation that he inherited from the patristic and medieval tradition. His synthesis has concrete effects for his understanding of how that temptation takes place and for his assessment of the moral qualities of temptation.

Using the same approach as in chapter 2, my purpose in this chapter is to present the anthropological background that stands behind Thomas's view of Christ's temptation. First, I consider the created and fallen states of Adam and his progeny. Regarding the fallen state, Thomas's portrayal of Adam's punishment—including slavery to Satan—receives careful consideration. In the second section, I consider the two forms of temptation that pertain specifically to the fallen state in Thomas's theology: the *fomes peccati* and inner demonic temptation. I have argued that the first involves a mode of anthropological reflection that is distinctly Latin, having no direct parallel in Maximus's Greek context. I therefore give particular care to my treatment of that form of temptation, as its moral qualities affect Thomas's Christological reflection on that topic.

In my analysis of the second form, inner demonic temptation, I argue that Thomas recognizes a fallen form of temptation that is, in its subjective experience, similar to fleshly temptation but that remains distinct in precise moral theological terms. Further, such temptation is, for Thomas, only partly dependent on the corruption of the *fomes*. In the final section, I address two broader questions that occupied my presentation of Maximus as well: first, the compatibility of inner demonic temptation and perfect virtue, and second, the way Thomas conceives of God's permission of temptation as both leading human beings to, and hindering them from, their final end.

The Created and Fallen States

For Thomas as much as for Maximus, an account of the genesis of the human race is necessary for an adequate treatment of the reasons for Christ's coming into human nature. In my consideration of Thomas's protology, I address those topics that bear a significant relationship to the qualities of Christ's human nature and to his overcoming of the devil in and through that nature. I first consider the original state of Adam: his passionate faculties, his graced state, the order of his soul, and his immunity from deception. Secondly, I address two areas in which Adam's sin brought about altered conditions in his experience of human nature: the withdrawal of original justice and his enslavement to demonic powers.[1]

---

1. A characterization of the nature of Adam's first sin in itself or its cause is beyond the purview of this study. As was the case with my presentation of Maximus in chapter 2, some of

The Unfallen Adamic State

The unfallen state, as conceived by Thomas, is the original, graced state of humankind. Though Adam enjoyed certain privileges (including immortality and incorruptibility)² in this state, this condition was not one of perfect beatitude or absolutely perfected grace. At the very least, Adam had not yet received certain graces of perfection, such as the beatific vision, and he possessed other virtues that indicate for Thomas a certain imperfection, such as faith.³ From this original condition, Thomas concludes that Adam awaited a "confirmation in righteousness," a term used to denote the final perfections that did not exist in the beginning:

> the rational creature is confirmed in righteousness [*in iustitia confirmati*] through the beatitude given by the clear vision of God ... as soon as Adam had attained to that happy state of seeing God in His Essence, he would have become spiritual in soul and body; and his animal life would have ceased.⁴

Since Adam is immortal in the original condition, this transition to a state of perfect beatitude would not be accomplished through the process we describe as death. However it would have taken place, the existence of this transition indicates that with regard to God's grace, the created state rests somewhere between the fallen and glorified state, enjoying certain supernatural graces but not yet perfected according to God's ultimate plan for humankind. Such was also the case for Maximus's account of the created state.

Particularly significant among the characteristics of the unfallen state is the existence of a certain sort of passibility in Adam. Thomas argues that the sensitive appetite, being constitutive of human nature from the beginning, was a faculty that was activated in the beginning only at the command of Adam's reason and will: "In the state of

---

the philosophical questions about the relationship of will and intellect would take me too far from the central subject matter of Christ's temptation.

2. *ST* I 97.1 and *ST* I 102.4. Unless otherwise noted, English translations are from Thomas Aquinas, *Summa Theologiae: First Complete American Edition*, 3 vols., trans. Fathers of the English Dominican Province (Cincinnati, Ohio: Benziger Brothers, 1947).

3. *ST* I 94.1 and *ST* I 95.3.

4. *ST* I 100.2.

innocence the inferior appetite was wholly subject to reason: so that in that state the passions of the soul existed only as consequent upon the judgment of reason."[5] In other words, there was in Adam absolutely no involuntary or irrational movement of his sensitive nature prior to the Fall.[6] Thomas has no difficulty (unlike Maximus) describing the unfallen Adam as passible. In part, Thomas's position comes from a consistent measured criticism of the Stoic position that had intermittently influenced Maximus's presentation of human affectivity. The Aristotelean sources of Thomas's position do not conceive of the passions as innately disordered or sinful; thus it is easier for Thomas to recognize their presence in the unfallen Adamic condition than it was for earlier ascetic tradition and for Maximus.[7]

Since no corporeal evil existed to elicit fear in Adam's original condition, the movement of the irascible portion of his sensitive appetite (a faculty somewhat parallel to Maximus's category of aversion)[8] was limited but not absent. Most notably, the irascible passion of hope was present in the original Adamic state.[9] There were, on the other hand, many spiritual goods that Adam voluntarily and rationally recognized as desirable in and through his concupiscible appetite (parallel to Maximus's category of desire):

But those passions which regard present good, as joy and love; or which regard future good to be had at the proper time, as desire and hope that casteth not down, existed in the state of innocence.[10]

---

5. *ST* I 95.2; throughout, Latin versions of Thomas's works are found at http://www.corpust homisticum.org/iopera.html.

6. One should note that Adam's prelapsarian condition can also be described as one of political governance, but one in which all the members support the rule of reason, whereas after sin, they do not. See the contrast that Thomas draws between Adam's state and our own at *ST* I 95.2, response. This presentation of Adam's created state also stands in notable parallel with Thomas's presentation of Christ's sensitive faculty, which also obeys perfectly the command of his reason; see chapter 6.

7. For more on Thomas's criticism of the Stoics, see Nicholas E. Lombardo, *The Logic of Desire: Aquinas on Emotion* (Washington, D.C.: The Catholic University of America Press, 2011), 40, 76.

8. See my explanation of their different senses in chapter 2, n. 6.

9. See *ST* I-II 25.3. While Thomas will argue that Adam did not have passions with regard to evil at *ST* I 95.2, he qualifies this claim in *ST* I 95.3, ad. 2, where he acknowledges that Adam could have hated the devil in the original state.

10. *ST* I 95.2.

The goods that Thomas lists here are primarily spiritual in nature—that is, they do not appear primarily with regard to worldly goods. Thus, while Thomas believes that Adam had need of food prior to his sin, Adam did not suffer from hunger in the primitive state.[11] Insofar as his desires were directed toward worldly things, they existed in view of and in perfect subjection to Adam's rational and volitional self-direction toward his final end.[12]

Having noted the positive role of human affectivity in Thomas's thought, one should take note of the creativity and positive import of Thomas's articulation of human affectivity in his own time. Thomas's affirmation of human affectivity in the Adamic condition rises out of Thomas's consideration of the affections that runs throughout his corpus. As has been noted by Nicholas E. Lombardo, Thomas's account of the passions in the *Summa Theologica* was probably the most extensive theological treatment of the topic written up to that point. It draws on and synthesizes a breadth of previous accounts of the passions. Without precedent, his account grounds the passionate and affective life in a careful exposition of theological anthropology.[13]

All of these factors establish Thomas as an essential medieval voice regarding the affective life. Notably for this study, his approach leads him into a consistently positive assessment of the passions that proved impossible for Maximus in the midst of the Stoic components of his sources. Despite Maximus's relative hesitancy regarding the specifically *passionate* nature of humanity from its creation, however, both Thomas and Maximus affirm the innateness and goodness of the broader reality of affectivity in human existence. No insurmountable differences arise between Maximus and Thomas in the preceding material.[14]

Thomas is clear that the reason for the rectitude of body and soul

---

11. *ST* I 97.3.

12. Thus, while Thomas's affirmation of passibility may at first appear to be in tension with Maximus's claim that passibility is a consequence of the Fall, Thomas's view in fact coincides closely with Maximus's presentation, wherein a primarily spiritual object of desire and aversion was envisioned in the unfallen state.

13. See the review of literature provided by Lombardo, *The Logic of Desire*, 107.

14. Thomas argues that his disagreement with the Stoics is about terminology rather than substance (Lombardo, *The Logic of Desire*, 76).

in Adam's original condition is a privileged state of supernatural grace. Thomas states:

> Now it is clear that such a subjection of the body to the soul and of the lower powers to reason, was not from nature; otherwise it would have remained after sin [*non erat naturalis, alioquin post peccatum mansisset*];... Hence it is clear that also the primitive subjection by virtue of which reason was subject to God, was not a merely natural gift, but a supernatural endowment of grace [*secundum supernaturale donum gratiae*]; for it is not possible that the effect should be of greater efficiency than the cause.[15]

For this reason, Adam's condition at the beginning can be called the *original* state of human nature, but it would be inaccurate to describe it as his *natural* state; God provided Adam with supernatural gifts that Thomas describes as a state of original justice and sanctifying grace.[16] Especially through original justice, there is a twofold ordering, both of the soul to God and of the body to the soul.

For this study, a final notable component of Adam's original, graced condition is his immunity to intellectual "deception (*deceptio*)"[17] and to temptation "by inward suggestion (*interiori suggestione*),"[18] each of which I treat in turn. Regarding the first, Thomas does not discuss the identity of the deceiver, but based on his replies, one can surmise that he intends to include both human and demonic sources in this treatment. While Thomas entertains distinctions that would permit a certain, imperfect form of deception before sin, he ultimately rejects them, clarifying that even Eve's deception was possible only *after* an interior act of pride.[19] Thomas concludes that "the rectitude of the primitive state was incompatible with deception of the

---

15. *ST* I 95.1.
16. Justice is not the only virtue that is conveyed in this original state; it also includes prudence, fortitude, temperance, and a grace that acted to protect Adam's imagination from demonic manipulation. I treat this final aspect next.
17. *ST* I 94.4.
18. *ST* II-II 165.2.
19. *ST* I 94.4., ad. 1. In the response to this question, Thomas argues that "whatever deception occurs must be ascribed to some lower faculty, such as the imagination or the like." Because of the clarification about Eve, however, one should take the deception through imagination as descriptive of the postlapsarian state; no deception seems possible prior to any sort of sinful consent. Thomas confirms this immunity again at *ST* II-II 165.2.

intellect."[20] From these considerations, Thomas equates the unfallen state of humanity with a basic freedom from evil intellectual influence. Just as Thomas denies that the devil could convince Adam of any false opinion in his intellect,[21] he similarly denies that any evil could enter Adam's body, answering in a reply that "were anything presented to the imagination or sense of the first man, not in accordance with the nature of things, he would not have been deceived, for his reason would have enabled him to judge the truth."[22]

Regarding the second component, inner temptation, Thomas considers the means of prelapsarian demonic attack in a question on temperance in the *Secunda Secundae*. Thomas argues there that "the devil had a minimum of power against man before sin, wherefore he was unable to tempt him by inward suggestion [*interiori suggestione*], but only by outward suggestion."[23] Thomas argues that this immunity to temptation comes as a result of "a special favor of grace."[24] Significantly, this grace protected other faculties of Adam's humanity, even ones that are not the subject of virtue and vice. The most important of these faculties is the imagination, which Thomas also argues would have remained without external influence. In short, before the Fall, Adam was immune to demonic attacks against his intellect, his appetitive faculties, and his imagination.

The Fall

Thomas's account of the Fall describes how Adam lost many of his created perfections as a consequence of sin. In this material—and, indeed, the rest of my treatment of Thomas—one may note a particular emphasis on the negative components of human emotionality in Thomas's account. Despite this largely negative focus, one should not lose sight of the positive characteristics of Thomas's account that

---

20. *ST* I 94.4, response.
21. *ST* I 94.4, response.
22. *ST* I 94.4, ad. 3. Thomas further denies that any such imaginative representation was possible in the original state in *ST* II-II 165.2.
23. *ST* II-II 165.2, ad. 2.
24. *ST* II-II 165.1, response. I consider this special grace again in the detailed analysis of inner demonic temptation in the second part of this chapter.

I outline above. As in the case of Maximus, the negative focus of this portrayal is necessitated by my central concern. In order to understand how Christ encounters, heals, and overcomes those most fundamentally disordered aspects of human affectivity in his own human experience of temptation, the disorder of human emotionality must be approached with open eyes and articulated accurately. For both Maximus and Thomas, Christ himself heals fallen human emotionality only by entering to some extent into its conditions; in tracing Christ's healing work, this study must follow the same course. For my purposes, then, two of the consequences of Adam's sin require careful attention: humanity's subservience to demonic powers and the internal appetitive disorder that entered human existence following Adam's sin. I treat each of these consequences and end with a discussion of the relationship between these two effects of sin in Thomas's corpus.

Thomas understands that when Adam sinned, this offense put him in a justly deserved servitude to demonic power. The theme is discussed in perhaps the most depth in Thomas's early *Commentary on Job*, though it can be seen with varying degrees of detail in portions of the *Summa Theologica* as well.[25] The content of this slavery will be considered at length in the analysis of demonic temptation that follows. For the moment, I wish to consider the justice of this bondage to the devil.

The nature of humanity's slavery or bondage to the devil, as presented by Thomas, is somewhat complex. On the one hand, Thomas argues that, consequent to Adam's sin, God justly punishes humanity. Any punishment from God that follows is, from humanity's perspective, unexceptionable. Moreover, it is within the bounds of justice for God to dispense this punishment through whatever vessels God

---

25. It is found in passing at *ST* I-II 80.4, but then later in more detail at *ST* III 48.4. The *Commentary on Job* is also particularly extensive on this point, found in Thomas Aquinas, *The Literal Exposition on Job: A Scriptural Commentary Concerning Providence*, trans. Anthony Damico (Atlanta, Ga.: Scholars Press, 1989). Though Thomas does not speak about this topic in his early *Summa contra Gentiles* at much length, I presume in this material a basic continuity in his thought on this subject. For the dating of Thomas's works, see Jean-Pierre Torrell, *Saint Thomas Aquinas: The Person and His Work, Revised Edition*, trans. Robert Royal (Washington, D.C.: The Catholic University of America Press, 2005), 330–61.

sees fit. Thus, God can rightly assign demons to plague humanity; he describes this arrangement through the analogy of a sovereign judge (God) and a torturer (the devil).[26] In this limited sense, humanity's sin incurs a double-debt to God and the devil. Indeed, Thomas calls humanity the devil's "bondsman" and states that "since the Devil had overcome man by inducing him to sin, man was subject to the devil's bondage."[27] Thomas maintains, however, that the power exercised by the devil over humanity is, from another perspective, manifestly *unjust* since the devil did not *earn* the right to enslave humanity. From the perspective of the devil, Thomas argues that the punishment the devil inflicts on human beings is *not* just.[28] Nevertheless, this distinction is important for Thomas because he wishes to avoid the implication that God could owe a debt to the devil or that Christ (by his passion and death) would in any way pay the devil for humankind.[29] In short, while humanity is *justly held*, the devil *holds unjustly*.

Thomas's early *Commentary on Job* ascribes a great deal of power to the devil over humankind. Because of the superiority of angelic natures over human nature, Thomas concludes an extended metaphorical reading of Leviathan with these lines:

> No human power is able to wound the devil or resist him, but all human power is considered by the devil as nothing.... No matter how much the strength and effort of humankind is exerted, it is disdained by the devil.[30]

Thus, if one were to construe the primary spiritual battle as between the devil and human beings left to their own power, there is no question who the victor would be. Divine aid is humanity's only recourse,

---

26. *ST* III 48.4, ad. 2.

27. *ST* III 48.4, ad. 2 and response, respectively.

28. There is some tension here, insofar as Thomas does not explain the authority by which the devil can be said to hold humanity in bondage in the passage quoted above. God is described as not merely *permitting* but even *ordaining* the penalty of demonic slavery (*ST* III 48.4, ad. 2). If God ordains the devil to inflict punishment on humanity, there seems to be something just, even from the perspective of the devil. Fundamentally, however, Thomas attempts to resolve the tension by arguing that the debt owed by humanity is to God alone and not to the devil, insofar as the devil attempts to collect this debt (for himself), his holding of humanity is unjust.

29. See *ST* III 48.4, ad. 3.

30. Aquinas, *Commentary on Job* 41 (found in Aquinas, *The Literal Exposition on Job*, 466, translation modified).

and that aid determines the boundaries of the battle waged against humankind.

Thomas argues that Adam's sin changed the *quality* and *means* of the devil's temptation. Considering Adam's changed moral circumstances after sin, Thomas writes that

> A suggestion whereby the devil suggests something to man spiritually, shows the devil to have more power against man than outward suggestion has, since by an inward suggestion, at least, man's imagination is changed by the devil; whereas by an outward suggestion a change is wrought merely on an outward creature.[31]

These changed moral circumstances for Adam's descendants are a concrete and palpable element of the devil's enslavement of humankind. Whereas prior to the Fall, Adam was largely immune to the devil's attack, Adam's sin results in new means of suggestion and temptation that were previously impossible. These means include an increased susceptibility in his internal faculties (including imagination and, in conjunction with the *fomes*, his sensitive appetite) as well as an exterior power over Adam's body. This latter power will be particularly significant for Thomas's Christological resolution in the next chapter. One can thus say that for Thomas, Adam's deliberate sin resulted in an unintended interior slavery to the devil: a position consonant with Maximus's view of Adam's sin from the first half. Thomas indicates that this slavery and susceptibility is the result of the withdrawal of grace that follows from Adam's sin, thereby becoming an intrinsic component of his condition after sin.[32] Adam's new susceptibility to inward demonic suggestion, however, was not the only consequence of his sin.

When Adam sinned, the supernatural graces that characterized his original state were withdrawn, consequently leading to the experience of inordinate desires.[33] Two changes occur. First, various forms

---

31. *ST* II-II 165.2, ad. 2.
32. *ST* II-II 165.1, response. Thomas only addresses, counterfactually, Adam's original immunity from temptation as a result of a special grace, but he implies thereby that after Adam consents to the temptation, that grace is removed.
33. For an account of the Fall that largely accords with that provided here, see Lombardo,

of both positive and negative affective states rush in. No longer does Adam experience only spiritual affectivity such as joy, love, and faith; for the first time, Adam involuntarily suffered passions that pertained to worldly needs, such as hunger. Second, these desires are no longer perfectly voluntary, becoming subject to a disordered political governance whereby they sometimes resist rational governance.

Because of the supernatural qualities of Adam's original state, he was left after sin in what Thomas calls a natural state of disorder. As just quoted above, Thomas says of this original rectitude that "such a subjection of the body to the soul and of the lower powers to reason, was not from nature; otherwise it would have remained after sin [*non erat naturalis, alioquin post peccatum mansisset*]."[34] With the withdrawal of the supernatural grace of the Adamic state, the various powers of the soul revert to their natural objects, resulting in moral disorder:

> Accordingly the privation of original justice, whereby the will was made subject to God, is the formal element in original sin; while every other disorder of the soul's powers, is a kind of material element in respect of original sin. Now the inordinateness of the other powers of the soul consists chiefly in their turning inordinately to mutable good; which inordinateness may be called by the general name of concupiscence. Hence original sin is concupiscence, materially, but privation of original justice, formally.[35]

The removal of God's supernatural aid results in the material consequence of a natural inordinateness and Augustinian "concupiscence," a term that, in this sense, Thomas uses interchangeably with the *fomes peccati*, the kindling of sin.[36] This way of construing the natural state of human desire is at odds with Maximus's understanding of natural

---

The Logic of Desire, 118–24. Thomas also discusses the natural consequences of the Fall in *ST* II-II 164.1.

34. *ST* I 95.1. One sees here how Thomas's approach to nature differs from that of Maximus, for whom virtue is described as natural.

35. *ST* I-II 82.1.

36. There is some lack of consistency in the translation of this phrase in modern secondary literature. Some modern scholars have taken to translating *fomes* as "spark." Lombardo, *The Logic of Desire*, 211, translates the phrase as "tinder of sin," which I take to be most accurate even in Thomas's usage. As I argue in this section, Thomas's native analogies present the devil as taking an intentional role in the production of "dry wood" for burning, so my preference for "kindling" or "tinder" stems from this aspect of Thomas's usage.

and imaginative appetites and the natural will (and, in turn, his dyothelitism); it is therefore important to consider why the two diverge here.[37]

By arguing that God provided supernatural aid to Adam in his original state, Thomas simultaneously anticipates two objections. First, he staves off the objection that God, from the beginning, did not provide Adam the necessary resources to successfully strive toward and attain absolute perfection insofar as this is possible within the confines of human nature. A trajectory of pure ascent toward God is conceivable from Adam's original condition; the Fall was by no means necessary.

Second, Thomas argues that the punishment of original sin is not, as it were, divinely inflicted corporal punishment or corruption. The punishment is not carried out through God's agency but instead flows from his (more passive) withdrawal of grace. This concern is seen especially strongly in Thomas's *Sentences Commentary*, in which he addresses whether original sin can be said to be "from God."[38] Following a distinction from Peter the Lombard seen in chapter 4, Thomas says that one must distinguish between original sin as fault and as punishment: insofar as original sin arises from Adam's willful transgression of God's commandment, it is not from God; insofar as it is a punishment, it is. But Thomas distinguishes even further so as to protect against the charge that God *inflicts* this punishment on humanity as a whole, that is, to make clear that this punishment flows from God's withdrawal of grace rather than from a distinct punitive action on God's part.

> But if it is considered insofar as it is a defect from some perfection, it is a punishment; and in this way, indeed, God is the cause of punishment. But it must be known that [God] is not the cause of all punishment in this way. For some punishment is through the infliction of some contrary torment or

---

37. Thomas invokes the category of "will as nature" in *ST* III 18.3 in a way that is consonant with Maximus's usage, but this distinction is absent from Thomas's purely anthropological reflection on nature, which instead reflects his Latin Augustinian heritage.

38. *Sent. Comm.* II 32.2.1, my translation. Citations of the *Sentences Commentary* are from https://www.corpusthomisticum.org/iopera.html.

corruption; and these latter punishments are by God's agency [*a Deo agente*], from whom all actions (insofar as they are orderly) and consequent sufferings take their principle. But all punishment, when it is just, is orderly. There is, however, some punishment which consists simply in a removal or a lack, as with the withdrawal of grace, and other things of this kind; and these kinds of punishments are from God, not indeed as from any agent [*non quidem sicut ab agente aliquid*], but rather as from the lack of influx of a certain perfection; because [to cause] to flow and not to flow are his [God's]; and his will is the cause of both.[39]

Thomas is careful to argue that while both kinds of punishment come from God's will, the kind of punishment involved in original sin is not *inflicted* by God but is merely a passive *withdrawal* of something beyond nature, undeserved. Perhaps Thomas might illustrate: as parents may give their children an allowance that exceeds what they have earned, the parents, when displeased with the children, may withhold the allowance without inflicting punishment, since the original gift was already unearned. Because he distinguishes the punishment of original sin from a just and orderly active infliction, Thomas implies that it would *not* be just for God to will some active punishment of original sin in Adam's descendants:

if the *fomes* is considered insofar as it is a punishment, it cannot be said that some punishment is inflicted (because a supernatural principle is not subjected to anything positive in man) but pertains to the same genus of punishment as that which consists only in defect [*in solo defectu*].[40]

To reiterate, the passivity of God's punishment in this line of reasoning is important. Since the withdrawal of something supernatural is in no sense owed, God does not actively inflict some further punishment that would drive the creature from God. Even though God's will is the cause of both punishments, the punishment of original sin does not come from God's will in the same way as does the latter kind of punishment. While one can see in this argument an echo of Maximus's distinction, seen in chapter 2, between God's permissive will and his

39. *Sent. Comm.* II 32.2.1, response, my translation.
40. *Sent. Comm.* II 32.2.1, response, my translation.

will of good pleasure, Maximus's understanding of the Fall remains less punitive and more pedagogical than does Thomas's.

The negative and formal aspect of concupiscence, however, is only half of Thomas's thought on the matter. He also considers a positive, material element that is more active in its separation of the human being from its final end. Thomas lays the blame for the positive proclivity or tendency that separates humanity from God at Adam's feet, through whom it is passed on to the rest of the species. Since the origin of the *fomes* is only negatively and formally ascribed to the agency of God, Thomas provides a parallel explanation of the material component, which can be described as "something positive" in concupiscence. Thomas explains this material component in a variety of ways: it can be called a "corrupt habit" and a sickness that is "as if in nature (*quasi in naturam*)."[41] Neither of these explanations, however, should be taken too literally because the phenomenon that Thomas describes here is *sui generis*. Even though it passes to other human beings as to the members of the body (in a way parallel to an acquired habit), in this context, he speaks of habit analogously and not in the full sense of an acquired habit.[42] Similarly, Thomas does not think that this disorder is fully natural—the *quasi* in the above affirmation is essential.[43] Instead, the material component of concupiscence is what Thomas most accurately describes as a "sickness" brought about by Adam's fault. This sickness is primarily and formally the lack of supernatural aid, but the establishment of any positive, seminatural component in it is attributed by Thomas to Adam. By placing the positive origin of the *fomes* in Adam's intentional sin, Thomas mitigates some of Maximus's objections to a natural power inclining against its source, thereby leaving some space for an orthodox dyothelite resolution to their

---

41. *ST* I-II 82.2.

42. Thomas claims in *ST* I-II 82.1, ad. 3 that original sin is an acquired habit "by the act of our first parent, but not by our own act." Since that is not how habits are normally acquired, Thomas prefers to call this habit "inborn due to our corrupt origin" (*ST* I-II 82.1, ad. 3). For his understanding of acquired habits and why original sin should not be formally understood as one, see also *ST* I-II 82.2, ad. 1; *De Malo* IV.2, ad. 5; and *ST* I-II 51.3, response.

43. In *De Malo*, Thomas states that this habit is neither natural nor infused by God (*De Malo* IV.2, in Thomas Aquinas, *The De Malo of Thomas Aquinas*, trans. Richard Regan (New York: Oxford University Press, 2001); text includes Thomas's Latin.

disagreements.[44] Nevertheless, there remains a significant disjunction between Thomas and Maximus about what a natural power should do in relation to humankind's final end.

Further, in Thomas's estimation, Adam did not act alone in his transgression, as he had the devil to help him. In his questions on concupiscence and original sin, Thomas only considers the ways in which these realities relate to human and divine agency, but following at least implicitly both Augustine and Peter the Lombard, Thomas elsewhere considers an *evil* intentional force in relation to the origin of the *fomes peccati*. In the final material of this section, then, I address those other texts to show how Thomas views the devil to be active alongside Adam in the material disordering of human nature that Thomas calls the *fomes*.

The strongest textual evidence in Thomas's corpus linking the devil to concupiscence appears in passages based on Genesis 3 where Thomas considers whether the devil can be said to be the cause of all sin: one article in the *Summa Theologica* and another in the *De Malo*. In both of these passages, Thomas draws on the analogy of kindling and fire to explain the way in which the devil can legitimately be called the cause of all sin. Since concupiscence (in the sense of disordered desire) is the "kindling of sin," Thomas's analogy of firewood prepared by the devil takes on important overtones.[45] I quote both passages before discussing them. First, in the *Summa Theologica*, Thomas states that

44. According to the reasoning of the *Sentences Commentary*, if God does anything *positive* in the punishment of original sin, this action would be tantamount to God habitually driving the creature farther from the Creator: something that Thomas believes would be unjust. However, if the positive element of original sin (concupiscence) were to be traced back to the nature that God covered from the beginning with his supernatural grace, one must still see that "natural" constitution as one that is indifferent to or even inclines against its Creator. If one were to consider this constitution as a part of God's providential plan, God's justice in creating a nature that would *naturally* rebel against God is not clear and remains in significant tension with Maximus's view of the natural will. For this reason, Thomas blames Adam for the positive and material component of the *fomes peccati*, which mitigates the extent to which this rebellious inclination can be called natural.

45. As discussed in a note above, the theological reality that the *fomes* attempts to describe is inherently analogical and evocative. From the beginning of this tradition, the use of the term *fomes* requires a close analysis of the analogy of fire, wood, burning, sparks, and of the different kinds of agency involved with those objects. What follows is an attempt to trace some of the Thomistic strains of this analogy.

the devil is the occasional and indirect cause of all our sins, in so far as he induced the first man to sin, by reason of whose sin human nature is so infected, that we are all prone to sin: even as the burning of wood might be imputed to the man who dried the wood so as to make it easily inflammable [*sicut diceretur esse causa combustionis lignorum qui ligna siccaret, ex quo sequeretur quod facile incenderentur.*].[46]

Second, in the *De Malo*, Thomas says that

We can speak in two ways of something causing something else: in one way directly; in the second way indirectly. Something indeed causes indirectly, as we say that a cause causing a disposition to an effect causes the effect as the occasion for the effect and indirectly [*sicut cum aliquod agens causat aliquam dispositionem ad aliquem effectum, dicitur esse occasionaliter et indirecte causa illius effectus*]. For example, such would be the case if we should say that one who dries out pieces of wood provides the occasion for burning the very wood [*sicut si dicatur quod ille qui siccat ligna est occasio combustionis ipsorum*]. And we need to say in this way that the devil causes all our sins, since he himself incited the first man to sin, from whose sin a proneness to every kind of sin resulted in the whole human race.[47]

Two major issues need to be addressed in these analogies: first, the *intention* of the devil, and second, the *agency* of the devil. The one who dries wood has a goal in mind. They do not do so indiscriminately, but precisely so that the wood might be burnt more easily. This agent does not directly cause the wood to be burnt, but he alters the composition or qualities of the wood with that end in mind. Similarly, the devil's actions would function with such subsequent burning as his intent.[48] That is, by tempting Adam, the devil intends not only to bring Adam to sin but also to make it easier for all Adam's progeny to do so as well.[49]

---

46. *ST* I-II 80.4., response.
47. *De Malo*, III 5., response.
48. In some passages in the *Sentences Commentary*, Thomas appears to deny that the devil has such a long-term goal in mind when he tempts Adam to sin. I discuss those passages in the section on temptation, but, to anticipate, the reason for this denial has to do with Thomas's early classification of the devil's temptation as a species of temptation "from the world."
49. One can note a similar account of a long-term demonic action in the *Commentary on Job* 41, in *The Exposition on Job: A Scriptural Commentary Concerning Providence*, trans. Anthony Damico (Atlanta, Ga.: Scholars Press, 1989), 467, though this text does not clearly relate to any action that might be analogous to kindling.

TABLE 5-1. Thomas's Demonic Allegory of the *Fomes Peccati*

	(1)	(2)	(3)	(4)
(a)	The dryer:	The act of drying:	Dried wood:	Burning of wood::
(b)	The devil:	Tempting Adam:	Proneness to sin:	Culpably sinful desire

On the second question of agency, one must be careful not to take Thomas's analogy too literally. The analogy indicates a *direct* agency in the drying of the wood, but the situation is different in the case of the devil's temptation of Adam—a difference that is obscured in the analogy itself.

In the passage from *De Malo*, the components of the analogy align as seen in table 5-1: In (a), the agent (1) performs an action (2) with a material object as the intentional goal (3) that results in or tends to an action carried out by another agent (4). In line (b), however, something more intervenes between (2) and (3) than in line (a). That is, the wood dries in (a) as a direct consequence of the act of drying;[50] the proneness to sin in (b) does not follow directly and necessarily from the act of tempting Adam. One must qualify that this temptation must be *successful*, that this quality only attains when Adam cooperates with the devil's temptation. For this reason and beyond the grasp of Thomas's analogy, the devil's agency in the origination of the *fomes* remains *indirect* in the sense that the devil cannot act alone in bringing it about, whereas Adam, in theory, could have acted alone in doing so. Adam's agency is the most important cause of the *fomes*. Nevertheless, the fact remains that in these passages, Thomas ascribes to the devil an indirect and intentional agency in the origin of humanity's general inclination toward sin.

Thomas's *Commentary on Job* also uses similar images. Thomas, for example, describes the experience of Adam's fallen progeny, and in so doing, he explores the description of Leviathan in the book of Job as

---

50. Thomas does not say explicitly that the "wood [*ligna*]" from (a) is equivalent to the *fomes* from (b), but his closing of the analogy refers to the wood as the "proneness to every kind of sin [*pronitas ad omnia peccata*]," which is unmistakably the language of concupiscence and the *fomes*.

a figure of the devil who tempts fallen human beings. In the course of this description, Thomas interprets certain "flaming pine logs" related to Leviathan's mouth as originating from demonic attack against Adam's fallen progeny:

> They are compared to a lit pine-pitch torch because of their redolence, as was said. Now by this verse is designated that the devil enkindles men to an eager desire for sin [*Diabolus ad concupiscentiam peccati homines incendit*] through a showing of some good as if through a kind of redolence.[51]

He later describes the devil's breath in similar metaphors:

> Since an animal breathes not only through his nostrils but also through his mouth, He adds fifth the operation of the mouth, saying *His breath*, that is, the exhalation proceeding from his mouth, *makes live coals glow*, that is, it is so hot and strong that it would be sufficient to light coals. For He speaks in a metaphor of those who light coals by blowing under them. Hence, He adds *and flame comes out of his mouth*, namely, since the vapor coming from his mouth is so hot and fiery that it can deservedly be compared to flame. Now by all these verses is designated the fact that the devil, by his concealed or manifest suggestions, kindles in man the fire of perverse desire [*Diabolus sua occulta vel manifesta suggestione perversae cupiditatis ignem in homine accendit*].[52]

This text appears to ascribe yet more to the devil's power than the texts quoted earlier. Most importantly, in both of these passages, Thomas uses a verb indicating the lighting of a fire (*incendere* and *accendere*, respectively) to describe the devil's activity in fallen humankind. Thus, while in the passage above the devil—in tempting Adam—was only said to prepare wood for burning (which human beings must themselves light), Thomas describes the devil as himself lighting the fire of desire in human beings who live in weakened moral circumstances after Adam's fall. Since fallen human beings share in the separate defect of the *fomes*, the "lighting" is likely interconnected with the "kindling" of the *fomes*.

---

51. Thomas, *Commentary on Job* 41, in *Exposition on Job*, 463. Given that this passage describes the postlapsarian condition, Thomas is no longer speaking about the devil's confection of the *fomes*; instead, he describes the devil's efforts to cause that previously prepared tinder to burn.

52. Thomas, *Commentary on Job* 41, in *Exposition on Job*, 463.

A final example of the symbolic overlap between Thomas's demonology and theory of the *fomes* is seen in his *Commentary on Romans*. There, a personified interpretation of the flesh and of sin is not out of the question.[53] In his treatment of Romans 7:7–13, and again in 14–20, three distinct references to the devil or to the devil's temptations appear in the symbolic structure of flesh and sin, one of which is significant here.[54] While a demonic interpretation of "sin" is not Thomas's preferred reading, Thomas finds it convenient to include this interpretation when Paul describes sin in highly personified and intentional categories, as in Romans 7:8:

> Thus, he first says that sin, taking occasion through the law (namely the law prohibiting sin) worked in me all concupiscence. But by sin here may be understood the Devil according to an emphatic locution, because he himself is the beginning of sin. And according to this, he works in human beings all desire for sin: "The one who sins is from the Devil, because the Devil sinned from the beginning" (Jn 3:8).[55]

Thomas initially refers this malice to a positive intentional agent. He decides that this reading is not to be preferred, however, "because the Apostle had not mentioned the devil here,"[56] and moves on to the more likely interpretations of actual or original sin, downplaying the apparently intentional and personified characteristics ascribed to sin by Paul.[57]

Outside his systematic questions that focus on original sin and concupiscence, then, Thomas recognizes a significant overlap between the influence of the devil and the influence of the "flesh." This recognition significantly expands on Thomas's more systematic questions on concupiscence and, moreover, shares commonalities with Maximus's Greek approach. Though the nature of humanity's wound is under-

---

53. See Bernhard Blankenhorn, "Aquinas on Paul's Flesh/Spirit Anthropology in Romans," in *Reading Romans with St. Thomas Aquinas*, ed. Matthew Levering and Michael Dauphinais, 3–4 (Washington, D.C.: The Catholic University of America Press, 2012).

54. These references appear in Aquinas's *Commentary on Romans* 7.2 (on Rom 7:9b, §563).

55. Thomas, *Commentary on Romans* 7.2, my translation.

56. Thomas, *Commentary on Romans* 7.2.

57. One might note the contrast on this point with John of Damascus from chapter 4, where John maintained the personification of the "law of sin" quite strongly.

stood differently by each thinker, both recognize the devil's intentional efforts to separate humankind from its final end. For Thomas, this means that the devil has an indirect agency in the origin of the *fomes* and that the devil enkindles desire in Adam's fallen progeny. Further, Thomas at times reads Paul's theory of the flesh and sin as indicating the devil and his works. In linking the origin of human sinfulness with the devil, Thomas's reading is drawn into substantive contact with Maximus' view of human sinfulness.

While Thomas's full understanding of the *fomes* is not succinctly summarized in any single text, its various components outlined above form a coherent whole. In particular, his view of the *fomes* as privation (as in Thomas's questions on concupiscence) is compatible with his view that it is partly demonically inspired (as in Thomas's questions on the devil). Thomas wishes to preserve the passivity of Adam's punishment by God. By the time of the *Summa Theologica*, therefore, Thomas ascribes the positive and more active aspect of original sin—concupiscence—to the agency of Adam *as well as* the devil (albeit in a subordinate way). In that way, Thomas argues that there is a malicious, intentional agent attempting to provide humanity with enduring tendencies toward evil, as if they were from *within* fallen human nature. Since the devil can be seen as the one who plays a unique role in "drying the kindling wood" of the *fomes*, God's role in original sin is preserved as a passive and formal withdrawal of original justice. God's agency is never involved in the movement of the creature from its final end; such movement comes directly from Adam's agency with the indirect, intentional aid of the devil. The differences between Maximus and Thomas on these matters are important. Thomas's primarily anthropological framework of the *fomes* is foreign to Maximus's prevailing demonological approach to human sinfulness. In contrast to Thomas's punitive approach to the Fall, Maximus's approach focuses more on the pedagogical function of the apparent punishment. And, most importantly, Maximus would insist much more heavily on the fundamental orientation of nature to its final end than does Thomas, for whom human nature can appear indifferent to its final end. Nevertheless, these remarks show that a generous reading of Thomas is in some ways compatible with Maximus's view of human nature.

Fleshly and Internal Demonic Temptation

In order to prepare for the particular question at the heart of this study, I trace Thomas's account of two different kinds of postlapsarian temptation: that arising from the flesh and that from the devil. When considering Maximus's account of demonic temptation in chapter 2, I considered tracing the question of human *culpability* for inner dispositions that were brought about by external, malicious forces.[58] Similarly, my treatment of Thomas's theory of temptation is intended to address what makes the human subject culpable for certain affective responses but not culpable for certain others. There are three steps in this argument. First, an analysis of Thomas's typology of temptations is necessary because Thomas's thought on this subject develops through his corpus, in which he provides substantially different typologies in the *Sentences Commentary*, his scriptural interpretation, the *Summa Theologica*, and his *Commentary on the Our Father*. After I discuss these typologies, I proceed to a treatment of each of the two postlapsarian forms of temptation.[59]

Typologies of Temptation in Thomas Aquinas

As shown in chapter 4, the medieval tradition that preceded Thomas had developed an elaborate typology of temptation that accounted for a number of sources, means, and moral characteristics for various forms of temptation. Following a typology originating in Hugh of St. Victor, the most common way of speaking about temptation pur-

---

58. Since demonic temptation cuts to the heart of Maximus's understanding of the moral act, I had to trace the progression of that act in detail. In Thomas's case, however, this same line of culpability is traced precisely in considering the sinfulness of the *fomes peccati*, the first of Thomas's forms of temptation.

59. These two forms—the *fomes peccati* and demonic temptation—are the only ones that bring about a direct inclination toward evil, as I show in my analysis of Thomas's typology. Other things that Thomas categorizes as temptation do not tempt directly in this way: human beings who tempt others to sin are only instruments of the devil's temptation; God's "temptation," on the other hand, is only in order to approve the one tested.

sued three main avenues: inner temptation from the flesh, exterior temptation by the devil, and interior temptation by the devil. I trace Thomas's own appropriation of this tradition through the works in which he addresses different kinds of temptation at some length: first, the *Sentences Commentary*; second, the *Summa Theologica, Commentary on 1 Thessalonians*, and the *De Malo*; and third, the *Commentary on the Lord's Prayer*.

From the beginning of Thomas's consideration of temptation, he shows a willingness to modify the typology provided in Peter the Lombard's *Sentences*. At this early stage, Thomas's classification of demonic temptation is buried among the distinctions in his typology. While Thomas acknowledges temptations coming from each of the different sources that Peter notes, Thomas's classification of these temptations (or tests) uses criteria that are distinct from Peter's:

> Three things come together in the perfect notion of temptation [*ad perfectam rationem tentationis*]. First, that through temptation some doubtful thing can be taken into knowledge; second, that such [temptation] be intended by the one who tempts [*ut hoc sit intentum ab eo qui tentat*]; third that the same one who tempts wants to take that thing into knowledge.[60]

By assigning three criteria to the proper nature of temptation, Thomas limits the sense in which the term temptation can be applied to scenarios that do not meet all these criteria. Thomas continues by considering different sources of temptation and their relationship to these criteria. His three main headings are: human beings; God; and the flesh and the world (these last two being considered together). The whole typology is visualized in figure 5-1.

As Thomas explains, only temptation from other human beings meets all three of his criteria and is thus the truest form of temptation. The second temptation, from God, meets the first two criteria but fails the third since God learns nothing by the trial.

The third kind of temptation (from the flesh and the world) only meets the first criterion: the thing tempting does not *intend* the trial; and the thing tempting does not learn anything about the thing

---

60. *Sent. Comm.* II 21.1.1, my translation.

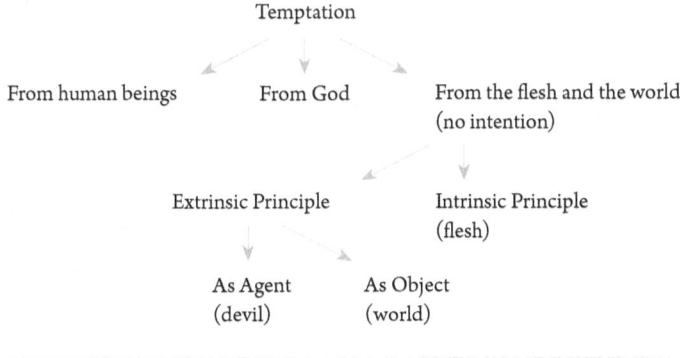

FIGURE 5-1. Thomas's Typology of Temptation in His *Sentences Commentary*

tempted.[61] This latter criterion is particularly important. As Thomas illustrates,

> the flesh or the world is said to tempt, because in this, the virtue or infirmity of the mind is manifestly made known, as in war the virtue of a soldier is made known, even though the enemy did not attack so as to know, but so as to conquer, whence the attack of virtue itself is called temptation.[62]

Thus, for sources of temptation in this third category, the trial as such is incidental to the purposes of the thing that tempts. That is, neither the flesh nor the world *intend* to try the one tempted. Thomas then introduces a distinction between such temptations that come from an internal principle and those that come from an external one, corresponding to the distinction between the flesh and the world.[63] This distinction

---

61. Thomas reiterates this point in one of his responses to *Sent. Comm.* II 21.1.1: "the flesh does not intend this, but rather to enjoy knowledge of pleasure [*caro non intendit [occidendi hominem per peccatum], sed delectabili cognito perfrui*]."
62. *Sent. Comm.* II 21.1.1.
63. *Sent. Comm.* II 21.1.1. In his *Commentary on Job*, Thomas also uses the interior/exterior distinction that will appear in his later Christological reasoning about temptation. Thomas does not appear to expound a full typology of temptation in this work, so I leave its brief discussion to this note. First, interior temptation is as follows: "just as a garment is consumed by a worm which is born of it, so the justice of man is consumed by those things which are in man like inflamed tinder [*corruptio fomitis*]—evil thoughts and other such things [*sicut enim vestimentum consumitur a tinea quae ex eo nascitur, ita iustitia hominis consumitur ex his quae in homine sunt sicut est corruptio fomitis, malae cogitationes et alia huiusmodi*]" (Thomas, *Literal Exposition*

between "inner" and "outer" is important in Thomas's later Christological reflections on temptation, so it is noteworthy that this distinction is present from Thomas's earliest typology of temptation. Finally, the latter category (the world) is subdivided into two final categories:

> Because that which is exterior is either an attack by way of object, and this is temptation from the world, by which things the heart of the human being is enticed to sin; or it is an attack by way of agency, which draws to sin by persuasion, by frightening, by flattering, and so with others, and this is said to be temptation from the enemy, namely the devil, and from those who are his members.[64]

By placing the devil at this juncture of his typology, Thomas has significantly restricted the meaning of the devil's temptation, ruling out that the devil *intends* to tempt. Instead, he argues, the ultimate end of the devil is to *deceive (fallere)* and to *lead into sin (inducere ad peccatum)*; the trial is only incidental to this ultimate goal.[65] This categorization leaves out the devil's attempts to ascertain those sins to which an individual is inclined, which would be a full "test" in this typology.[66]

In the *Summa Theologica, Commentary on 1 Thessalonians*, and *De Malo*, Thomas's definition of temptation shifts significantly and, consequently, so does his typology. Instead of the three criteria for a temptation expounded above, one finds in these works a simple, concise definition of temptation: "'to tempt' means to make a test of something",[67] or, translating differently, "to tempt is, properly speaking, to make trial of something."[68] This more compact definition gives Thom-

---

of Job 4, in *Exposition on Job*, 124). The exterior temptation receives no lengthy description in this passage.

64. *Sent. Comm.* II 21.1.1.

65. *Sent. Comm.* II 21.1.1, obj. 2.

66. Thomas recognizes that the devil has such a smaller, more proximate end in temptation (*Sent. Comm.* II 21.1.1). Structurally, however, this trial is instrumental to the real attack. The devil, at that stage, only wants to figure out what sins a person is likely to commit. Once that has been determined, the real attempt to drive on toward that sin begins.

67. Excerpts and quotations from Thomas Aquinas, *Commentary on the Letters of Saint Paul to the Philippians, Colossians, Thessalonians, Timothy, Titus, and Philemon*, trans. F. R. Larcher (Lander, Wyo.: Aquinas Institute for the Study of Sacred Doctrine, 2012), 173–74: "*Tentare est experimentum de aliquo sumere.*"

68. *ST* I 114.2: "*tentare est proprie experimentum sumere de aliquo.*"

TABLE 5-2. Thomas's Later Typology of Temptation

The Tester	Who Learns	For What End
God	Others	(In order to approve)
Human beings	The tester	To approve or reprove
Devil	The tester	To reprove

as the ability to assign a proper definition of temptation to a broader array of phenomena than he could in the *Sentences Commentary*. Most importantly, this changed definition requires a specific *intention* on the part of the thing tempting. This fact is borne out in the examples he gives of the full sense of temptation, each of which is a personified, intentional being: God, human beings, and demons.

For each of these three subjects of temptation, Thomas considers two questions that enable him to distinguish how each is distinct. First, he considers *who* gains knowledge through the test, and second, he considers *what ends* the tester seeks through the trial. Together, these three works represent Thomas's more developed understanding of temptation. Their typology can be summarized in table 5-2 above.

According to the second column, Thomas argues that God's testing can be differentiated from that of human beings and the devil, since God tests only so that *others* might know the quality of the person tested. The other two types of testers do so in order to find out for themselves. According to the third column, the testing of human beings can be differentiated from that of demons: whereas human beings can test either to approve or reprove, demons test only for the latter reason.[69] Although left implicit, Thomas's reasoning suggests that God tests only in order to approve. God's intention is never that the one tested would *fail,* and indeed, Thomas elsewhere states that the one tested in this way *never* fails.[70]

While these three subjects are the main and proper tempters in

---

69. In *ST* I 114.2, Thomas argues that when human beings test in order to reprove, they do so "as minister of the devil [*hoc agit inquantum est minister Diaboli*]."

70. I include this detail in the figure above despite its merely implicit presence in these texts. As seen immediately below, Thomas later explicitly affirms that God tests only to the *good.*

Thomas's later typology, Thomas also includes two subordinate sources of temptation that do so "instrumentally or materially": the flesh and the world.[71] This change is an inversion of what he argued in his early *Sentences Commentary*. At that time, he wrote that demonic temptation was a subspecies of "temptation from the flesh and the world," yet now, fleshly temptation has taken a subordinate and inferior role to temptation from the devil.

As a final aspect of this typology, Thomas indicates in important passages in both the *Summa Theologica* and *De Malo* that the internal/external distinction generally used to differentiate between fleshly and demonic temptation is not clean. In both texts, Thomas argues that the devil can tempt fallen human beings internally by the manipulation of one's imagination, senses, and any other faculty that makes use of a bodily organ.

Finally, Thomas addresses a categorization of temptations in a somewhat more modest fashion in his late *Commentary on the Our Father*. In the sixth petition of this text ("lead us not into temptation"), Thomas treats in detail the question of temptation toward evil. Thomas's definition of temptation here is slightly different than in the previous two texts but retains most of its meaning: "To tempt someone is to prove his virtue."[72] But virtue requires two things: to do good and avoid evil. In explaining this distinction, Thomas avows that God tries only for the good: "Therefore God often sends tribulations to the just, so that, while he patiently upholds them, their virtue may be made clear and [so that] they may grow in virtue."[73] Further, God has no part in the other temptation toward evil: "God tempts no one in this way."[74] Echoing the observations of the first part of this chapter, Thomas insists that God's role in evil must be purely passive or permissive, offering nothing that intentionally would lead one away from God.

---

71. *ST* I 114.2; see also the *1 Thessalonians* commentary, 3.1, where their temptation is described as material [*materialiter*].

72. Thomas, *Commentary on the Our Father*, pet. 6: "tentare hominem est probare virtutem eius." Before stating this definition, Thomas also articulates his more common definition: "to tempt is nothing other than to test or to prove [*tentare nihil aliud est quam experiri seu probare*]."

73. Thomas, *Commentary on the Our Father*, pet. 6.

74. Thomas, *Commentary on the Our Father*, pet. 6.

Instead, temptation toward evil is accomplished in three ways: by the flesh, by the devil, and by the world. The first of these is described by Thomas as "extremely severe" because "our enemy, the flesh, is united to us."[75] One should not read too much into Thomas's use of "enemy (*inimicus*)" to describe the flesh here; it certainly does not mean a facile negativity toward the body. This fact is made clear by Thomas's description of the next temptation, which appears to be even stronger than the first:

> Even after the flesh is treated with contempt, another [enemy] arises, namely the Devil, against whom we have a great struggle. Our struggle is not against flesh and blood, but against principalities and powers, against the rulers of the world of this darkness" (Eph 6:12).[76]

The invocation of Ephesians 4:12 in this context is significant. Thomas's invocation (along with his chronological comparative) implies that any *internal* struggle in human beings is in some sense minor in comparison to the struggle human beings must have with *angelic* powers. Thus, if the flesh is the "enemy," it is only so in a relative sense: only the devil is the real Enemy of humankind.

Thomas consistently recognizes throughout his corpus that temptation arises from a variety of sources, both internal and external. When it comes to temptation toward evil, the flesh and the devil take the most prominent locations. Thomas's relative assessment of the flesh and the devil, however, shifts after the *Sentences Commentary*. Thomas grants demonic temptation a more prominent place in later works than he did in that early work and even inverts the relationship between the flesh and the devil, ultimately granting the latter a deeper participation in the nature of temptation than the former.

Thomas stands in continuity with the earlier medieval tradition in his dependence on a distinction between internal and external temptation, often superficially correlated with the distinction between fleshly and demonic temptation. Thomas's formal typologies

---

75. Thomas, *Commentary on the Our Father*, pet. 6.
76. Thomas, *Commentary on the Our Father*, pet. 6. As with Maximus's stages of asceticism, one should not take Thomas's chronological comparative ("even after" ... "another arises") literally.

of temptation do not address the *internal* temptation of the devil, but this kind of temptation constitutes an important aspect of his developed thought concerning the devil and humankind. After considering fleshly temptation in more detail, Thomas's way of distinguishing it from internal demonic temptation will conclude this section.

Temptation from the Flesh in Aquinas's Thought
By way of anticipation, Thomas's assessment of the *fomes peccati* (or disordered concupiscence) leads him to conclude that this form of temptation cannot be present in Christ. Despite the fact that this topic plays no positive role in Thomas's Christology, much can be learned from the negative role it plays. I have taken care in chapter 2 to consider the anthropological structures that lay beneath temptation for Maximus, for whom the devil's sharpest temptation arose from natural appetites that were incited or inflamed by demons and thereby encouraged to develop in sinful ways. These appetites, for Maximus, were deeply embedded in the faculties of will and wish, which rise out of the natural, rational, and volitional nature of humankind. Thomas, however, frames the anthropological basis of passionate temptation in a different way, arguing that the appetitive faculties themselves function as a source of temptation in their natural state. That Thomas describes the functioning of the sensitive appetite as "tempting" is a direct consequence of the *fallenness* of the faculty; as discussed above, the sensitive appetite in no way tempted Adam prior to the Fall. Thomas calls this temptation from the sensitive appetite disordered concupiscence, or the *fomes peccati*. To understand his anthropological arrangement, I explain how Thomas conceives of this species of temptation, including its place in his postlapsarian anthropology and its object; its action as a conjoined activity of body and soul; why it is called temptation and how it tempts; and what theological ends this category serves in Thomas's thought.

The Place and Object of the *Fomes* in Fallen Humanity. Following Aristotelian categories, Thomas considers the human soul to be composed of three components: nutritive, animal, and rational. These three components are distinct in their powers but are still conceived as a totality, comprising a single soul. The sensitive appetite, whose role in the *fomes* is central, rises from the animal aspect of the soul, though it is transformed by its conjunction with reason in the human soul. The sensitive appetite takes its object primarily from the apprehension of a perceived or apparent bodily good. This action is itself passive, receiving the data of its act from outside (i.e., from the powers of apprehension), and the three sources that Thomas recognizes for this passive component are the imagination, the senses, and the estimative power (which in rational beings is called the cogitative power). The sensitive appetite, in turn, uses the data provided from these sources to form an appropriate appetitive reaction.

These reactions are categorized by Thomas into two forms (the desirable and the difficult), which are ascribed to two subfaculties within the appetitive faculty (the concupiscible and the irascible, somewhat comparable to Maximus's view of desire and aversion).[77] Since Thomas argues that all irascible movement is reducible to concupiscible movement, the distinction between these faculties is not absolute.[78]

Thomas understands the sensitive appetite to be conjoined to reason and will through the cogitative power. By means of this conjunction, the sensitive appetite is made rational by participation in human beings; it is not a merely "animal" instinct as it is in nonrational beings. Most importantly, because of the conjunction of the sensitive appetite with reason and will, the sensitive appetite is capable of formation (or malformation) by the human subject's highest faculties and can therefore be the indirect subject of sin when it is not formed correctly.[79] That is, when reason fails to resist, restrain, and even foresee the irrational or immoderate movement of the sensitive appetite, the appetite, insofar as it is conjoined to reason, is said to have a sinful movement.[80]

---

77. See Lombardo, *The Logic of Desire*, 50–54. As I noted earlier in this chapter and argued in chapter 2, n. 6, however, Thomas may at times understand the action of these faculties differently than Maximus. While these differences do not seriously affect my argument, they lead me to distinguish the terminology I use for each figure.

78. See ST I-II 22–25 for Thomas's introduction to the passions; ST I-II 23.4 presents Thomas's full list of passions, and ST I-II 25.1 and ST I-II 82.3, ad. 2, explain how the irascible passions can be reduced to concupiscible ones.

79. ST I-II 74.3, ST I-II 74.4, and ST I-II 77.

80. On the interplay of reason and will in the origin of sinful action, see Denis J. M. Bradley,

Such irrational movement is possible, as discussed above, because of the disordered inclination of the *fomes peccati*, a disorder that is understood by Thomas to be *intrinsic*, meaning that the *fomes* is not an external force acting on the sensitive appetite but instead *is* the appetite itself in a habitually disordered state. Thomas defines this disordering role in these terms:

> The fomes is nothing but a certain inordinate, but habitual, concupiscence of the sensitive appetite.... Now sensual concupiscence is said to be inordinate, insofar as it rebels against reason; and this it does by inclining to evil, or making the good difficult. Consequently, it is essential to the *fomes* to incline to evil or make it difficult to do good.[81]

When this habit moves forward into act, it is called actual concupiscence, the experience of which is unavoidable in the fallen state.[82] In fact, Thomas explicitly argues that while reason is capable of restraining and anticipating any particular irrational movement of the sensitive appetite, reason is incapable of foreseeing and forestalling *every* such movement. Reason is overwhelmed by the variety of irrational movements that assail it.[83] Thomas states the same with equal candor in his question on sin in the sensitive appetite: "a man cannot avoid all such movements [*non potest homo vitare omnes huiusmodi motus*]." After describing the act of the faculty itself, I will return to the moral imputability of these movements.[84]

The Act of the *Fomes* as a Conjoined Act of Body and Soul. There is a psychic and a physical component to every passion. The precise relationship of these two is particularly important for the way in which one should conceive of demonic temptation. Indeed, Robert Pasnau and Robert Miner have disputed how one should conceive of the bodily nature of the passions. Robert Pasnau offers an argument that the

---

"Aquinas on Weakness of the Will" in *Weakness of Will from Plato to the Present*, ed. Tobias Hoffmann, 100–105 (Washington, D.C.: The Catholic University of America Press, 2008).

81. *ST* III 27.3, response.
82. *ST* III 27.3, response.
83. *ST* I-II 74.3, ad. 2.
84. *ST* I-II 74.3, ad. 2 and ad. 3. See below and Odon Lottin's analysis in *Psychologie et Morale aux XIIe et XIIIe Siècle*, vol. 2, part 1 (Louvain: Abbaye du mont César, 1948), 579–84.

passions of the sensitive appetite should be conceived in a materialistic fashion.[85] Pasnau argues that at least part of the unruly aspect of the passions is a direct consequence of bodiliness; we do not have absolute control over our bodily states, so we do not have absolute control over our passions.[86] Since the sensitive appetite also takes its movement from other nonrational capacities in human nature (such as sense and imagination), we cannot govern our sensitive appetite perfectly.[87]

In response, Robert Miner has proposed that the movement of the sensitive appetite and the concomitant bodily change should be related as *form* and *matter*.[88] Miner believes that Pasnau and others are guilty of a crude reading of Thomas's view of movement here, equating "movement" with locomotion.[89] He points out that Aristotle and Aquinas have three senses of movement: motion in respect of quality, motion in respect of quantity, and motion in respect of place (locomotion).[90] The first two forms of movement, Miner argues, can be ascribed to the formal cause as such, and thus the "movement" of the sensitive appetite need not be considered as identical to the bodily motion in the sense organ.[91] Miner's counterproposal is that Thomas describes these two movements of the passions as "conjoined," not as identical. Thus, in any passion, the psychic movement is the formal cause and the bodily movement is the material cause. Miner is careful to note that the formal cause does not imply *efficient* causality;

---

85. Robert Pasnau, *Thomas Aquinas on Human Nature: A Philosophical Study of* Summa theologiae Ia 75–89 (Cambridge: Cambridge University Press, 2002), 252–64.

86. Pasnau, *Thomas Aquinas on Human Nature*, 257. Pasnau fails to account for the unfallen Adamic state in his account of Thomas; Adam had such perfect control, yet his sensitive appetite was certainly *material* even in that condition.

87. Pasnau argues that "since the mind cannot control what we perceive, it cannot entirely control the sensory appetite" (Pasnau, *Thomas Aquinas on Human Nature*, 258). To agree partially, I argue below that the fallen person's control of imagination is also apparently incomplete, as it is capable of movement by or through demonic forces.

88. Robert Miner, *Thomas Aquinas on the Passions: A Study of* Summa Theologiae Ia2ae 22–48 (Cambridge: Cambridge University Press, 2009), 38–46.

89. Miner attributes this mistaken position to D'Arcy as well; see Miner, *Thomas Aquinas on the Passions*, 40.

90. Miner, *Thomas Aquinas on the Passions*, 39–40. Aristotle's different forms of movement can be found at *Physics* 3.1 and 8.7.

91. I argue below that Thomas's conception of this motion is at least partly local. The kind of motion in the devil's power is local motion and Thomas argues that such local motion can cause the movement of the sensitive appetite.

the movement's beginning in the formal cause does not mean that the material cause follows as the movement of a pool ball follows from the impact of a cue.[92]

This debate about the bodily and psychic components of the passions matters a great deal with regard to fallen human beings' affectivity when the problem is related to inner demonic temptation. For both Pasnau and Miner, the material movement of the sensitive appetite results in passionate motion. If the devil can cause the former, though, what is the moral character of any resulting appetitive movement? Thomas's questions on the devil's inner temptation will demonstrate the importance of this conjunction of material and formal causes of the passions.

How the *Fomes* Tempts. Thomas consistently categorizes the irrational or immoderate movement of the sensitive appetite as a form of *temptation*, but like Peter the Lombard, he indicates that it is often culpably sinful as well. The primary reason why the *fomes* is considered by Thomas (especially by the time of the *Summa Theologica*) to be venially sinful is that human subjects are capable of foreseeing and preventing individual irrational movements; a failure to do so is a venial sin of omission.[93] Such inordinate desires that precede the judgment of reason are what Thomas calls the "antecedent" passions, which, as Paul Gondreau argues, are solely the activity of the *fomes*.[94] While Thomas sees these movements as disordered, he specifies that the ability to foresee these irrational antecedent movements is essential to their culpability. Citing Augustine, Thomas states that "no man sins in what he cannot avoid" and clarifies in his response that "the *fomes* does not hinder man from using his rational will to check individual inordinate movements, *if he be presentient of them*."[95]

---

92. Miner, *Thomas Aquinas on the Passions*, 45.
93. *ST* I-II 74.3, ad. 2. As Odon Lottin argues in *Psychologie et Morale*, vol. 2, part 1, 579–84, Thomas's early *Sentences Commentary* may differ on this question—meaning that he would have followed Peter and Alexander in arguing that *any* irrational movement of the sensitive appetite would have been venially sinful. But as I argue here, Thomas's mature position is distinct.
94. Paul Gondreau, *The Passions of Christ's Soul in the Theology of St. Thomas Aquinas* (Scranton, Pa.: University of Scranton Press, 2009), 337–49.
95. *ST* I-II 74.3, obj. 2 and ad. 2, emphasis added.

Conversely, however, lacking this presentience, especially if no presentience were possible, Thomas implies that there is no culpability on the part of the one who experiences the movement.[96] It is thus possible for antecedent passions to be morally blameless. This commonly occurs when disordered movements work in close proximity or even in conjunction with one another. Thomas gives an example of such a situation: an individual first successfully foresees and prevents a movement of lust but then (precisely *because of* this prevention) experiences an unforeseen movement of vainglory. Thomas concludes from this example that "man cannot avoid all such movements," which, taken in light of his Augustinian objection that "no man sins in what he cannot avoid," implies that those unavoidable movements are not even venially sinful—though they are still disordered movements that arise from the corruption of the *fomes*.[97] In order to remain morally blameless in such a case, one would have to resist the movement and keep it from overwhelming one's reason. Thomas explicitly endorses such a spiritual pedagogy in similar questions on internal demonic temptation.[98]

By describing the experience of the *fomes* in this way, Thomas indicates that there are two distinct ways in which the disorder becomes morally reprehensible or culpable. Most commonly, the experience of moral lapse is found in a failure of reason and will to anticipate, prevent, and cut off the irrational motion before it begins.[99] In this form, the *sinful* aspect of the *fomes* is chronologically the first component of the disorder, and the *tempting* aspect is subsequent, since the

---

96. Lottin, *Psychologie et Morale*, vol. 2, part 1, 579–84, disagrees with this assessment, arguing that Thomas's constant teaching is that any irrational movement arising from the sensitive appetite (what, at the time of the *Sentences Commentary*, is called the *secundo primi* movement) is venial sin (see especially 579). Lottin cites *ST* I-II 74.3, ad. 3 for his claim, but he ignores the significant caveat to this position in the second objection and reply. Thus, while Lottin emphasizes the continuity of Thomas's teaching, he overlooks the importance of the component of *unpreventability* that Thomas later recognizes in certain situations.

97. Thomas appears to reiterate this position when he discusses the movement of the sensitive appetite caused by the devil (*ST* I-II 80.3, ad. 3), but offers a not-easily reconciled exposition in other places, such as in his question on the Virgin Mary's relation to the *fomes* (*ST* III 27.4, obj. 1; see also the reply). A similar difficult passage is found at *ST* I-II 17.7, where even sudden movements are treated as if they may be preventable (and thus culpable).

98. *ST* I-II 80.3, ad. 3.

99. Again, Thomas's examples in *ST* I-II 74.3, ad. 2 bear out the requirement that sinfulness be strictly a matter of foresight and prevention.

venial sin of omission pushes one on toward a fully elicited, rationally chosen sin.[100] On the other hand, if one has done everything in one's power to foresee and prevent irrational movement of the sensitive appetite, some irrational movements will still "get by" one's first line of defense since, as Thomas argues, the fallen human being is constitutionally incapable of avoiding all such movements. In such an instance (as in Thomas's example of unpremeditated vainglory), moral blamelessness could be preserved by resisting the movement to the extent that one's reason is not enraptured by the passion. In this less common case, the unforeseeable movement is chronologically first and acts as a temptation; culpable sin arises only when this first movement is not properly resisted.

In the experience of temptation from the *fomes*, an irrational experience of passion thus arises in two ways, one venially sinful and one (in theory) morally blameless. In both cases, the desire that arises proceeds to distort and confuse the rational faculty, inclining reason to pursue a merely apparent good. While reason was at first unaffected by passion, these irrational movements make it difficult to pursue the true good—a more serious and difficult moral quandary since the individual's reason and will then become inordinately drawn by passion to an object that cannot be pursued licitly. But unless the human subject is so "possessed" by the passion that reason and will are completely fettered, there is still a moral battle to be fought. To explain this battle, I outline how for Thomas, passion affects the decision of the will.

Thomas argues that the influence of passion on the will is indirect, and in two ways: by distraction and by way of object.[101] Distraction is simply a matter of focus and intentionality. Human beings can hold only so much in their mind at one time, and if a passion enters into one's consideration, it eventually must take the place of some other consideration. The second of these ways, however, is bound to the question of how the will is moved by the object of its consideration.

---

100. Pasnau, *Thomas Aquinas on Human Nature*, 252–64, gives a direct consideration of concupiscence as a force of temptation. His analysis is much more in depth that what I present since disordered concupiscence is in the end somewhat tangential to the Christological center of this project.

101. *ST* I-II 77.1, response.

Importantly, Thomas does not consider the will to be *necessarily* moved by its object:

> the judgment of the estimative power follow[s] the passion of the sensitive appetite ... for which reason we observe that those who are in some kind of passion, do not easily turn [*non facile ... avertunt*] their imagination away from the object of their emotion, the result being that the judgment of the reason often [*plerumque*] follows the passion of the sensitive appetite, and consequently the will's movement follows it also, since it has a natural inclination always to follow the judgment of the reason.[102]

In the context of this quotation, Thomas invokes these considerations to draw attention to the distorting and disordering quality of the passions as they arise from the *fomes* and from acquired vice. Nevertheless, Thomas notes that there is some freedom of reason and will even in the grips of these antecedent passions, which he maintains in order to preserve the moral responsibility of the one who experiences such passions. In order for there to be a real temptation, there has to be an ability to do otherwise, to make a choice. Without this qualification, every instance of passion would involve a determinism leading without exception from an initial (and sometimes morally blameless) irrational motion to the final completion of the desire in action.

For this reason, one cannot say that the *fomes peccati* strictly binds the fallen human being to culpable sin. Instead, it is perhaps best to say, as Aquinas does, that the overall effect is a downward or evil inclination. Some antecedent movements are both sinful and tempting (when they could be prevented), and all such movements tend to divert reason and will from the true good. Because of this strong propensity toward sinful thoughts and deeds, these movements are an essential point of fragility in human nature in Thomas's anthropology; they constitute a deep brokenness and disorder of fallen humanity.

The Function of the *Fomes* in Thomas's Anthropology. The most obvious reason Thomas places so much emphasis on the *fomes* in his moral psychology is a broadly Augustinian conception of the human sub-

102. ST I-II 77.1, response.

ject, a conception that affirms the human being in the fallen and unredeemed state as *non posse non peccare*: not able not to sin.[103] Like Augustine, however, Thomas seeks to avoid any perfectly strict *necessity* of sin, especially for the baptized individual. Indeed, if one is constitutionally incapable of not performing an objectively sinful act, then one cannot be morally culpable for such an act since, as pointed out by Augustine and acknowledged by Thomas, one is morally praised or blamed only for something that is in one's power.[104] Although both Thomas and Augustine see disordered concupiscence as a stable aspect of human existence in this world, Thomas for his part accounts for human culpability by providing for the possibility of morally blameless prevention and resistance and by entirely excluding cases of strict constitutional necessity from moral culpability. Thus, a Thomistic affirmation of the fallen human subject as *non posse non peccare* must be qualified by these caveats. Thomas's thought in the *Summa Theologica* recognizes that in order for something to be sin, it must be in some way chosen or willfully omitted.

Thomas's understanding of what is in the human subject's power is crucial. On the one hand, Thomas argues that particular movements of the sensitive appetite are capable of rational control and prevention; on the other, he argues that all these movements, taken together, are *not* in the power of reason to control perfectly. Thomas is best understood in the *Summa Theologica* as arguing that culpable sensitive sin appears *only* when reason and will were capable of foreseeing and forestalling the irrational movement of the sensitive appetite, or when reason and will fail to resist it when such movement falls on one by constitutional necessity.

Culpable sin from the *fomes* is still ubiquitous; a merely descriptive *non posse non peccare* certainly holds for Thomas. Thomas recognizes the scriptural basis of this claim (as, for instance, 1 John 1:8) and seeks a theological framework that also affirms it. The *fomes* is for Thomas a

---

103. For an excellent study of the Augustinian conception of concupiscence, see Timo Nisula, *Augustine and the Functions of Concupiscence* (Boston: Brill, 2012).

104. Augustine states this in *On Free Will* III 18; Thomas cites this text at *ST* I-II 74.3, obj. 2. See also Timo Nisula, *Augustine and the Functions of Concupiscence* (Boston: Brill, 2012), 326, which argues that for Augustine, there can be "no necessity of sinning in a Christian person."

way of expressing that all are in need of divine aid and nearly constantly confronted with opportunity for and temptation toward sin. Significantly, and much like Maximus, Thomas avoids a perfectly strict moral fatalism; it is theoretically possible (even if never carried out in practice by fallen humanity) that one could avoid any culpable disordered movement of the sensitive appetite. In making such an affirmation, Thomas modified the schema of the medieval tradition that preceded him since, as mentioned in chapter 4, both Peter the Lombard and Alexander of Hales affirmed that the irrational movement of the sensitive appetite is *always* venially sinful (regardless of its preventability). Thomas makes this modification precisely in order to maintain the tradition's central claim: if an act cannot be called voluntary, it cannot be called culpable; thus, in order for there to be culpable sin in the sensitive appetite, its act must in some way be voluntary.

Demonic Temptation in Aquinas's Thought

Thomas sees the corruption of the *fomes peccati* as a corruption of the sensitive appetite that results from the withdrawal of original justice. However, as I have shown above, a susceptibility to interior demonic temptation is also, for Thomas, a result of the withdrawal of a "special favor of grace" when Adam sinned.[105] I have shown that the devil intended the *fomes*, yet the ongoing relationship between the devil's inner movement and that of the *fomes* requires further clarification. Indeed, Thomas holds that some, but not all, forms of inner demonic temptation are dependent on the presence of the *fomes* in the individual tempted.[106]

Thomas argues that there are four consequences resulting from the withdrawal of Adam's sanctifying grace, corresponding to a lack of the four cardinal virtues (justice, prudence, fortitude, and temperance). Thomas usually uses the phrase "original justice" to refer to this

---

105. *ST* II-II 165.1, response; *ST* II-II 165.2.
106. At the time of the *Sentences Commentary*, Thomas implicitly denies that the devil can tempt by way of passion outside of the corruption of the *fomes peccati* (see *ST* Supplement, 96.5, ad. 2). While the *fomes* is a necessary condition for the devil's passionate temptation, the devil also has the ability to work internally in the imagination, a faculty that is not governed by any virtue.

four-fold grace. The four consequences of its withdrawal, respectively, are malice, ignorance, weakness, and concupiscence.[107] In turn, these four defects correspond to the four faculties in which virtue resides for Thomas: the will, the reason, irascibility, and the concupiscible faculty (respectively). When Thomas describes Adam's original immunity to interior demonic temptation as such, however, he states that this effect is the product of a "special favor of grace [*Ex speciali ... beneficio gratiae*]"[108] that prevents the movement of Adam's *imagination* by the devil. In this case, Thomas describes a benefit of grace that cannot be categorized within the four sanctifying graces of virtue in his main account of Adam's privileges. Most significantly, the faculty of imagination has no corresponding virtue,[109] and yet by some original grace, Adam's imagination was immune from internal demonic attack. Though Thomas does not include the loss of this grace in his list concerning the consequences of Adam's sin, his reasoning elsewhere no less forcefully shows it to be a distinct gift of grace in the Adamic state that was consequently lost. This grace is, then, a component of Adam's original supernatural privileges that protected Adam in a unique way. For this reason, the grace that prevents interior demonic attack is of a different sort than the infused, sanctifying grace of temperance and original justice that, when absent, lead to the *fomes peccati*. In theory, then, Thomas affirms that one without the *fomes* could still be susceptible to interior demonic attack through the imagination. This combination of graces is visualized in figure 5-2.

With the addition of this grace of immunity from demonic attack, Thomas views the sensitive appetite as *doubly* corrupted by the withdrawal of original grace. Firstly, this withdrawal leads to a lack of perfect temperance and of original justice and, thereby, to the *fomes peccati* in the sensitive appetite. In this respect, Thomas speaks of the concupiscence listed among the effects of Adam's sin. Secondly, the withdrawal of original grace leads to a distinct ability of the devil to move

---

107. *ST* I-II 85.3.
108. *ST* II-II 165.1, response.
109. Thomas affirms that there is no virtue in the powers of apprehension at *ST* I-II 56.5; he likewise affirms that imagination is a power of apprehension at *ST* I 78.4, response.

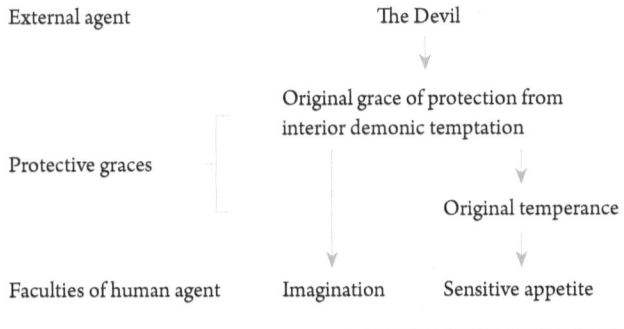

FIGURE 5-2. The Graces Protecting the Prelapsarian Condition from Demonic Attack

faculties of the body attached to sense organs such as imagination and the sensitive appetite. In no actual fallen human being are these two effects separated, yet neither should the two consequences be considered interchangeable. The grace that prevents the devil from directly moving the sensitive appetite is distinct from and acts by a different mechanism than the grace of original justice that holds the sensitive appetite inside the bounds of reason. Even if the devil never interiorly tempts an individual who does not have the *fomes peccati*, their coincidence does not make interior temptation absolutely subordinate to the *fomes peccati*. They are distinct disorders of the fallen condition.

That the devil is capable of tempting human beings interiorly, then, is properly understood by Thomas to be a consequence of the withdrawal of original grace but not completely reducible to a demonic ability to act on the basis of the *fomes peccati*. At the very least, Thomas envisions demonic movement of the imagination as a distinct phenomenon outside the corruption of the *fomes*. Given that Thomas's mechanism by which the devil moves the imagination is the same as that by which the devil moves the sensitive appetite, the phenomenon of interior demonic movement of the sensitive appetite remains distinct from the movements of the *fomes peccati*.[110]

---

110. This mechanism is discussed in a moment. Furthermore, and also discussed, an absolute perfection of temperance (and thus a lack of the *fomes peccati*) is sufficient to hold the

For these reasons, interior demonic temptation remains a significant component of Thomas's theory of the human act and cannot be dismissed as it has been in recent literature. To more adequately address this aspect of Thomas's moral psychology, I proceed in five parts. First, I explore Thomas's general affirmations about interior demonic attack. Second, I explain the technical mechanism by which Thomas believes this temptation takes place. Third, I lay out the two forms that this temptation takes in Thomas's mature accounts. Fourth, I argue that Thomas's portrayal of this attack remains temptation and is not a description of a form of possession. Fifth, I address the moral classification of the sorts of appetitive attacks that the devil can affect.

Thomas's General Affirmations Concerning Internal Demonic Attack. Thomas consistently holds that the relationship between demonic and fleshly temptation is complex. I begin with relevant passages from the *Commentary on Job* and then turn to Thomas's more systematic works.

As outlined earlier, Thomas's reflections on the devil in the *Commentary on Job* are found in a metaphorical description of Leviathan. In at least three places, Thomas's allegorical commentary on this passage indicates that the devil's temptation is a combined attack against both intellect and passion. Emphasizing the imaginative aspect of temptation, Thomas states that "the devil enkindles men to an eager desire for sin through a showing of some good."[111] There is thus a demonstrative or cognitive component to the devil's temptation, by which the devil indicates an aspect of the good to the one tempted. The devil's goals, though, are also with regard to human passion, for "through the disturbance of the devil's head, that is, through his temptations, a flash of fire, namely, of anger or of eager desire or even of vainglory, leaps forth."[112] In this passage, the devil's activity is some-

---

sensitive appetite within the bounds of reason. Thus, in a definitive sense, Thomas considers the devil's movement of the sensitive appetite to be secondary and subordinate to the presence of the *fomes peccati* in that individual and that appetite. Without the corruption of the *fomes* (and thus, with an absolute perfection of grace in the sensitive appetite), the devil cannot move sensibility.

111. *Commentary on Job* 41, in *Exposition on Job*, 463.
112. *Commentary on Job* 41, in *Exposition on Job*, 462.

what remote from the passion itself; the appetitive component arises through the devil's imaginative attack. But another example, already quoted above, shows that the devil's activity directly causes passion:

> Since an animal breathes not only through his nostrils but also through his mouth, He adds fifth the operation of the mouth, saying *His breath,* that is, the exhalation proceeding from his mouth, *makes live coals glow,* that is, it is so hot and strong that it would be sufficient to light coals. For He speaks in a metaphor of those who light coals by blowing under them. Hence, He adds *and flame comes out of his* mouth, namely, since the vapor coming from his mouth is so hot and fiery that it can deservedly be compared to flame. Now by all these verses is designated the fact that the devil, by his concealed or manifest suggestions, kindles in man the fire of perverse desire [*Diabolus sua occulta vel manifesta suggestione perversae cupiditatis ignem in homine accendit*].[113]

Here Thomas uses an ablative that he did not use in the previous quotation; the devil's suggestion is the direct *means* or *agent* of the "fire of perverse desire" in the human victim. Thomas sees a direct demonic agency in the origin of particular irrational movements of the sensitive appetite.

Thomas's more systematic writings argue similarly. In the *Sentences Commentary*, Thomas argues that "the Devil alone is said to tempt (*Diabolus solus dicitur tentare*)... because he himself uses the things of the world and of the flesh as instruments for the temptation of human beings."[114] This same affirmation is found in the *Summa Theologica*:

> The flesh and the world are said to tempt instrumentally or materially, that is in so far as one can know what kind of a person someone is, by seeing whether he follows or spurns fleshly desires and despises worldly prosperity and adversity. Also, such things are used by the devil for the purpose of tempting.[115]

Thomas indicates in this passage that the flesh is the instrument of the devil. Further, even if human beings use the flesh as a means to tempt other people, Thomas argues that they do so as servants of the

---

113. *Commentary on Job* 41, in *Exposition on Job*, 463.
114. *Sent. Comm.* II 21.1.1.
115. *ST* I 114.2, translation modified.

devil.[116] In both his exegetical and systematic works, then, Thomas recognizes that the devil brings about individual irrational movements of the sensitive appetite and movements of the imagination.

The Thomistic and Aristotelian Mechanism of Inner Demonic Temptation. While Thomas's Aristotelian cosmology is not the direct object of my investigation here, certain aspects of it are important in order to understand his conception of the action of angels and demons on human beings. First in *ST I* 110.3 and later in *ST I* 111 and 114, Thomas concludes that angelic natures are capable of moving material bodies by local motion. He states that "the corporeal nature has a natural aptitude to be moved immediately by the spiritual nature as regards place."[117] Thomas draws further concrete conclusions from this fact in his questions on angels and demons. This causal mechanism translates to an angelic ability to move any faculty or power of the human being that is attached to a corporeal body. Regarding angels, Thomas recognizes an ability to enlighten the human mind, change the imagination, and change human senses. Regarding demons, Thomas recognizes similar capabilities, stating that "the corporeal nature has a natural aptitude to be moved locally by the spiritual nature: so that the devil can produce all those effects which can result from the local movement of bodies here below."[118]

Through this local motion, Thomas further argues that angels and demons are able to cause indirectly the other two kinds of Aristotelian movement: those of quantity (magnitude) and quality (affection).[119] In response to an objection that concerns precisely those three different kinds of movement, Thomas states that "angels, by causing local motion, as the first motion, can thereby cause other movements [of quantity and quality]; that is, by employing corporeal agents to

---

116. As in the *Sent. Comm.* II 21.1.1, ad. 5.

117. *ST* I 110.3, response. Since this kind of motion is the "most perfect" kind of motion, Thomas argues that other kinds of inferior motion are also in the power of angels and demons; see *ST* I 110.3, obj. 2 and ad. 2. This fact is particularly important in light of Miner's objections—see n. 123

118. *ST* I-II 80.2, response. On angelic movement, see *ST* I 111.1, *ST* I 111.3, and *ST* I 111.4.

119. Thomas denies that demons can alter the substantial forms of creatures, which he sometimes classifies as a fourth kind of movement. See *De Malo* XVI 10, obj. 6, response, and ad. 6.

produce these effects, as a workman employs fire to soften iron."[120] Thus, while the devil's action in creating these other kinds of movement is indirect, it is no less intentional, purposeful, or capable than an ironworker in the forge.[121] This fact is important with respect to the devil's movement of the sensitive appetite. Given that Thomas sees the movement of the sensitive appetite as one of the three kinds of movement considered by Aristotle, and since the devil can cause (directly or indirectly) all three kinds of movement, the devil is able to cause the movement of the sensitive appetite—in both its bodily and psychic forms.[122]

Thomas's late systematic works bear witness to the devil's ability to arouse passion. Thomas states in *ST* I-II 80.2 that

> the operation of the devil seems to be confined to the imagination and sensitive appetite, by moving either of which he can induce man to sin [*inducere ad peccatum*]. For his operation may result in presenting certain forms to the imagination; and he is able to make it that the sensitive appetite is incited to some passion [*potest etiam facere quod appetitus sensitivus concitetur ad aliquam passionem*].[123]

Thomas does not restrict this activity to the bodily form of passion, later clarifying in that question that, while the devil's action begins in the bodily form, it results in "certain passions being aroused in the sensitive appetite."[124] Elsewhere, one finds the similar affirmation that "by the interior movement of the spirits and humors an angel can do some-

---

120. *ST* I 110.3, ad. 2.

121. Thomas seems to deny this power in *De Malo* XVI 10, response, but he only denies a *direct* power over those other movements. His statements in the *Summa Theologica* thus specify how the devil has *indirect* power over them.

122. These three kinds of motion are the only three recognized in his Aristotelian cosmology and demons are capable of causing (either directly or indirectly) all three. Thomas's reasoning thereby renders moot (for my purposes) the disagreement between Pasnau and Miner on this issue. Even if, as Miner argues, there is something analogous to the sense in which Thomas means "motion" when applied to passions (Miner, *Thomas Aquinas on the Passions*, 45–46), Thomas's explicit affirmation (seen below) is that regardless of which kind of motion the passions are, the devil can cause them.

123. *ST* I-II 80.2, response.

124. *ST* I-II 80.2, response. Note that he does not say certain *movements*, but rather, certain *passions*. "Movements" could be explained as bodily; passions pertain to the psychic act of the appetite as such. In any case, the further effects that he lists for these passions make it clear that he is describing a fully psychic event.

thing towards changing the act ... of the appetitive and sensitive power, and of any other power using a corporeal organ."[125] Against Alexander of Hales's limitation of demonic activity to apprehension, Thomas argues, like the early ascetic tradition, that the devil is able to stir up both images in the imagination and passions in the sensitive appetite.[126]

Apprehensive and Passionate Attack from the Devil.[127] In recent literature, the first of these two forms of attack has received some attention, but the latter form has been neglected.[128] Hence, I proceed to consider both forms of attack and trace certain developments between the *Sentences Commentary* and Thomas's mature writings, focusing on the subjective effects of these attacks.

Thomas treats the devil's apprehensive attack as related to an attempt to "darken" the human intellect. On the basis of angelic nature itself, this effect can be produced only indirectly, since Thomas denies that demons have a strictly *intellectual* form of attack. This restriction follows from Thomas's recognition that angels have only the natural power to *illuminate* the human mind with knowledge; since true knowledge is contrary to the devil's purposes, the devil does not produce the intellectual effects in humankind of which he is capable.[129] The only way that this darkening effect can be accomplished through the natural powers of angels is through manipulation of the imaginative power and sensitive appetite.[130]

Thomas argues that through the devil's movement of the bodily

---

125. *ST* I 111.4, ad. 2. See also *ST* I 111.2, where Thomas affirms simultaneously that the will is free and that angels can move the will externally through passion.

126. There are other related activities that could be cataloged alongside these two kinds of temptation. These activities tend to be sexual in nature: either causing or impeding (apparently male) sexual arousal. These activities are likely not distinct categories of temptation and thus can be taken as representative of the kind of power the devil has over powers conjoined to bodily organs. See *Sent. Comm.* IV 34.1.3, especially ad. 1 and ad. 4, and *ST* II-II 154.5, response. For an overview of the importance of this question in medieval canon law and marriage law, see Catherine Rider, *Magic and Impotence in the Middle Ages* (New York: Oxford University Press, 2006).

127. In distinguishing these two kinds of attack in these terms (apprehensive and passionate), I move beyond Thomas's explicit terminology; in the *De Malo*, Thomas uses the terms "persuasion" and "disposition" to designate these two attacks, and in the *Summa Theologica*, he simply discusses attacks against the imagination and against the sense appetite.

128. See the discussion of the literature in the introduction.

129. See *ST* I-II 80.2 and *De Malo* XVI 12.

130. *ST* I-II 80.2 and *De Malo* XVI 11.

components of the imagination, "certain forms are presented to the imagination" that can be used by the devil to deceive.[131] Thomas elsewhere explains how this effect serves the devil's purposes:

> as to a person's imagination or apprehension, that when it is strong, the senses or sensitive appetite is moved: which change is not without bodily alteration and the spirits of the body, as we see that with the apprehension of something pleasant the sensitive appetite is moved to desire, and from this the body is warmed.[132]

Similarly, one reads in the *De Malo* that good and bad angels

> somehow internally dispose and arrange forms of the imagination insofar as such dispositions and arrangements are appropriate for apprehending intelligible things. And good angels indeed arrange forms of the imagination for human beings' good. And devils do likewise for their evil. Devils arrange forms of the imagination whether to desire sin, namely, as the things human beings apprehend induce them to pride or some other sin, or to prevent true understanding itself, as things apprehended lead human beings into doubts that they do not know how to resolve, and then into error.[133]

In these passages, there are two goals that Thomas indicates in this apprehensive attack: a goal of deception and an appetitive goal. For the first, there is a sort of confusion that the devil hopes to encourage. By presenting things to the mind that it cannot or does not understand, the devil leads into intellectual error and presumably, thereby, eventually into moral error as well.

For the second goal, the intended effect is to move the one tempted from apprehension to appetition. In this form, Thomas's consideration of an imaginative attack aligns with an argument seen in Alexander of Hales, namely that demons present objects to the imagination in order to learn about the passions toward which humans are *already* inclined.[134] For Thomas, the spiritual pedagogy implied by this rea-

---

131. ST I-II 80.2: "*aliquae formae repraesententur imaginationi.*"
132. *Commentary on Galatians* 3.1, my translation. The Latin is found at https://www.corpusthomisticum.org/cgl.html. This same argument is found in *De Malo* III 4, where an apprehended object is used by demons to try to elicit passion.
133. *De Malo* XVI 12, response. *De Malo* XVI 11 also contains extensive discussion of demonic attack against the imagination.
134. One sees this explanation in *De Malo* III 4, response: "we call the devils tempters since

soning is one of *resistance* to demonically inspired images. Thomas states that this resistance is proper to reason alone and cannot be caused or hindered by the devil. Thus, were one not to resist the image, such an omission would be morally reprehensible in the human subject experiencing such temptation. It would be this lack of resistance that constitutes for Thomas the first *sinful* movement toward the apprehended object.[135]

In acknowledging a second, directly passionate form of demonic temptation, Thomas moves beyond the apprehensive/appetitive distinction invoked in the attack against the imagination and thus diverges from the position of Alexander of Hales, who maintained the relative culpability of demonic and fleshly temptation by means of this distinction. Since the passions are elicited by a faculty conjoined to a bodily organ, Thomas argues that demons can bring them about without any image presented to the imagination.[136] Thomas considers the demonic intentions in this situation in three short passages, one each in the *Sentences Commentary*, the *Summa Theologica*, and *De Malo*. In the *ST passage*, Thomas states that

> through certain passions being aroused in the sensitive appetite, the result is that man more easily perceives the movement or sensible image which is brought in the manner explained, before the apprehensive principle.... It also happens, through the rousing of a passion, that what is put before the imagination, is judged, as being something to be pursued, because, to him who is held by a passion, whatever the passion inclines him to, seems good.[137]

---

they learn through the actions of human beings to which emotions the human beings are more subject, so that the devils may thereby more effectively impress on the imagination of those individuals what they intend." This same distinction between apprehension and appetition is found in *Sent. Comm.* II 21.1.2, ad. 4.

135. If this interpretation is accurate, it can be understood to resemble Maximus's spiritual pedagogy of separating images from passions discussed in chapter 2. Thomas describes this pedagogy only as "resistance" without explaining what that resistance looks like. For Maximus, it is a process of separating images and passions that is described in many of Maximus's ascetic works. Even if these theories are not identical, it is noteworthy that there may be a Thomistic parallel to the earlier ascetic discipline.

136. *Sent. Comm.* II 21.1.2, ad. 5. In that response, Thomas considers the mode of demonic instigation of desire, but his explanation does not easily cohere with his later explanation in the *De Malo* and *ST*. In the *Sentences Commentary*, he describes a "purely natural" movement of the sensitive appetite in which there is no sin, alongside another in which there is.

137. *ST* I-II 80.2. In *De Malo* III 4, response, Thomas merely describes the mechanism; he does not describe what further ends this disposition serves for the devil.

The first demonic goal Thomas describes is precisely the obverse side of the goal described in the imaginative attack above: the devil hopes to cause the one tempted to relate a passionate disposition to images presented to the imagination (either from real external objects or from implanted demonic images). As early as the *Sentences Commentary*, Thomas recognizes that "the devil is unable to extort this [conjoining] motion" whereby a concupiscible movement is connected to the apprehension of some desirable thing, thereby delineating the aspect that remains within human power and responsibility.[138] That is, since Thomas conceives this movement that associates images with irrational movements of passion to be proper to reason and will alone, this activity is the first sinful or culpable movement toward the object presented and passion elicited.

The second goal from the *Summa Theologica* quotation above, however, is concerned with another matter: the judgment of a desirable thing as something to be pursued. Clearly, this act of judgment is proper to the reason and will of the one tempted, thereby showing that there must be freedom to resist. But Thomas also describes the one tempted by such a demonic passion as being "held by a passion (*a passione detinetur*)," which indicates that the temptation puts significant pressure upon one's free will. Because of this pressure, the relationship of such temptation with the distinct phenomenon of *possession* requires clarification.

Inner Demonic Temptation and Possession. For the medieval tradition leading up to Thomas, I have shown that irrational movements of the sensitive appetite are venially sinful. In that context, it was impossible to affirm that the devil could cause this movement, since that would be to say that the devil could *cause* a human subject to sin. At best, one whose appetite was thus inflamed would be described as possessed and thus not culpable for the irrational movement that is, properly speaking, in the genus of objective sin. As shown above, however, Thomas does not believe *every* irrational movement of the sensitive appetite to be culpably sinful; there are movements based on the cor-

138. *Sent. Comm.* II 21.1.2, ad. 5.

ruption of the *fomes peccati* that are constitutionally unpreventable and therefore cannot be even venially sinful. For this reason, Thomas is able to describe inner demonic temptation of a human's concupiscible power without the implication that the devil causes an act in the genus of sin.

Thomas's analysis of this phenomenon in both the *Summa Theologica* and *De Malo* draws this temptation into close relationship with possession, but he also distinguishes possession from the cases he calls temptation. Thomas states that the distinctive feature of a true possession is that "the use of reason is completely fettered."[139] In such a case, the devil "can compel anyone to do an act which, in its genus, is a sin," though such an act is not imputed to the human who performed it because they retained no rational or volitional freedom in its performance.[140] True compulsion to acts in the genus of sin is strictly tied to the *complete* binding of reason and thereby will. In such a case, the one so compelled is properly described as possessed, not as tempted or sinning.

It turns out, then, that "lesser" movements of the sensitive appetite caused by the devil are the most morally significant for the one experiencing them. Thomas maintains that such cases where reason is not completely bound should be considered temptation instead of possession, precisely because "devils can sometimes move internal vapors and fluids without fettering reason" in individuals who "are awake and enjoy the use of reason."[141] In such cases, Thomas argues that "insofar as [reason] is free, it can resist sin."[142] Most significantly, Thomas argues that in the case of demonically incited passion,

The lusting of the flesh against the spirit, when the reason actually resists it, *is not a sin* [*non est peccatum*], but is matter for the exercise of virtue. That reason does not resist, is not in the devil's power; wherefore he cannot bring about the necessity of sinning."[143]

139. *De Malo* III 4, response: "*totaliter usus rationis ligetur.*" The same is seen in the relevant *Summa Theologica* question; see *ST* I-II 80.3.
140. *ST* I-II 80.3, response.
141. *De Malo* III 4, response.
142. *ST* I-II 80.3, response.
143. *ST* I-II 80.3, ad. 3, emphasis added. One finds a parallel passage in *De Malo* III 3, ad. 8.

Thus, in the case of a demonically incited passion, Thomas argues that virtue is exercised in the resistance of reason to that which is proposed by passion. "*Non est peccatum*": there is no sin.

Thomas maintains this position because such demonically inspired movements are unpreventable; as seen above, what cannot be prevented cannot be sin. Much like Maximus, Thomas consistently speaks only of *resisting* inner demonic temptation and not of *preventing* it.[144] In short, the natural "data" (from the apprehensive power) that inform the sensitive appetite in irrational antecedent movements of passibility are not present in the case of demonic temptation. Since those data provide reason and will the necessary information to cut off irrational movement before it begins, the absence of that information results in an inability to predict, foresee, or prevent its movement. Equivalently, since the agent acting on the sensitive appetite in this case is greater than the human subject, there is a constitutional inability on the part of the human subject to understand or foresee the occult movement of the devil.[145]

Again, in the *De Malo*, the devil's "disposition" of a human subject to sin (by which disposition human passions are elicited) is distinguished from a case wherein the devil causes an act in the genus of sin. After describing the mechanism of demonically inspired passion, Thomas concludes that "it is evident that the devil internally incites to sin by persuading and disposing but *not by bringing about sin*."[146] The distinction that he draws is between "inciting (*instiget*)" and "bringing about (*perficiendo*)" sin or, in the terms used in the *Summa Theologica*, between "inducing to sin" and inducing by necessity.[147] Both of the former terms (inciting and inducing) presume that the tempted human has not performed an act in the genus of sin; only the latter terms (*perficiendo* and *necessitatem inducere*) indicate that something in the

---

Thomas exhibits development on the particular matter of whether temptation is material for the exercise of virtue; for his earlier position, see *Sent. Comm.* II 21.1.3, ad. 3.

144. *ST* I-II 80.3, ad. 2 and ad. 3.
145. Thomas recognizes the superiority and inscrutability of demonic activity in *De Malo* XVI 7 and 8.
146. *De Malo*, III 4, response.
147. *ST* I-II 80.2 and 3, respectively.

genus of sin had occurred. Thomas consistently denies that the devil does these latter two acts in proper cases of inner demonic temptation.

In light of these considerations, inner demonic temptation is truly and only that; Thomas argues that such temptation does not cause acts in the genus of sin and does not bind reason or will. While Thomas believes the devil to be capable of possessing someone with a passion, the smaller demonically inspired movements categorized as temptation require close moral discernment since they can be and must be resisted.[148] In this discernment, one can see remarkable parallels with Maximus's ascetic practices.

Demonic Passion as Quasi-Antecedent Propassion. In Thomas's moral theological terms, two pairs of terms require consideration in attempting to classify demonically inspired passion: *full* passion or *pro*passion, on the one hand; and *antecedent* or *consequent* passions, on the other.[149] I deal with each of these pairs of terms in order.

I have noted earlier that when a Christian writer accepts a Stoic definition of passion, propassions are introduced as a way to recognize a morally neutral (or potentially positive) form of affectivity that does not hinder proper moral discernment. As noted in the first half, Maximus sometimes reflects this Stoic definition in his anthropological material, yet he avoids it in his Christological reflection. In light of Thomas's broadly Aristotelian aims, Thomas's acceptance of the category of propassion is somewhat surprising, precisely because it rests on a Stoic conception of passion that he generally resists. Still, in order to categorize demonic passion in Thomas's thought, it is enlightening to consider how a full passion and a propassion are distinguished in the prior tradition.

As discussed in Paul Gondreau's work, the generally acknowledged difference between full passions and propassions is whether

---

148. See Roger A. Couture, *L'Imputabilité Morale des Premiers Mouvements de Sensualité* (Rome: Presses de l'Université Grégorienne, 1962), 229–30, for a list of unimputable acts that includes these demonic activities.

149. For Thomas's distinction between antecedent and consequent passion, see *De Malo*, XII 1. For further discussion of passion and propassion, see Gondreau's discussion in *Passions of Christ's Soul*, 337ff.

they disturb or cloud the mind.[150] Peter the Lombard, reflecting a Stoic conception of passion passed down through Origen and Jerome, distinguishes between a propassion that "does not disturb the intellectual faculties from rectitude or from contemplation of God"[151] and a full passion that does. This disruption of rationality is what makes passions so morally problematic, yet by way of contrast, it is unclear whether propassions reach the mind or soul *at all*. As explained above, the way that Thomas describes demonically inspired passion places it along a spectrum in which reason and will retain some freedom to perform their proper acts, but the purpose and indeed effect of the devil in this temptation is to cause *some* movement in the soul as a distraction from one's final end.

For Thomas, however, inner demonic temptation (not possession) does not fetter or cloud the mind in the way that a full passion does. In the *De Malo*, one reads that "devils can sometimes move internal vapors and fluids without fettering reason" in individuals who "are awake and enjoy the use of reason."[152] The freedom left to reason and will thereby indicate that proper instances of inner demonic temptation are *not* full passions but rather somewhere in the range of those affective movements that are called propassions.

The distinction between antecedent and consequent passion corresponds to the way in which different passions arise, respectively, either before or after the judgment of reason. Thomas argues that antecedent passions have the characteristic feature that they "always prevent judgments of reason."[153] As just seen, however, Thomas claims that reason and will retain some freedom to perform their proper acts in these cases, and Thomas's treatment of antecedent passions indicates that they arise directly and exclusively from the *fomes peccati*.[154] The origin or root source of demonically inspired passion, however,

---

150. See Gondreau, *Passions of Christ's Soul*, chapters 1 and 2, especially 67–68, 84–85, and 130–31.
151. Peter the Lombard, *Sentences* III 15.2.
152. *De Malo* III 4, response.
153. *De Malo* XII 1.
154. Such in any case is Gondreau's explanation of antecedent passion; Gondreau argues that "at the root source of the antecedent passion is what Aquinas.... identifies as the *fomes peccati*" (Gondreau, *Passions of Christ's Soul*, 342).

cannot be attributed to the *fomes* in this way; as shown above, the *fomes* is a necessary but not sufficient condition to such demonic movement. The devil exploits the constitutional lack of governance that comes with the *fomes* and defective forms of temperance, but the movement should not be said to come *from* that corruption per se. Indeed, the circumstances in which the movement of the *fomes peccati* is not venially sinful are relatively limited, whereas *any* movement caused directly by the devil is inculpable for the one experiencing the passion. Insofar as antecedent passions bind reason and have their root cause in the *fomes*, demonic passions should not be considered interchangeably with them.

On the other hand, demons are not consulting human rationality before eliciting these movements; such consultation with reason is what constitutes a consequent passion. In balance, the lack of rational consultation renders these passions much closer to antecedent passions. While not fully in conformity with an antecedent passion, inner demonic passions do share with antecedent passions an intention by their author to incite sin and the net effect of making it difficult to do good.[155] Based on these considerations, inner demonic temptation of the sensitive appetite appears to be a propassion (as opposed to a full passion) and similar to (but not identical to) antecedent passion. Consequently, they may stand as a different species of passion alongside antecedent and consequent passions that is not fully described in Thomas's corpus.

Thomas's cumulative argument is as follows. By means of apprehensive and appetitive attacks, the devil is capable of producing images in the mind and can simultaneously pair—though not conjoin—these images with a passion that would often accompany that image. The simultaneous movement of both the imagination and sensitive appetite would appear to be the most difficult form of demonic temptation to resist. Notably, this combined attack is, subjectively speaking, nearly indistinguishable from the sorts of appetitive movements

---

155. *ST* III 27.3, response. These two features are also necessary for Thomas's definition of the *fomes* and thereby of antecedent passion.

that come from the *fomes*; Lombardo is correct in this component of his analysis of demonic temptation.[156] An antecedent passion from the *fomes*, like demonic passion, occurs with a simultaneous image in the imagination with an accompanying passion in the sensitive appetite. What is formally lacking in demonic passion, however, is a *direct*, conjoined relationship of the imagination with the appetite: the apprehensive movement is not the immediate *cause* of the appetitive movement, as it would be in the case of a movement from the *fomes peccati*. Resistance to demonic passion associated with images, then, would often take the shape of resisting the association of images with desires. This resistance to the association of images and passions remains in the power of reason and will, which can either resist or concede to their movement. In doing so, one might turn one's thoughts to something else in order to drive away the image and distract from the passion; or one might think about the image in a contemplative manner, thereby stirring up contrary passions that remain within the bounds of reason. Such suggestions look quite similar to Maximus's ascetic heuristics and Maximus's spiritual pedagogy of the passions outlined in chapter 2.

Demonic Temptation, Virtue, and Providence

In this final section, I consider two of the broader implications of Thomas's theory of interior demonic temptation. First, the foregoing presentation of interior demonic temptation entails a corollary in Thomistic virtue theory, namely, that fallen human beings (even ones with the infused virtue of temperance) are not always able to maintain their sensitive appetite perfectly under the ordination of reason. I therefore address the various forms of temperance recognized by Thomas and ask whether and how they might be compatible with inner demonic temptation. Second, I consider the ways that Thomas views the providential arrangement of temptation in relation to the final end of humanity.

156. Lombardo, *The Logic of Desire*, 123.

Internal Demonic Temptation and Virtue, Especially Temperance

Thomas's account of the virtue of temperance is multifaceted, allowing it to take a variety of forms.[157] The virtuous pagan has an acquired form of temperance, whereas the baptized Christian in a state of grace has an infused (and perhaps also an acquired) form of it; in the resurrected state, those who come into the beatific vision enjoy such a perfected form of temperance that it is no longer capable of defect. I wish to consider how and to what extent Thomas believes temperance to be possible for graced yet fallen human beings in this life. I first consider the relationship between demonic powers and a fallen human being's corporeal organs and then contrast this form with Thomas's view of the unfallen form of temperance. This latter, conditionally perfect form of temperance will be most relevant to the discussion of Thomas's Christological reflections in the next chapter.

In the confrontation of inner demonic temptation with temperance in the fallen condition, there is a tension between the powers of two rational agents. On the part of the demonic agent, Thomas argues that demons have a natural power over any and all corporeal objects, including conjoined organs of human faculties (once the original grace that prevented this movement was removed). On the part of the human agent, Thomas considers temperance to be the rational moderation of the sensitive appetite with regard to natural pleasures such as the desire for food, drink, and sex.[158] In this struggle to control the same matter, Thomas argues that, left to themselves, the devil's abilities overpower the human being's. The organ moves whether the human subject likes it or not since the fallen human's governance of his or her sense passions (even with some degree of temperance) is not complete.[159] Further, since the movement of the sensitive appe-

---

157. In considering the relationship between inner demonic temptation and virtue, I have noted above the two virtues that govern the irascible and concupiscible faculties: fortitude and temperance. Since Thomas considers all passions to be reducible to those of the concupiscible appetite, I examine only temperance here. The case of fortitude would be parallel. See Thomas Aquinas, *Disputed Questions on Virtue*, trans. Ralph McInerny (South Bend, Ind.: St. Augustine's Press, 1999), 22–29.

158. ST II-II 141.4, response.

159. See *Commentary on Job* 41, in *Exposition on Job*, 466: "no human power is capable

tite *is* the movement of the bodily organ, temperance consists in the transformation of the activities of that organ in conformity with the rule of reason. If the organ is not thus transformed, one cannot be said to be perfectly temperate. Even when combined with a theoretically possible sinlessness, the continual movement of the appetite outside of reason's command means that one's temperance lacks absolute perfection.[160]

In contrast to the fallen condition, unfallen human nature enjoyed privileged moral circumstances regarding these appetites.[161] As explained above, unfallen human beings—Adam and Eve—were free from interior demonic temptation due to the grace of original justice. As such, Adam and Eve could not be presented by the devil with false images in their imagination or with irrational passions in their sensitive appetite. For Thomas, furthermore, the unfallen individual's intellectual faculties thoroughly penetrate into the entirety of the sensitive appetite, resulting (both by sanctifying grace and by nature upheld by original justice) in a conditionally perfect temperance. In the Adamic state, the soul enjoyed supreme rational governance, so that sensitive movements were completely rationally governed.[162] Thomas thereby

---

of wounding the devil or resisting him, but every human power is reckoned by the devil as naught.... No matter how much the strength and effort of man is extended, it is held in contempt by the devil." Also: angels have an "immediate presidency" over corporeal bodies (*ST* I 110.1, ad. 2) since "corporeal nature is below the spiritual nature" (*ST* I 110.3, response). Thomas places some restrictions on this power over fallen humanity, but those restrictions do not pertain to the sensitive appetite or imagination. Only those actions that are not conjoined to corporeal organs are outside of the power of demons; hence the will, for instance, is completely beyond their direct grasp. See *ST* I 111.2 and *ST* I-II 80.2. There is at least one Thomistic reason to place limits on the demonic power even over fallen human beings: Thomas himself argues that such power remains under God's providential rule. Thomas consistently qualifies this demonic activity with the phrase "unless he [the devil] be restrained by God" (*ST* I-II 80.3, response; *ST* I-II 80.2, response; and *De Malo* III 4, response), thus indicating that the strict boundary on demonic action within fallen human beings is God's permission.

160. To be demonically tempted from within is "material for the exercise of virtue" (*ST* I-II 80.3, ad. 3), but the virtue that is exercised is thereby demonstrated not to be absolutely perfected. See also *ST* II-II 155.1–3.

161. That temperance and the *fomes* are inversely related is seen in *ST* III 15.2, response. There remains some difficulty on this point; when discussing the effects of baptism, Thomas argues that the baptized receives "the fullness of virtues" (*ST* III 69.4, response) and that the *fomes* is not the negation of virtue (*ST* III 69.4, ad. 3). The habit of temperance (while somehow imperfect) is thus present in the baptized in conjunction with disordered concupiscence.

162. In defense of Thomas's arrangement and placement of temperance precisely in the sensitive appetite, see Romanus Cessario, *The Moral Virtues and Theological Ethics*, 2nd ed. (Notre Dame, Ind.: University of Notre Dame Press, 2009), 65–66.

shows that the virtue and grace enjoyed in the Adamic state unfailingly prevent demonically inspired passion and imaginative deception. For this reason, Thomas's account of unfallen temperance holds demonic temptation through the sensitive appetite to be incompatible with this conditionally perfect virtue.

In these considerations, Thomas's conception of temperance is distinguished from that seen in Maximus's thought. In chapter 2, I described Maximus's version of temperance as non-eschatological, extrinsic, and historically realized. Thomas's, by contrast, is *eschatological, intrinsic,* and *historically unrealized* (at least outside of Christ). Thomas's definition of temperance is eschatological in that an absolutely perfected temperance that does not and cannot attain in fallen humanity is the measure of all other forms that the virtue may take.[163] For Thomas, temperance is intrinsic because it resides precisely in the concupiscible faculty and wholly conforms that faculty to the rule of reason. If an individual's concupiscible faculty is not wholly conformed to reason, that fact is simply a different way of saying that the individual is not absolutely perfectly temperate. Finally, temperance's intrinsic quality (coupled with the universality of the *fomes* prior to the eschaton) means that temperance will never be fully realized by fallen human beings this side of the eschaton: disordered movements cannot be wholly prevented, and so temperance remains in some sense imperfect. While the believer is still called to imitate Christ, this imitation cannot be perfectly successful. Only Christ—the head whose virtue flows to the body and the first fruits of the eschaton—proleptically demonstrates this absolutely perfected form of virtue.

Providence and Temptation in Thomas

Thomas addresses God's purposes for temptation in the *Sentences Commentary* and in the *Summa Theologica*. In both works, Thomas acknowledges that temptation endures throughout this life and is in some sense unavoidable; accordingly, Thomas balances an affirmation

---

163. Thus, in contrast to Maximus's reticence in describing the eschatological conditions of humanity, Thomas demonstrates a greater confidence in saying what form virtue takes in the final condition of humankind.

of the bad qualities of temptation (inclining to sin) against its positive qualities (leading one to salvation). I consider first Thomas's portrayal of the *fomes peccati* and then turn to demonic temptation.

In his *Sentences Commentary*, Thomas gives evidence that he conceived of temptation at that time as at least partly permitted by God for the punishment of humankind; in such an explanation, temptation is ultimately tangential to the goal of the spiritual and virtuous life. Thomas addresses this question in the *Sentences Commentary* by asking whether temptation is something that a human being should *seek*. His answer is that

> temptation in itself is ordained to the perdition of the human being [*tentatio per se ordinata est ad hominis perditionem*]; but it is only ordained to salvation accidentally, namely from that which is conquered through the help of divine grace: and thus simply to be tempted is not to be sought; but to be tempted and to conquer when taken together is to be sought. But the victory is exceedingly doubtful [*nimis dubia*] because of our fragility, therefore it is safer to flee than to search out.[164]

Thomas's judgment on the matter is prudential in nature. Given fallen human weakness, the Christian has no guarantee of victory over temptation. In fact, since victory is "exceedingly doubtful" because of the *fomes*, Thomas encourages human beings to flee from temptation.[165] This interpretation indicates that the goal of temptation in itself is *evil* and thus that God's permission of it is punitive or negative; nevertheless, it *can be* part of God's plan to save humankind, when it is successfully conquered.

A similar balance is found in Thomas's answer in one of the objections to this same question, though not without certain difficulties. There, Thomas's objector invokes 2 Timothy 2:5 to support a certain view of temptation, wherein temptation is a necessary step toward salvation. The objector notes:

---

164. *Sent. Comm.* II 21.1.3, response.
165. Thomas compares the one who seeks temptation to one who eats poison; seeking temptation for itself is asking for spiritual death.

that without which [*sine quo non*] one cannot enter the kingdom is to be greatly sought. But temptation is of this kind; because one will not be crowned unless they have fought according to the rules (2 Tim 2:5). But there is no spiritual combat without temptation. Therefore temptation is to be sought.[166]

That is, temptation, in the eyes of the objector, is *necessary* for salvation. Thomas's answer to this objection works toward the same balance as in his response above. He answers on the one hand that temptation is not strictly necessary to enter the kingdom but concedes, on the other, that one cannot get through life without temptation:

Temptations are not necessary to enter the kingdom, unless by conditional necessity; thus, namely, so that if temptations come, one does not enter the kingdom unless they are conquered. But for temptations to come is not absolutely necessary, *unless according to the corruption of our present state* [*nisi secundum corruptionem status praesentis*], *from which follows the battle of flesh against the spirit, which is called temptation.*[167]

His answer is that there is *no absolute necessity* for temptation in this life; it is in this way that Thomas maintains that temptation is not a *sine qua non* of salvation. But Thomas admits with perfect candor that fleshly temptation is unavoidable and thus necessary in our corrupt state. Perhaps Thomas can say that this temptation is not absolutely necessary because it is possible to envision a form of human life (perhaps an Adamic scenario) wherein one would not necessarily encounter temptation, but Thomas does not consider the fact that even Adam experienced temptation prior to his sin.[168] Thomas's early position thus encounters various difficulties.

Later, in the *Summa Theologica*, Thomas reflects further on God's drawing good out of evil (in this case, the evil of disordered concupiscence) through his providence. Thomas asks whether baptism should remove all the consequences of sin, including disordered con-

---

166. *Sent. Comm.* II 21.1.3, obj. 4.
167. *Sent. Comm.* II 21.1.3, ad. 4, emphasis added.
168. As I discuss below, Thomas may modify this claim by the time of the *Summa Theologica*; there, he admits that even in the original Adamic state, God arranged for the devil to tempt humanity for nonpunitive reasons.

cupiscence. In his reply, Thomas states that it is fitting that baptism *not* remove concupiscence because "this is suitable for our spiritual training: namely, in order that, by *fighting* against concupiscence ... man may receive the crown of victory."[169] Here, Thomas first affirms God's way of working through our disordered concupiscence to enable us to achieve good: the one who fights against concupiscence will be rewarded for doing so. Yet the negative aspect does not disappear here; throughout the article, this concupiscence (along with the other defects from Adam's sin) is described as the "debt of punishment" for Adam's sin. And while the *fomes* remains before the final resurrection, Christ's victory over it is absolute; Thomas argues that even now, this victory is seen in that Christians "should no longer be in fear" of such consequences.[170]

Thomas's view of the temptation from the *fomes* thus holds at once to the punitive *and* pedagogical role it plays in the spiritual life. Thomas believes that a complete and perfect victory *will be* possible in the end, but he defers the complete destruction of the *fomes* until the final resurrection.[171] While Thomas affirms that God brings about positive consequences from the struggle with the flesh (to the extent that he can say that the Christian should no longer fear the struggle), this affirmation should be understood in terms of God's ability to extract a good from a humanly caused evil. Fleshly temptation is not part of God's original plan for Adam and Eve in the garden; that it became a part of their moral life must be seen as a departure from that original plan. The redemptive purposes of the *fomes peccati* appear ancillary to their primarily punitive function in Thomas's thought.

In Thomas's early treatment of the defeat of the devil through Christian practice, the emphasis falls heavily on the role of the *teacher*

---

169. *ST* III 69.3, response. There is some ambiguity in Thomas's thought about whether it is the struggle or the victory that wins the crown. Both before and after the composition of this passage, Thomas argues that it is the *victory* (and not merely the struggle) that earns the crown (see *Sent. Comm.* IV 49.5.3.1 and *Commentary on the Our Father*, pet. 6). In this case, in order to argue for God's justice in allowing the *fomes* to endure after baptism, Thomas argues that, although the *fomes* still constitutes an obstacle that cannot be perfectly overcome, one is rewarded by God for fighting against it.

170. *ST* III 69.3, ad. 3.

171. *ST* III 69.3, response. See also, for instance, Thomas's *Commentary on Romans* 7.4 (§593).

as the devil's adversary. For Thomas (himself an educator), the teacher defeats the devil in the same way that one who spreads the truth is opposed to a sower of lies.[172] While this opposition between the teacher and the devil may have significant consequences for the way Thomas conceives of the spiritual journey, the communal role of the teacher in the defeat of the devil should not be understood as opposed to the personal role of the spiritual combatant.[173] While Thomas may not initially consider the place of spiritual combat in the defeat of the devil, Thomas's reflections in the *Summa Theologica* primarily address the *moral* (as opposed to doctrinal) struggle against personified evil.

Demonic temptation rests on different foundations than fleshly temptation in Thomas's thought. Thomas recognizes that demonic temptation existed even before Adam's sin, and for that reason, he admits that the phenomenon is not primarily punitive.[174] Thomas's thought in the *Summa Theologica* addresses this matter so as to avoid any sort of cosmological dualism wherein the devil's temptations would not be directed by God's plan for human salvation.[175] In this way, Thomas indicates that demonic temptation in general is not punitive in the way that fleshly temptation is. In notable contrast, however, the specific phenomenon of internal demonic temptation *is* punitive in much the same way as fleshly temptation.

In a question on the devil's temptation of human beings, Thomas explores God's providential permission of demonic temptation both before and after Adam's sin.[176] The question is prompted by Thomas's

---

172. In the *Sentences Commentary*, Thomas may consider heresy to be the most powerful temptation that the devil can level against humankind; see *Sent. Comm.* IV 49.5. Thus, whereas Maximus saw the defeat of the devil in terms of personal spiritual warfare, Thomas tended to see it in terms of doctrine. This shift could reflect a broad contemporary shift in medieval Christianity; see Jeffrey Burton Russell, *Lucifer: The Devil in the Middle Ages* (Ithica, N.Y.: Cornell University Press, 1984), 100, 103, 190, and 299. It also reflects the personal biographies of both men.

173. As discussed in chapters 1 and 2, for the Origenistic tradition of spiritual combat, 2 Timothy 2:5 was one of the most important verses used to justify the monastic lifestyle. For Origen, and in turn Maximus, this verse meant that near-constant temptation was an essential component of spiritual progress. The monk, more than any other sort of person, was the one who underwent such temptation in order to defeat the devil in his own life. The monk was therefore in a privileged place to earn the crown promised in 2 Timothy.

174. *ST* II-II 165.2, obj. 3 and ad. 3.

175. Thomas emphasizes that all demonic action against human beings takes place under God's authority (*Commentary on Job* 41, in *Exposition on Job*, 464).

176. *ST* I 64.4.

observation that not all demons are in hell: some are instead permitted to remain in the air, tempting human beings to sin. The broad cosmological nature of this question makes it understandable why Thomas moves so easily into a consideration of providence and justice. If demons are supposed to be *punished* for their sin, why are they allowed to do what apparently would *please* them? Thomas answers with his deepest and most profound consideration of the purposes of demonic temptation in his later corpus. God providentially arranges that superior creatures are used to procure the welfare of inferior creatures, both directly and indirectly. The direct procurement is that by which good angels are sent to protect humanity from evil and bring them to good. Indirectly, however, God providentially procures human welfare

> as when anyone assailed is exercised by fighting against opposition. It was fitting for this procuring of man's welfare to be brought about through the wicked spirits, lest they should cease to be of service in the natural order. Consequently a twofold place of punishment is due to the demons: one, by reason of their sin, and this is hell; and another, in order that they may tempt men, and thus the darksome atmosphere is their due place of punishment. Now the procuring of men's salvation is prolonged even to the judgment day: consequently, the ministry of the angels and wrestling with demons endure until then. Hence until then the good angels are sent to us here; and the demons are in this dark atmosphere for our trial.[177]

As in Thomas's reflections on fleshly temptation in the *Sentences Commentary*, Thomas argues that it is good and fitting for the human subject to struggle against temptation as the indirect means for God's procurement of human welfare. Human beings will continue to be saved until the end of time, and precisely in view of that goal of salvation, demons are used by God to bring about that end. Thomas thus argues that this form of temptation is providentially fitting, resulting in a presentation of demonic temptation that is more positive than the *fomes peccati*.[178]

---

177. *ST* I 64.4. A similar line of reasoning can be seen in *ST* I 114.1, ad. 3.
178. A similar statement in support of the necessity of temptation is found in the *Commentary on the Our Father*, petition 6: "it is human to be tempted, but to give consent is demonic [*tentari humanum est, sed consentire diabolicum est*]."

In temptation from the *fomes peccati*, God extracts salvation from temptation precisely as God brings a human good from a human-originated evil. In demonic temptation, however, God brings about human salvation from a broader cosmological situation for which human beings are not responsible: a world in which there are angels who have rebelled against their Creator. Originally, God permitted humans to be tempted by the devil when they were innocent; they had the ability to resist this temptation, and through this resistance they would have merited. After the Fall, humans suffer from the *fomes peccati*, and God also permits them to be tempted by demons, not only as part of the human beings' punishment but also as a path toward merit.

For this reason, Thomas's primary distinction regarding demonic temptation concerns two ways in which God seeks human welfare: the first directly by bringing humans good things and withholding them from evil, and the second indirectly by the strengthening that occurs through a permitted attack. The latter of these involves a real evil, for opposition and attack occur only where beings are not united in love and worship. The proportionality of this punishment rests for Thomas in his observation that demons have *nothing else to do,* and so God puts them to the best use possible. Thus, by the writing of the first part of the *Summa Theologica*, Thomas understood demonic temptation primarily as a means of human welfare and salvation that follows from God's will to save humankind in whatever way God deems to be most fitting.

One can note, finally, that there is still a negative component in the specific phenomenon of internal demonic temptation. Thomas elsewhere carefully defines what makes a temptation punitive: "an assault is penal if it be difficult to resist it: but, in the state of innocence, man was able, without any difficulty, to resist temptation."[179] In this sense, the internal demonic temptation that follows from Adam's sin is most certainly punitive, since it is altogether more difficult to resist than was the first temptation in the garden.

While both the pedagogical and punitive roles are present in the

---

179. *ST* II-II 165.1, ad. 3.

fallen human's experience of demonic temptation, its first and original function is God's desire to save humankind, not to punish it. Indeed, that original desire penetrates through even the postlapsarian forms of demonic temptation since "the procuring of men's salvation is prolonged even to the judgment day."[180] In light of these considerations, Thomas's mature thought finds a place for the individual's personal spiritual warfare against the devil alongside the teacher's duty to proclaim the truths of the faith. The role of this temptation is marked by a confidence in God's providential arrangement of the cosmos both before and after sin, though tempered with an acknowledgement that human sin has made even that struggle more difficult than God originally intended. Thus, while one should not be over-confident of one's defeat of the devil, Thomas would recognize that the defeat and frustration of the demons—along with the graced triumph of humans—is God's fundamental and original intent for the struggle of human beings with angelic powers.

A summative contrast: Fleshly temptation exists *only* after Adam's sin and is primarily brought about through Adam's own agency. God permits it to arise as a humanly caused evil that can be used accidentally by God for human salvation. As such, fleshly temptation punishes and provides an opportunity for moral strengthening—in that order. Demonic temptation inverts this order, at least with respect to God's providential arrangement. Since this temptation exists (albeit in different forms) both before and after sin, God's permission is different and, at the beginning, nonpunitive. It originally existed as a means for Adam and Eve to grow from grace to glory. When Adam sinned, the temptation became more internal, more difficult to resist, and consequently punitive but still belonging within the overarching framework of God's salvific plan. Consequently, demonic temptation provides an opportunity for moral strengthening and punishment—in that order.

Thomas shares with Maximus a recognition that God puts the devil to use for the purpose of human salvation. This pedagogical purpose for temptation was first and foremost in Maximus's view of the temp-

---

180. *ST* I 64.4, response.

tation as a whole. Thus, when Thomas proposes forms of temptation that are primarily punitive, he parts ways with Maximus's approach. Maximus holds out hope that all forms of temptation are ultimately part of God's economic will—that God allows all tests as necessary steps in accomplishing human salvation. Thomas, by contrast, views both the *fomes peccati* and internal demonic temptation primarily as just punishments that only incidentally bring about human salvation.

Both forms of postlapsarian temptation in Thomas's thought are a sign of one's wayfarer state, in which one's possession of grace and virtue remains at least somewhat imperfect. Even so, the experience of these temptations is not for Thomas a strict moral fatalism; through a combination of prevention and resistance to individual irrational movements of the sensitive appetite, one can constantly strive toward moral perfection. Both internal demonic temptation and the *fomes peccati* are permitted by God for human punishment. However, God can also use both forms of temptation to strengthen the individual's virtue and lead one to salvation. Given these categories of fallen temptation, the final chapter considers how, in Thomas's thought, Christ takes on something of this temptation.

6

THOMAS'S VIEW OF CHRIST'S TEMPTATION

I have noted throughout the preceding chapters how various figures have attempted to affirm a multifaceted Christological synecdoche, wherein Christ identifies with both the prelapsarian and postlapsarian conditions of human existence. Through each successive historical figure, I have argued that the prelapsarian Christological synecdoche has expanded while that of the postlapsarian condition has comparatively shrunk. Indeed, by the time of Peter and Alexander, no component of Christ's temptation makes explicit contact with the fallen circumstances of humankind. For his part, Thomas insists that Christ should embody the various states of human existence, even in his temptation: thus, in comparison with his immediate high medieval predecessors, he commendably expands the postlapsarian synecdoche. Yet Thomas's most detailed treatments of Christ's temptation prioritize Christ's identification with the prelapsarian condition over his identification with fallen humankind. In this way, Thomas's affirmations in this regard remain more modest than those of Maximus. Thomas's Christological analysis of the three general forms of temptation affirms that Christ's temptation closely resembles Adam's prelapsarian condition while continuing to share some aspects of the postlapsarian condition.

To demonstrate Thomas's position, I first consider passages that treat Thomas's broad understanding of the purpose and means of

Christ's temptation (his saving action). In this material, Thomas affirms that Christ's temptation stands both in a typological relationship with Adam's unfallen temptation and in an intimate and sympathetic relationship with fallen forms of temptation. Second, I trace the Christological foundations of these claims by summarizing Thomas's claims about the person and natures of Christ (his ontological constitution), with special concern for the perfections and voluntary defects of Christ's humanity. Third, on the basis of this analysis of Christ's constitution, I turn to Thomas's treatment of Christ's salvific act found specifically in his temptation. In that final section, I survey each of the three medieval forms of temptation (the *fomes*, external demonic temptation, and internal demonic temptation) and Thomas's reasons for affirming or denying them in Christ.

Christological Synecdoche in Thomas's Soteriology of Temptation

In contrast to many voices from the earlier Latin tradition, Thomas assigns a distinct soteriological value to Christ's temptation by the devil. Thomas conceives of Christ's saving work, in part, as an act of liberation from the powers that held humankind in bondage following Adam's sin. In that liberating act, Thomas distinguishes two moments: temptation and death. That is, Thomas argues that Christ's defeat of the devil is accomplished in these twin acts, whereby Christ appears to (and in a sense does) submit himself to the devil's power.[1] In addition to Christ's death, then, Thomas conceives of Christ's temptation itself as salvific, a means by which Christ *satisfies* for human sin

---

1. A superficial reading of Thomas's soteriology might appear to attach the actual accomplishment of human salvation from the devil exclusively in the event of the crucifixion and death of Christ. For instance, Thomas's *Commentary on Hebrews* focuses nearly exclusively on Christ's death (and not his temptation) as the locus of Christ's redeeming work from the devil. See his comments on Hebrews 2:17–18, in Thomas Aquinas, *Commentary on the Epistle to the Hebrews*, trans. Chrysostom Baer (South Bend, Ind.: St. Augustine's Press, 2006). As I discuss below, however, one passage from this commentary also includes Christ's temptation among the properly liberating events of Christ's life. See also Matthew Levering, *Christ's Fulfillment of Torah and Temple: Salvation According to Thomas Aquinas* (Notre Dame, Ind.: Notre Dame University Press, 2002); Levering's work has focused on the liberating nature of Christ's death in Thomas's thought.

and redeems humankind from the devil. Following the synecdochal structure seen throughout this study, Thomas treats the salvific quality Christ's temptation in terms of its *unfallen* and *fallen* characteristics.

The Adam-Christ Typology and Christ's Unfallen Temptation

Thomas considers Christ's temptation as unfallen when he places it in a typological relationship with the temptation of Adam.[2] In so doing, Thomas views Christ's temptation as an undoing or reversing of Adam's failure.[3] Thomas notes that the order of Christ's temptations in Matthew's account parallels the temptations of Adam, moving successively from a temptation to gluttony, to vainglory, and finally to ambition. In the *Summa Theologica* (*ST*), Thomas explains the devil's reasoning in pursuing this pattern of temptations:

> The devil does not straight away tempt the spiritual man to grave sins, but he begins with lighter sins, so as gradually lead him to those of greater magnitude.... Thus, too, did the devil set about the temptation of the first man.... This same order did he observe in tempting Christ.[4]

In order to undo Adam's temptation, Christ needed to undergo the same sort of experiment that Adam endured at the beginning. Thomas's reasoning implies that the moral circumstances of Christ's temptation were at least in part similar to those of Adam's original temptation.

---

2. There are scriptural reasons for expositing Christ's temptation in a typological relationship with the various tests that Israel underwent, but to my knowledge, Thomas does not invoke this typological relationship. See Thomas Aquinas, *Commentary on the Gospel of St. Matthew*, trans. Paul M. Kimball (Camillus, N.Y.: Dolorosa Press, 2011), 122. At the same time, Thomas usually collapses the details of the temptation narrative so that what was simultaneously the temptation of Adam *and* Eve is treated as if it were only Adam's temptation. There is one instance in which Thomas also speaks briefly of an "Eve/Christ" typology; see the *Commentary on Matthew* 4: "Just as the devil willed to tempt the woman, he also did to Christ, promising spiritual things" (in Aquinas, *Commentary on Matthew*, 114). This example is an exception to the predominant Adam/Christ typology.

3. Thomas holds, with the majority Dominican position, to this "reversal" explanation in *ST* III 1.3. For that reason, Thomas would not abstractly put forward Adam's unfallen condition—or, consequently, Christ's sharing in an unfallen condition—as a reason for Christ's incarnation (as in the minority Franciscan position). For Thomas, both aspects are ordered in different ways to the reversal of sin. Maximus had articulated a position more in line with the Franciscan position, since Maximus had identified more concretely ways in which Christ's incarnation, even independently of Adam's sin, would have improved the prelapsarian condition.

4. *ST* III 41.4, response. See also *ST* III 41.2, response and the *Commentary on Matthew* 4, in Aquinas, *Commentary on Matthew*, 114, 116.

To emphasize how important this typology and parallel pattern are for Thomas, it is worth noting that he is willing to sacrifice the psychological intensity of Christ's temptations in order to preserve them. As Thomas explains, "temptation which comes from the enemy takes the form of a suggestion," and this suggestion "must arise from those things towards which each one has an inclination."[5] In Adam's case, according to Thomas, the devil was able to proceed through three suggestions, each with an increased psychological severity: gluttony, vainglory, and pride or ambition. The order of Adam's temptation is tuned to his original integrity; only "lighter sins" were suggested at the outset. Only then could the idea of the great sin of pride—that "in which ... only carnal men have a part"—be suggested.[6] In Christ's case, the devil proceeds through the same order, but since Christ remains perfectly "spiritual" during the first two temptations, the third is no real temptation at all:

> Thirdly, he [the devil] led the temptation on to that in which no spiritual men, but only carnal men, have a part—namely, to desire worldly riches and fame ... [the third] is inapplicable to spiritual men.[7]

There is a divergence between the experiences of Adam and Christ as the temptations proceed; whereas in Adam the first two temptations toward light sins prepared his mind for his concession to a great sin, Christ holds his mind from such preparation so that he remains a

---

5. *ST* III 41.4, response. Thomas also addresses this order in *ST* II-II 163.1, obj. 2 and ad. 2, where he qualifies the first temptation to gluttony as not coming from within but only externally.

6. See *ST* II-II 163.1, response and ad. 2, for Thomas's statement of Adam's first proper sin. The order matters for Thomas in *ST* III 41.4, response. The nature of Adam's "carnality" prior to his sin of pride may be precisely the devil's attempt to draw his attention to "carnal" things in the first two temptations. One should not misread Thomas's claim as indicating that Adam's first sin was gluttony or vainglory. The order can be important even if the first temptations were not yet sin. The first two suggestions paved the way in Adam and Eve's mind for the Fall into pride: the devil "begins with [temptations toward] lighter sins, so as gradually to lead him to those of greater magnitude" (*ST* III 41.4, response). On a critical note, Thomas cites Gregory's *Moralia*, where the only interpretation that coheres with an application to the prelapsarian Adam is an identification of the devil with "vice" (*ST* III 41.4, response). Since Adam (prior to his pride) had no vices, the only thing that can "insinuate" into Adam's mind is the devil's suggestion. There remains tension here, however, insofar as Thomas also denies that the devil was able to deceive Adam before his sin of pride (see *ST* I 94.4) or to work interiorly in Adam at all.

7. See *ST* II-II 163.1.

"spiritual man" going into the third temptation. Indeed, since a tempting suggestion "must arise from those things towards which each one has an inclination," Christ's third temptation is only nominally so. Thus, Thomas regards Christ's precise reproduction of the form and order of the Adamic temptation (and Christ's blameless response to it) as salvific; the psychological intensity of the tests which Christ endured is not significant at this juncture.

Thomas repeats the claim that Christ's temptation shares in unfallen characteristics in the *De Malo*, where he considers the mode of the devil's suggestion to be the same for Christ as it was for Adam. The devil

> persuades human beings to things in two ways: visibly and invisibly. He persuades visibly as when he sensibly appears to human beings in some form and sensibly speaks with them and persuades them to sin. For example, he tempted the first human being in the garden of paradise in the form of a serpent, and he tempted Christ in the desert in some visible form.[8]

In this respect, Thomas has maintained the synecdochal character of Christ's identity with the prelapsarian condition in his temptation.

The Soteriological Importance of Christ's Postlapsarian Temptation

In other passages, Thomas indicates that Christ's temptation should not be completely identical to that of Adam. One sees, for instance, in the *Commentary on Matthew* that Christ's temptation is not only about undoing *Adam's* sin but also about reversing by experience the fallen aspects of the temptation of Adam's progeny:

> For He willed to be tempted so that, just as by His death He conquered ours, so by His temptation He might overcome all our temptations [*tentatione sua superet omnes tentationes nostras*].[9]

---

8. *De Malo* III 4, in Thomas Aquinas, *The De Malo of Thomas Aquinas*, trans. Richard Regan (New York: Oxford University Press, 2001).

9. *Commentary on Matthew* 4, in Aquinas, *Commentary on Matthew*, 112. He repeats this description and claim through a quotation of Gregory at *ST* III 41.1, response. The parallel between temptation and death is even stronger in this latter passage, though Thomas does not put it in his own words.

Christ undergoes this temptation in order to undo not just those temptations that pertained to Adam's integral state but also "all our temptations."[10] Just as death did not pertain to the Adamic state (but yet is taken on by Christ in order to conquer ours), so too the temptation that Christ undergoes pertains to the *postlapsarian* state. This statement may be Thomas's clearest and most direct affirmation of the soteriological function of Christ's postlapsarian temptation, but other passages provide further clarity. Thomas elsewhere argues that Christ shares in a "fallen" experience of temptation when he considers its salvific and particularly satisfactory character and Christ's compassion with fallen humanity.

In the *Tertia Pars* of the *Summa Theologica*, Christ's passion and death play a pivotal role in Thomas's understanding of Christ's "satisfaction" for humanity's sins, yet in a way that includes a "satisfactory" role for Christ's temptation. In an explanation of Hebrews 2:17–18 in the *Tertia Pars*, Thomas comments that "by his temptation [*sua tentatione*] and passion Christ has succored us by satisfying for us."[11] For two reasons, it is evident that Thomas has in mind a defect of Christ's human nature when considering this satisfactory role for Christ's temptation. First, he makes this statement in a question on Christ's assumption of human defects of soul that come from Adam's sin. Second, he also states in that question that Christ "assumed our defects that He might satisfy for us,"[12] so that it is clear that Thomas ranks a component of Christ's temptation among those defects. I elaborate those "satisfactory" components below.[13]

In two places in the *ST*, Thomas offers mutually reinforcing expla-

---

10. *Commentary on Matthew* 4, in Aquinas, *Commentary on Matthew*, 112. Christ does not experience all forms of fallen temptation, but he does experience *some* form; see below.

11. *ST* III 15.1, ad. 3: "*Christus sua tentatione et passione nobis auxilium tulit pro nobis satisfaciendo.*"

12. *ST* III 15.1, response: "*Christus suscepit defectus nostros ut pro nobis satisfaceret.*"

13. To anticipate the full treatment of this question below, Thomas's explanation in the *Summa Theologica* and *Commentary on Matthew* make it clear that the relevant defect in Christ's humanity is hunger in the first temptation and Christ's exterior susceptibility to bodily movement by the devil in the latter two temptations (see *ST* III 41.1, ad. 2). The devil did not have this latter power over Adam in the garden; it is a distinctly *postlapsarian* aspect of Christ's temptation. Thomas thereby indicates that Christ's temptation is not a mere re-enactment of Adam's prelapsarian experience in the Garden but an entering into some of the conditions that Adam's temptation and subsequent failure entailed for his progeny.

nations of what it means to satisfy for another person. In *ST* III 14.1, Thomas offers this definition of satisfaction: "one satisfies for another's sin by taking on himself the punishment due to the sin of the other."[14] In *ST* III 48.2, Thomas offers this alternative explanation:

> He properly atones [*satisfacit*] for an offense who offers something which the offended one loves equally, or even more than he detested the offense. But by suffering out of love and obedience, Christ gave more to God than was required to compensate for the offense of the whole human race.[15]

These two definitions address, respectively, the prospective and retrospective nature of satisfaction, a view Thomas first articulated in the *Sentences Commentary*.[16] According to the first, Christ's satisfaction acts as a safeguard against future sin by addressing its causes. According to the second, Christ's satisfaction superabundantly compensates for sin already committed. Each of these aspects contributes to Thomas's understanding of Christ's temptation. The latter, retrospective definition shows that Christ's temptation gave something that was desired (by God) more than the sin committed was hated. By his postlapsarian temptation, Christ "suffers out of love and obedience," thereby satisfying for past sin. On the other hand, the former, prospective definition indicates that the satisfactory nature of Christ's temptation requires that Christ take on something of the punishment for sin on himself. That is, since Thomas knows that Christ satisfies by his temptation, he equally knows that something in Christ's temptation must resemble the punishment that followed from Adam's sin.

Having established that Thomas treats Christ's temptation as satisfactory, one can in turn conclude that Thomas's discussion of the

---

14. *ST* III 14.1, response.

15. *ST* III 48.2, response. At the time of *Sentences Commentary*, Thomas demonstrates familiarity with the definition of satisfaction from Augustine (see *ST* Supplement, 12.3, obj. 1) repeated by Peter the Lombard as well as the definition offered by Anselm (see *ST* Supplement, 12.3, obj. 5). Thomas argues that these two definitions are essentially consistent (*ST* Supplement, 12.3, ad. 5): the former is an aid in preventing future sin and the latter corrects for sins already committed (*ST* Supplement, 12.3, response). This same parallel can be seen in the two definitions above: by taking on punishment, he addresses the causes of sin in ourselves and acts to prevent them in the future; by offering up something loved, he compensates (superabundantly) for sins already committed.

16. *ST* Supplement 12.3, response; see also the previous note.

effects of Christ's passion in *ST* III 48 can largely be applied to Christ's temptation as well.[17] That is, Christ's temptation involves his *suffering out of love*, but Thomas further states that suffering out of love is a necessary condition for two of the other ways in which Christ's death was salvific: by way of merit and by way of sacrifice. As for Christ's merit, Thomas states that "whosoever suffers for justice's sake ... merits his salvation thereby."[18] Concerning the passion's sacrificial character, Thomas states that it was "the sacrifice of suffering out of love."[19] Thus, since Christ's temptation also involved his suffering out of love, it follows that Christ's temptation merits human salvation and constitutes a sacrifice for human sin.[20] In summary, Thomas treats Christ's temptation as *satisfactory* and *sacrificial* for human sin and *meritorious* for human salvation, all by means of an acceptance of something of the postlapsarian conditions of temptation.

Thomas further assigns an important role to Christ's fallen temptation in his explanation of Christ's merciful regard for fallen humanity. I consider in turn Thomas's understanding of "mercy" and "compassion" as applied to God and then their use regarding Christ.

---

17. Since the evidence is clearest with regard to satisfaction, it is best to focus the substance of my argument on that point; I note the other ways in which Christ's death is salvific for completion.

18. *ST* III 48.1, response. Thomas's reference is to meriting for oneself, but in context, Thomas clarifies that the merit of Christ, in his role as the Head of the Church, overflows to the body as well. See Joseph P. Wawrykow, *God's Grace and Human Action: 'Merit' in the Theology of Thomas Aquinas* (Notre Dame, Ind.: University of Notre Dame Press, 1995), 238–47 (which does not address, however, whether Christ's temptation is meritorious).

19. *ST* III 48.3, reply 3: "*ex caritate patientis fuit sacrificium.*" Here, the suffering is the object of the sacrifice, but it stands to reason that, for Thomas, Christ would offer any of his suffering (not just the Passion itself) for human salvation.

20. There is some thin evidence from the *Sentences Commentary* that Thomas may also consider Christ's temptation as "a redemption that conquers": "Christ redeemed [*redimit*] us by that which he did and endured in human nature; through which he both made satisfaction [*satisfecit*] to the Father for all humankind and conquered [*vicit*] the enemy, resisting his temptation" (*Sent. Comm.* III 19.1.4.2, response [my citations of the *Sentences Commentary* are from https://www.corpusthomisticum.org/iopera.html, my translations]). The location of the phrase concerning Christ's temptation makes it difficult to ascertain whether Thomas would place it in connection with redemption, but such remains a possibility. The idea of redemption is essentially one of slavery [*servitus*] and liberation through the paying of a price [*pretium*] (*ST* III 48.4; for Thomas's demonological usage of *vincere*, see *ST* III 46.3, *ST* III 47.2, *ST* III 49.2, and *ST* III 52.1. As an example of a different usage, in *ST* III 46.11, it is used in reference to Christ's defeat of death). The redemptive aspect of Christ's temptation would lie in the "payment" to the Father that Christ makes by demonstrating the devil's lack of justice in trying to hold Christ in bondage, thereby leading to God's removal of the devil from his role as a tormentor of humankind.

God is from eternity good and loving; these attributes are the essential and sufficient cause of any act of God that is called "merciful."[21] The goodness of God is the foundation of the acts that Thomas calls the "effects of mercy," which Thomas explains by reference to the etymology of mercy, *misericordia*:

> a person is said to be merciful [*misericors*], as being, so to speak, sorrowful at heart [*miserum cor*]; being affected with sorrow [*tristitiam*] at the misery of another as though it were his own. Hence it follows that he endeavors to dispel the misery of this other, as if it were his; and this is the effect of mercy. To sorrow, therefore, over the misery [*miseria*] of others belongs not to God; but it does most properly belong to Him to dispel that misery, whatever be the defect we call by that name.[22]

These effects of mercy are traced to God's goodness because Thomas believes that mercy, understood as an affection of passion rooted in sorrow, does not exist in the divine nature.[23] God's goodness infinitely exceeds any affective movement human beings can have. Indeed, the incarnation of Christ is itself the greatest demonstration of the merciful effects arising from God's goodness. This arrangement between God's goodness and Christ's mercy is clear in the *Summa Theologica*, where Thomas argues that God's judgment takes place through Christ "so that [God's] judgment to men might be sweeter [*suavius*]."[24] By judging us through Christ's mediatorial action, God shows a greater effect of mercy than if God had judged us in another way. It is, however, precisely God's goodness and love that ground God's choice to judge us through Christ.

Christ, on the other hand, has mercy as a human in a sense that God does not: as an affection of passion and as a virtue subordinate to charity.[25] Thomas affirms that Christ's soul, being passible, was capable of sorrow. Thomas likewise acknowledges that mercy is sorrow at

---

21. *ST* I 21.4, response. In that response, the divine attribute of justice is correlated with the attribute of goodness—and not with mercy—for reasons that will become clear in a moment.
22. *ST* I 21.3, response.
23. *ST* I 21.3, response.
24. *ST* III 59.2.
25. See *ST* II-II 30.3, response, where the affect and virtue are distinguished.

the misfortune of another.[26] In similar terms, Thomas defines human mercy (*misericordia*: literally, distress of heart) as "compassion for another's affliction,"[27] and so Thomas's treatment of Christ's compassion (to "suffer with [*compatior*]" another) is in essence a discussion of his human mercifulness as well.

In Christ's case, this affective mercy is perfectly governed by the intellectual appetite (the will), in which mercy can also be present as a rational appetite. Thomas describes this rational disposition as an intellectual recognition whereby "one person's evil is displeasing to another."[28] Because the sensitive affect can be governed by reason, mercy is called a virtue, and like all virtues, it is found perfectly in Christ from the moment of his conception.[29] Nevertheless, Christ's experience of human misery is the cause of his active feeling of *misericordia*, his sorrow at heart at another's misfortune. While the following quotation does not speak directly of Christ's temptation, it serves as something of a primer to the nature of Christ's sympathy. He

> is ready and apt to come to assistance, and this because he knows by experience [*per experientiam*] our misery, which as God he knew from eternity by simple knowledge [*per simplicem notitiam*].[30]

In Christ's human life, there is a different mode of mercy, one that acts by experience of our misery. Since the virtue involved is the rational governance of one's sorrow in the face of another's misfortune, one's sorrow is rightfully greater as one's confrontation with the other's misfortune increases. Thomas would see this response embodied in the Gospel of John's account of the raising of Lazarus (Jn 11:1–44). Christ knows from a distance that Lazarus has died (v. 14), and even upon entering the town, there is no indication of Christ's sorrow (vs. 17–32).

---

26. For Christ's sorrow, see *ST* III 15.6. For the definition of mercy, see *ST* II-II 30.1, sed contra and *ST* II-II 30.1, response.

27. *ST* II-II 30.1, ad. 2: "*compassio miseriae alterius.*" In the same article's response, he cites Augustine's parallel definition.

28. *ST* II-II 30.3, response.

29. *ST* III 7.2 and 12. I discuss Christ's perfections of virtue in the next section.

30. *Commentary on Hebrews* 4.3, in Aquinas, *Commentary on Hebrews*, 108. One might also note in this context Thomas's affirmation in *ST* III 41.4, response, where Christ's *humanity* appears as the proximate cause of the defeat of the devil.

However, when confronted with the sorrow of Mary, Lazarus's sister, Christ is "deeply moved in spirit and troubled" (v. 33). When he begins to approach the tomb, Christ weeps (v. 35). Christ's virtue is perfect throughout, yet the virtuous affective response (sorrow at another's misfortune or, equivalently, mercy) is greater when confronted experientially with sorrow and death. Thus, while Christ's *virtue* of mercy is not greater because of his experience of our misery, his rationally governed affective response (his *feeling* of compassion or mercy) is rightfully greater in and through that direct experience of our misery.

In the above citations, Thomas speaks generally of Christ's humanity and human *experience* as the ground for a unique affective and virtuous mercy in Christ. However, Thomas also speaks of Christ's *temptation* as an essential component of that experience of misery. In the Hebrews commentary, one finds the strongest affirmation of the role of Christ's temptation in his compassion with fallen humanity:

> He was tempted, so that He might be like to us as much in temporal things as in all other things, except in sin alone. For if He would have been without temptations, He would not have known them by experience, and thus He would not have been compassionate [*Si enim fuisset sine tentationibus, non fuisset eas expertus, et sic non compateretur*].[31]

Through a direct confrontation with some of our miserable conditions in his own temptation, Christ's virtuous affective response to that misery is greater than if he had not experienced such temptation. Thomas thereby directly links three realities in a unique way: temptation, experience, and compassion. Temptation and experience increase Christ's rationally governed sorrow concerning our misery to the extent that, within God's plan to save humanity through Christ, these temptations are the economic *sine qua non* of his "suffering with" human misery: without them, "he would not have compassion," that is, the feeling of compassion.

On the one hand, Thomas's Adam/Christ typological reading of Christ's temptation establishes a framework for Christ's temptation that views it from the perspective of Christ's unfallen experience of

---

31. *Commentary on Hebrews* 4.3, in *Commentary on Hebrews*, 109.

temptation. On the other hand, the soteriological reflections outlined above indicate that Christ's temptation also involved a certain fallen experience of temptation that can be seen to satisfy for human sin and to lead to a greater rationally governed feeling of compassion and mercy with our fallen lot.

Having established Thomas's *purposes* for Christ's temptation, I turn next to Thomas's consideration of the ontological constitution of Christ as the ground for this experience of temptation.

Christ's Perfections and Voluntary Defects

Thomas's understanding of Christ's ontological constitution is the basis of his reflection on what Christ accomplished in his life, temptation, and death. This arrangement is simply another way of saying that for Thomas, being precedes act, both for mere human beings and for Christ. I have indicated in the first section that Thomas's conception of the salvific nature of Christ's temptation is predicated on two comparisons: Christ's likeness to the prelapsarian Adam and to fallen humanity. In this section, I show that these affirmations in Thomas's theory of Christ's *action* can be traced to affirmations in Thomas's understanding of Christ's *constitution*. Thomas's soteriology in this regard is a version of the synecdochal character of Christ's humanity, composed of *aspects* of the different historical states of human nature.[32] Thomas balances claims of Christ's perfections as a "comprehensor" with claims of Christ's human defects as a "wayfarer."

In this material, I first discuss Christ's role as a *comprehensor*, wherein Christ's ontological constitution shares in the unfallen states of humankind (whether original or glorified). Second, I consider those aspects of Christ's constitution that Thomas considers "fallen" or, in his language, characteristic of Christ's state as a *wayfarer*. Third, I treat the way in which Thomas affirms these wayfarer attributes be to fully *voluntary* in Christ.

---

32. I have noted in chapter 3, n10, that Adams, *What Sort of Human Nature?* 67, describes my "Christological synecdoche" as Christological "telescoping."

Christ the Comprehensor: Christ's Human Perfections

Thomas categorizes Christ's human perfections along two lines: perfections of knowledge and perfections of grace. Thomas recognizes a soteriological orientation in these perfections; since Thomas conceives of Christ's mission as one of satisfying for sin and reconciling to God, these characteristics are indispensable to his work. In order for Christ's life to be of greater value to God than human sin, Christ must offer back to God a life of perfection: he is utterly upright, aware of his purpose, and able to proclaim truthfully the coming of God's reign.[33] I consider in turn the perfections of Christ's knowledge and grace, as these constitute for Thomas a limit on any defects that might exist in his human nature.

Thomas first affirms that Christ's mission of bringing humankind into union with God requires that he share from the beginning that knowledge of God that will be shared by the blessed and "comprehensors" in heaven. Thomas reasons that this *visio Dei* should be given to Christ because "the cause ought always to be more efficacious than the effect."[34] That is, since Christ's redemption causes us to enter into the beatific vision, Christ himself should possess that knowledge of God in abundance. Thomas clarifies that Christ's human knowledge of God does not violate the innate limitations of his human nature.[35] This knowledge is indeed given to Christ as grace, but even then, it is not the same knowledge that the Word has by virtue of the divine nature; "the uncreated knowledge [of God from eternity] is in every way above the nature of the human soul," so Christ's human soul, strictly speaking, does not participate in this uncreated divine self-knowledge.[36]

Secondly, beside the beatific vision of God, Christ also possessed two other forms of knowledge (infused and acquired) that correspond

---

33. See *ST* III 48.2, response, where it is Christ's "exceeding charity" (his virtue) that makes his sacrifice superabundant.

34. *ST* III 9.2, response. For further detail of Thomas's thought on this subject, see *ST* III 10.

35. Thomas's doctrine of Christ's *visio Dei* is sometimes misunderstood as violating Christ's human finitude. For an excellent, sympathetic discussion of Thomas's doctrine of the *visio Dei* in Christ, see the work of the late Edward Oakes, *Infinity Dwindled to Infancy* (Grand Rapids, Mich.: William B. Eerdmans Publishing Company, 2011), 210–21, especially 220.

36. *ST* III 9.2, ad. 3.

to two cognitive faculties constitutive of human nature (passive and active intellect). According to the first, infused knowledge, Christ was granted knowledge of all intellectual species capable of comprehension by a human mind in his passive intellect. Thomas draws a parallel here between Christ and the angels; just as the latter were infused at their creation with all "intelligible species" capable of comprehension by their individual natures, so too Christ was granted "an infused or imprinted knowledge, whereby He knows things in their proper nature by intelligible species proportioned to the human mind."[37] Here again, this knowledge is bounded in a sense by the finitude of Christ's human mind; the species of his knowledge are "proportioned to [his] nature," so that this knowledge is not absolutely identical to the knowledge that God has of creation from eternity or even, indeed, to the infused knowledge of angelic natures.[38] Thomas is careful to point out that this infused knowledge also bears a relation to Christ's mission, so that he might know and thereby be able to teach "all things made known to man by Divine revelation."[39] Essentially, in order for Christ to reconcile humanity to God, Christ must understand the relationship between the two (humanity and God), comprehend his role in bringing about that reconciliation, and impart that knowledge to his followers. In this affirmation, Thomas understands Christ's knowledge in a way similar to Maximus, who equally saw Christ's knowledge as an important part of his saving work.

Thomas's affirmation of Christ's full humanity, however, leads him to argue for an understanding of Christ's knowledge that Maximus's account lacked. By the time of the writing of the *Summa Theologica*, Thomas argues that Christ possessed an acquired human knowledge that differs in its origin from Christ's infused knowledge.[40] Thom-

---

37. *ST* III 9.3, response. See also *ST* III 11.
38. See *ST* III 11.4, where Thomas distinguishes one sense in which Christ's human knowledge is greater than the knowledge of the angels and another in which it is comparatively limited by the nature of human knowledge in relation to angelic knowledge. See also *ST* III 11.1, where Thomas also avows that this knowledge of Christ is a strictly *human* knowledge, proportioned to the human sciences and divine revelation.
39. *ST* III 11.1, response. See also *ST* III 7.7, response.
40. *ST* III 9.4, response. Thomas acknowledges here that in the *Sentences Commentary*, he had argued otherwise. See also *ST* III 12.

as's reasoning is based on the utility of all aspects of human nature. Christ had in his passive intellect a comprehension of all those sorts of knowledge a human being can understand, but Thomas notes that human nature also has the distinct ability in its active intellect to abstract knowledge or intellectual species from the impression of phenomena on the sense organs. Since Christ has that active intellect by virtue of the incarnation (that is, because it is an essential feature of human nature), Thomas reasons that it would not be fitting if Christ were not to make use of that faculty, since "God and nature make nothing in vain."[41] Thus, during the course of his human life on earth, Christ was able to grow in knowledge by abstracting intellectual species from the impression of sensory data.[42] This form of knowledge expresses Thomas's strongest affirmation of the natural functioning of Christ's human cognition, and in this affirmation, his recognition of the powers of human nature may exceed that of Maximus, who rested simply in an affirmation of Christ's omniscience.

Still, taken together, Thomas's claims about Christ's knowledge amount to a denial that Christ could properly be called ignorant.[43] Each of the three forms of Christ's knowledge contributes in its own way to Christ's saving mission. Christ's beatific knowledge proleptically displays what all the blessed will enjoy in heaven; Christ's infused knowledge allows him to carry out his mission with a full understanding of his purpose and role and also to share that knowledge with his followers; and Christ's acquired knowledge reveals the fittingness of all the parts of Christ's human intellect, so that no part of his humanity would be without purpose in the course of his human life. In the first two affirmations, Thomas is largely compatible with Maximus's views of Christ's knowledge.[44] In the third, Thomas's theory of Christ's

41. *ST* III 9.4, response.
42. See *ST* III 12.2, where he explains that the kind of growth he means exceeds that of "comparing the infused intelligible species with what He received through the senses for the first time," which was his previous position. In that view, Christ played a sort of intellectual matching game in which what he already knows is paired with what is presented to him and in turn abstracted to an intellectual species. In his developed thought, Christ's knowledge can increase "in essence" and "in the soul of Christ there was a habit of knowledge which could increase by the abstraction of species."
43. This claim is made explicit in *ST* III 14.4, response.
44. When I presented Maximus's understanding of Christ's knowledge in chapter 3, I dealt

acquired knowledge, recognizing the faculties and limits of human knowing, likely surpasses any discussion of Christ's human knowledge found in Maximus's corpus.

As for Christ's perfections of grace, I focus on two aspects of this perfection: the graces of virtue and the "gifts" of grace. First, Thomas states that

> since the grace of Christ was most perfect, there flowed from it, in consequence, the virtues which perfect the several powers of the soul for all the soul's acts; and thus Christ had all the virtues.[45]

In light, again, of my ultimate aim, the most prominent of those virtues in Christ's soul is the virtue of temperance residing in the sensitive appetite. Thomas takes particular care to affirm this virtue in Christ:

> Christ had no evil desires whatever, as will be shown; yet He was not thereby prevented from having temperance, which is the more perfect in man, as he is without evil desires.[46]

It is important to note that Thomas's demonstration of Christ's lack of evil desire does not address all the cases of inner temptation I discussed in the previous chapter. When Thomas addresses Christ's lack of evil desire, he considers two cases: outright sin and the presence of the *fomes*, both of which he emphatically denies as present in Christ.[47] One sees this same denial of the *fomes peccati* when Thomas denies that Christ had any "proneness towards evil [*pronitas ad malum*]" or any "difficulty in well-doing [*difficultas ad bonum*]."[48] Since inner passionate temptation from the devil is subordinated to the presence of the *fomes*, these qualifications suffice to deny evil *desire* in Christ. Yet as noted in chapter 5, Thomas recognizes that the devil also works internally through the *imagination*; Thomas does not fully explain Christ's relationship with the grace that prevents that attack.

---

with the abstract compatibility between temptation and omniscience. That problem was more acute in Maximus's writings than it is in Thomas's, so it needs no repetition here.

45. *ST* III 7.2, response.
46. *ST* III 7.2, ad. 3. Fortitude (which governs the irascible faculty) need not be treated here, as it is parallel to temperance (which governs the concupiscible faculty).
47. *ST* III 15.1 and 2.
48. *ST* III 14.4, response.

A second aspect of Christ's "fullness of grace" further illuminates how Thomas may resolve the question of a demonic imaginative attack against Christ. Thomas argues that in Christ, all the graces capable of flowing into the human soul were present to a maximal degree and with a maximum of power so that it might "overflow" from Christ to the rest of humanity. In order to pass grace on to the rest of humankind, Christ must possess it fully and superabundantly. Thus Thomas affirms that "His grace extends to all the effects of grace, which are the virtues, gifts, and the like."[49] In this light, one should remember from chapter 5 that Adam's original condition had a "special favor of grace" that prevented the devil from harming him interiorly; the existence of such a grace should thus predispose one to think that Thomas would deny an inner demonic attack against Christ's imagination as well as against his sensitive appetite.

Christ the Wayfarer: Christ's Human Defects

Thomas explains the importance of Christ's human defects in three ways. First, by them, Christ's takes on the punishment of another. This reason is familiar; it also appears in Thomas's understanding of the salvific character of Christ's temptation. Second, the assumed defects demonstrate the reality of the incarnation by giving Christ a humanity that is recognizable to fallen human beings. Third, Christ thereby gives his followers a clear "example of patience by valiantly bearing up against human passibility and defects."[50] I have reason to return to Thomas's account of Christ's exemplarity below. Together, these reasons indicate that without these defects, Christ's saving mission would have been somewhat impeded.

Two of Christ's human defects are particularly related to the devil's power in relation to Christ and his temptation. First, the devil is granted a certain exterior authority over Christ's body, whereby he is able to change Christ's physical location.[51] I elaborate this defect further

---

49. *ST* III 7.9, response.
50. *ST* III 14.1, response.
51. This defect must be construed from the account to follow; see below. It corresponds to Adam's freedom from demonic attack (and subsequent postlapsarian susceptibility) mentioned in chapter 5.

on. Second, Thomas affirms that Christ assumed what Thomas calls the "natural and indetractible passions." By them, Christ experiences things that did not attain in the prelapsarian condition, most importantly hunger. These two postlapsarian defects are what the devil makes use of when he tempts Christ. By them, Thomas attempts to affirm the postlapsarian Christological synecdoche traced throughout this study. While the phrase "natural and indetractible passions" has its origin in Maximus and comes to Thomas through John of Damascus, Thomas's interpretation of it has significant consequences for the Christological synecdoche that he constructs. For that reason, I consider this phrase for the remainder of this section.

In the *De Fide Orthodoxa*, John of Damascus, borrowing from Maximus, had written that Christ assumed the "natural and blameless passions" of human nature.[52] For Maximus, these passions indicated Christ's double-descent into the ambiguous moral circumstances of fallen humankind. John maintains this sense, indicating that these passions included the ability of Christ to be attacked by the devil through his passions in a distinctly postlapsarian way. Burgundio of Pisa's Latin translation of this passage, in turn, calls them "the natural and indetractible [*indetractibilis*] passions." While "blameless" is within the range of meanings for *indetractibilis*, the term (primarily denoting an inability to be removed) creates interpretive difficulties for Burgundio's reader. This difficulty is exacerbated by Burgundio's minimization of the demonic associations of the natural and blameless passions as understood by John and (more remotely) Maximus.

These differences lead Thomas to diverge from Maximus's approach to these passions. While Thomas recognizes that something in these passions relates to the fallen condition (like Maximus), Thomas modifies Maximus's sense by referring them back to an unfallen characteristic of Christ's humanity as well. Thomas approaches the term looking for something related to Christ's passions that "cannot be taken away," as indetractible denotes. Thomas finds an answer in

---

52. *De Fide Orthodoxa*, III 20 (PG 94:1081–2); see chapter 4 as well. John of Damascus, *De Fide Orthodoxa: Versions of Burgundio and Cerbanus*, ed. Eligius M. Buytaert (St. Bonaventure, N.Y.: Franciscan Institute, 1955).

Christ's knowledge and grace, both of which were uniquely perfect in Christ and thus unable to be fittingly removed from him.[53] Through these perfections, Christ demonstrates an aspect of human affectivity unencumbered by humanity's fallen circumstances. In so reading this term, Thomas strays from the most likely grammatical sense of Burgundio's text. In Burgundio's text, it is the *passions* (which are "morally blameless" and indicative of the *postlapsarian* condition) that are described as indetractible, but in Thomas's reading, the term is applied to Christ's *knowledge* and *grace* (which "cannot be taken away" and are thus indicative of the *unfallen* condition).

Thomas's relative emphasis on Christ's human perfections can also be seen elsewhere in Thomas's reflection on the topic. In the quotation below, Christ's mission requires the *fullness* of grace and knowledge but only a *portion* of the defects of fallen humanity:

The fullness of all grace and knowledge was due to Christ's soul of itself... and hence Christ assumed all the fullness of knowledge and wisdom absolutely. But He assumed our defects economically, in order to satisfy for our sin, and not that they belonged to Him of Himself. Hence it was not necessary for Him to assume them all, but only such as sufficed to satisfy for the sin of the whole nature.[54]

Thomas justifies this limited contact with the fallen condition by arguing that the defects Christ experiences (passibility and corruptibility, especially) are the root cause of the other defects, thereby rendering the assumption of these other defects irrelevant:

"Since Christ healed the passibility and corruptibility of our body by assuming it, He consequently healed all other defects."[55] He heals these aspects precisely because he did not assume the other defects that would interfere with his perfections of knowledge and grace. Other defects, as understood by Thomas, simply are not compatible with Christ's manifest perfections of grace and knowledge: if grace increases, those defects decrease.

---

53. *ST* III 14.1, response.
54. *ST* III 14.4, ad. 2.
55. *ST* III 14.4, ad. 1.

Thomas's standard for measuring Christ's contact with the postlapsarian conditions of temptation stands at a midpoint among the positions seen throughout this work. On the one hand, Thomas has included explicit space for a fallen mode of temptation in Christ's affective life. In this affirmation, he has notably improved on the positions articulated by Peter the Lombard and Alexander of Hales. Yet, Thomas's settled position is still significantly shy of the claims made by John of Damascus and Maximus. To say that Christ's passions are blameless (with Maximus) means one thing; to say that his passions do not detract from his knowledge and virtue (with Thomas) means something different. Essentially, whereas in Maximus's thought the "natural and blameless passions" indicate *only* Christ's synecdochal contact with the *fallen* conditions of human passibility, for Thomas the "natural and indetractible passions" straddle the line between fallen and unfallen. To Thomas, they express Christ's synecdochal contact both with fallen experience (namely, hunger) and with the fullness of grace experienced in the *unfallen* condition.

Maximus undoubtedly agrees that Thomas is right to invoke Christ's perfections of knowledge and grace as an essential part of Christ's saving mission. The problem, however, is that Thomas has strayed from the elaboration of Christ's human defects to which *ST* III 14 is devoted. Just when Thomas undertakes an exposition of Christ's defects, he instead offers a consideration of Christ's perfections. By inverting the question, Thomas offers a disjunction where Maximus had insisted on a conjunction. For Thomas, one must choose: *either* Christ enjoyed a perfection of grace and virtue *or* Christ experienced human passibility in the way fallen humanity experiences it. At this precise juncture, Maximus, in a very different idiom, instead tried to hold them together: Christ *both* enjoyed a fullness of virtue *and* experienced human passibility in its weakened state after the Fall.

Christ's Voluntary Assumption of Human Defects
Following a tradition of reflection that goes back to at least John of Damascus, Thomas affirms that Christ's assumption of human defects is not the same as a fallen human's contraction of those defects from

Adam. Since Christ's origin is unique (not arising from carnal concupiscence), his humanity is not bound to the effects of Adam's sin that other human beings acquire simply because they originate from an act that binds them to Adam's transgression.[56] Because of this absolute freedom, Christ takes on the characteristics of our wounded nature as an act of perfect gratuity.

As pointed out in chapter 4, an orthodox articulation of Christ's *voluntary* assumption of human defects requires more precision than had been offered up to this point in the medieval tradition because the unique person of Christ has not one will but two. There are certain natural boundaries to the problem. On the one hand, Christ's human will cannot be said to act toward some effect when that will does not itself exist; any act that describes the decision to take a certain *form* or *condition* of human nature would therefore *a priori* appear to describe the divine will alone in the eternal decision to undertake the incarnation. On the other hand, orthodox dyothelitism requires that both wills (human and divine) be in accord; it would not do to say that Christ as God willed something that Christ as human did not (or *vice versa*), as that would rupture Christ's hypostatic unity.

Thomas addresses this issue in both the *Sentences Commentary* and the *Summa Theologica*. In approaching the general question of the voluntary nature of the assumption of human defect, Thomas articulates a distinction between assumption and contraction.[57] One who "contracts" a defect does so out of necessity:

In the verb "to contract" is understood the relation of effect to cause, i.e. that is said to be contracted which is derived of necessity together with its cause. Now the cause of death and such like defects in human nature is sin.... And hence they who incur these defects, as due to sin, are properly said to contract them.[58]

So human beings whose origin stands in connection to Adam's original sin are bound by a strict necessity in taking on the defects conse-

---

56. *ST* III 14.3 discusses the way in which Christ "assumed" but did not "contract" his bodily defects.
57. This distinction is found first in the *Sent. Comm.* III 15.1.3.
58. *ST* III 14.3, response.

quent to his sin. But Christ did not share this relationship to Adam's sin and was therefore free to either assume the defects or not:

> For He received human nature without sin, in the purity which it had in the state of innocence. In the same way He might have assumed human nature without defects. Thus it is clear that Christ did not contract these defects as if taking them upon Himself as due to sin, but by His own will.[59]

This mode of taking on defects is what Thomas calls "assumption," and Thomas surpasses John of Damascus's treatment by affirming that this action is properly ascribed to the divine will alone, since the action is concerned with the *creation* of Christ's human will.[60] The decision to enter into the conditions of human defect is made before Christ's human will exists, so Christ's human willing of these defects must conform to the constitutional limitations of his human will.

Thomas's further reflections on the matter explicitly consider only Christ's mortality—the relationship of Christ's human will to his own death—and leave the parallel case of his passibility largely implicit. At the time of the early *Sentences Commentary*, Thomas restricts to the divine will alone the power to change the normal course of nature, including altering the natural progression toward death:

> Only he is [said] to change the established law and course of nature who instituted and ordained nature; which God alone accomplished. And thus no other bodily, spiritual, animate, or angelic power, not even the soul of Christ [*nec etiam animae Christi*], could change the divinely established law of nature, except by way of prayer or intercession.[61]

There is a constitutional limitation on the power of Christ's human soul considered in itself; since the divine will had established that Christ's humanity would suffer from certain defects such as mortality, the ability to avoid death is not properly attributed to Christ's soul. Thomas affirms this explicitly:

---

59. *ST* III 14.3, response.
60. *ST* III 14.2, ad. 2.
61. *Sent. Comm.* III 16.1.3, response.

as the death of Christ's body followed according to the law and course of nature (as is said and as the Teacher says in the text), it must be said that the necessity of dying in Christ was not subject to his human will, but only to the divine [*necessitas moriendi in Christo non subdebatur voluntati ejus humanae, sed solum divinae*], as one opinion says.[62]

In the *Sentences Commentary*, then, the divine will alone could prevent Christ's death by establishing his humanity at the moment of the incarnation in an unfallen condition. In this sense, Thomas's early thought is clear that Christ's mortality (and, by analogy, passibility) is "not subject to his human will." Nevertheless, these claims are clarified in the *Summa Theologica* in such a way that it is still possible to affirm the fully voluntary (nonconstrained) character of Christ's human corruptibility, mortality, and passibility.

In the *Summa Theologica*, Thomas equally denies that Christ's human soul was omnipotent since human nature is necessarily finite.[63] Thomas goes on to clarify the positive sense in which Christ's death was in the power of his human soul and thus fully voluntary. Thomas considers three different kinds of creaturely change and addresses whether Christ's soul was capable of performing each: a natural transmutation of creatures (such as using a hand to pick up a cup); a miraculous transformation (such as raising the dead); and the creation and destruction of creatures (such as in Genesis).[64] The first of these is unquestionably in the power of Christ's soul, as such actions pertain to the normal relationship between soul and body in human nature; the third of these is described by Thomas as absolutely beyond the power of Christ's human soul.

The second case, however, is crucial to the way in which Thomas affirms that Christ willingly accepts human defects: Thomas affirms that Christ's human soul has an "instrumental power" to raise the dead insofar as it is conjoined to the Word. This instrumental power is later affirmed by Thomas as the means by which Christ can be said to be omnipotent with regard to his human body.

62. *Sent. Comm.* III 16.1.3, response.
63. *ST* III 13.1.
64. *ST* III 13.2.

Christ's soul may be viewed as an instrument united in person to God's Word; and thus every disposition of His own body was wholly subject to His power. Nevertheless, since the power of an action is not properly attributed to the instrument, but to the principal agent, this omnipotence is attributed to the Word of God rather than to Christ's soul.[65]

There is, again, a certain limit to this power; the "principal agent" of the act remains the Word of God and not Christ's human soul. But Thomas is willing to extend this instrumental power to the extent that Christ's soul can be affirmed as capable of preventing his death: "His spirit had the power of preserving His fleshly nature from the infliction of any injury; and Christ's soul had this power, because it was united in unity of person with the Divine Word."[66] This affirmation makes particular sense when conceived in a "top-down" manner. If the Word were to determine in a particular instance that his body should not be harmed, his divine and human natures would both act together in preventing that harm, the omnipotent divine will carrying it out directly and the human will instrumentally agreeing to it and wishing it in human fashion.

The *voluntary* character of Christ's assumption of defect requires that the Word of God—the single person who performs all the acts of the God-man—has the power to do otherwise, even as human—otherwise, the hypostatic union itself would be torn apart into a duality of subjects. To be sure, Christ's human will accepts death. As Thomas states in the *Summa Theologica*, "insofar as such necessity [of constraint] is opposed to the will, it is clear that these defects were not in Christ by necessity, either with respect to the divine will nor with respect to the human will absolutely, as following the deliberation of reason."[67] Essentially, Christ does accept death, but Christ does not *merely* accept death—his human soul instrumentally *allows* it. One can accept death without the ability to prevent it, but such is not what Thomas says of Christ in the *Summa Theologica*; there is a more active, instrumental permission that, because of the hypostatic union,

---

65. *ST* III 13.3.
66. *ST* III 47.1.
67. *ST* III 14.2, translation modified.

is essential in order for Christ to undergo any of the defects fittingly ascribed to Christ. Without this human and instrumental permission (which concurs with the divine will), Christ would not have undergone these defects. Such an affirmation would also transfer to Thomas's view of Christ's passions, which would also share this instrumental permission. The divine will and human will perfectly concur in every human act of Christ. Were the Word to determine that a particular affective response should not take place, his divine and human wills together act to ensure that it does not; conversely, the Word's determination that an affective response is appropriate leads his human and divine wills to concur in the allowance of the passion.

Christ's Temptation and the Three Medieval Temptations

I structure this final discussion around each of the three main kinds of temptation recognized by Thomas and the medieval tradition, considering along the way the most relevant passages from Thomas's corpus: *ST* III 41 and the fourth chapter of Thomas's *Commentary on Matthew*. In my treatment of each of these kinds of temptation, I address why Thomas believes it to have been present or absent in Christ. By doing so, I hope to explain how Christ's status as both wayfarer and comprehensor affect Thomas's presentation of the purpose and means of Christ's temptation.

Thomas's Denial of the Fomes Peccati in Christ

Thomas consistently denies Christ to have been infected or consequently tempted by the *fomes peccati*. Thomas's argument for the exclusion of the *fomes peccati* from Christ is first and foremost rooted in his observation that this defect is "not ordained to satisfaction," meaning that were Christ to have it, he would be less—not more—capable of acting as the mediator between humanity and God.[68] It would detract from Christ's offering of something "more loved" in place of the

---

68. *ST* III 15.2, response.

offenses committed by humankind.[69] While this rejection of the *fomes* is consistent throughout Thomas's writings, the reasons Thomas offers for it differ slightly in his corpus. In *ST* III 15, Thomas argues that the *fomes peccati* in Christ would contradict Christ's *absolutely perfected virtue*; in *ST* III 41, by contrast, he argues that this defect would contradict Christ's *sinlessness*.

In *ST* III 15.2 Thomas invokes Christ's virtue as the sole criterion by which the *fomes* must be denied in Christ. I have noted in chapter 5 that Thomas sees an inverse relationship between virtue and the *fomes peccati*. As the movement of the *fomes* increases, one's virtue decreases. Since for Thomas, the virtue of temperance resides precisely in the sensitive appetite, the opposition between virtue and the *fomes* can be stated even more specifically: the stronger the *fomes*, the weaker one's temperance; the stronger one's temperance, the weaker the *fomes*. Since Christ had the fullness of virtue and an absolutely perfected temperance (as an aspect of his status as a comprehensor), the *fomes* was as weak as possible, which is to say, nonexistent: "since in Christ the virtues were in their highest degree, the *fomes* of sin was nowise in Him."[70]

This position coincides with Thomas's presentation of the virtue of temperance in chapter 5. Because Thomas invokes Christ's virtue here and not his sinlessness, Thomas indicates that Christ's freedom from morally culpable error is not immediately and necessarily contradicted by the presence of the *fomes*. The same was the case for Thomas's presentation of the *fomes* in general; the constitutional lack of governance over the sensitive appetite does not (and cannot) require an absolute necessity of culpable sin in the one so inflicted. But nonetheless, no one contracts the *fomes* in a world without sin, and so its status as part of the *reatu poenae* (the debt of punishment) is crucial. Even if one can resist the movement of the *fomes* in a morally blameless fashion, its presence is still a mark of a fallen, sinful human nature that lacks a fullness of virtue. While a fallen human being might not be culpable for certain movements, the *fomes* remains opposed to

---

69. See the discussion of satisfaction in the first part of this chapter.
70. *ST* III 15.2, response.

a human nature in possession of its original integrity and of an absolutely perfected virtue.

One must also understand Thomas's second denial of the *fomes* from Christ in light of the place of the *fomes peccati* as a component of the *reatu poenae*. This second denial appears to begin from a different premise: instead of Christ's virtue, it invokes Christ's sinlessness. One reads in *ST* III 41 that

> Christ wished to be *tempted in all things, without sin*. Now, temptation which comes from an enemy can be without sin: because it comes about by merely outward suggestion. But temptation which comes from the flesh cannot be without sin, because such a temptation is caused by pleasure and concupiscence.[71]

At a glance, Thomas's explanation appears to draw on the prior medieval tradition's view that the *fomes peccati* is *always* culpably sinful (as for Peter the Lombard and Alexander of Hales and discussed in chapter 4), but Thomas's appropriation of this tradition is more complicated. For Alexander of Hales, Christ cannot be tempted from within (either demonically or from the flesh) because the *fomes* as such would contradict Christ's freedom from culpable sin; Alexander held that a suggestion begins to be sin when one experiences desire for it.

Thomas, however, should not be understood to follow Alexander in this narrow sense of the word "sin," whereby it signifies "culpable."[72] Rather, Thomas's citation of Hebrews and his subsequent discussion of "sin" should be construed broadly, such that one cannot be tempted from the flesh while lacking the *reatu poenae*. Essentially, temptation from the enemy can and did come without sin (see Adam and Eve's temptation before the Fall); yet the temptation from the flesh only came after that sin. Thus, when Thomas says that fleshly

---

71. *ST* III 41.1, ad. 3. A similar explanation drawing on the sinfulness of "pleasure" is found in the *Commentary on Matthew* 4 (in Aquinas, *Commentary on Matthew*, 112), where Thomas almost surely draws from the Halesian reading of Gregory the Great.

72. The "because" clauses in *ST* III 41.1, ad. 3 can also be read in a protological way: *because* Adam and Eve's first temptation was by merely external suggestion, and *because* disordered concupiscence only appears in a world into which sin has entered. This usage is the same as that which the Council of Trent commends in the *Decree on Original Sin*, in which disordered concupiscence is called sin in a broader, metaphorical way.

temptation cannot be "without sin," this description signifies something about protology and not moral psychology or culpability.[73] By construing "sin" in this broad way, Thomas does not reverse his earlier articulation of non-morally culpable movements of the *fomes*. A fallen subject could remain free of moral culpability for movements of the *fomes* (in a narrow sense 'sinless'), but by definition no one infected by the *fomes* could remain untouched by those deleterious consequences of sin. It is these consequences, in turn, that detract from Christ's mission of guiding humankind to a final blessed state (with its concomitant fullness of grace). Such an explanation is fully consonant with Thomas's mature thought about the *fomes* and with his explanation of the absence of the *fomes* from Christ in *ST* III 15.2.

These two explanations, then, ultimately coincide and can be summarized in one affirmation: Christ, in order to pass a final blessedness on to his followers, was free of the *reatu poenae* with regard to the *fomes peccati*. Thomas could articulate this claim in two distinct ways: either by pointing to Christ's virtue as proleptically that of a *comprehensor* or by recognizing Christ's absolute separation from sinful humanity that comes to him by the same proleptic grace. In both explanations, Thomas is concerned with a careful delineation of what sort of human existence Christ would lead in order to satisfy for human sin and lead humankind to its final end.

The Devil's Exterior Temptation in Thomas's Account

Thomas's explicit account of Christ's demonic temptation only speaks of an external, visible temptation.[74] I will address in the final sub-

---

73. This reading admittedly adds a different difficulty to the above quotation, which begins with the affirmation of Hebrews 4:15 that Christ is tempted like us in every way, yet without sin. If "sin" is taken in the same sense as I have outlined here, this affirmation would contradict Thomas's claim that Christ experiences any postlapsarian form of temptation, that is, that Christ was tempted in every way that Adam was before he sinned. Thomas thus has to use the term "sin" equivocally in this passage to remain consistent.

74. The *Commentary on Hebrews* (in the passage on Hebrews 4:15) offers an interesting account of Christ's temptations that might allow for the devil to work hiddenly through the Pharisees and other events near the end of Christ's life; see *Commentary on Hebrews*, 108. This possible reading is also in substantive agreement with Maximus in *The Ascetic Life*. However, because Thomas's description of Christ's temptation "by terrifying... with adversity" is not explicitly demonic, I do not treat this passage as significant for Thomas's understanding of Christ's temptation by the devil.

section whether Thomas could also support an invisible or internal temptation from the devil. At the present juncture, three final matters about Thomas's positive affirmations need consideration. First, I address how Christ's external temptation is affirmed as a form of punitive or postlapsarian temptation. Second and most extensively, I examine Thomas's conception of Christ's visible temptation by the devil as exemplary for human temptation in general. In this material, I have recourse to the claims above about the *voluntariness* of Christ's temptation in relation to Thomas's later treatment of the idea of an *occasion of sin*. Third and briefly, I review how Christ's external temptation accomplishes a defeat of the devil.

As seen in the previous chapter, Thomas sees the *fomes peccati* and internal demonic temptation primarily as punitive. If Christ's "satisfaction" for sin by temptation implies that he takes on something of that punishment on himself, however, it is important to clarify how the external temptation Christ endured might also be somehow punitive, even if it does not include the other distinctly postlapsarian modes of temptation. As discussed in chapter 5, the phenomenon of external temptation as such is decidedly *not* punitive; it occurred in the Garden before sin, but I also noted that the conditions of external temptation are changed by sin so that even a purely external assault can still be described as punitive (and thus, when taken on by Christ, satisfactory). Thomas states that "the devil had a minimum of power against man before sin, wherefore he was [able to tempt] ... only by outward suggestion,"[75] but after his sin, Adam's body was rendered susceptible to external manipulation by demonic force. Further, since Christ experienced hunger as one of the natural and indetractible passions, the devil, while remaining completely external to Christ's body, could also exploit that natural defect in the first temptation that Christ experienced.

Christ's outward temptation by the devil, then, does not reproduce completely Adam's prelapsarian temptation. First, Christ's experience of hunger differed from that of Adam in the garden; the temptation that follows from that hunger is thus also different (and arguably

75. *ST* II-II 165.2, ad. 2.

more intense) than Adam's. Second, in the second and third temptations, Thomas points out that Christ "suffered from the devil in being 'taken up' on to 'the pinnacle of the Temple' and again 'into a very high mountain.'"[76] Such bodily transportation exceeds the conditions of temptation that Adam experienced in the garden and thus constitutes a distinctly postlapsarian component of Christ's experience of temptation. Christ's hunger and his bodily transportation together constitute the postlapsarian component of Thomas's Christological synecdoche, which brings about all the salvific effects of Christ's temptation described in the first portion of this chapter: satisfaction, sacrifice, merit, and compassion.

Secondly, the *exemplarity* of Christ's temptation for his followers is limited in Thomas's presentation by the uniqueness of Christ's saving mission. For Thomas, in fact, Christ's followers are commended *not* to imitate some aspects of his temptation. The central issue may be illuminated beginning with some exposition of Thomas's *Commentary on Matthew*. There, Thomas explores the possibility that it would not have been sinful for Christ to have changed the stones into bread.[77] Thomas goes on to argue that Christ refuses this demonic suggestion in order to give "instructions which ought to be followed by the one who has been tempted."[78] Thomas states:

Man ought to do nothing at the devil's choice. Vegetius said, "A wise leader ought to do nothing at the choice of his enemy [*ad arbitrium sui hostis*], even if it seem to be good." And thus, although the Lord would have been able to change the rocks into bread without sin, He was not willing to do so because the devil was suggesting it [*suggerebat*].[79]

---

76. *ST* III 41.1, ad. 2. In another text, Thomas has Christ walk to these locations; presumably, Thomas means to say that only the end of these journeys was accomplished through such bodily violence.

77. In the *Summa Theologica*, Thomas argues that it would be pointless for the devil to propose something morally indifferent; the devil only "tempts in order to induce us to sin" (*ST* III 41.4, obj. 1.). For this reason, Thomas argues in the *Summa Theologica* that it would have been inordinate (read: sinful) for Christ to have performed a miracle when he could have simply done what John the Baptist did: eat locusts and honey (*ST* III 41.4, ad. 1). Regardless of whether Thomas ultimately considers the first temptation to be toward something sinful or not, Thomas never contradicts Vegetius's advice and presumably always holds that it is best for fallen humans to avoid even apparently good suggestions from the devil.

78. *Commentary on Matthew* 4, in Aquinas, *Commentary on Matthew*, 114.

79. *Commentary on Matthew* 4, in Aquinas, *Commentary on Matthew*, 115.

Thomas argues that even though it may not have been sinful, Christ's example still demonstrates something important to his followers: *not to cooperate with the devil's suggestion, even concerning an apparent good.* In this example, Christ constitutes a clear example to be imitated by his followers. However, this clear form of exemplarity is not present in Christ's actions in the second and third temptations.

Within the bounds of the *Commentary on Matthew*, Thomas takes care to avoid various senses in which the devil would be said to do violence to Christ. Thomas refers to Jerome's opinion that "Christ virtuously permitted" the devil to tempt him, so that even things that the devil thought he was "forcing" Christ to do were in fact permitted by Christ. Thomas's exegesis limits this permission in a number of ways, so that the devil has a minimum of power over the mind and body of Christ. For instance, Thomas prefers to deny that the second and third temptations are "according to the manner of an imaginary vision" that would have appeared only to Christ or "according to the manner of a corporeal vision" that would have appeared objectively to anyone who had been in the desert.[80] Following the explicit affirmation of Matthew (and thus primarily as a matter of exegesis), Thomas argues that the first temptation was in the desert but that the other two took place in the physical localities described by the text, *outside* the desert. Thomas wonders: How did Christ get to those places?

I have delineated above how Thomas argues for a certain suffering of the devil's power, whereby the devil is responsible for moving Christ's body to the top of the Temple and to the mountain. Concerning the movement of Christ's body into the city of Jerusalem, Thomas considers two options: either he was carried by the devil (and that Christ permitted this carrying) or Christ went by his own power and wisdom. In other words, Christ walked. Thomas, following the reasoning that limits the power that the devil has over Christ's body (because it seems unfitting that Christ be carried such a long distance by Satan), prefers the latter option:

---

80. *Commentary on Matthew* 4, in Aquinas, *Commentary on Matthew*, 116.

How did he take Him [to Jerusalem]? Some say that he carried Him upon himself. Others say (and indeed better), that *by exhorting he persuaded Him that He go to this place* [*exhortando induxit ad hoc quod iret*]; and Christ from the disposition of His wisdom [*ex dispositione suae sapientiae*], went into Jerusalem.[81]

The exemplarity of Christ in the first temptation (that one not cooperate with the devil even in apparent goods) recedes in the second temptation, when the "disposition of Christ's wisdom"—Christ's elicited decision—agrees with the devil's exhortation to proceed into Jerusalem. Thus, even if Christ's movement toward Jerusalem is morally neutral and blameless, the exemplarity commended by Thomas in the first temptation is no longer present in the second. In this instance, Christ has gone against the advice of Vegetius: "A wise leader ought to do nothing at the choice of his enemy, even if it seem to be good." While Christ makes his way to the Temple in Jerusalem at the devil's suggestion, Thomas's earlier advice would leave Christ's followers back in the desert.

Thomas can argue in this way because what would be an occasion of sin for others is not for Christ. As Thomas stated in his *Commentary on Matthew*, Christ "would not have been able to commit a fault [*offendere*] by an occasion of some sin."[82] Christ can cooperate in such morally neutral suggestions from the devil because he is impeccable; his followers *cannot* because they *are* not.

In the *Summa Theologica*, Thomas treats a similar question about the occasion of sin with perhaps a greater attentiveness to the way in which Christ's temptation should be considered exemplary for his followers. In this passage, Thomas does not consider the manner of Christ's movement to the temple and mountain but rather the more general observation that Christ entered the desert to be tempted in the first place. The objector asks:

---

81. *Commentary on Matthew* 4, in Aquinas, *Commentary on Matthew*, 117, translation modified. This claim is in tension with the claim that the devil did physical violence to Christ in the last two temptations, but they are not incompatible. Thomas could have Christ walk most of the way and the devil move him to the summit of the Temple and mountain.

82. *Commentary on Matthew* 4, in Aquinas, *Commentary on Matthew*, 118, translation modified: "*non poterat offendere occasione alicuius peccati.*"

It seems that, by going into the desert to be tempted, He exposed Himself to temptation. Since, therefore, His temptation is an example to us, it seems that others too should take such steps [*se ingerere*] as will lead them into temptation. And yet this seems a dangerous thing to do, since rather we should avoid the occasion of being tempted.[83]

Thomas's answer introduces a distinction that accounts for Christ's exemplarity in a slightly different way than did the *Commentary on Matthew*. There are, Thomas argues, two occasions of temptation: one "on the part of the devil" and one "on the part of man." Each of these occasions requires comment. The circumstances of the first are described in these terms:

Such occasions of temptation are not to be avoided [*non est vitanda*]. Hence Chrysostom says: "Not only Christ was led into the desert by the Spirit, but all God's children that have the Holy Ghost. For it is not enough for them to sit idle; the Holy Ghost urges them to endeavor to do something great [*urget eos aliquod magnum apprehendere opus*]: which is for them to be in the desert from the devil's standpoint, for no unrighteousness, in which the devil delights, is there."... Now, there is no danger [*non est periculosum*] in giving the devil such an occasion of temptation; since the help of the Holy Ghost, who is the Author of the perfect deed, is more powerful than the assault of the envious devil.[84]

According to this commentary, what Thomas calls an occasion "on the part of the devil" might be more accurately described as an occasion on the part of the Holy Spirit, since it is first and foremost the Spirit that leads both Christ and other humans into such experiences. They are led there not in order that they might fail but in order that they might "do something great." With such direct guidance from the Spirit, however, cooperation in an occasion of demonic temptation is permissible both for Christ and for his followers. The reasoning here is different than in the *Commentary on Matthew*; there, the priority of the devil's intentions lead Thomas to affirm that the occasion should be avoided (at least in the case of Christ's fallen disciples), but here, the

---

83. *ST* III 41.2, obj. 2.
84. *ST* III 41.2, ad. 2.

priority of the Spirit's intentions leads Thomas to affirm that the occasion should not be avoided.[85] Because the Spirit led Christ to the desert (and presumably to the Temple and mountain), Christ and his followers both should follow the Spirit's prodding. The result will be that, empowered by the Spirit, even Christ's followers will "do something great." Between the *Commentary on Matthew* and the *Summa Theologica*, Thomas does not give clear criteria by which to judge which temptations come from the Spirit (and should therefore be sought) and which, if any, come only from the devil (and should therefore be avoided), but such is not the object of his concern in these passages. One might think that Thomas has in mind a process much like that envisioned by the desert fathers and Maximus: a discernment of spirits whereby the intention of the Spirit might be rightly determined and sifted from the prodding of the devil. Whatever spiritual pedagogy may be involved, Christ's temptation is thus an example of virtuous accomplishment of the good that others should imitate under the Spirit's direction and against the devil's wiles.

On the other hand, even in Thomas's presentation in the *Summa Theologica*, Christ's impeccability still somewhat limits the sense in which Christ's temptation can be exemplary for his followers. The second occasion of temptation "on the part of man" occurs when "a man causes himself to be near to sin by not avoiding the occasion of sinning [*occasiones peccandi non evitans*]."[86] Since Christ "would not have been able to commit a fault [*offendere*] by an occasion of some sin,"[87] so neither can he be "near to sin," with the result that there is no occasion "on the part of man" for Christ to avoid. In this way, Christ inculpably "of His own free-will exposed Himself to be tempted by the devil" and goes to the desert "as to a field of battle" because he knows he will conquer.[88] Thus, events and scenarios that would

---

85. It should also be noted, though, that Thomas's answer here does not directly confront the objection, which asks if the one tempted should "take steps (*se ingerere*)" to enter into temptation. He only argues here that such demonic temptation is "not to be avoided [*non est vitanda*]"—he does not address whether it should be *sought*.

86. *ST* III 41.2, ad. 2.

87. *Commentary on Matthew* 4, in Aquinas, *Commentary on Matthew*, 118, translation modified.

88. Thomas reaffirms the sense of Christ's inability to sin at *ST* III 18.4, obj. 3 and ad. 3. Christ's will is "determined to the good" and could not become determined to evil. See also

be potentially dangerous for those inflicted with the *fomes peccati* —events and scenarios that should be fled—are not dangerous for Christ, who needs not flee them. It is not that Christ breaches the boundaries of the occasion of temptation on the part of man but rather that, for Christ in otherwise morally neutral situations, there is no boundary to breach. Christ is separated from sinners and in no way near to an occasion of some sin. For Christ utterly to defeat the devil, he must be able to go and conquer where others should not go and cannot conquer. This arrangement stands in significant contrast to the early monastic tradition, which was quick to see in all Christ's actions a model for direct imitation by his followers. The positive necessity of temptation in the moral life was admitted more readily in the ascetic tradition, often entailing a brazen attempt to attract the demons' attention. They did so, they thought, following in the footsteps of their exemplar, who commanded them to take up their cross and follow him. Thomas's account of temptation, by contrast, treads Christ's footsteps in the desert much more cautiously.

Thomas qualifies the exemplarity of Christ's temptation precisely in order to safeguard another soteriological fact: Christ forges the way to the future state of humankind in heaven. Since Christ is a comprehensor, he shows humanity here on earth the kind of freedom with which we will be endowed in the next life: an absolute freedom from difficulty in striving after the good. While Christ may not point the way through the morally ambiguous minutiae of our own fallen temptations, he nevertheless imparts hope to his followers that these temptations will fall away and that we will someday have no cause to fear the devil at all.

Finally, the voluntary quality of Christ's temptation is essential to the way in which it brings about a defeat of the devil. Just as Christ willingly suffered death, Thomas argues that Christ had to willingly expose himself to the devil's attack: "that He allowed Himself to be

---

the discussion of Christ's impeccability in Reginald Garrigou-Lagrange, *Reality: A Synthesis of Thomistic Thought*, trans. Patrick Cummins (St. Louis, Mo.: B. Herder Book Co., 1950), 224–27, especially 226; the French is in Reginald Garrigou-Lagrange, *La Synthèse Thomiste* (Paris: Desclée de Brouwer, 1946), 349–54.

tempted was due to His own will."[89] Without this voluntary permission, "the devil would not have dared to approach Him."[90] Nor was Christ free only before he allowed the devil's approach; he remained free throughout the "sufferings" that the devil inflicted in the course of the temptations:

And we understand Him to have been taken up by the devil [to the Temple and mountain], not, as it were, by force, but because, as Origen says, "He followed Him in the course of His temptation like a wrestler advancing of his own accord."[91]

The militaristic or agonistic image for this event is common in Thomas's presentation. In the *Commentary on Matthew*, Christ enters into "single combat (*singular certamen*) with the devil,"[92] and in the *Summa Theologica*, he went out "as to a field of battle (*campum certaminis*)" against the devil.[93] In all these images, Thomas's emphasis on Christ's freedom in and through the battle with the devil ensures that the battle imagery does not imply that the result was uncertain. Christ always battles freely and with an assurance of victory.

Christ's apparent submission to the devil's power paradoxically conquers the devil: "Christ came to destroy the works of the devil, not by powerful deeds, but rather by suffering from him and his members, so as to conquer the devil by righteousness (*iustitia*), not by power."[94] As I argued in chapter 5, this demonstration of Christ's justice is part of the overthrowing of the devil. The devil always implicitly holds humankind unjustly (without respect for the bounds of his conditional permission from God to punish humankind for sin), but this injustice is demonstrated publicly to God the moment that the devil attempts to claim an individual who proves himself to be without sin. God is thus perfectly in the right to remove the devil from the subordinate position he had theretofore occupied, even if the complete overthrow-

---

89. *ST* III 41.1, ad. 2; see also *ST* III 41.2, response.
90. *ST* III 41.2, response.
91. *ST* III 41.1, ad. 2.
92. *Commentary on Matthew* 4, in Aquinas, *Commentary on Matthew*, 111.
93. *ST* III 41.2, response.
94. *ST* III 41.1, ad. 2.

ing of the devil is delayed until the final judgment. Christ's confrontation with the devil occurs so that he might render humankind free from all temptation.[95]

In all these reflections, Thomas is concerned to maintain the dual affirmation that Christ is, even on earth, simultaneously a wayfarer and a comprehensor—both "on the way" and already sharing the final blessings of heaven. As a wayfarer, he shares in fallen conditions of temptation, allows the devil to tempt him with hunger, and allows the devil to do violence to his body. As a comprehensor, he shares in humanity's unfallen qualities, has a perfect inability to sin, and thereby gives a sign of hope to those who follow his footsteps. He conquers the devil perfectly by marching onto the "battlefield" of temptation and standing fast in the devil's attack. While this status and mission grants Christ the ability to approach the devil in ways that his followers in this life cannot imitate without danger, the voluntary quality of all Christ's temptations and of his mission to defeat the devil requires that he "provoke" the devil's attack by willingly exposing himself to the devil's temptation.[96] Thus, the uniqueness of Christ's mission, for Thomas, ultimately undergirds the difference between Christ's temptation and that of other human beings.

The Possibility of Christ's Inner Demonic Temptation in Thomas's Corpus

In the preceding, I have established that the punitive temptation from the flesh is absent from Christ and that the external temptation Christ endures is punitive precisely in light of Christ's hunger and the violence done by the devil in taking Christ to the top of the Temple and to the mountain. However, in order to comprehensively consider the ways in which Christ's temptation might be considered to be punitive, I address whether the final form of temptation Thomas recognizes as primarily punitive—inner demonic temptation—can be found in Christ. This task is particularly difficult in light of Thomas's neglect of

---

95. *ST* III 41.1, response. See also *Commentary on Matthew* 4, in Aquinas, *Commentary on Matthew*, 112.

96. *ST* III 41.2, response, which is in a citation from Ambrose.

internal demonic temptation in his Christological reflection on temptation:

> Temptation which comes from an enemy can be without sin: because it comes about by merely outward suggestion. But temptation which comes from the flesh cannot be without sin, because such a temptation is caused by pleasure and concupiscence.... And hence, Christ wished to be tempted by an enemy, but not by the flesh.[97]

Since Thomas himself does not address this question directly, this third category of temptation is rarely discussed in the secondary literature. Nevertheless, its place remains important in an estimation of the "satisfactory" nature of Christ's temptation. Because of this neglect in both Thomas's own writings and the secondary literature, any proposed answer to the question of Christ's inner temptation must be somewhat speculative.

There are two aspects to this question, pertaining to the two faculties that Thomas admits to be susceptible to the devil's internal attack: the *sensitive appetite* and the *imagination*. I do not need to consider the first of these in detail; I have clarified in chapter 5 that the devil can only interiorly attack the sensitive appetite of an individual whose temperance is not absolutely perfect. Christ's, however, *is* absolutely perfected.[98] For this reason, a passionate interior attack from the devil is not possible in Christ. The imagination is a different case, as noted by Jean-Pierre Torrell's work on Christ's temptation. While Torrell's suggestions are happily taken as broadly Thomistic, however, he is willing to diverge from Thomas's own treatment in some ways.[99] For this reason, I briefly present Thomas's statements on this matter and show that their cumulative force indicates that Thomas would not affirm that Christ was tempted through his imagination by the devil.

---

97. *ST* III 41.1, ad. 3.
98. While Paul Gondreau does not explicitly address the action of the devil in this matter, he has considered whether it is possible to affirm, in the Thomistic corpus, that Christ was tempted by his passions. His conclusions are appropriately tentative and, as he admits, indicate some tensions in the Thomistic corpus. See Paul Gondreau, *The Passions of Christ's Soul in the Theology of St. Thomas Aquinas* (Scranton, Pa.: University of Scranton Press, 2009), 309–10, 317, 340, and 359–60.
99. See the discussion of the literature in the introduction.

As noted above, Thomas's explicit statements about Christ's temptations only affirm that the devil appeared to him in some visible form. The *Commentary on Matthew* affirms this visibility in a few places. Most obviously, Thomas speaks of the "corporeal form" that the devil took when tempting Christ.[100] Similarly, following a usage of the "stages" of sin from Gregory the Great and as interpreted by Alexander of Hales, Thomas indicates that any "interior" movement of the devil would have to come with pleasure and thus would begin to be sin.[101] Finally, I noted above that the *Commentary on Matthew* uses the plain sense of Matthew's text to produce an exegesis that argues against the idea that the devil could produce an image or mirage to Jesus's imagination or senses in the desert.[102]

The evidence of the *Summa Theologica* on this point is sparse. The affirmation at *ST* III 41.1, reply 3 explains Christ's assumption of demonic attack by observing that it "comes about by merely outward suggestion," and for that reason, one might presume that Thomas believes the devil's attack to have been only exterior.[103] Perhaps the strongest evidence—and the only evidence that discusses Christ's temptation in any proximity to Thomas's affirmation of internal demonic temptation—comes from a passage of the *De Malo* already quoted in chapter 5. There, in the midst of his question on the internal instigations of the devil, Thomas states:

He persuades human beings to things in two ways: visibly and invisibly. He persuades visibly as when he sensibly appears to human beings in some form and sensibly speaks with them and persuades them to sin. For example, he tempted the first human being in the garden of paradise in the form of a serpent, and he tempted Christ in the desert in some visible form. But we should not think that he only persuades human beings in this way.[104]

---

100. *Commentary on Matthew* 4, in Aquinas, *Commentary on Matthew*, 113.
101. *Commentary on Matthew* 4, in Aquinas, *Commentary on Matthew*, 112.
102. *Commentary on Matthew* 4, in Aquinas, *Commentary on Matthew*, 116–17.
103. *ST* III 41.1, ad. 3 and *ST* III 41.3, ad. 2 should, in all likelihood, not be read as affirming an interior temptation because (1) these "other assaults" are not described as "invisible," so there is no positive reason to believe that is the nature of the contrast Thomas is drawing; and (2) the "visibility" of these temptations may refer simply to their presence in the Gospel texts (and thus "visible" to the reader).
104. *De Malo* III 4, response.

The contrast that Thomas draws is fairly clear; if Thomas had wanted to affirm that the devil had tempted Christ in some internal way, this passage would have been an ideal place to do so. Instead, precisely as Thomas distinguishes between internal and external forms of demonic suggestion, he limits Christ's temptation to the external or visible form. On this limited, though fairly significant, evidence it seems that Thomas would intend to exclude any interior imaginative temptation from Christ.

One could further speculate that Thomas argues in this way in order to maintain the fullness of grace in which Thomas knows Christ to have existed. I have argued in chapter 5 that there was a distinct Adamic grace that protected the protological couple from an imaginative attack from the devil, so that the devil had a "minimum of power" against humankind before sin.[105] Since Thomas shows interest in limiting the power of the devil over Christ's mind and body,[106] it would be consonant both with that limitation and with Christ's possession of the fullness of grace that the devil would not have this power over Christ. In this way, Christ's freedom from such attack would come to him as part of his status as a comprehensor who imparts hope in his followers by showing them the future condition of heaven.

Thomas's presentation of Christ's temptation by the devil shares the synecdochal characteristics seen throughout this study. From Maximus onward, the central thinkers discussed throughout constitute Christ's humanity in such a way as to draw in aspects of both prelapsarian and postlapsarian human nature. The presence of these aspects makes the whole of each condition present in its entirety: a Christological synecdoche. In each successive transmission of this synecdoche, from Maximus until Thomas's predecessors, however, there was a tendency to hedge successively against any presentation of Christ's temptation that might implicate him in sinful disorder. Combined with the refinement of the concept of disordered concu-

---

105. *ST* II-II 165.2, ad. 2.
106. As in the *Commentary on Matthew* 4, in Aquinas, *Commentary on Matthew*, 116–17.

piscence, this led Thomas's predecessors to a progressive shrinking of Christ's contact with the fallen conditions of human temptation. Indeed, in Peter and Alexander, no distinctly fallen features remain in their understanding of the means of Christ's temptation.

Thomas, for his part, affirms the prelapsarian synecdoche of Christ's temptation through an exposition and affirmation of an Adam/Christ typology. Precisely by reproducing the form and order of Adam's temptations, Christ's temptation undoes Adam's, as the condition of the possibility of fallen temptation in his descendants. The two distinct categories of fallen forms of temptation (the *fomes peccati* and internal demonic temptation) are rejected in Christ's case on the grounds that they would not contribute to Christ's satisfaction for sin and would detract from his status as a comprehensor who shares proleptically in the glorified condition of humankind.

As for the postlapsarian synecdoche, Thomas's recognition lies somewhere between the strongest and weakest articulations plotted through this study. Thomas's theoretical grounding of the importance of Christ's fallen temptation far surpasses his high medieval predecessors, who had nothing positive to say in relation to Christ's postlapsarian experience of temptation. In content, however, the hunger of Christ and Christ's bodily transportation by the devil are far from the passions that attack Christ in the *De Fide Orthodoxa* and, moreover, from the spiritual warfare of the mind described in the writings of Maximus. In Thomas's account, a relatively heavy soteriological weight thus hangs on these two aspects of Christ's temptation.

CONCLUSION ✧ CHRIST IN CHRISTIAN
TRADITIONS OF TEMPTATION

As the Roman persecutions of Christianity ended during the fourth century, many of those who sought to be witnesses to their faith found their way into the desert. While these aspiring martyrs no longer faced bodily harm at the hands of the ruling governmental principalities, they believed that their witness to their faith required them to fight in the battle against principalities and powers of the spiritual realm. It was no mistake that they fled to the desert, because doing so concretely imitated the example proposed by Christ, who had done precisely the same when he undertook his own battle against personified spiritual evil. Christian cosmology—as exemplified relatively early in the thought of Origen of Alexandria—left these spirits with significant ongoing moral influence even after Christ's desert confrontation, both within and beyond the Christian community. In figures such as Evagrius, this Origenist cosmology became a fully articulated plan for spiritual warfare, unveiling the devil's plan of attack, detailing the demons' power over human passibility, and prescribing apotropaic spiritual and mental practices to help the monk discern when desire was demonic and when it was spiritually beneficial. If there was a battle against the flesh in these monastic communities, it took place in the context of a cosmology wherein angelic beings had a sometimes alarming influence over human bodies, flesh, and minds.

In this tradition, reflection on human passibility was intricately linked to reflection on Christ. Evagrius identified three primary spiritual "battlefronts" for the monk and placed these fronts in correspondence with the demonic temptations Christ experienced in the desert. Such an understanding of temptation functioned in several ways. First, it placed the primary battle against the devil inside the human experience of passibility. Second, it helped the monk to identify and address the root causes of his own spiritual failings. Third, it offered a coherent interpretation of Hebrews 4:15 by affirming that Christ experienced every genus of temptation that did not require Christ to give in to some prior temptation. Fourth, as I identified in chapter 1, this view emphasized the exemplarity of Christ in the monk's personal moral struggle and concrete discernment of God's will. Before Maximus, however, the link between Christ and the monk in this tradition could have been criticized as *merely* exemplary: that Christ was simply the first holy man to retreat to the desert and that he only indicated the independent and prior truth that victory against the demonic was possible for all.

Within this demonological tradition of human passibility, Maximus's most significant contribution may have been a thoroughgoing articulation of Christ's *empowering* exemplarity for monastic spiritual struggle. In his exposition, Maximus demonstrates how Christ's experience and subsequent defeat of the demons of desire and aversion—Maximus's version of the Evagrian emotional categories—effected the liberation of all those who would follow after him from the demons' snares and enabled the defeat of their own temptations. In Maximus's framework, Christ's experience of human passibility stands in solidarity with the fallen experience of his followers, who routinely must discern their desires and seek to activate them according to nature. At the end of this world, this process of discernment will no longer be necessary, since the demons' temptations will be brought to an end as the saints are crowned for "competing according to the rules" (2 Tim 2:5). Through his progressive "putting off" the principalities and powers, Christ inaugurates this eschatological mode of human passibility in his own existence. In this sense, Christ experiences each of these distinctive stages of human nature as it is drawn toward its final end.

Christ has thereby concretely drawn humanity into the fullness of its expression that God had always intended for humanity to share with God in heaven.

While this tradition emphasizes Christ's solidarity with the fallen condition, it does so by limiting the penetration of virtue during one's earthly existence into the human emotional faculties, which remain the central spiritual battlefield on this side of the eschaton. For Maximus, demonic temptation through desire and aversion requires that demons retain significant power in those faculties. As I have noted in chapter 2, this arrangement renders Maximus's conception of temperance *noneschatological, external,* and *historically realized.* Refusing to speculate about the final eschatological state of humanity, Maximus settles for a noneschatological vision of temperance that pertains to this life. Yet in this life, human virtue can extend only as far as human power. Since, for Maximus, passibility remains somewhat out of human control in this life, so too are human temperance and patience theoretically limited to a rational and external control of faculties that remain somewhat ungovernable in this life. Christ can be affirmed as sinless and perfectly virtuous in this framework precisely because the categories of culpable sin and virtue do not extend into complete governance of the emotional faculties during this life. The precise location of temperance and patience in this scheme is thus a matter for further investigation, yet it should also be clarified that a complete penetration of virtue into these faculties is concretely inaugurated in Christ, as his human life draws demonic temptation to a complete and final end, as the emotional faculties return to their original, divinely intended purpose. In this sense, Maximus would allow for Christ to "progress" in virtue (understood interchangeably with the progress of spiritual combat against personified evil) as he concretely moves affectivity from its earthly to its eschatological form through his desert temptations, public ministry, and passion. At the same time, this arrangement articulates the virtue of temperance in a way that allows the monk even now to realize, imitate, and share with Christ.

Before Maximus had accomplished his articulation of Christ's temptation by the devil, the Latin West had already begun synthesizing the Greek ascetic view with a distinctively Latin view of human fallenness. In particular, Gregory the Great's reflection on human temptation had already begun to meld Maximus's predecessors in the Greek tradition with anthropological material from Augustine. The ascetic tradition in part found its way into Gregory's work through John Cassian, who had transmitted much of the Greek tradition of demonic temptation to Latin-speaking Christianity.[1] Demonic suggestion thereby finds its place as the first stage of sin in Gregory's moral psychology. Further, Gregory holds that such suggestion can at times reach as far as the direct stimulation of desire in the flesh of the human victim. Helping to shape the Latin tradition, Augustine had articulated a view of fallen human affectivity that attributed sinful human propensities to an inner division within the human will. Influenced in part by Paul's struggle recounted in Romans 7, Augustine saw human sinfulness as rooted in disordered concupiscence, whereby the human subject was drawn inordinately toward illicit goods through the lower appetites, the flesh. Due to Augustine's influence, the flesh and its desires primarily find expression in the second stage of Gregory's progression of sin. With a leg in both the Greek- and Latin-speaking Christian worlds, Gregory's spiritual theology thus stands at a crucial juncture in the development of Latin theories of human temptation.

High medieval reception of Gregory's thought progressively diminished the significance of the ascetic view and leaned more and more on Augustine's anthropology of the Fall, especially in later medieval Christological reflection. Hugh of St. Victor, Peter the Lombard, and Alexander of Hales each contributed to this diminishment of Christ's synecdochal contact with fallen human temptation. For them, the influence of malicious spirits was seen as peripheral to a purely anthropological and internal moral conflict between the higher

---

1. See, for instance, John Cassian, *Conferences*, trans. Colm Luibheid (New York: Paulist Press, 1985), 53, 57–58, and 67. Rufinus's translations of Evagrius may also play a role here; see Richard Sorabji, *Emotion and Peace of Mind: From Stoic Agitation to Christian Temptation* (Oxford: Oxford University Press, 2003), 357. For discussion of Cassian's role in transmitting Greek asceticism to the West, see Conrad Leyser, *Authority and Asceticism from Augustine to Gregory the Great* (Oxford: Oxford University Press, 2000), especially 36–38, 160–71. Leyser is concerned with coenobitic innovations from Cassian's eremitic traditions, but he acknowledges Gregory's general indebtedness to Cassian throughout.

and lower parts of the human being. When human fallenness came to be viewed as internal strife instead of cosmic warfare, Christ's contact with it was necessarily limited to maintain his own moral rectitude. When the ascetic view was presented anew for Latin-speaking Christians in Burgundio's translation of John of Damascus's *De Fide Orthodoxa*, it had little impact on the prevailing Augustinian conception of human sinfulness.

As articulated by the Latin medieval tradition, humanity's fallen moral struggle (cast as anthropology) appears experientially similar to the sort of moral struggle recounted in the ascetic tradition (cast as demonic combat), yet the differences are brought to light especially well in the way each tradition related Christ to this fallen human struggle. For Augustine and his successors, Christ's rectitude of soul ruled out the internal division characteristic of the battle between the flesh and the spirit; a Christ who is divided and struggling against his own flesh would be in no position to save others from this struggle. And since Christ could not fittingly have been tempted by his own humanity, this tradition became wary of ascribing to Christ any phenomenon that might resemble the fallen conflict between spirit and flesh. Hence, Augustine, Gregory the Great, and Alexander of Hales deny that the devil could have had any interior influence on Christ's mind. For Alexander, this denial stands tensely alongside the affirmation that this precise kind of temptation can occur blamelessly in other human beings. For neither Peter nor Alexander does Christ's temptation share any discernable contact with any fallen form of temptation. Christ's synecdochal contact with fallen temptation receded entirely from view.

Thomas's thought on Christ's temptation, while standing broadly in this Latin tradition of reflection on the topic, corrects some of the Christological errors of his proximate predecessors. Most importantly, Thomas affirms that Christ's human existence—including his temptation—shares synecdochally in both the unfallen and fallen states of human existence. The presence of these fallen characteristics remains important for Thomas's soteriology as a whole and marks a unique Latin attempt to realign Christ's affectivity with those whose affectivity stands in greatest need of healing.

CONCLUSION 289

The distinctive differences in Thomas's account, *vis-à-vis* Maximus, arise from Thomas's differing conception of virtue. As stated in chapter 5, Thomas' view of virtue is *eschatological*, *intrinsic* to the appetitive faculties, and *historically unrealized* apart from Christ himself. Taking Christ's human life as a demonstration of the way humankind will exist in the eschaton, Thomas articulates an idealized vision of temperance that is different than the examples put forward even by the saints, who were still afflicted with the *fomes* during their earthly life. In this vision of temperance, the virtue resides inside the faculty itself, fully penetrating the most animal parts of human nature. But because fallen human beings—even if they perfectly avoid culpable affective sin—can never realize this ideal in history, Thomas limits the exemplary character of Christ's human existence. Christ's unique grace and virtue allow him to proceed blamelessly where fallen human beings, afflicted with the *fomes peccati*, would be imprudent to follow. Were a fallen human being to attempt to confront the devil just as Christ did, it would be a sign of—and likely exacerbate—a lack of virtue. In comparison to the ascetic tradition, Thomas's relative limitation of the *imitatio Christi* is a real disadvantage.

As a further, related disadvantage, Christ's synecdochal contact with postlapsarian forms of temptation is significantly more limited in Thomas's account than in that of Maximus. In Thomas's presentation, this contact rests entirely in Christ's hunger and his being forcibly taken by the devil to the top of the Temple and to the mountain. Christ's hunger is, admittedly, an important way in which he shares in something of fallen temptation; Thomas here preserves the disciple's call to imitate Christ's example. But as for Thomas's account of Christ's bodily transportation by the devil, can this detail truly be said to affect his temptation in a substantive way? Does such bodily transportation bring Christ into real contact with humanity's fallen experience of temptation? In response to the complex nexus of fallen affective experiences that attain alongside hunger, is Christ's solidarity and compassion with our lot (Heb 4:15) adequately captured by Christ briefly allowing the devil to pick him up and carry him? If answered negatively, these questions would seriously challenge the consistency of Thomas's soteriological account of Christ's temptation.[2] It remains an open question whether the general Latin limitation of Christ's synecdochal identity with fallen humanity can adequately preserve the patristic understanding of Christ's substantive entering into the fallen conditions of human temptation as a whole.

To state this concern concretely, Maximus's vision for Christ's temptation is starkly different than Thomas's, as each works on different assumptions about what aspects of human fallenness can rightly and fittingly be taken on by Christ. Rather than tracing a straight line through Thomas to an ideal articulation of this soteriological problem today, it may be necessary to reexamine some of his assumptions about Christ's fullness of grace to arrive at a position fully consonant with the patristic witness to Christ's temptation. Instead of Thomas's disjunction (Christ's fullness of grace *or* his fallen experience of temptation), how do we return to Maximus's conjunction: Christ's fullness of virtue *and* a fallen experience of temptation?

If I have reached back to criticize Maximus and Thomas, it is only fair to let them reach forward to challenge us. The present work has shown that centuries of Christian reflection on this topic, in a way that is perhaps disconcerting to a modern reader, have leaned heavily on the reality of the devil and a vast army of evil spirits. In the Greek ascetic tradition, this army stands behind the everyday moral experiences of the monk. To remove consideration of the demonic is to deprive the monk of any coherent, overarching account of temptation—either Christ's or their own. In the high medieval Latin tradition, the devil is the sole source of Christ's temptations. For this tradition, a "reverse-reading" of Hebrews 4:15 (from Christology back to anthropology) would result in a necessary consideration of how the devil tempts other human beings as well. If the modern reader feels the need to maintain a skepticism regarding the existence of the devil and the demonic, that reader will ultimately need to recognize that they

---

2. J. P. Torrell's broadly Thomistic suggestion of an interior imaginative attack against Christ is therefore happily received as more consonant with the approach of the Greek tradition.

can no longer fully inhabit either the monk's or the scholastic's moral or theological world.

If a Christian reader decides to part from demonological realism, however, the critical problems in moral theology exposed in this study are no closer to resolution than they were at any stage of the tradition's reflection. The demythologizing reader today must still decide how to account for human responsibility in relation to their own emotional states and make a determination about the limits of human power in such affairs (τὰ ἐφ' ἡμῖν). Yet this reader must now make these determinations without the resources that the tradition of moral discernment has brought to bear on the question. In its place, this reader is likely to substitute traditional judgments in the moral sphere with supposedly "objective" scientific ideas derived from modern psychology. If we cannot have full-throated inner demons, we end up stammering about "inner demons": inclinations, instincts, and impulses that have no clear footing or relationship to good and evil. Without an avowed relationship with ethics, psychology ceases to aid personal discernment. In dealing with the mind as an object instead of as a subject, its effort to describe human behaviors may be wholly accurate, but it cannot prescribe: it can no longer tell us what we must do, what we must avoid.

Further, if psychology is today to be a proxy for ethics, the "objectivity" of such a scientific framework is necessarily limited in exactly the same way as that of the monks in the desert: human subjects in human communities must still carry out this diagnostic work. The issues of authority, self-interest, and self-justification that could plague a monastic community do not disappear in any modern academe. Instead, these problems are merely rendered in an even more insoluble secular mode whose cries of "objectivity" ensure only that it will always refuse to recognize the self-interested character of the subjects involved in the work. In this regard, modern psychological claims are at a distinct disadvantage in comparison to the reflection of the tradition, which always recognized that it was human subjects with real moral failings who, despite these failings, have to try to reach past their self-interest and self-justification to do good and avoid evil. The self-scrutiny of the demonological worldview (innately functioning as a remedy to moral self-justification) has no parallel in a modern scientific psychology. While the ongoing attempt to ascertain the limits of human power can surely be aided by modern scientific psychology, the path that abandons the old to embrace the new has its own perils.

Even if one takes the leap to consider demonology seriously, the critical task is far from over. Thomas's and Maximus's differing cosmological and anthropological frameworks each have serious and divergent consequences for the articulation of Christ's saving life and death and for the practical responses that Christians today should have to their temptations. Ecclesiologically, the diverging concepts of nature and providence (which also mingle with conceptions of the demonic) present in these two thinkers will surely continue to have ramifications for the ongoing relationship between Greek and Latin Christian traditions.[3] It remains a matter of systematic, pastoral, and ecumenical importance to consider whether human beings are primarily tempted by their own humanity or by personal angelic beings.

While the resolution of these challenges is a complicated systematic and historical task, I remain convinced that they are not intractable. From a modern Thomistic perspective, the work of J. P. Torrell on Christ's temptation is a significant step toward a differentiated consensus between the two traditions' conceptions of Christ's temptation. Torrell's account of a demonic imaginative attack against Christ allows for a Christological consideration of at least one aspect of the ascetic tradition. There are limits to this solution, however, since this Thomistic solution continues to follow Alexander of Hales's moral distinction between intellectual and appetitive attack. Torrell's solution therefore lacks the appetitive component that is central to Maximus's account of Christ's temptation. From a modern Maximian perspective, the continued focus must be on an investigation of the nature of the virtues that govern human appetitive life. Anthropologically, the central questions for Maximus concern where patience and temperance are

---

3. See Andrew Louth, "Introduction," in *A Saint for East and West: Maximus the Confessor's Contribution to Eastern and Western Christian Theology*, ed. Daniel Haynes, xix–xxv (Eugene, Ore.: Cascade Books, 2019), which I also discussed in my introduction.

located in the human soul. In a Christological mode, how does the ascetic tradition affirm that Christ is fully in possession of patience and temperance if he does not possess their eschatological form in his earthly life? Answers to these questions would help to address the central concerns of the Latin perspective on Christ's temptation.

Finally, a thorough ecumenical investigation of the Council of Trent—especially its decree on original sin—will be a fruitful locus of discussion for ecclesial negotiation of this study's anthropological difficulties. I have suspicions that Trent's affirmations about original sin are not wholly at odds with an Evagrian or Maximian framework for fallen human temptation. If such accommodation is possible, Eastern Rite and Eastern Orthodox faithful—and, for that matter, Pentecostals—may find Trent's claims about human fallenness surprisingly hospitable. A differentiated consensus between Orthodoxy and Catholicism on this point would be highly significant, especially for traditionally divisive topics such as the Immaculate Conception of Mary. And given the global growth of Pentecostalism, renewed consideration of spiritual warfare on the part of Roman Catholicism may become an indispensable ecumenical task.

Regardless of the way forward in mutual understanding and in the articulation of Christ's saving work, Christ's relationship with fallen human emotionality—in all its soteriological complexity—must continue to guide Christian reflection on Christ's temptation. Even if Maximus and Thomas cannot themselves fully resolve these problems for the modern reader, the return to the Maximian and Thomistic sources of these traditions is nevertheless an essential step toward a proper diagnosis of the problem and, thereby, a step toward its resolution.

BIBLIOGRAPHY

Adams, Marilyn McCord. *What Sort of Human Nature? Medieval Philosophy and the Systematics of Christology*. Milwaukee, Wis.: Marquette University Press, 1999.
Adriaen, Marci, ed. *Gregorii Magni: Moralia in Iob*. Corpus Christianorum: Series Latina. Vol. 143–143b. Turnholt: Brepols, 1985.
Alexander of Hales. *Summa Theologica*. Vol. 3. Edited by P. Bonaventurae Marrani. Florence: Typographia Collegii S. Bonaventurae, 1930.
Aquinas, Thomas. *Commentary on the Epistle to the Hebrews*. Translated by Chrysostom Baer. South Bend, Ind.: St. Augustine's Press, 2006.
———. *Commentary on the Gospel of St. Matthew*. Translated by Paul M. Kimball. Camillus, N.Y.: Dolorosa Press, 2011.
———. *Commentary on the Letters of Saint Paul to the Philippians, Colossians, Thessalonians, Timothy, Titus, and Philemon*. Translated by F. R. Larcher. Lander, Wyo.: Aquinas Institute for the Study of Sacred Doctrine, 2012.
———. *The De Malo of Thomas Aquinas*. Translated by Richard Regan. New York: Oxford University Press, 2001.
———. *Disputed Questions on Virtue*. Translated by Ralph McInerny. South Bend, Ind.: St. Augustine's Press, 1999.
———. *The Literal Exposition on Job: A Scriptural Commentary Concerning Providence*. Translated by Anthony Damico. Atlanta, Ga.: Scholars Press, 1989.
———. *Opera Omnia*. http://www.corpusthomisticum.org/iopera.html.
———. *Quaestiones Disputatae*. Vol. 2. Rome: Marietti, 1949.
———. *Summa Theologiae: First Complete American Edition*. 3 vols. Translated by Fathers of the English Dominican Province. Cincinnati, Ohio: Benzinger Brothers, 1947.
———. *Treatise on Human Nature: The Complete Text*. Translated by Alfred J Freddoso. South Bend, Ind.: St. Augustine's Press, 2010.
Augustine of Hippo. *Concerning the City of God against the Pagans*. Translated by Henry Bettenson. St. Ives: Penguin Books, 1972.

———. *Earlier Writings*. Translated by John H. S. Burleigh. Philadelphia: Westminster Press, 1953.

———. *On Christian Belief*. Translated by Matthew O'Connell. Hyde Park, N.Y.: New City Press, 2005.

———. *On Genesis*. Translated by Edmund Hill. Hyde Park, N.Y.: New City Press, 2002.

———. *On the Trinity: Books 8–15*. Edited by Gareth B. Matthews. Translated by Stephen McKenna. Cambridge: Cambridge University Press, 2002.

——— *Responses to Miscellaneous Questions*. Translated by Boniface Ramsey. Hyde Park, N.Y.: New City Press, 2008.

———. *The Retractions*. Translated by Mary Inez Bogan. Washington, D.C.: The Catholic University of America Press, 1968.

———. *The Trinity*. Translated by Edmund Hill. Brooklyn, N.Y.: New City Press, 1991.

Aulén, Gustaf. *Christus Victor*. Translated by A. G. Herbert. New York: Macmillan Company, 1956.

Ayres, Lewis. "Christology as Contemplative Practice: Understanding the Union of Natures in Augustine's *Letter* 137." In *In the Shadow of the Incarnation: Essays on Jesus Christ in the Early Church in Honor of Brian E. Daley*, edited by Peter W. Martens, 190–211. Notre Dame, Ind.: University of Notre Dame Press, 2008.

Bak, John S. "Christ's Jungian Shadow in *The Last Temptation*." In *God's Struggler: Religion in the Writings of Nikos Kazantzakis*, edited by Darren J. N. Middleton and Peter Bien, 153–68. Macon, Ga.: Mercer University Press, 1996.

Baker, Richard R. *The Thomistic Theory of the Passions and their Influence Upon the Will*. Published diss., University of Notre Dame, 1941. Ann Arbor, Mich.: Edwards Brothers, Inc., 1941.

Balthasar, Hans Urs von. *Cosmic Liturgy: The Universe According to Maximus the Confessor*. San Francisco: Ignatius Press, 1988.

———. *Presence and Thought: Essay on the Religious Philosophy of Gregory of Nyssa*. Translated by Mark Sebanc. San Francisco: Ignatius Press, 1988.

———. *Theo-Drama: Theological Dramatic Theory* II. Translated by Graham Harrison. San Francisco: Ignatius Press, 1990.

———. *Theo-Drama: Theological Dramatic Theory* III. Translated by Graham Harrison. San Francisco: Ignatius Press, 1992.

———. *Theo-Drama: Theological Dramatic Theory* IV. Translated by Graham Harrison. San Francisco: Ignatius Press, 1994.

Bañez, Domingo. *Comentarios Ineditos a la Tercera Parte de Santo Tomas*. Vol. 1. Edited by Vincente Beltran de Heredia. Burgos: Matriti, 1951.

Barad, Judith. "Aquinas on the Role of Emotion in Moral Judgment and Activity." *The Thomist* 55, no. 3 (1991): 397–413.

Barnes, Corey L. *Christ's Two Wills in Scholastic Thought: The Christology of Aquinas and Its Historical Contexts*. Toronto: Pontifical Institute of Mediaeval Studies, 2012.

Barnett, S. A. *'Instinct' and 'Intelligence': The Science of Behavior in Animals and Man.* London: MacGibbon and Kee, 1967.
Barth, Karl. *Church Dogmatics.* Vol. I.2. Translated by G. T. Thomson and Harold Knight. Peabody, Mass.: Hendrickson Publishers, 2010.
Basil of Caesarea. *The Letters.* Translated by Roy J. Deferrari. Cambridge, Mass.: Harvard University Press, 1961.
———. *On the Human Condition.* Translated by Nonna Verna Harrison. Crestwood, N.Y.: St. Vladimir's Seminary Press, 2005.
Bathrellos, Demetrios. *The Byzantine Christ: Person, Nature, and Will in the Christology of St. Maximus the Confessor.* New York: Oxford University Press, 2004.
———. "Passions, Ascesis, and the Virtues." In *The Oxford Handbook of Maximus the Confessor,* edited by Pauline Allen and Bronwen Neil, 287–305. Oxford: Oxford University Press, 2015.
Bausenhart, Guido. *"In allem uns gleich außer der Sünde": Studien zum Beitrag Maximos' des Bekenners zur altkirchlichen Christologie.* Mainz: Matthias-Grünewald-Verlag, 1992.
Behr, John. "The Word of God in the Second Century." *Pro Ecclesia* 9, no. 1 (Winter 2000): 85–107.
Bélanger, Rodrigue. "La dialectique Parole-Chair dans la christologie de Grégoire le Grand." In *Gregory the Great: A Symposium,* edited by John Cavadini, 82–90. Notre Dame, Ind.: University of Notre Dame Press, 1995.
Benedict XVI, Pope. *Jesus of Nazareth: From the Baptism in the Jordan to the Transfiguration.* New York: Doubleday, 2007.
Berndt, Rainer, SJ, ed. *Hugonis de Sancto Victore: De Sacramentis Christiane Fidei.* Aschendorff: Monasterii Westfalorum, 2008.
Bertrand, Dominique. "Origène et le Discernement des Esprits." In *Origeniana Octava,* Vol. 2, edited by L. Perrone, 969–75. Leuven: Leuven University Press, 2003.
Billot, Ludovico. *De Personali et Originali Peccato: Commentarius in Primam Secunae et in Tertiam Partem.* Rome: Apud Aedes Universitatis Gregorianae, 1931.
Billuart, F. C.-R. *Summa Sancti Thomae.* Vol. 6. Paris: Victorem Palmé, 1872.
Blankenhorn, Bernhard. "Aquinas on Paul's Flesh/Spirit Anthropology in Romans." In *Reading Romans with St. Thomas Aquinas,* edited by Matthew Levering and Michael Dauphinais, 1–38. Washington, D.C.: The Catholic University of America Press, 2012.
Blowers, Paul M. *Exegesis and Spiritual Pedagogy in Maximus the Confessor: An Investigation of the Quaestiones ad Thalassium.* Notre Dame, Ind.: University of Notre Dame Press, 1991.
———. "Realized Eschatology in Maximus the Confessor, *Ad Thalassium* 22." *Studia Patristica* 32 (1995): 258–63.
———. "Gentiles of the Soul: Maximus the Confessor on the Substructure and Transformation of Human Passions." *Journal of Early Christian Studies* 4, no. 1 (Spring 1996): 57–85.

———. "The Passion of Jesus Christ in Maximus the Confessor." *Studia Patristica* 37 (2001): 361–77.

———. "The Dialectics and Therapeutics of Desire in Maximus the Confessor." *Vigiliae Christianae.* 65, no. 4 (2011): 425–51.

———. "Maximus the Confessor and John of Damascus on Gnomic Will (γνώμη) in Christ: Clarity and Ambiguity." *Union Seminary Quarterly Review* 63, no. 3–4 (2012): 44–50.

———. "On the 'Play' of Divine Providence in Gregory Nazianzen and Maximus the Confessor." In *Re-Reading Gregory of Nazianzus: Essays on History, Theology, and Culture*, edited by Christopher A. Beeley, 199–217. Washington, D.C.: The Catholic University of America Press, 2012.

———. *Maximus the Confessor: Jesus Christ and the Transfiguration of the World.* Oxford: Oxford University Press, 2016.

Blowers, Paul, and Robert Louis Wilken. "Introduction." In *On the Cosmic Mystery of Jesus Christ: Selected Writings from St Maximus the Confessor*. Translated by Paul M. Blowers and Robert Louis Wilken. Crestwood, N.Y.: St. Vladimir's Seminary Press, 2003.

Bonaventure. *Opera Omnia.* Vol. 3. Edited by Adolphe Charles Peltier. Paris: Vivès, 1845.

Botha, T. J. "An Analysis of Ephrem the Syrian's Views on the Temptation of Christ as Exemplified in his Hymn De Virginitate XII." *Acta Patristica et Byzantina* 14 (2003): 39–57.

Bradley, Denis J. M. "Aquinas on Weakness of the Will." In *Weakness of Will from Plato to the Present*, edited by Tobias Hoffmann, 70–91. Washington, D.C.: The Catholic University of America Press, 2008.

Bradshaw, David. *Aristotle East and West: Metaphysics and the Division of Christendom.* New York: Cambridge University Press, 2004.

Brakke, David. *Demons and the Making of the Monk: Spiritual Combat in Early Christianity.* Cambridge, Mass.: Harvard University Press, 2006.

Branick, Vincent. "The Sinful Flesh of the Son of God (Rom 8:3): A Key Image of Pauline Theology." *Catholic Biblical Quarterly* 47, no. 2 (1985): 246–62.

Briel, Matthew. *A Greek Thomist: Providence in Gennadios Scholarios.* Unpublished diss., Fordham University, 2016.

Bright, Pamela. "The Combat of the Demons in Anthony and Origen." In *Origeniana Septima*, edited by W. A. Bienert and U. Kühneweg, 339–43. Leuven: Leuven University Press, 1999.

Burns, J. Patout. "Augustine on the Origin and Progress of Evil." *Journal of Religious Ethics* 16, no. 1 (1988): 9–27.

Caietanus, Thomas de Vio. *Summa totius theologiae S. Thomae de Aquino.* Vols. 2/1, 2/2, and 3. New York: Georg Olms Verlag, 2000, 2001, 2002.

Capelli, Piero. "The Outer and the Inner Devil: On Representing the Evil One in Second Temple Judaism." In *"The Words of a Wise Man's mouth are Gracious"*

(QOH 10,12): Festschrift for Günter Stemberger on the Occasion of this 65th Birthday, edited by Pauro Perani, 139–52. New York: Walter de Gruyter, 2005.

Capreolus, John. *On the Virtues*. Translated by Kevin White and Romanus Cessario. Washington, D.C.: The Catholic University of America Press, 2001.

Carluccio, Gerard G. *The Seven Steps to Spiritual Perfection according to St. Gregory the Great*. Ottawa: University of Ottawa Press, 1949.

Carroll, E. R. "Recapitulation in Christ." In *New Catholic Encyclopedia: Second Edition*, vol. 11, edited by Thomas Carson and Joann Cerrito, 952–53. New York: Thomson Gale, 2003.

Casidy, A. M. *Evagrius Ponticus*. New York: Routledge, 2006.

Cassian, John. *Conferences*. Translated by Colm Luibheid. New York: Paulist Press, 1985.

Cates, Diana Fritz. *Aquinas on the Emotions: A Religious-Ethical Inquiry*. Washington, D.C.: Georgetown University Press, 2009.

Catholic Church. *Catechism of the Catholic Church*. 2nd ed. Vatican: Libreria Editrice Vaticana, 2012.

Cessario, Romanus. *The Moral Virtues and Theological Ethics*. 2nd ed. Notre Dame: University of Notre Dame Press, 2009.

Colish, Marcia L. *Peter Lombard*. 2 vols. New York: E. J. Brill, 1994.

Cooper, Adam G. *The Body in St. Maximus the Confessor: Holy Flesh, Wholly Deified*. New York: Oxford University Press, 2005.

———. "Freedom and Heteronomy: Maximus and the Question of Moral Creativity." In *A Saint for East and West: Maximus the Confessor's Contribution to Eastern and Western Christian Theology*, edited by Daniel Haynes, 85–101. Eugene, Ore.: Cascade Books, 2019.

Corpus Christianorum, Series Graeca. Vols. 7, 10, 18, 22, 23. Leuven: Brepolis, 1991f.

Corrigan, Kevin. *Evagrius and Gregory: Mind, Soul and Body in the 4th Century*. Burlington, Vt.: Ashgate Publishing Company, 2009.

Couture, Roger. *L'Imputabilité Morale des Premiers Mouvements de Sensualité de Saint Thomas aux Salmanticenses*. Rome: Presses de l'Universit Grégorienne, 1962.

Coyle, J. Kevin. "Early Monks, Prayer, and the Devil." In *Prayer and Spirituality in the Early Church*, vol. 1, edited by Pauline Allen, Raymond Canning, and Lawrence Cross, 229–49. Everton Park, Queensland: Watson Ferguson and Company, 1998.

Crisp, Oliver. "Did Christ have a *Fallen* Human Nature?" *International Journal of Systematic Theology* 6, no. 3 (July 2004): 270–88.

Crouzel, Henri. *Origen*. Translated by A. S. Worrall. San Francisco: Harper and Row Publishers, 1989.

Cullen, Christopher M. *Bonaventure*. New York: Oxford University Press, 2006.

Daley, Brian. "A Humble Mediator: The Distinctive Elements in Saint Augustine's Christology." *Word and Spirit: A Monastic Review* 9 (1987): 100–117.

———. "Divine Transcendence and Human Transformation: Gregory of Nyssa's Anti-Apollonarian Christology." In *Re-thinking Gregory of Nyssa*, edited by Sarah Coakley, 497–506. Malden, Mass.: Blackwell Publishing, 2004.

———. *Gregory of Nazianzus*. Oxfordshire: Routledge, 2006.
Daniélou, Jean. *Origen*. Translated by Walter Mitchell. New York: Sheed and Ward, 1955.
Danker, Frederick William. *A Greek-English Lexicon of the New Testament and other Early Christian Literature*. 3rd ed. Chicago: University of Chicago Press, 1979.
Davidson, Ivor J. "Pondering the Sinlessness of Jesus Christ: Moral Christologies and the Witness of Scripture." *International Journal of Systematic Theology* 10, no. 4 (October 2008): 372–98.
Davies, Brian, ed. *Thomas Aquinas: Contemporary Philosophical Perspectives*. New York: Oxford University Press, 2002.
Deferrari, Roy J. *A Latin-English Dictionary of St. Thomas Aquinas*. Boston: St. Paul Editions, 1960.
Doucet, Marcel. *Dispute de Maxime le Confesseur avec Pyrrhus: Introduction, Texte Critique, Traduction et Notes*. 2 vols. Unpublished diss., Institut d'Études Médiévales at the University of Montréal, 1972.
———. "Vues Récentes sur les 'Métamorphoses' de la Pensée de Saint Maxime le – Confesseur." *Science et Esprit* 31, no. 3 (1979): 269–302.
———. "La Volonté Humaine du Christ, Spécialement en son Agonie. Maxime le Confesseur, Interprète de l'Écriture." *Science et Esprit* 37, no. 2 (1985): 123–59.
Dressler, H. "Irenaeus, St." In *New Catholic Encyclopedia: Second Edition*, vol. 7, edited by Thomas Carson and Joann Cerrito, 570–72. New York: Thomson Gale, 2003.
Driscoll, Jeremy, OSB. *Steps to Spiritual Perfection: Studies on Spiritual Progress in Evagrius Ponticus*. New York: Newman Press, 2005.
Dubarle, André Marie. "La Tentation Diabolique dans le Livre de la Sagesse (2:24)." In *Mélanges Eugène Tisserant*. vol. 1, 187–95. Rome: Biblioteca Apostolica Vaticana, 1964.
Dudden, F. Homes. *Gregory the Great: His Place in History and Thought*. New York: Russell and Russell, 1905.
Edwards, Jr., Mark U. "Luther and the Servants of Satan." *Lutheran Theological Seminary Bulletin* 69, no. 1 (1989): 16–26.
Ellul, Jacques. *If You Are the Son of God: The Suffering and Temptations of Jesus*. Translated by Anne-Marie Andreasson-Hogg. Eugene, Ore.: Cascade Books, 2014.
Engberg-Pedersen, Troels. "Stoicism in Early Christianity: The Apostle Paul and the Evangelist John as Stoics." In *The Routledge Handbook of the Stoic Tradition*, edited by John Sellars, 29–43. New York: Routledge, 2016.
Erismann, Christophe. "A Logician for East and West." In *A Saint for East and West: Maximus the Confessor's Contribution to Eastern and Western Christian* Theology, edited by Daniel Haynes, 50–65. Eugene, Ore.: Cascade Books, 2019.
Field, Anne. *The Binding of the Strong Man: The Teaching of St. Leo the Great*. Ann Arbor, Mich.: Word of Life Press, 1976.
Fitzpatrick, Edmund J. *The Sin of Adam in the Writings of St. Thomas Aquinas*. Mundelein, Ill.: St. Mary of the Lake Seminary, 1950.

Flannery, Kevin L. *Acts Amid Precepts: The Aristotelian Logical Structure of Thomas Aquinas's Moral Theory*. Washington, D.C.: The Catholic University of America Press, 2001.

Forbes, Chris. "Paul's Principalities and Powers: Demythologizing Apocalyptic?" *Journal for the Study of the New Testament* 23, no. 82 (2001): 61–88.

———. "Pauline Demonology and/or Cosmology? Principalities, Powers and the Elements of the World in Their Hellenistic Context." *Journal for the Study of the New Testament* 24, no. 3 (2002): 51–73.

Garrett, Susan R. *Demise of the Devil: Magic and the Demonic in Luke's Writings*. Minneapolis, Minn.: Fortress Press, 1990.

———. *The Temptations of Jesus in Mark's Gospel*. Grand Rapids, Mich.: William B. Eerdmans Publishing Company, 1998.

Garrigou-LaGrange, P. Reg. *La Synthèse Thomiste*. Paris: Desclée de Brouwer, 1946.

———. *Christ the Savior: A Commentary on the Third Part of St. Thomas' Theological Summa*. Translated by Bede Rose. St. Louis, Mo.: B. Herder Book Co., 1950.

———. *Reality: A Synthesis of Thomistic Thought*. Translated by Patrick Cummins. St. Louis, Mo.: B. Herder Book Co., 1950.

Garrigues, Jean-Miguel. *Maxime le Confesseur: La Charité, avenir divin de l'homme*. Paris: Beauchesne, 1976.

———. *Le Dessein Divin d'Adoption et le Christ Rédempteur à la lumière de Maxime le Confesseur et de Thomas d'Aquin*. Paris: Éditions du Cerf, 2011.

Gauthier, R.-A. "Saint Maxime le Confesseur et la Psychologie de l'acte humain." *Recherches de Théologie Ancienne et Médiévale* 21, no. 1 (1954): 51–100.

Gennadius. "Liber Ecclesiasticorum Dogmatum." *Journal of Theological Studies* 7, no. 25 (October 1905): 78–99.

Gerson, Lloyd P. *The Passions of Christ's Soul in the Theology of St. Thomas Aquinas*. Scranton, Pa.: University of Scranton Press, 2009.

———. "Plotinus and the Platonic Response to Stoicism." In *The Routledge Handbook of the Stoic Tradition*, edited by John Sellars, 44–55. New York: Routledge, 2016.

Gillman, Florence Morgan. "Another Look at Romans 8:3: 'In the Likeness of Sinful Flesh.'" *Catholic Biblical Quarterly* 49, no. 4 (1987): 597–604.

Gillon, Louis B. *Christ and Moral Theology*. Staten Island, N.Y.: Alba House, 1967.

Gilson, Étienne. *Le Thomisme: Introduction à la Philosophie de Saint Thomas d'Aquin*. Paris: Librairie Philosophique J. Vrin, 1947.

Giulean, Dragos-Andrei. "The Watchers' Whispers: Athenagoras's *Legatio* 25, 1–3 and the *Book of the Watchers*." *Vigiliae Christianae* 61, no. 3 (2007): 258–81.

Godin, André. "Tentation." In *Dictionnaire de Spiritualité*, vol. 15, edited by A. Derville, P. Lamarche and A. Solignac, 888–90. Paris: Beauchesne, 1991.

Gondreau, Paul. "The Passions and the Moral Life: Appreciating the Originality of Aquinas." *The Thomist* 71, no. 3 (2007): 419–50.

———. "St. Thomas Aquinas, the Communication of Idioms, and the Suffering of Christ in the Garden of Gethsemane." In *Divine Impassibility and the Mystery of*

Human Suffering, edited by James F. Keating and Thomas Joseph White, OP, 214–45. Grand Rapids, Mich.: William B. Eerdmans Publishing Company, 2009.

———. *The Passions of Christ's Soul in the Theology of St. Thomas Aquinas*. Scranton, Pa.: University of Scranton Press, 2009.

Granados, Luis. "The Action of the Holy Spirit in Christ, according to Saint Maximus the Confessor." In *A Saint for East and West: Maximus the Confessor's Contribution to Eastern and Western Christian Theology*, edited by Daniel Haynes, 115–33. Eugene, Ore.: Cascade Books, 2019.

Grant, Robert M. *Irenaeus of Lyon*. New York: Routledge, 1997.

Green, Bernard. "The Theology of Gregory the Great: Christ, Salvation, and the Church." In *A Companion to Gregory the Great*, edited by Bronwen Neil and Matthew Dal Santo, 133–56. Boston: Brill, 2013.

Gregory of Nazianzus. *On God and Christ: The Five Theological Orations and Two Letters to Cledonius*. Translated by Frederick Williams and Lionel Wickham. Crestwood, N.Y.: St. Vladimir's Seminary Press, 2002.

Gregory of Nyssa. *Homilies on Ecclesiastes*. Translated by Stuart George Hall and Rachel Moriarty. Berlin: Walter de Gruyter, 1993.

———. *Homelies sur Ecclesiaste*. Translated by Françoise Vinel. Paris: Éditions du Cerf, 1996.

———. *Life of Moses*. Translated by Abraham J. Malherbe and Everett Ferguson. New York: Paulist Press, 1978.

———. *On the Soul and the Resurrection*. Translated by Catharine P. Roth. Eugene, Ore.: Wipf and Stock, 1992.

———. *Opera Omnia*. Vol. 3. https://books.google.com/books?id=fvfuD2TKz_wC.

Gregory the Great. *The Book of the Pastoral Rule*. Translated by George E. Demacopoulos. Crestwood, N.Y.: St. Vladimir's Seminary Press, 2007.

———. *Forty Gospel Homilies*. Translated by Dom David Hurst. Kalamazoo, Mich.: Cistercian Publications, 1990.

———. *Morals on the Book of Job*. 4 vols. London: John Henry Parker, 1844–1850.

Guillaumont, Antoine and Claire. "Démon: Dans la Plus Ancienne Littérature Monastique." In *Dictionnaire de Spiritualité*, 189–212. Paris: Beauchesne, 1957.

Guiu, Adrian. "Eriugena's Appropriation of Maximus Confessor's Anthropology." In *A Saint for East and West: Maximus the Confessor's Contribution to Eastern and Western Christian Theology*, edited by Daniel Haynes, 3–30. Eugene, Ore.: Cascade Books, 2019.

Hardy, Edward Rochie, ed. *The Christology of the Later Fathers*, Louisville, Ky.: Westminster John Knox Press, 1954.

Hayes, Zachary. *The Hidden Center: Spirituality and Speculative Christology in St. Bonaventure*. New York: Paulist Press, 1981.

Haynes, Daniel, ed. *A Saint for East and West: Maximus the Confessor's Contribution to Eastern and Western Christian Theology*. Eugene, Ore.: Cascade Books, 2019.

Heiko, A. Oberman. "Luther and the Devil." *Lutheran Theological Seminary Bulletin* 69, no. 1 (1989): 4–11.
Hibbs, Thomas, ed. *Thomas Aquinas on Human Nature*. Indianapolis, Ind.: Hackett Publishing Company, 1999.
Hilaire de Poitiers. *La Trinité*. Vols. II–III. Translated by George-Matthieu de Durand, Gilles Pelland, and Charles Morel. Paris: Éditions du Cerf, 2000, 2001.
Hofer, Andrew. *Christ in the Life and Teaching of Gregory of Nazianzus*. Oxford: Oxford University Press, 2013.
Hugh of St. Victor, *On the Sacraments of the Christian Faith*. Translated by Roy J. Deferrari. Eugene, Ore.: Wipf and Stock Publishers, 1951.
Jankowiak, Marek, and Phil Booth. "A New Date-List of the Works of Maximus the Confessor." In *The Oxford Handbook of Maximus the Confessor*, edited by Pauline Allen and Bronwen Neil, 19–83. Oxford: Oxford University Press, 2015.
Jenson, Robert W. "Evil as Person." *Lutheran Theological Seminary Bulletin* 69, no. 1 (1989): 33–40.
Jensen, Steven J. "The Error of the Passions." *The Thomist* 73, no. 3 (2009): 349–79.
John of Damascus. *Opera Omnia*. Vol. 1. https://books.google.com/books?id=x8AUAAAAQAAJ.
———. *De Fide Orthodoxa: Versions of Burgundio and Cerbanus*. Edited by Eligius M. Buytaert. St. Bonaventure, N.Y.: Franciscan Institute, 1955.
———. *La Foi Orthodoxe*. Vols. 1–2. Translated by P. Ledrux. Paris: Les Éditions du Cerf, 2010.
———. *Writings*. Translated by Frederic H. Chase, Jr. Washington, D.C.: The Catholic University of America Press, 1958.
Kalleres, Dayna S. "Demons and Divine Illumination: A Consideration of Eight Prayers by Gregory of Nazianzus." *Vigiliae Christianae* 61, no. 2 (2007): 157–88.
Kapic, Kelly M. "The Son's Assumption of a Human Nature: A Call for Clarity." *International Journal of Systematic Theology* 3, no. 2 (July 2001): 154–66.
Kappes, Christiaan. *The Immaculate Conception: Why Thomas Aquinas Denied, While John Duns Scotus, Gregory Palamas, and Mark Eugenicus Professed the Absolute Immaculate Existence of Mary*. New Bedford, Mass.: Academy of the Immaculate, 2014.
Keech, Dominic. *The Anti-Pelagian Christology of Augustine of Hippo 396–430*. Oxford: Oxford University Press, 2012.
Kelly, Henry Ansgar. *Satan: A Biography*. Cambridge: Cambridge University Press, 2006.
Kelly, Joseph F. "The Devil in Augustine's Genesis Commentaries." *Studia Patristica* 33 (1997): 119–24.
Kingston, Charlotte Emily. *The Devil in the Writings and Thought of Pope Gregory the Great (590–604)*. Unpublished diss., University of York, Department of History, 2011.
Konstantinovsky, Julia. *Evagrius Ponticus: The Making of a Gnostic*. Burlington, Vt.: Ashgate Publishing Company, 2009.

Lampe, G. W. H. *A Patristic Greek Lexicon.* Oxford: Clarendon Press, 1968.
Lange, A., and H. Lichtenberger, eds. *Die Daemonen: die Daemonologie der israelitisch-juedischen und fruehchristlichen Literatur im Kontext ihrer Umwelt.* Tuebingen: Mohr Siebeck, 2003.
Larchet, Jean-Claude. *La Divinisation de l'Homme Selon Saint Maxime le Confesseur.* Paris: Éditions du Cerf, 1996.
———. "Ancestral Guilt According to St. Maximus the Confessor: A Bridge between the Eastern and Western Conceptions." *Sobornost* 20, no. 1 (1998): 26–48.
———. *Maxime le Confesseur: Médiateur entre l'Orient et l'Occident.* Paris: Éditions du Cerf, 1998.
———. "The Mode of Deification." In *The Oxford Handbook of Maximus the Confessor,* edited by Pauline Allen and Bronwen Neil, 341–47. Oxford: Oxford University Press, 2015.
Lashley, Karl S. *Instinctive Behavior: The Development of a Modern Concept.* Translated by Claire H. Schiller. New York: International Universities Press, Inc., 1964.
Layton, Richard A. "Propatheia: Origen and Didymus on the Origin of the Passions." *Vigiliae Christianae* 54, no. 3 (2000): 262–82.
Leclercq, Jacques. "La Tentation." In *Pastorale du Péché.* Tournai, Belgium: Desclée, 1961.
Léthel, Francois-Marie. "La Prière de Jésus à Gethsémane." In *Maximos Confessor: Acts du Symposium sur Maximue le Confesseur Fribourg, 2–5 septembre 1980,* edited by Felix Heinzer and Christoph Schönborn, 207–14. Fribourg: Éditions Universitaires, 1982.
Levering, Matthew. *Christ's Fulfillment of Torah and Temple: Salvation According to Thomas Aquinas.* Notre Dame, Ind.: University of Notre Dame Press, 2002.
Lévy, Antoine. *Le Créé et l'Incréé: Maxime le Confesseur et Thomas d'Aquin: Aux Sources de la Querrele Palamienne.* Paris: Vrin, 2006.
Lollar, Joshua. *"To See into the Life of Things": The Contemplation of Nature in Maximus the Confessor's "Ambigua to John."* Unpublished diss., University of Notre Dame, 2011.
———. "Christ and the Contemplation of Nature in Maximus the Confessor's *Amibigua to John.*" In *A Saint for East and West: Maximus the Confessor's Contribution to Eastern and Western Christian Theology,* edited by Daniel Haynes, 245–59. Eugene, Ore.: Cascade Books, 2019.
Lombard, Peter. *The Sentences.* 4 vols. Translated by Giulio Silano. Toronto: Pontifical Institute of Mediaeval Studies, 2007–2010.
———. *Sententiae in IV Libris Distinctae.* 3 vols. Grottaferrata: Editiones Collegii S. Bonaventurae Ad Claras Aquas, 1971.
Lombardo, Nicholas E. *The Logic of Desire: Aquinas on Emotion.* Washington, D.C.: The Catholic University of America Press, 2011.
Lottin, Odon. *Psychologie et Morale aux XIIe et XIIIe Siècles.* Vol. 2, Part 1. Louvain: Abbaye du Mont César, 1948.

Loughlin, Stephen. "Similarities and Differences between Human and Animal Emotion in Aquinas's Thought." *The Thomist* 65, no. 1 (2001): 45–65.
Louth, Andrew. *Maximus the Confessor*. New York: Routledge, 2006.
———. "Introduction." In *A Saint for East and West: Maximus the Confessor's Contribution to Eastern and Western Christian Theology*, edited by Daniel Haynes, xix–xxv. Eugene, Ore.: Cascade Books, 2019.
Mangenot, E. "Démon d'après les Pères." In *Dictionnaire de Théologie Catholique*, vol. 4, edited by E. Amann, 339–84. Paris: Librairie Letouzey et Ané, 1908.
Mark the Monk. *Counsels on the Spiritual Life*. Translated Tim Vivian and Augustine Casiday. Crestwood, N.Y.: St. Vladimir's Seminary Press, 2009.
Martin, Dale Basil. "When Did Angels Become Demons?" *Journal of Biblical Literature* 129, no. 4 (2010): 657–77.
Mateo-Seco, Lucas Francisco, and Giulio Maspero, eds. *The Brill Dictionary of Gregory of Nyssa*. Boston: Brill, 2010.
Maximus the Confessor. *Ambigua*. Translated by Emmanuel Ponsoye. Paris: Éditions de l'Ancre, 1995.
———. *Ambigua to Thomas and Second Letter to Thomas*. Translated by Joshua Lollar. Turnhout: Brepols, 2009.
———. *The Ascetic Life and the Four Centuries on Charity*. Translated by Polycarp Sherwood. New York: Newman Press, 1955.
———. *The Church, the Liturgy, and the Soul of Man: The Mystagogia of St. Maximus the Confessor*. Translated by Dom Julian Stead. Still River, Mass.: St. Bede's Publications, 1982.
———. *Dispute de Maxime le Confesseur avec Pyrrhus: Introduction, Texte Critique, Traduction et Notes*. Vol. 2. Translated by Marcel Doucet. Unpublished diss., Institut d'Études Médiévales at the University of Montréal, 1972.
———. *Lettres*. Translated by Emmanuel Ponsoye. Paris: Éditions du Cerf, 1998.
———. *The Life of the Virgin*. Translated by Stephen J. Shoemaker. New Haven, Conn.: Yale University Press, 2012.
———. *On Difficulties in Sacred Scriptures: The Responses to Thalassios*. Translated by Fr. Maximos Constas. Washington, D.C.: The Catholic University of America Press, 2018
———. *On Difficulties in the Church Fathers: The Ambigua*. 2 vols. Translated by Nicholas Constas. Cambridge, Mass.: Harvard University Press, 2014.
———. *On the Cosmic Mystery of Jesus Christ: Select Writings from St. Maximus the Confessor*. Translated by Paul M. Blowers and Robert Louis Wilken. Crestwood, N.Y.: St. Vladimir's Seminary Press, 2003.
———. *Opera Omnia*. Vol 1. https://books.google.com/books?id=8aoWAAAAQAAJ.
———. *Opera Omnia*. Vol 2. https://books.google.com/books?id=NsPUAAAAMAAJ.
———. *Opuscules Théologiques et Polémiques*. Translated by Emmanuel Ponsoye. Paris: Éditions du Cerf, 1998.

———. *The Philokalia*. Vol. 2. Edited and translated by G.E.H. Palmer, Philip Sherrard, and Kallistos Ware. New York: Faber and Faber, 1981.

———. *Questions à Thalassios*. Translated by Emmanuel Ponsoye. Malon: Éditions de l'Ancre, 1992.

———. *Questions à Thalassios*. Vols. 1–3. Introduction and notes by Jean-Claude Larchet. Translated by Françoise Vinel. Paris: Éditions du Cerf, 2010, 2012, 2015.

———. *Questions and Doubts*. Translated by Despina D. Prassas. DeKalb, Ill.: Northern Illinois University Press, 2010.

———. *Selected Writings*. Translated by George C. Berthold. New York: Paulist Press, 1985.

———. *Vie de la Vierge*. Translated by Maichel-Jean van Esbroeck. Louven: Corpus Scriptorum Christianorum Orientalium, 1986.

Maxwell, David R. "What Was 'Wrong' with Augustine: The Sixth-Century Reception (or Lack Thereof) of Augustine's Christology." In *In the Shadow of the Incarnation: Essays on Jesus Christ in the Early Church in Honor of Brian E. Daley*, edited by Peter W. Martens, 212–27. Notre Dame, Ind.: University of Notre Dame Press, 2008.

McFarland, Ian A. "'Naturally and by Grace': Maximus the Confessor on the Operation of the Will." *Scottish Journal of Theology* 58, no. 4 (2005): 410–33.

———. "Fallen or Unfallen? Christ's Human Nature and the Ontology of Human Sinfulness." *International Journal of Systematic Theology* 10, no. 4 (2008): 399–415.

McKinley, John E. *Tempted for Us: Theological Models and the Practical Relevance of Christ's Impeccability and Temptation*. Colorado Springs, Colo.: Paternoster, 2009.

———. "Four Patristic Models of Jesus Christ's Impeccability and Temptation." *Perichoresis* 9, no. 1 (2011): 29–66.

Meyendorff, John. "Free Will in Saint Maximus the Confessor." In *The Ecumenical World of Orthodox Civilization: Russia and Orthodoxy*, vol 3, edited by Andrew Blane, 71–75. Paris: Mouton, 1974.

Miner, Robert. *Thomas Aquinas on the Passions: A Study of* Summa Theologiae 1a2ae 22–48. Cambridge: Cambridge University Press, 2009.

Minns, Denis. *Irenaeus*. Washington, D.C.: Georgetown University Press, 1994.

———. *Irenaeus: An Introduction*. New York: T & T Clark, 2010.

Nellas, Panayiotis. *Deification in Christ: Orthodox Perspectives on the Nature of the Human Person*. Crestwood, N.Y.: St. Vladimir's Seminary Press, 1987.

Nichols, Aidan. *Byzantine Gospel: Maximus the Confessor in Modern Scholarship*. Edinburgh: T and T Clark, 1993.

Nielsen, Jan Tjeerd. *Adam and Christ in the Theology of Irenaeus of Lyons: An Examination of the Function of the Adam-Christ Typology in the Adversus Haereses of Irenaeus, against the Background of the Gnosticism of His Time*. Assen, Netherlands: Van Gorcum & Company, 1968.

Nieuwenhove, Rik van. "'Bearing the Marks of Christ's Passion': Aquinas' Soteriology." In *The Theology of Thomas Aquinas*, edited by Rik van Nieuwenhove and

Joseph Wawrykow, 277–302. Notre Dame, Ind.: University of Notre Dame Press, 2005.

Nieuwenhove, Rik van, and Joseph Wawrykow, eds. *The Theology of Thomas Aquinas.* Notre Dame, Ind.: University of Notre Dame Press, 2005.

Nisula, Timo. *Augustine and the Functions of Concupiscence.* Boston: Brill, 2012.

Nemesius of Emesa. *On the Nature of Man.* Translated by R. W. Sharples and P. J. Van Der Eijk. Liverpool: Liverpool University Press, 2008.

Oakes, Edward. *Infinity Dwindled to Infancy.* Grand Rapids, Mich.: William B. Eerdmans Publishing Company, 2011.

Okholm, Dennis. *Dangerous Passions, Deadly Sins: Learning from the Psychology of Ancient Monks.* Grand Rapids, Mich.: Brazos Press, 2014.

O'Laughlin, Michael. "The Anthropology of Evagrius Ponticus and its Sources." In *Origen of Alexandria: His World and His Legacy,* edited by Charles Kannengiesser and William L. Petersen, 357–73. Notre Dame, Ind.: University of Notre Dame Press, 1988.

O'Meara, Thomas F. *Thomas Aquinas: Theologian.* Notre Dame, Ind.: University of Notre Dame Press, 1997.

Origen of Alexandria. *Commentary on the Epistle to the Romans.* Translated by Thomas P. Scheck. Washington, D.C.: The Catholic University of America Press, 2001.

———. *Commentaire sur l'Épitre aux Romains.* Vol. 3. Translated by Luc Bresard and Michel Fedou. Paris: Éditions du Cerf, 2011.

———. *Contra Celsum.* Translated by Henry Chadwick. Cambridge: Cambridge University Press, 1965.

———. *Homilies on Ezekiel.* Translated by Thomas P. Scheck. New York: Newman Press, 2010.

———. *Homilies on Genesis and Exodus.* Translated by Ronald E. Heine. Washington, D.C.: The Catholic University of America Press, 1982.

———. *Homilies on Joshua.* Translated by Barbara J. Bruce. Washington, D.C.: The Catholic University of America Press, 2002.

———. *Homilies on Judges.* Translated by Elizabeth Ann Dively Lauro. Washington, D.C.: The Catholic University of America Press, 2010.

———. *The Song of Songs Commentary and Homilies.* Translated by R. P. Lawson. New York: Newman Press, 1957.

Osborn, Eric. *Irenaeus of Lyons.* New York: Cambridge University Press, 2001.

Osborne, Catherine. *Eros Unveiled: Plato and the God of Love.* Oxford: Oxford University Press, 1994.

Pagels, Elaine. *Origin of Satan: How Christians Demonized Jews, Pagans, and Heretics.* New York: Vintage Books, 1996.

Partoens, Gert, and Anthony Dupont. "*Sed de quo peccato?* Augustine's exegesis of Rom. 8:3 in *sermo* 152, 9–11." In *Vigiliae Christianae* 66, no. 2 (2012): 190–212.

Pasa, Zeljko. *The Influence of Evagrius Ponticus on the Thought of Maximus the Confessor: A Comparison of Three Spiritual Struggles in the Works of Evagrius*

Ponticus and Maximus the Confessor. Rome: Pontificium Institutum Orientale, 2010.

Pasnau, Robert. *Thomas Aquinas on Human Nature: A Philosophical Study of Summa theologiae Ia 75–89.* New York: Cambridge University Press, 2002.

Pauw, Amy Plantinga. "Where Theologians Fear to Tread." *Modern Theology* 16, no. 1 (2000): 39–59.

Pesthy, Monka. "*Logismoi* Origéniens—*Logismoi* Évagriens." In *Origeniana Octava*, vol. 2, edited by L. Perrone, 1017–22. Leuven: Leuven University Press, 2003.

Pinckaers, Servais. *The Pinckaers Reader: Renewing Thomistic Moral Theology.* Edited by John Berkman and Craig Steven Titus. Washington, D.C.: The Catholic University of America Press, 2005.

———. *Passion and Virtue.* Translated by Benedict M. Guevin. Washington, D.C.: The Catholic University of America Press, 2015.

Piret, Pierre. *Christ et la Trinité selon Maxime le Confesseur.* Paris: Beauchesne, 2012.

Plested, Marcus. *Orthodox Readings of Aquinas.* Oxford: Oxford University Press, 2014.

———. "The Ascetic Tradition." In *The Oxford Handbook of Maximus the Confessor*, edited by Pauline Allen and Bronwen Neil, 164–76. Oxford: Oxford University Press, 2015.

Portaru, Marius. "Classical Philosophical Influences: Aristotle and Platonism." In *The Oxford Handbook of Maximus the Confessor*, edited by Pauline Allen and Bronwen Neil, 127–47. Oxford: Oxford University Press, 2015.

Porter, Jean. "Right Reason and the Love of God: The Parameters of Aquinas' Moral Theology." In *The Theology of Thomas Aquinas*, edited by Rik van Nieuwenhove and Joseph Wawrykow, 167–91. Notre Dame, Ind.: University of Notre Dame Press, 2005.

Principe, Walter H. "Some Examples of Augustine's Influence on Medieval Christology." In *Collectanea Augustiniana: Melanges T.J. Van Beval*, vol. 2, edited by Bernard Bruning, Mathiis Lamberigts, and Jozef Houtem, 955–74. Leuven: Leuven University Press, 1990.

Quay, Paul M. "Angels and Demons: The Teaching of IV Lateran." *Theological Studies* 42, no. 1 (1981): 20–45.

Renczes, Philipp Gabriel. *Agir de Dieu et Liberté de l'Homme: Récherches sur l'Anthropologie Théologique de Saint Maxime le Confesseur.* Paris: Éditions du Cerf, 2003.

Reynolds III, Bennie H. "Understanding the Demonologies of the Dead Sea Scrolls: Accomplishments and Direction for the Future." *Religion Compass* 7, no. 4 (2013): 103–14.

Rhonheimer, Martin. *The Perspective of the Acting Person: Essays in the Renewal of Thomistic Moral Philosophy.* Edited by William F. Murphy, Jr. Washington, D.C.: The Catholic University of America Press, 2008.

Rider, Catherine. *Magic and Impotence in the Middle Ages.* New York: Oxford University Press, 2006.

Riou, Alain. *Le Monde et l'Église selon Maxime le Confesseur*. Paris: Beauchesne, 1973.
Rousseau, Philip. *Ascetics, Authority, and the Church of Jerome and Cassian: Second Edition*. Notre Dame, Ind: University of Notre Dame Press, 2010.
Russell, Jeffrey Burton. *The Devil: Perceptions of Evil from Antiquity to Primitive Christianity*. Ithica, N.Y.: Cornell University Press, 1977.
———. *Satan: The Early Christian Tradition*. Ithica, N.Y.: Cornell University Press, 1981.
———. *Lucifer: The Devil in the Middle Ages*. Ithica, N.Y.: Cornell University Press, 1984.
———. *Mephistopheles: The Devil in the Modern World*. Ithica, N.Y.: Cornell University Press, 1986.
———. *The Prince of Darkness: Radical Evil and the Power of Good in History*. Ithica, N.Y.: Cornell University Press, 1988.
Rosen-Zvi, Ishay. "Two Rabbinic Inclinations? Rethinking a Scholarly Dogma." *Journal for the Study of Judaism* 39, no. 4–5 (2008): 513–39.
Schaff, Philip, ed. *Nicene and Post-Nicene Fathers*. Vol. 9. New York: Charles Scribner's Sons, 1899.
Schoenborn, Christoph. "Plaisir et Douleur dans l'Analyse de S. Maxime, d'après les Quaestiones ad Thalassium." In *Maximus Confessor*, edited by Felix Heinzer and Christoph Schoenborn, 273–84. Fribourg: Éditions Universitaires Fribourg Suisse, 1982.
Schoors, A., and P. Van Deun. *Philohistor: Miscellanea in Honorum Caroli Laga Septuagenarii*. Leuven: Uitgeverij Peeters, 1994.
Scott-Macnab, David. "St. Augustine and the Devil's 'Mousetrap.'" In *Vigiliae Christianae* 68, no. 4 (2014): 409–15.
Sellars, John. "Introduction." In *The Routledge Handbook of the Stoic Tradition*, edited by John Sellars, 1–13. New York: Routledge, 2016.
Senchuk, Dennis M. *Against Instinct: From Biology to Philosophical Psychology*. Philadelphia: Temple University Press, 1991.
Sherwood, Polycarp, OSB. "An Annotated Date-List of the Works of St. Maximus the Confessor." *Studia Anselmiana*. Vol. 29. Rome: Pontificium Institutum S. Anselmi, 1952.
———. "Introduction." In *Maximus the Confessor, The Ascetic Life, The Four Centuries on Charity*, translated and annotated by Polycarp Sherwood, 3–102. Westminster, Md.: Newman Press, 1955.
Sinkewicz, Robert E. *Evagrius of Pontus: The Greek Ascetic Corpus*. New York: Oxford University Press, 2003.
Smith, J. Warren. *Passion and Paradise: Human and Divine Emotion in the Thought of Gregory of Nyssa*. New York: Crossroad Publishing Company, 2004.
Sorabji, Richard. *Emotion and Peace of Mind: From Stoic Agitation to Christian Temptation*. Oxford: Oxford University Press, 2003.
Steenberg, M. C. *Irenaeus on Creation: The Cosmic Christ and the Saga of Redemption*. Boston: Brill, 2008.

Steiner, M., OFM. *La Tentation de Jesus dans l'Interpretation Patristique de Saint Justin à Origene.* Paris: Librairie Lecoffre, 1962.

Stone, Michael E. *Adam's Contract with Satan: The Legend of the Cheirograph of Adam.* Bloomington: Indiana University Press, 2002.

Straw, Carole. "Gregory's Moral Theology." In *A Companion to Gregory the Great,* edited by Bronwen Neil and Matthew J. Dal Santo, 177–204. Boston: Brill Publishers, 2013.

Rist, John. "On the Platonism of Gregory of Nyssa." *Hermathena,* no. 169 (Winter 2000): 129–51.

Te Velde, Rudi A. "Evil, Sin, and Death: Thomas Aquinas on Original Sin." In *The Theology of Thomas Aquinas,* edited by Rik van Nieuwenhove and Joseph Wawrykow, 143–66. Notre Dame, Ind.: University of Notre Dame Press, 2005.

Thielicke, Helmut. *Between God and Satan.* Translated by C. C. Barber. Grand Rapids, Mich.: William B. Eerdmans Publishing Company, 1960.

Thunberg, Lars. *Microcosm and Mediator: The Theological Anthropology of Maximus the Confessor.* Lund: Hakan Ohlssons Boktryckeri, 1965.

Tollefsen, Torstein T. "The Metaphysics of Maximus: Becoming One with God." In *A Saint for East and West: Maximus the Confessor's Contribution to Eastern and Western Christian Theology,* edited by Daniel Haynes, 223–30. Eugene, Ore.: Cascade Books, 2019.

Toorn, Karel van, Bob Becking, and Pieter von der Horst, eds. *Dictionary of Deities and Demons.* Leiden: Brill, 1998.

Toronen, Melchisedec. *Union and Distinction in the Thought of St. Maximus the Confessor.* New York: Oxford University Press, 2007.

Torrell, Jean-Pierre. *Le Christ en ses Mystères: La vie et l'oeuvre de Jésus selon saint Thomas d'Aquin.* Vol. 1. Paris: Desclée, 1999.

———. *Saint Thomas Aquinas: The Person and His Work Revised Edition.* Translated by Robert Royal. Washington, D.C.: The Catholic University of America Press, 2005.

Vandenbroucke, Francois. "Démon." In *Dictionnaire de Spiritualité,* vol. 3, 218–19. Paris: Beauchesne, 1980.

Vann, Gerald, and P. K. Meagher. *The Temptations of Christ.* New York: Sheed and Ward, 1957.

Vos, Nienke. "Demons Without and Within: The Representation of Demons, the Saint, and the Soul in Early Christian Lives, Letters and Sayings." In *Demons and the Devil in Ancient and Medieval Christianity,* edited by Nienke Vos and Willemien Otten, 3–36. Boston: Brill, 2011.

Vos, Nienke, and Willemien Otten, eds. *Demons and the Devil in Ancient and Medieval Christianity.* Boston: Brill, 2011.

Ware, Kallistos. "The Imitation of Christ according to Saint Maximus the Confessor." In *A Saint for East and West: Maximus the Confessor's Contribution to Eastern and Western Christian Theology,* edited by Daniel Haynes, 69–84. Eugene, Ore.: Cascade Books, 2019.

Warren, E. Janet. "'Spiritual Warfare': A Dead Metaphor?" *Journal of Pentecostal Theology* 21, no.2 (2012): 278–97.

Wawrykow, Joseph P. *God's Grace and Human Action: 'Merit' in the Theology of Thomas Aquinas*. Notre Dame, Ind.: University of Notre Dame Press, 1995.

———. *The Westminster Handbook to Thomas Aquinas*. Louisville, Ky.: Westminster John Knox Press, 2005.

Weinandy, Thomas. *In the Likeness of Sinful Flesh: An Essay on the Humanity of Christ*. Edinburgh: T and T Clark, 1993.

Williams, Rowan Douglass. "Augustine's Christology: Its Spirituality and Rhetoric." In *In the Shadow of the Incarnation: Essays on Jesus Christ in the Early Church in Honor of Brian E. Daley*, edited by Peter W. Martens, 176–89. Notre Dame, Ind.: University of Notre Dame Press, 2008.

———. "'Tempted as we are': Christology and the Analysis of the Passions." *Studia Patristica* 44 (2010): 391–404.

Wright, Archie T. "Some Observations of Philo's *De Gigantibus* and Evil Spirits in Second Temple Judaism." *Journal for the Study of Judaism* 36, no. 4 (2005): 471–88.

Zernheld, Claire-Agnes. "Le Double Visage de la Passion: Malédiction due au Péché et/ou Dynamisme de la Vie." In *Philohistor: Miscellanea in Honorem Caroli Laga Septuagenarii*, edited by A. Schoors and P. Van Deun, 361–80. Leuven: Uitgeverij Peeters, 1994.

INDEX

Akrasia, 67, 109

Alexander of Hales, 132, 157n66, 158, 162, 166, 168–78, 215, 223–24, 262, 269, 281, 287–88; and appetitive temptation, 169–72; and imaginative temptation 172–75; and Christ's temptation 175–78

Apollinarianism, 42n80, 48, 1

Appetite (ὄρεξις), 57, 95n164; as natural 53, 63–6, 71, 78–81, 105–6, 114–16, 118–19, 127, 134–36; as unnatural or against nature, 77–78, 135–36, as violent, 77–79, 105, 119, 127

Appropriation: essential, 99–100, 104–6, 128; relational, 99–101, 105, 120

Avarice, 33, 40–41, 61

Aristotle, 58n35, 179, 206, 209, 228; and the three kinds of movement, 220–21

Askesis, 32n40, 35, 39–40, 76n91, 82–88, 129, 205n76, 224n135, 228, 231 287n1

Augustine of Hippo, 10, 57, 132, 148–57, 160–3, 193, 210, 214, 287–88; and concupiscence, 151; and interior temptation 149–52; and temptation of Christ, 152–54

Baptism. *See sacraments*

Blowers, Paul M., 6–8, 11–12, 29n32, 51n4, 51n6, 63n56, 87n137, 114n45, 119n55

Burgundio of Pisa, 20, 133–35, 139n25, 141, 144n33, 147–48, 260–61, 288

Choice (προαίρεσις), 25, 27, 30–31, 37, 39, 58, 64n58, 65–68, 109, 112–20, 134, 136–37, 141–43, 148, 213

Christ: and choice, 112–20; compassion or mercy of, 168, 248, 250–54, 272, 289; defects of, 251, 259–62; external temptation of, 10, 13, 58, 70–71, 145, 154, 160–61, 175–77, 270–79, 282; hunger of, 125, 248n13, 260, 262, 271–2, 279, 283, 289; impeccability of, 28, 66, 99, 101n7, 106, 112–20, 276; knowledge of, 109–12, 255–57; natural and blameless passions of, 105, 141, 143–44, 147, 260, 262; perfections of, 106–20, 254–59, 262; virtue of, 106–8, 253, 268–70; voluntary defects or passions of, 108, 143, 146–47, 254, 262–66, 279; sinlessness of, 7, 44, 47, 99, 106n25, 110–12, 177, 268–69; and temptation by pain, 108, 125–30; and temptation by pleasure, 125–30; and satisfaction for human sin, 248–50, 267, 271–72, 283; as unfallen or as *comprehensor*, 99–102, 144–5, 255–62; and *visio Dei*, 255; as *wayfarer* 259–62; weakness and confusion of, 43–46, 101–6

313

Christological synecdoche, 47, 102, 143, 145–46, 148, 166, 177–78, 243–45, 247, 254, 260, 262, 272, 282, 287–90
Communicatio idiomatum, 110
Concupiscence. See *fomes peccati*
Corruptibility, 55, 60n41, 100–101, 120–22, 261, 265

Demons: ability to affect human bodies, 34, 152, 220–2, 232n159, 284; appetitive or passionate attack from, 18, 73, 77n97, 159, 169–72, 210, 219, 222–25, 292; army of, 33, 35, 85, 108, 290 ; as deceptive, 73, 81–82, 91, 102, 109, 223, 234; enslavement to, 54, 129–30, 180, 187–88, 250n20; imaginative attack from 171–5, 218–9, 222–5, 234, 259, 282, 292; injustice of, 187, 193, 278; intellectual attack from, 30, 82, 92, 169–70, 184–85, 222–23, 292; knowledge of, 151–52; as preternatural agents, 15–16; specialties of, 33, 40; and thoughts, 33–34, 37–41, 62, 72, 76, 79–87, 96, 128, 144–45, 150–51, 157–60, 173–74, 178; and 2 Timothy 2:5, 35, 91, 96, 235–6, 285; as vices, 11n24, 34, 40–41, 76n91, 88n138, 246n6
Devil: as author of *cheirograph*, 75; confrontation or combat with Christ, 1, 3, 10, 40, 74, 120–30, 278–9, 284, 286; as serpent or Leviathan, 35, 43, 76–77, 144, 155, 158, 187, 196, 218–19, 281; opposed by teachers, 237–8. See also demons
Deliberation, 25, 27, 30, 31, 53n15, 58, 64–6, 69, 78, 80, 112, 114, 116, 118, 136, 142, 164, 266
Dispassion, 29, 83–85, 95–96
Dyothelitism, 9, 13, 49, 63, 124–25, 127–28, 135, 146, 168, 190–92, 263. See also monothelitism

Elect, 149, 152–58, 161–62
Eros, 29n32, 51
Eschatology, 31n39, 50, 84, 89n147, 90, 95, 118n53, 119n55, 130, 142, 234, 285–86, 289, 293
Eucharist. See sacraments
Eupatheia. 28, 31n38
Evagrius of Ponticus, 22, 36–41, 58, 61–62, 76, 150n46, 151, 178, 284, 285, 287n1
Fall, 3, 19, 28, 43, 45, 53–58, 72–75, 90–91, 94, 97–99, 120–21, 133, 141, 145, 148–49, 154, 156, 162, 163, 176, 178, 180, 182, 185–99, 206, 240, 262, 269, 287
Exemplarity. See *imitatio Christi*

Fomes peccati, 3, 10n22, 13, 71, 149, 151, 163–5, 167, 170, 172n109, 175n121, 178, 189, 192–95, 197–98, 206, 208, 212n100, 214, 216, 233n161, 236–37, 263, 269, 280, 287
Fortitude, 51n7, 184n16, 215, 232n157, 258n46

Gauthier, R.-A., 4–5, 133–34
Genesis, 50, 53, 180. See also Kenesis and Stasis
Gethsemane, 6–7, 9, 11n23, 12–13, 64n59, 103, 126–28, 175
Gluttony, 40, 61
Gnomic will (γνώμη), 7, 11–12, 57, 59, 63–64, 83, 101n7, 130–31, 136n15
Gondreau, Paul, 17–18, 132n1, 134, 137–38, 145n35, 146n37, 210, 229n154, 280n98
Grace, 6, 13, 53n16, 85, 142, 166, 181, 184–85, 188–91, 215–27, 232–35, 241–42, 250, 255, 258–62, 270, 282, 289–90
Gregory of Nazianzus, 41, 45–47
Gregory of Nyssa, 28–31, 41–45, 59, 61, 67n64, 95n164, 96n166
Gregory the Great, 81, 132, 148, 154–61, 177–78, 269n71, 281, 287–88

Hugh of St. Victor, 163, 199, 287
Human being: aversion (θυμός) of, 23–25, 29, 36–38, 51, 55, 57, 59, 61, 71, 76–77, 88–93, 97, 124n68, 125n69, 126–31, 182–83, 207, 285; as body and soul, 58–62, 183, 206, 208; concupiscible faculty of, 182, 207, 216, 225–26, 232, 234; confusion in nature of, 77, 103–4, 223; desire (ἐπιθυμία) of, 23–5, 29, 36–8, 51–5, 57, 59, 61, 63, 74, 76–81, 84, 87, 90, 97, 125–31; flesh of, 169, 206; imagination of, 16–18, 22–24, 37, 58, 62–64, 78–9, 169, 172–73, 184n16, 185, 188, 204, 207, 209, 213, 216–17, 220–25, 230–33, 258–59, 280–81; irascible faculty, 23n6, 51n6, 182, 207, 216, 232n157, 258n46; as rational, 22–23, 27–28, 36, 55, 62, 66, 74, 78, 112, 115, 134–35, 165, 169, 181, 206–7, 210, 212, 226, 232–3, 252, 286; weakness of, 44, 45, 53n16, 131, 149, 150, 167, 216, 235
Humility, 87, 88, 93

Ignorance, 26, 58, 67–68, 74–75, 77, 82–84, 109–12, 119–20, 123–24, 136, 142, 167, 216
Imitatio Christi, 2, 3, 19, 39–40, 48, 98–99, 120, 129, 178, 234, 259, 272–77, 279, 285–86, 289
Impulse (ὁρμή), 11n23, 24n14, 29–31, 60–1, 77, 107, 138, 291

John Cassian, 157n67, 178, 287, 260
John of Damascus, 5, 64, 105n24, 112n38, 133–45, 162–63, 166, 168, 177, 197n57, 262, 264, 288
Justice, 186 193n44, 237n169, 239, 250n20, 278; original, 180, 184, 189, 198, 215–17, 233

Kinesis, 50. *See also* genesis and stasis

Law of sin, 54n18, 60n41, 96–97, 130, 140–41, 144–45, 148, 165n86, 197n57. *See also* human being
Logos (λόγος), 8n14, 12, 52–4, 57n34, 58–9, 63, 65, 95, 100, 103, 106, 110–11, 115–16, 121n61, 128, 136n13, 143
Lombardo, Nicholas, 14–16, 183, 189n36, 231
Louth, Andrew, 8, 292n3

Macrina the Younger, 28–31
Maximus the Confessor, 2–13, 21–131, 133–43, 145–48, 154, 158, 166, 176–83, 186, 188–93, 197–99, 206–7, 215, 227–28, 231, 234, 241–43, 245n3, 256–8, 260, 262, 270, 276, 282–83, 285–293
Monasticism, 12, 37–41, 48, 50, 80, 82–87, 95, 124, 151, 174, 178, 238, 277, 284–86, 291; and contemplation, 78, 84–88, 93
Monothelitism, 48–49, 67, 112–13, 124–25, 127–28. *See also* dyothelitism
Mortality, 55, 91, 100–101, 120–21, 129, 150, 154, 264–65

Natural will. *See* will (θέλησις)
Nemesius of Emesa, 22–28, 30–31, 37, 59, 63, 65–66, 68, 115, 137
Nestorianism, 48–9, 113–14, 119–20, 128

Origen of Alexandria, 22, 32–36, 39, 61n46, 96, 108, 178, 229, 278, 284

Passibility, 2–3, 55–57, 61, 72, 75–76, 81, 98, 100–105, 119–25, 129–30, 143, 146, 181, 227, 259, 261–62, 264–65, 284–86
Passion: antecedent, 210–11, 213, 227–31; consequent, 182, 228–30; as dishonorable, 60, 117; as indetractible, 144n33, 260–62, 271; as natural and blameless, 94n162, 105, 134, 141, 143–44, 147, 260,

Passion: as natural and blameless, (*cont.*) 262; presentience of, 210–11; as punitive, 60; as unnatural or contrary to nature, 56, 60, 79–81, 87, 105, 125–26

Pain (ὀδύνη), 51n6, 53n12, 54, 56, 61, 69–71, 77n99, 83, 88, 91–94, 100, 108, 125–30

Patience, 70, 88, 90, 108, 259, 286, 292–93

Peter the Lombard, 132, 146, 162–70, 178, 190, 193, 210, 215, 229, 262, 269, 287

Plato, 24, 26, 51, 57, 59

Pleasure (ἡδονή), 61, 68–71, 83, 91–4, 100, 108, 122, 125–30

Possession, 72n75, 81n115, 82n118, 171, 218, 225–29

Providence, 90–6, 139, 231, 234–42, 292

Psychology, modern, 291

Reatu poenae, 268–70

Reprobate, 153–58

Sacraments, 35, 84–85, 97, 107, 153, 233n161, 236–37

Satan. *See* devil

Sensitive appetite. *See* concuspicible faculty *and* irascible faculty

Sin: generations or stages of, 81, 84, 128, 155–58, 281; occasion of, 271, 274–77

Stasis, 50, 53n14, 97. *See also* Genesis and Kenesis

Stoicism, 9, 21–24, 28, 30, 37, 57, 60–61, 83, 95, 137–38, 176, 182–83, 228–29; and "what is up to us" (τὰ ἐφ᾿ ἡμῖν), 9, 11, 21, 34, 63–65, 68, 116

Supernatural, 15, 130, 181, 184, 188–92, 216; and natural, 59n38, 64n59, 127n73

Synod of Dort, 154n57

Temperance, 70, 88, 90, 106, 184–85, 215–17, 230–34, 258, 268, 286, 289, 292–93

Temptation: external, 10, 58, 63, 71, 160, 169, 205, 271, 279; and Hebrews 4:15, 1, 41, 71, 97, 99, 111, 160, 285, 289–90; internal, 15, 18, 149, 161, 164, 166, 169–70, 172, 174, 206, 271; from within, 67, 83, 154, 160, 164, 175, 198, 269; from without, 67–71, 160, 164

Thomas Aquinas, 2, 4, 6, 14–20, 39n72, 47, 51n6, 81n115, 87–8, 90, 95, 105n24, 106, 112n38, 132–33, 137, 144n33, 145n35, 148–52, 154–55, 162–63, 165–6, 177, 179–283, 288–93

Thoughts, 33–4, 37–41, 62, 72, 76, 79–80, 84, 86–7, 96, 98, 128, 144–5, 150–1, 156–60, 169, 173–74, 177–78, 201n63, 213, 231. *See also* demons

Torrell, Jean-Pierre, 17–19, 292

Trent, Council of, 293

Tropos (τρόπος), 12, 52–4, 58–9, 83, 97, 101, 130–31, 136n13, 143

Unwillful (ἀκουσίων): actions as, 26; passions as, 68–71, 77–78; ignorance as, 26, 68, 109–11. *See also* willful

Vainglory, 40–41, 61, 86, 88, 92–93, 211, 212, 218, 245–46

Vice, 15–6, 21, 34, 40n74, 76, 131, 185, 213

Virgin birth, 100–101, 122

Virtue, 3, 8, 11, 15–16, 21, 28–30, 52, 69–70, 84–85, 88–90, 93, 99, 106–8, 110, 123, 131, 164, 180, 201, 204, 216, 226, 231–34, 242, 251–55, 258, 262, 268–70, 286, 289–90

Ware, Kallistos, 1, 6, 9

Will (θέλησις), 8, 63–4, 66–7, 78, 80, 105, 114, 124, 128, 135, 190

Will, divine, 48–9, 103, 142, 146–47, 263–67. *See also* providence

Willful (ἑκουσίων): actions as, 25–27, 68, 82, 190; passions as, 68–71, 77–78; ignorance as, 68, 109–11. *See also* unwillful

Wish (βούλησις), 53, 64–66, 78–80, 105, 125, 127, 134–36, 142, 147, 206

Salvation through Temptation: Maximus the Confessor and Thomas Aquinas on Christ's Victory over the Devil was designed in Arno with Givry display type and composed by Kachergis Book Design of Pittsboro, North Carolina. It was printed on 55-pound Natural Offset and bound by Maple Press of York, Pennsylvania.

www.ingramcontent.com/pod-product-compliance
Lightning Source LLC
Chambersburg PA
CBHW022031290426
44109CB00014B/826